WHOSE BOSNIA?

WHOSE BOSNIA?

Nationalism and
Political Imagination
in the Balkans,
1840–1914

EDIN HAJDARPASIC

CORNELL UNIVERSITY PRESS
ITHACA AND LONDON

Cornell University Press gratefully acknowledges receipt of a subvention from Loyola University Chicago which aided in the publication of this book.

First published 2015 by Cornell University Press
Printed in the United States of America

Library of Congress Cataloging-in-Publication Data

Hajdarpasic, Edin, 1977– author.
  Whose Bosnia? : nationalism and political imagination in the Balkans, 1840–1914 / Edin Hajdarpasic.
    pages cm
  Includes bibliographical references and index.
  ISBN 978-0-8014-5371-7 (cloth : alk. paper)
  1. Bosnia and Hercegovina—Politics and government—19th century. 2. Bosnia and Hercegovina—Politics and government—20th century. 3. Nationalism—Bosnia and Hercegovina—History—19th century. 4. Nationalism—Bosnia and Hercegovina—History—20th century. I. Title.
  DR1725.H35 2015
  320.540949742'09034—dc23   2015013325

Cornell University Press strives to use environmentally responsible suppliers and materials to the fullest extent possible in the publishing of its books. Such materials include vegetable-based, low-VOC inks and acid-free papers that are recycled, totally chlorine-free, or partly composed of nonwood fibers. For further information, visit our website at www.cornellpress.cornell.edu.

Cloth printing   10 9 8 7 6 5 4 3 2 1

To Azem, Mergima, Enes, Alice, and Malik

Contents

Figures and Maps

Acknowledgments

Many institutions generously supported this work. I would like to thank the Social Science Research Council, the Fulbright-Hays Research Program, the German Marshall Fund of the United States, and the University of Michigan Institute for the Humanities for enabling me to research and write earlier versions of this book. Fellowships from the American Council of Learned Societies and Loyola University Chicago research leaves and a book subvention grant provided crucial and generous help in the later stages of writing. At Cornell University Press, I especially thank John Ackerman and Roger Haydon for their enthusiastic support of this project; Karen Laun and Mary Petrusewicz provided excellent editorial oversight in preparing the manuscript for publication. I could not have wished for a better experience. I am deeply grateful to the two anonymous reviewers for Cornell University Press for comments and advice that greatly improved the manuscript; one reader's insights were exceptionally inspiring in the revisions process.

Special gratitude goes to the staff of the archives that provided the sources for this book. Archival work in postwar Bosnia is challenging and I was able to complete this book only thanks to the hard work of librarians, archivists, and collectors across the country. In Sarajevo, I thank: the National Museum, the National Library, the Historical Institute, the Bosniak Institute, the Museum of Literature and Performing Arts (especially to Šejla Šehabović), the Media Center (with gratitude to Dragan Golubović), the City Archive, and the Archive of Bosnia-Herzegovina (especially to Mina Kujović). I am grateful to the staff of the Archive of Herzegovina in Mostar and the Archive of the Tuzla Canton in Tuzla. I greatly appreciate the help of several Bosnian Franciscans, particularly Ivan Šarčević and Mato Perić, who allowed me to consult monastery collections in Fojnica, Kreševo, Tolisa, Sarajevo, and Kraljeva Sutjeska.

I could take advantage of these amazing resources thanks to the graciousness of several friends who hosted me on several of my research trips. I am grateful to Nevena Ivanović and Dubravka Stojanović for welcoming me to Belgrade, where I worked at the Archive of Serbia, the Serbian National Library, and the Archives of the Serbian Academy of Arts and Sciences. I also thank the Archive of the Croatian Academy and the Croatian National Library, both in Zagreb; the Boğaziçi University Library in Istanbul; and the Austrian State Archives in Vienna.

Proper acknowledgment of the many colleagues and friends who helped me to write this book seems like an impossible task. At the University of Michigan, Geoff Eley, John Fine, Katherine Verdery, Brian Porter, and Michael Kennedy shaped my formative research questions through their generous mentorship and thoughtful comments. Ann Arbor provided vital intellectual inspiration and an exceptionally supportive community, and I am grateful to Lenny Ureña, Ema Grama, Juan Hernández, Marie Cruz, Chandra Bhimull, Nita Luci, Tijana Krstić, Bhavani Raman, Frank Cody, and Olivera Jokić for enriching my life. Special thanks go to Emil Kerenji, whose friendship and conversations about history, film, books, and politics sparked countless stimulating ideas over the years.

I consider myself lucky to have ended up at Loyola University Chicago. Barbara Rosenwein and Tony Cardoza welcomed me to Loyola six years ago and I thank them and the history department as a whole for creating such a nurturing and productive work environment. I am especially grateful to Suzanne Kaufman and Tim Gilfoyle for their unflagging support, which made a huge difference in making me feel at home in Chicago.

I could not have written this book without the support of family and friends who encouraged me as I traveled and wrote in Bosnia, Kosovo, Florida, Michigan, Utah, New York, California, and of course, Chicago. This project owes a great deal to Farah Tahirbegović, Imrana Kapetanović, Amer Kapetanović, Admir Jugo, Damir Žiško, and Rea Maglajlić; I continue to look to their tireless intellectual and artistic engagements for inspiration. Damir Imamović influenced this book more than he probably knows. His creativity and always brilliant comments on several drafts helped me sharpen my arguments and finish this book. I am grateful to Max Bergholz for critical feedback on the manuscript as a whole, which greatly benefited from his astute suggestions and expertise in Yugoslav histories. My colleagues Holly Case, Theodora Dragostinova, Pieter Judson, and Tara Zahra discussed parts of my work at conferences, workshops, and dinners with enthusiasm and kindness. Larisa Kurtović, Sasha Hemon, Srdjan Vučetić, and Robert Donia read and commented on different chapters and I am grateful to them for their useful feedback. I thank Elissa Helms, Risto Pekka Pennanen, Maximilian Hartmuth, Omer Hadzišelimović, Maurus Reinkowski, Snježana Buzov, Dubravko Lovrenović, Vjekoslav Perica, Florian Bieber, Elma Hašimbegović, Ivan Lovrenović, Azra Hromadžić, Andrew Gilbert, and Bodo Weber for conversations that pointed me to helpful sources, contacts, and ideas during my research. I also want to thank many individuals whose friendship and generosity helped shape this work: Hajro Bojadžić, Tidža, Sakib, Meho, and Nedim Bahtić, Nina Wieda, Sneža Žabić, Vedran Rešidbegović, Adela Sajdel, Carolyn Zola, and Damir Arsenijević.

Finally, I thank my family: Mergima, Azem, Enes, Alice, and Malik. This book exists only due to their boundless support and love. I dedicate this work to them.

WHOSE BOSNIA?

Whose Bosnia?

B y the end of the nineteenth century—an era marked by the
rise of new nation-making projects worldwide—patriotism
had become a ubiquitous point of reference, "a general spice
for everything," Milutin Garašanin wrote in 1892. As a leading Serbian
diplomat, publicist, and minister of the interior, Garašanin spent much of
his career trying to cultivate new national attachments to Serbia and to
expand the state's realms to neighboring Balkan regions.[1] But at the same
time, Garašanin was exasperated by the intractable proliferation of patriotic
phrases, symbols, gatherings, and activities that enabled so many actors to
claim to have become "ever more patriotic." "Instead of laboring to bring
ourselves up to [patriotism], we have found that it is much more practical and much easier to pull it from the upper reaches down toward us,"
Garašanin complained; "we have debased it from deed to desire." And it is
the endlessness of patriotic desires that Garašanin found especially unsettling: "If, for example, you wish for Serbia to be an empire, and you see that
this is not enough, you can immediately wish for a *great* empire; and if that
is also too little, you wish for it to be *twice as great* an empire; and when
you're bored with that, you wish for *three times as great*, and so on until
infinity. Within the limits of desires for patriotism, there are no limits."[2]

This book is about the proliferation and compulsion of patriotic desires.
Garašanin's nineteenth-century observations are a good place to begin exploring these issues because they articulate both a patriotic compulsion to
continually expand national spaces and a frustration with patriotism itself,
which is characterized as inadequate, incomplete, and not powerful enough
to fulfill its lofty mission.

First, there is what one could call the proliferation of nationalist cultural
forms. In this regard, Garašanin emphasized the rapid multiplication of
"ready-made patriotic phrases," creating "a kind of patriotic menu" from
which one could choose how to present oneself as a national subject in
nineteenth-century Serbia (often by invoking the "unliberated" lands of
Kosovo, Macedonia, and Bosnia).[3] Garašanin's descriptions made it clear
that this phenomenon was not limited to official political discourse. "One
patriotizes in music notes," in business deals, dance halls, and government
offices, in social gatherings, lunches, and dinners, spawning new patriotic
expressions, Garašanin wrote; they "seep into everything" and reshape how

people speak, socialize, and behave themselves as proper nationals. Like other popular "phraseologies," Garašanin suggested, this profusion of patriotism was a transnational phenomenon, one that "travels from one state to another; it has not yet been established whether it is carried by the winds or whether people transfer it."[4] In many ways, this observation resembles Benedict Anderson's idea of the nation as a "modular" template that had become "available for pirating" since the early nineteenth century.[5] While giving support to such interpretations, Garašanin's notes emphasize even more strongly the open-endedness of nationalism, especially its ability to produce an enormous array of expressions and thus keep national forms open to further variations and appropriations across different political contexts.

This proliferation of nationalism is distinct from a second major phenomenon that one can observe in Garašanin's work. The mass spread of patriotic forms, in Garašanin's view, could only create a nationalism that is shallow and inadequate, encouraging impossible patriotic desires. Having condemned his Serbian compatriots for their superficial zeal, Garašanin then called for an urgent renewal of "true" patriotism that would exceed its popular iterations and create an even more deeply patriotic Serbian nation. "Could there be a more magnificent and more patriotic vision than when new activists, new patriots, new preachers of Serbian life" emerge, Garašanin wrote, when activists "create even the slightest cracks through which Serbian thought could radiate outside of Serbia," allowing its nationalism to "burst out with its full power" and "stun the world." What is remarkable about this account is its demonstration of the compelling force of nationalist frustrations and visions. Garašanin simultaneously denounces popular desires for more patriotism as shallow, insatiable, and "infinite," and he himself urgently calls for more and more patriotism. The arc of this logic is important to note: it begins with the premise of flawed patriotism of one's co-nationals and then moves to resolve this foundational disappointment by creating an ever more powerful national project.

A number of analysts have already noted the significance of such pressures and discontents for the formation of new nationalist projects. Homi Bhabha has described nationalism as "an idea whose cultural compulsion lies in the impossible unity of the nation as a symbolic force."[6] Étienne Balibar has highlighted an enduring problem of nation-making in which states and "nationalist ideologies *almost succeed, but not quite . . .* and this situation unleashes a permanent process of displacement and escape. You need more nationalism. You need a nationalism which is, so to speak, more nationalistic than nationalism itself." In this way, "we meet again with the fact that there is no intrinsic end to this process." This phenomenon, as Balibar suggested, is difficult to name; indeed, there are no clearly established terms in critical literature for these dynamics.[7] I propose here a term like "nation-compulsion" as a shorthand for these pressures: a compulsion not in a pathological sense, but something closer to a set of political and moral imperatives that one grapples with as part of becoming and maintaining oneself as a proper patriot.

Focusing on nationalist contestations over Bosnia as its terrain, this book examines the proliferation of national forms and the patriotic compulsion that these forms have historically exerted in an attempt to explain the resilience of nationalism since its emergence in the nineteenth century. The following analysis generally emphasizes two distinct ways in which nationalist politics have remained so open-ended and prolific in their output. On the one hand, this study investigates and specifies the generative processes, such as the ones described by Garašanin, that have helped propel national projects onward by creating new expressions, projects, and variations of national forms in and around Bosnia-Herzegovina. On the other hand, in order to understand what I have called the nation-compulsion, it delves into a number of particular subjects that nationalists in the nineteenth-century Balkans found especially compelling—subjects like "the people," national suffering, youth. Working together, the proliferation and compulsion of nationalism have made it an immensely dynamic and open-ended force, one that eludes any clear sense of historical closure.

Bosnia is an ideal place for exploring these issues. As the site of the 1914 assassination that triggered the First World War and the territory where the term "ethnic cleansing" was invented during the Yugoslav wars of the 1990s, Bosnia has become a global symbol of nationalist conflict and ethnic division in the twentieth and twenty-first centuries. But the formative nationalist contestations over this land began well before 1914, emerging with the rise of new political movements during the long nineteenth century. This book turns to this often-overlooked historical terrain to explore the formation and proliferation of patriotic attachments to this contested national space.

The Approach: Grounded Theory in the Modern Balkans

This approach differs from other accounts of nation-making in several ways, but its fundamental departure is in its insistence on the open-endedness of nationalism that enables it to remain such a vital political project. To grasp the implications of this view, it is necessary to reconsider the often unstated assumptions that underpin textbook accounts of nation-formation. Most scholarly narratives of nation-making trace how certain elites tried to spread and establish their patriotic programs among target populations, such as populations within or around existing state boundaries, or populations seen as the basis for a future, though not yet realized, state. In what is one of the best-known such typologies, the historian Miroslav Hroch presented a three-stage model of the development of nationalism among the "small nations" of Eastern and Northern Europe, progressing from elite scholarly patriotism (phase A) to nationalist advocacy in the public sphere (phase B) to the emergence of a mass political movement (phase C).[8] Dealing not with "small nations" but with great powers of Western Europe, other studies—like Eugen Weber's classic history of French nation-making— explored how already strong states possessing key instruments of nationalization (the army, school, and administration) steadily turned "peasants into Frenchmen." These influential arguments, of course, have been challenged by subsequent scholarship, which has critiqued the "ethnicist" and "statist" assumptions of this historiography.[9] Yet even the arc of most critical studies reinforces, however unwittingly, a core aspect of national narratives: a guiding focus on the final outcome, namely, the long-term consolidation of national identities (including regional counter-identities), a process usually drawing to a close with the establishment of stable state institutions.

It is in this sense that such accounts outline a kind of "completist" paradigm of nation-formation. It is a narrative paradigm in which scholars diagnose and explain the historical factors, obstacles, and phases that made—or failed to make—various populations into nationals, thus completing the process of nationalization in one way or another. The story usually ends there, with Frenchmen, Turks, Serbs, and other nationals clearly established, or with failures like Yugoslavia plainly apparent to us today. Nation-formation in this paradigm is acknowledged as immensely complex, but it is still conceived in terms of finite outcomes, ends achieved or not achieved: languages standardized, masses nationalized, states established, etc. While there is considerable room for gradations, including different sequences, stages, or weak and strong processes, such analyses still pose nation-making as a more or less completable process, with failure usually being read as a self-evident mark of closure.

In the following pages I propose a different approach to understanding the dynamics of nationalism. Can the process that Eugen Weber called the "internal colonialism" of nation-building—in his view a clearly positive development—ever be truly complete? When South Slavic activists like the twentieth-century writer Pero Slijepčević urged that national consciousness must be "foisted directly and forcefully from the outside" on "our own people," what kind of political relations did this activism entail?[10] How and when does one come to know who are, and who are not, one's "own people"? In taking up such questions, this book understands the project of nationalizing one's "own people" not as a passing stage but as the basic structural condition on which national projects are founded and continually renewed.

To get at these issues, I approach national politics in Bosnia using what Claudio Lomnitz has characterized as "grounded theory." In his historical-anthropological studies of nationalism, Lomnitz wrote of the challenge of making "provincial" findings—in his case based on research across

Mexico—speak to a wider range of theoretical and methodological issues. "As opposed to England, France, Germany, or the United States," Lomnitz wrote, knowledge produced in a "provincial" context like Mexico "is usually thought to be parochial and prosaic," lacking the power to set "world-historical" trends or to reshape broad theories of national phenomena.[11] Although Lomnitz wrote of these challenges with Mexico and Latin America in mind, this predicament has also been noted by scholars working on Eastern Europe, Southeast Asia, and other "areas" once marked as non-Western—or insufficiently Western—and thus incapable of generating universalizing principles.[12] As Maria Todorova has shown, the ambiguous geopolitical position of the Balkans—a region long described as geographically European but as historically, economically, and culturally non-European—has similarly ensured that "lack," "lag," and "backwardness" have remained the dominant tropes of analyses of nationalism in this area.[13]

As a way of transcending the limitations usually imposed on provincial knowledge, Lomnitz developed the notion of a "grounded theoretical" analysis of nationalist politics. Such an approach is "grounded because it works through a vast and dense set of facts, and grounded because it has to confront, and hopefully to transgress, an order of confinement" to its provincial locale. It is at the same time theoretical since it seeks to identify and interpret the underlying assumptions and relationships that constitute nationalist politics in a given historical context.[14]

This grounded theoretical approach is especially useful for studying nationalism's cultural forms in and around Bosnia-Herzegovina, allowing us to delve into what Garašanin described as a patriotism driven by endlessly multiplying desires and compelling demands. These distinct phenomena require a kind of historical analysis that differs from the familiar blow-by-blow accounts of nation-building events (e.g., establishment of parties, acquisition of territories, institutional reorganization, etc.), which in themselves cannot adequately capture the development of enduring national forms, subjectivities, and practices. To get at this kind of history, I return to the groundwork of South Slavic national activists—ethnographers, insurgents, teachers, academics, poets, politicians, and other actors often grouped together as "intellectuals"—in order to closely read the archives that they produced and to analyze the issues that they struggled with as they claimed Bosnia for different causes. To call these actors "elites" is, of course, accurate in the obvious sense of this term; emerging nineteenth-century patriots certainly constituted and proclaimed themselves to be a distinct social formation that led and organized nation-making projects. In substantial part, this study is thus a contribution to understanding the cultural and intellectual production of nationalism.[15] But insofar as it invokes hierarchical models of top-down dictation, the term "elites" also risks distorting our focus and obscuring more interesting questions about the workings of nationalism, including questions about how one becomes a patriot, how national forms spread, and what makes nation-making seem, in the eyes of nationalists themselves, so grievously incomplete and so promisingly open-ended.[16]

If some of the key debates in the following pages appear abstract, it is largely because the work of nationalists themselves is inescapably abstract, based as it is around foundational abstractions like "the people," "our brothers," and "national destiny."[17] Instead of avoiding such issues or trying to assign fixed meanings to patriotic subjects, I consider precisely their inhering ambiguities and trace the historical contexts that made them possible. By unpacking recurring concerns of South Slavic activists, I hope to outline research questions that—grounded as they are in the Bosnian terrain—may be useful in other contexts as well.[18]

The Setting: Bosnia-Herzegovina as a National Question

As a province ruled by both the Ottoman and Habsburg Empires during the long nineteenth century—Ottoman until 1878, Habsburg from 1878 to 1914—Bosnia presents a fascinating site of transnational and transimperial competition and mutual influence. At the outset of the nineteenth century, Bosnia was an Ottoman borderland, the Porte's westernmost European province. The province's boundaries were forged in the aftermath of the long Habsburg-Ottoman wars, beginning in the seventeenth and extending into the eighteenth century, when a series of diplomatic treaties set stable borders between the two empires. Bosnia was the name of the larger province that absorbed the southeastern region of Herzegovina after it was reorganized several times and disbanded in 1865, later resulting in the official designation of the land as Bosnia-Herzegovina; the name Bosnia was a common shorthand for the entire region.[19] By the mid-nineteenth century, the rise of the Serbian principality and the strengthening of Montenegro to Bosnia's east and southeast gave the province the outlines that the country roughly holds today (see map I.1).[20] The Ottoman Empire ruled Bosnia until 1875–1878, when a series of peasant uprisings and international conflicts forced Istanbul to cede control of Bosnia to the Habsburg Monarchy. Invoking the international mandate to occupy and "civilize" the province, Austria-Hungary administered Bosnia from 1878 until the First World War, when both Ottoman and Habsburg states collapsed and new states, including Yugoslavia, were created in their wake.

Perhaps the most discussed facet of this land, the one constantly revisited by politicians and scholars alike, was its "national" or "ethnic" composition. Such phrases seem self-evident, evoking confident projections of clear-cut population counts, but the numbers themselves necessarily conflate a vast array of social relations into deceptively solid "ethnic" categories. In Ottoman-era official registers, the key criterion of intercommunal difference was confessional affiliation, usually assessed for the purposes of

Map I.1 "Changes in Turkey in Europe, 1856–1878." In this rendering, Bosnia's position as the outermost Ottoman periphery is emphasized by its borders jutting out of the map frame. From John G. Bartholomew, *A Literary and Historical Atlas of Europe* (New York: Dutton, 1912).

taxation. In nineteenth-century Ottoman Bosnia, population estimates for the province (there were no systematic surveys as such) agree that the Orthodox accounted for the largest number, followed by Muslims, Catholics, Jews, and Roma.[21] Beginning in the 1850s, Ottoman population estimates for the entire province usually cited a figure of about a million inhabitants; the numbers almost doubled during the Habsburg period and reached just under two million inhabitants by 1914. The extensive census counts carried out by the Habsburg administration after 1878 inherited the earlier Ottoman templates, officially using religion as the primary category of difference and treating the resulting groups as autonomous political constituencies. This development is especially significant in light of Habsburg policies elsewhere in the Dual Monarchy, which used language as the basic census category. In Habsburg Bosnia, however, "language" appeared less relevant as a census rubric because most of the population spoke a variant of the same South Slavic dialect, leaving "confession" as the most conspicuous marker of difference.[22]

The last Austro-Hungarian census in Bosnia in 1910 reported approximately the following scheme (by group count and percentage of total population): 434,000 (22%) Catholic, 825,000 (44%) Orthodox, 612,000 (31%) Muslim, and 26,000 (3%) so-called others. Even at the time, the rubric "confessional" was often read as "national"; Orthodoxy was equated with Serbs, Catholicism with Croats, and Islam with Bosniaks or Bosnian Muslims—but nationalists themselves contested these conflations. In 1911, the Habsburg administration produced for its own imperial use one of the first "ethno-confessional" maps of Bosnia: a color-coded, expertly shaded vision of difference mapped onto neatly bounded districts (see map I.2).

Such mappings and numbers, of course, primarily reflect political obsessions rather than the more tangible factors—physical geography, local affiliations, economic relationships—that could be said to "compose" a place. Already in the 1890s, Serbian and Greek geographers openly wrote that their practice of assigning a different color for each ethnic group was "not done in an *ethnographic*, but in a distinct, so to say *ethnocratic* way," denoting not who actually lived in a given area, "but which group is dominant in a given colored area."[23] As many scholars have long stressed, statistics claiming to represent nationality tend to treat groups as homogeneous and permanent, thus concealing other social dynamics and identifications both across and within these categories. Fluctuating census numbers (e.g., showing a rise in the Catholic population during the Habsburg period) can hint at deeper social transformations (population growth, migration changes, conversions, etc.), but they also reinforce the basic rubrics themselves.[24]

During the nineteenth century, emerging national activists projected claims of both unifying sameness and radical difference onto this Bosnian context. Since the 1840s, budding South Slavic patriots—overwhelmingly based in neighboring Serbia and Croatia, where processes of "national

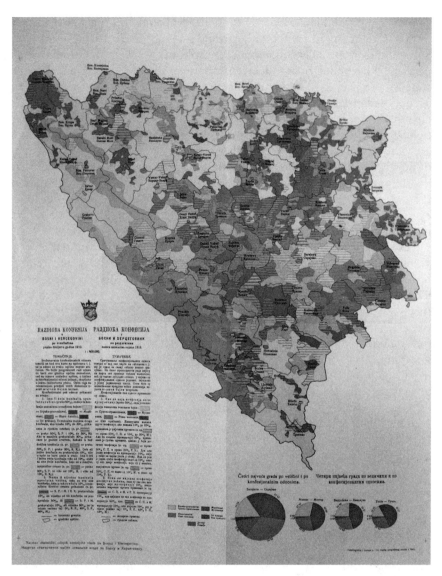

Map I.2 "Division of Confessions by Census," The Statistical Department of the Austro-Hungarian Provincial Government of Bosnia and Herzegovina, 1911. With permission from the Archive of Bosnia-Herzegovina, Sarajevo.

awakening" were already flourishing—looked to the "unawakened" Bosnia as a space where new patriotic sentiments would spread and lead to some kind of national unification. Based in the Habsburg realms, Croatian patriots declared Bosnia and its inhabitants natural parts of their national community, invoking bonds of language, history, and folklore. At the same time,

Serbian nation-builders used very similar arguments to proclaim the same terrain as rightly their own, but they could also rely on a major resource: the autonomous principality of Serbia that broke away from the Ottoman Empire at the beginning of the nineteenth century and became an independent state by 1878. Like Greece and Bulgaria, Serbia claimed many populations around its borders as "Serbian" and sought to expand its territory, particularly in Macedonia (which Serbia partly conquered in 1912) and Bosnia (which remained under Habsburg rule). Since the 1860s, many Yugoslav activists, even as they disagreed with earlier Serbian claims, shared this view of Bosnia as an unliberated land central to their projects. Thus both Serbian and Croatian patriots, including those from Bosnia itself, often appointed themselves as guardians and awakeners of a land that remained—in their eyes—"unawakened," silent, suffering, and generally unable to realize its national potential without its bigger Serbian and Croatian brothers.

European statesmen, journalists, and political figures were intensely invested in the formation of new nations in the Balkans, actively intervening in some situations and generally keeping a close watch over these processes. The Serbian and Greek revolutions at the beginning of the nineteenth century (1804–1817 and 1821–1830, respectively) and the subsequent growth of national movements elicited a tremendous amount of Western European interest and captured the attention of writers from Lord Byron to Leopold von Ranke to Karl Marx.[25] This international framework meant that South Slavic national activists—as well as Ottoman and Habsburg officials—always carried out their work with "Europe" in mind, explicitly appealing to transnational audiences and liberal opinion across England, France, Germany, and Russia.[26]

It is important to remember that Serbian and Croatian movements were inseparably intertwined projects that developed shared repertoires, aims, and practices, especially as they concerned Bosnia-Herzegovina. Leading South Slavic figures frequently depicted Bosnia as a space of Serbo-Croatian national convergence, a process that promised to sweep across the province's different confessions, thus demonstrating the power of the emerging national movements. At the same time, however, rival nationalist claims explicitly opposed each other, claiming Bosnia exclusively for one or the other side and thus envisioning a Serbian-Croatian confrontation over the province.

In declaring national disputes as inevitable, many actors (as well as outside observers) simply pointed to the intercommunal differences—Muslims, Croats, Serbs, and "others" occupying the same place—as guarantees of present or future problems. In these winner-take-all understandings, the diagnosis of difference itself portends division. The history of twentieth-century partitions, designed to identify and separate groups according to various criteria, seems only to reinforce the notion that "different peoples" ultimately cannot live together (e.g., Protestants and Catholics in Ireland,

Hindus and Muslims in India, Serbs and Croats in Yugoslavia, etc.). Although Samuel Huntington's "clash of civilizations" is one recent example of this kind of thinking, the tradition is longer and is familiar to students of Eastern Europe, the Middle East, and other areas where communal differences are cited as insurmountable obstacles to lasting peace. In 1944, a leading Harvard scholar explicated such assumptions in the title of one of the first American surveys of southeast Europe—*The Balkans: Many Peoples, Many Problems.*[27]

The question that arose in the nineteenth century—whose is Bosnia?—captures some of the key assumptions behind nationalist disputes across Eastern Europe. By the 1870s, this question became a ubiquitous staple of Serbian and Croatian polemics, which passionately rehearsed arguments over slogans like "Bosnia is Serbian" and "Bosnia is Croatian."[28] At the turn of the twentieth century, mirroring claims over the same peoples became more intense, assuming languages of "anthropological" and "racial" difference at the same time that Serbian, Muslim, and Croatian activists forged new alliances in the name of Yugoslav unity.[29] Not only Croatian and Serbian, but also Ottoman and Habsburg imperial officials as well as Yugoslav Communists entered these debates, reinterpreting "the Bosnian question" and mapping their own political visions—frequently by appropriating already established patriotic idioms—onto this contested terrain throughout the twentieth century.[30]

Over the past two hundred years, these varied political projects have waxed and waned, with Bosnia erupting to the forefront of particular international crises (as in 1875, 1908, 1914, or 1992) and receding to the background at other times. At certain junctures, especially in the 1930s and the 1990s, plans for a Serbian-Croatian partition of Bosnia were advocated as "solutions" to the persisting "national question in Yugoslavia." Others condemned such attempts as violations of "a historical entity which has its own identity and its own history."[31] Amid the violent dismemberment of Yugoslavia, the Dayton Peace Accord ended the Bosnian War (1992–1995) by instituting de facto partition within the now-independent country (see map I.3). In the wake of ethnic cleansing, Bosnia's status as a "no man's land" has fascinated filmmakers, policy experts, philosophers, and historians across the world.[32] Many also saw the best qualities of socialist Yugoslavia embodied in this place. Slavoj Žižek was certainly not the only thinker to argue in the 1990s that "what could be said to embody the positive legacy of Titoist Yugoslavia—its much-praised multiculturalist tolerance—was ('Muslim') Bosnia."[33]

Since Bosnia was the target of so many rival projects, scholars often confront temptations—sometimes outright requests—to mediate among the competing sides, to bring out alternative voices that speak against nationalist divisions, or to rescue from oblivion some dimension of this land that has been silenced by ethno-national narratives. While I understand these temptations,

Ethnic composition in 1998

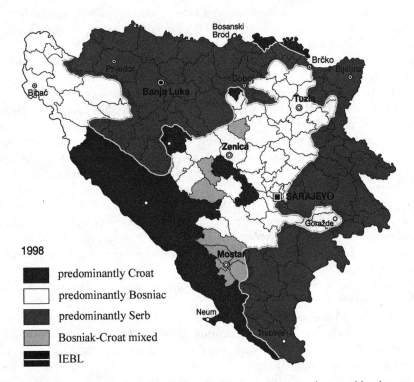

Map I.3 Inter-entity boundary lines of Bosnia-Herzegovina as implemented by the Dayton Peace Agreement, which ended the war in Bosnia (1992–1995). Map provided by the Office of the High Representative, Sarajevo.

and while national and imperial forces have often suppressed different kinds of politics, this book does not claim to speak for some "silent" Bosnia, nor does it aim to recover a Bosnia that is somehow "better"—that is, less nationalist and more liberal—than its past or present.[34] Instead, this book focuses on the dominant forms of nationalist politics, asking what demands, practices, and forces have historically shaped the proliferation of nationalist projects on this terrain, marked as it is by tropes of awakening, silence, and suffering. This book consequently takes a broad view of "the Bosnian question," tracing a wide range of actors and movements that have produced its various iterations. Its key protagonists are not only Bosnians who worked in this province but also actors like Serbian statesmen, Croatian writers, and Ottoman and Habsburg officials who forged intense political attachments to this land and thus made themselves central to its history.

Having passed through hundreds of arguments, visions, and revisions, the nineteenth-century question, "whose is Bosnia?" became a habituated expression of nationalist dispute, a metonym for the more general history of South Slavic national contestations. Precisely because of its deeply engrained status in political discourse, this question deserves closer scrutiny to reveal its assumptions and implicit narrative codes.

The Code of Questions: The Plan of the Book

To ask the question, whose is Bosnia? (or, whose is Kashmir? or, whose is Cyprus?) is to pose an already coded prompt, a riddle that structures expectations and presupposes certain kinds of explanations and answers.[35] The question, whose is Bosnia? presents an apparent enigma that already anticipates contestations, partial solutions, interruptions, and complications between many sides: Serbs, Croats, Muslims, Ottomans, Habsburgs, Yugoslavs, Communists, American peacemakers, and so on. Crucially, such questions presuppose that, after all the entanglements and twists of history, there are answers that provide the satisfaction of having an end to the story. Histories of national questions have often been written with such narrative expectations of *drama* in mind — unresolved question, complicating delays, and answer that reveals the truth and restores clarity.[36]

There are many examples of history written with such narrative expectations in mind. Writing in a series of articles in 2000, for instance, Timothy Garton Ash characterized the toppling of Slobodan Milošević as "the last revolution" that not only concluded the Yugoslav Wars but also signified "*the end* of an even longer and larger story: the two-centuries-old, delayed, and long-interrupted process of the formation of modern European nation-states out of the ruins of the Ottoman Empire."[37] Historians like Gale Stokes similarly found that "solving" the Yugoslav wars required the recognition that the nationalist projects, for better or worse, continue to be the only "realistic" options around. The wars were appalling, of course, but they were simply "*the final working out* of a long European tradition of violent ethnic homogenization," a protracted process of the "redrawing of state borders onto ethnic lines" over the last two centuries. Nationalist partition, however tragic, here appears as narrative relief: the resolution of a number of long-standing historical questions (the Eastern Question, the Bosnian question, the Yugoslav question, etc.).[38] That once-perplexing riddle, whose is Bosnia?, the evasive problem that vexed so many statesmen, observers, and writers since the nineteenth century, thus abruptly arrives at its ultimate settlement in the 1990s through violence, war, and partition. The history of Bosnia told in this key is basically dramatic.

But there are always other ways of reading this history. Instead of playing out the suspense of the dramatic plotline culminating in the present, this book strives to reopen those critical situations where different kinds of national tensions take place, something closer to Brecht's "epic" than to the "dramatic" staging of riveting tragedies.[39] Such an analysis treats "national questions" not as settleable territorial disputes that can be resolved through border changes and power-sharing agreements, but as deeper questions that inhere in nationalist concerns with producing and reproducing proper patriotic subjects. Far from "solving" such questions in the Yugoslav space, the violence of the twentieth century has only intensified and reinvented them for new post-1990s generations. A sustained look at the processes of identification with one's co-nationals reveals the reversible course of these practices, thus removing the aura of inevitability fostered by dramatically coded questions and inviting a more active engagement with nationalism as a living problem.

I write as someone whose personal background is shaped by these histories. I was born in Sarajevo, Yugoslavia, and lived in that city until the outbreak of war in 1992. A year and a half later, my family and I, like many citizens of the newly formed Bosnia-Herzegovina, came to the United States through its refugee resettlement program. I received my professional training and employment as a historian at various American institutions. It will surprise no one that I have deep attachments to Bosnia, Yugoslavia, and the United States. This personal background is, for me, more than a link that connects the autobiographical and the historiographical by way of their shared site; it also made me more aware of the possibilities and limitations of history as a discipline that usually touches only certain senses of the past. This particular project is born out of the conviction that we badly need new narratives not only of Bosnia's national space but also of nationalism as a political force. My aim here is thus not to settle nationalist disputes, but rather to raise research questions about how we, as students of nationalism, can productively study this very much living phenomenon.

The issues that I present in the following chapters are arranged thematically. They are the result of my close reading of nationalist works in nineteenth-century Bosnia, where certain issues kept reappearing in various guises. By following these archival traces, I found myself assembling something like a formative repertoire of nationalist concerns, which constitute the core subjects of this book: "the people," suffering, activism, youth, and imperial rivalry.

Chapters 1 and 2 analyze the emergence of Bosnia as a space central to South Slavic national identifications and patriotic sentiments. Chapter 1 explores how folkloric pursuits in Bosnia and Herzegovina, often dismissed as a passing romantic stage of nationalism, were in fact crucial to the self-fashioning of national activists, enabling them to develop new ethnographic-populist practices and to outline the subject of their activity: the *narod* or "the people." Alongside folklore, Serbian and Croatian activists discovered in Bosnia another core concern: the suffering of the Bosnian

Christians under Turkish rule. As Chapter 2 shows, the vast body of patriotic writing on this subject powerfully reconfigured South Slavic categories of identification and established suffering as a foundational—and continually renewable—sentiment of national consciousness.

The following three chapters analyze struggles over the organization of national activism. Chapter 3 turns to the impact of the Serbian nationalizing mission in Bosnia. It explores the anxieties raised by the process of nation-formation in this province, especially as it concerned the possibility of nationalizing Bosnian Muslims and the disappointments that this project continually produced. Chapter 4 charts the rise of the nationalist youth or *omladina* movements among the South Slavs, paying special attention to the linkages of youth and heroism at the turn of the century. This development, exemplified by the rise of the Young Bosnia movement, not only bolstered political attacks—the 1914 assassination happened "when Gavrilo Princip decided to show Franz Ferdinand whose is Bosnia," one Young Bosnian wrote—but also intensified the nationalist anticipation of youth as an extraordinary but not fully formed political element.[40] Chapter 5 turns to the Ottoman and the Habsburg Empires and their appropriation of nationalist cultural forms; these processes show how these states, often perceived as being "anational" or "supra-ethnic," created patriotic programs in Bosnia from the 1860s onward and made crucial contributions to the proliferation of nationalist politics. The epilogue offers some reflections on these themes more broadly.

Each chapter can be read as a thematic essay in itself, or as a part of an overarching exploration of the formative concerns of nation-making.

Findings: The Co-National as *(Br)other*

Bosnia's history has often been told as either a chronicle of long-simmering ethnic tensions and conflict or as a story attesting to enduring solidarity and peaceful coexistence between Serbs, Croats, and Muslims. Rather than take sides in this debate, this book reconsiders the historical formation of these foundational categories and focuses on the recurring slippages between otherness and sameness, division and unity, in national projects revolving around Bosnia.

The relationship of the Serbian and Croatian movements to Bosnian Muslims provides an especially productive terrain for such an analysis. Like other national movements that rose in the nineteenth-century Balkans, Serbian and Croatian projects defined themselves against the background of "the Turkish yoke," appealing to Christian (both Orthodox and Catholic) peasants to rise up against "the Turks" and their oppression. Yet even as they explicitly named "the Turks" as their mortal enemy, many Serbian-Croatian patriots simultaneously described Bosnian "Turks" or "Muhammedans" as their "brothers," pointing to shared language, customs, and ancestry and calling for a cross-confessional expansion of patriotic sentiments. Many Serbian-Croatian nationalists envisioned a national future where Bosnian Muslims would shed their "backward" qualities and embrace the ethos of South Slavic unity, thus demonstrating the power of patriotism to triumph over political divisions. In 1850, Ivan Franjo Jukić, a leading national activist in Bosnia, summed up these tensions thus: Bosnian Muslims are "the greatest enemies of their own people and their own same-blooded brothers."[41]

My argument here is not that the position of Bosnian Muslims was somehow exceptional, but rather that struggles around Muslims' status as potential *co-nationals* outline an exemplary and central figure of nation-making, a figure that is neither enemy nor ally, neither "ours" nor "theirs," neither "brother" nor "Other"—an undecidable figure that I have called *(br)other*.

To understand the centrality of the (br)other to the work of nationalism, it is helpful to contrast it with another common understanding of relations between co-nationals. The nation is an imagined community, Benedict Anderson famously wrote, "imagined because the members of even the smallest nation will never know most of their fellow-members . . . yet in the minds of each lives the image of their communion." Anderson stressed "fraternal," "horizontal comradeship" as the defining quality of the national community, "regardless of the actual inequality and exploitation that may prevail in each." But in their emphasis on the crucial idea of comradeship, Andersonian accounts tend to frame national bonds in binary terms, resulting in relations that are either "brotherly" or "unbrotherly," harmonious or conflictual, united or ultimately divided.[42] A closer look at these relations reveals a much more interesting and dynamic picture of patriotic brotherhood, one fraught with abiding anxieties over recognizing, identifying, and relating to one's "fellow members," be they peasants, or women, or children, or, in the South Slavic context, Muslims—that is, people continually depicted as backward, ignorant, hostile, disappointing, and otherwise insufficiently patriotic, yet at the same time acknowledged as indispensable to the national future.

The co-national, in this understanding, is the national (br)other: signifying at the same time the potential of being both "brother" and "Other," containing the fantasy of both complete assimilation and ominous, insurmountable difference—and thus making visible a range of passages between seeming opposites. Brothers and brotherhood are deeply naturalized figures in histories of nationalism; part of their power resides in their habitual characterizations of national relations as brotherly, implying or at least expecting a sense of shared ancestry, intimacy, and fellowship among its overwhelmingly male members. This "familial, fraternalist and thus androcentric configuration of politics," as Jacques Derrida and Mona Ozouf have shown, has inscribed particular Christian understandings of fraternity into modern conceptions of democracy, privileging certain genealogies and senses of brotherhood as seemingly universal and self-evident.[43] While Andersonian accounts of "imagined communities" have long viewed the nation as a historical construct, they have nonetheless left intact its crucial assumption of the nation as a self-evident "brotherhood." One task of this book is to bring into sharper focus the brother, this naturalized—and therefore often overlooked—subject of national histories.

Drawing on the writings of Zygmunt Bauman and Jacques Derrida, I suggest the term "(br)other" as an interpretive device, a strategy of double writing that enables us to simultaneously hold two terms that usually have opposite meanings. Taking advantage of the accidental overlap of two terms in English, "(br)other" designates neither a new content nor a third term separate from the foundational binary.[44] It is instead an analytical practice that brings out other meanings, citations, and decisions that one makes in particular readings, a way of keeping in mind different possibilities that inhabit the brother and the Other. Such interpretive practices help us stay alert to the range and reversibility of processes of national identification.

The (br)other as an analytical strategy can be traced here only as an outline; its actual workings emerge more fully through deeper contextual exploration of national relations, which this book pursues in the following pages. Being the subject of different interpretations and interventions, the figure of the (br)other allows us to trace the formation of diverse political valences, relationships, and commitments. Given the assumptions of fraternity as an overwhelmingly male society, focus on the (br)other can also highlight the persistent concerns over the gendering of national subjects and patriotic norms.[45] One could, within the context of uneven power relations between different constituencies, also analyze gradations that make certain figures something like "little" or "big" (br)others.[46] This book cannot develop all of these possibilities of (br)otherhood; instead, it takes the history of Serbian-Croatian attempts to nationalize Bosnian Muslims as grounds for elaborating the meanings of the (br)other as a *co-national*.

Having (br)others for co-nationals exposes a peculiar quality of nationalism: its relentless and impossible drives to "finally" consolidate relations among co-nationals. Since the nineteenth century, countless patriotic projects have claimed to have "finally" settled who is a Serb, or a Croat, or a Muslim, and who is not, to have "finally" established a lasting sense of unity among "our people." Nonetheless, the (br)other reappears, undoing any permanent sense of closure of nation-making and unsettling proclaimed bonds of national unity. To read and write (br)others into histories of nationalism is thus to underline the matters that repeatedly expose this strangeness of "us" as a foundational category of nationhood.

CHAPTER ONE

The Land of the People

"The word *narod* has flooded our poetry, literature, sciences, not to mention our journalism," wrote the Croatian politician Ivan Lorković in 1898 in a reflection on the significance of this term—generally meaning "the people"—for the rise of nationalism in the Balkans. "This is the word that has inspired all the movements in different parts of our people in this century; yet the concept of 'the people' itself proved to be different in content and in scope" for various constituencies. For some, it meant "liberation from the Turks," for others, a folklorist celebration of vernacular "language and education," for others still, it signaled political autonomy in the Habsburg Empire. "But none of these has encompassed this concept in its complete extent or in its full meaning," Lorković concluded. "Every side viewed the people from another perspective, and none managed to fathom the secret depths of the national soul. It has remained unknown."[1]

Getting to the heart of "the people" preoccupied countless writers of the nineteenth century. In the South Slavic context alone, thousands of pages were filled by debates over the implications of the term *narod*, which has been variously translated as the people, nation, folk, population, ethnic community, and so on; in turn, this pivotal term spawned further political references like *narodnost* (nationality or national belonging) or *narodni* (folk or popular, as adjectives). In Serbia, elementary school primers in the 1870s tried to teach the meanings of the term *narod* to schoolchildren by staging inspirational conversations between a father and his son.[2] In Croatia, nineteenth-century scholars published lengthy accounts comparing different connotations of the term *narod* in different Slavic languages.[3] Collections of folklore and writings of romantic poets invariably extolled the *narod* as the indisputable source of the national spirit.[4] While the term *nacija* was also used, *narod* remained the sovereign term for matters relating to "the nation" in the South Slavic contexts. Indeed, when Serbian intellectuals engaged with Ernest Renan's famous lecture "What Is the Nation?" in the 1880s, they translated the question as, "What Is the *Narod*?"[5]

For many, it seemed that any attempt at a definition of either "the nation" or "the people" would result in needless confusion. In 1879, one Serbian theorist spent almost one hundred pages reviewing the "latest scientific research" on "the principle of nationality" only to see countless European writers "come to the strange conclusion that 'nationality' is actually not a defined notion that has stable characteristics or signs, but that the constitutive elements of nationality are very confused, volatile, and in a constantly fluid and unconsolidated state. . . . This seems to be a notion that is truly undetermined, diffuse, without a defined or stable content!"[6] Dizzy with definitional vertigo that usually followed the attempts to fill in this apparent void, most nineteenth-century nationalists resorted to tropes of naturalism that promised to restore self-evident truth to fundamental political categories. Thus the same Serbian scholar who decried the inadequacy of "certain international theories of the nation" concluded that *narod* and *narodnost* were "natural-historical facts" so obvious that they ultimately needed no explanation at all.[7]

If nationalists tended to mystify these concepts, later twentieth-century political scientists, sociologists, and other analysts often proposed critical classifications that distinguished different usages and meanings of terms like "the people," "the nation," or *narod*. Entries for these terms in *The Dictionary of Untranslatables*, an originally French- and later English-language compendium of major political concepts, indicate the key directions of such analyses. *Demos* and *ethnos*, for example, are widely seen as terms for very different political understandings of "the people," while *plebs, gens, populus, pueblo, Volk*, race, and other concepts demarcate still more meanings and possible political platforms. Each of these terms can denote a distinct type of community and can help outline different visions of "the people."[8] For students of nationalism, one of the most familiar questions has been whether a particular conception of "the people" resembles something like *demos* (conceived of as a community of political membership that is relatively expansive and reflective of Enlightenment notions of democracy) or *ethnos* (understood as a limited community of birth or cultural belonging, a concept often traced to central European romanticism).[9]

While such analyses have captured certain strands of political thought, they have also tended to overlook another sense of the notion of "the people," one that goes beyond given templates of *ethnos* or *demos* and instead points to "the people" as a site of *praxis*, a field of nationalist-populist activity where new political positions, subjectivities, and projects were developed throughout and well after the nineteenth century. Moving away from definitions of bounded social bases (communities of birth or membership) allows us to reinterpret the nineteenth-century preoccupations with "the people" as a crucial form of nationalist self-fashioning through particular practices and sensibilities. In a commentary on the works of Bronislaw Malinowski and Joseph Conrad, the anthropologist James Clifford has written of "ethnographic self-fashioning" as a creative historical project that brings into being both the ethnographer, the practitioner of a specific disciplinary code, and the ethnographer's subject. Rather than assuming a prior difference between "self" and "other" (or between European writers and their non-European subjects in Clifford's work), analytical questions about "self-fashioning" projects direct our attention to productive and transformative practices that can create and spread new cultural models, roles, and behaviors.[10]

My aim here is not to add yet another definition of the term *narod* as a given communal basis, but to outline how the nationalist discovery of "the people" constituted a new kind of political engagement—what I call "ethnographic populism"—that was accessible and extraordinarily adaptable, presenting a renewable set of political strategies that spurred on ever more patriotic missions and mutations. This approach allows us to rethink several crucial developments that marked the rise of national movements across Europe during the nineteenth century. In central and eastern Europe in particular, the production of folkloric and ethnographic studies has long been recognized as a quintessential "national science," a branch of knowledge that emerging patriots fervently embraced in the wake of Herder and related romantic inspirations of the late eighteenth century.[11] But the significance of such ethnographic activities has been often misunderstood. Scholars seeking to debunk harmful national myths have tended to see most nineteenth-century folkloric activities as examples of "the invention of traditions," that is, as deliberate nationalist efforts to invent and impose certain narratives and customs on particular constituencies.[12] The overwhelming focus on "fakelore," however, has blinded us to the deeper and more transformative projects of national self-fashioning, projects that enabled the constitution of new kinds of patriotic subjectivities and drove the creation of "the people" as an endless and impossible subject of national-populist pursuits.[13]

Because of its centrality in South Slavic imaginings of nationhood, Bosnia-Herzegovina is an ideal site for such discussions. Over the course of the nineteenth century, leading South Slavic activists—from the famed folklorist Vuk Karadžić to local collectors like Ivan Franjo Jukić—discovered Bosnia-Herzegovina as "the land of the people" and in the process helped develop new practices of national self-fashioning on this central ethnographic terrain.

A Man from the People

At the outset of the nineteenth century, there was little apparent reason why Bosnia and Herzegovina in particular should have attracted any more attention in Serbia and Croatia than other neighboring regions. Prior to the 1830s, in fact, few South Slavic intellectuals and writers expressed any abiding interest in these Turkish provinces. To be sure, there were many mentions of this province, its medieval history, and its conquest by the Ottomans, but on the whole it is difficult to find sustained discussions of these regions, particularly about their relation to areas like Serbia or Croatia.[14] The Serbian Enlightenment thinker Dositej Obradović, one of the first to take up the task of awakening "us Serbs," certainly counted on "the inhabitants of Montenegro, Dalmatia, Herzegovina, Bosnia, Serbia, Croatia (excluding the *kajkavian* speakers), Slavonia, Srem, Bačka, and Banat, except for the Vlachs there," to hear his pleas for Serbian unity; regarding Bosnia specifically, however, he had little to say. If anything, the conspicuous presence of "the Turks" in these areas gave Obradović an opportunity to expound an important point about his cross-confessional vision of the Serbian nation: "In speaking of the peoples in these kingdoms and provinces, I mean both the Greek and Latin Church followers, not excluding the Turks, Bosniacs, and Herzegovinians themselves, since confession and faith can be changed, but kin and language never (*rod i jezik nikad*)." These Turks, however, also had to be additionally explained as being the Bosnian Muslims, not "the real Turks [who] will go back to the state where they came from, while the Bosniacs will remain Bosniacs, and will be as their ancestors, that is, Serbs."[15] Despite providing a backdrop for these notable clarifications, Bosnia remained in Obradović's accounts an otherwise unremarkable "sister land" of the rising and clearly more promising Serbia.[16]

To most Croatian, Slavonian, or Dalmatian intellectuals as well, Bosnia seemed no more outstanding than other provinces in the South Slavic tableau at the turn of the nineteenth century. When Ljudevit Gaj, the leading figure of the Illyrian movement, issued his announcement of the first issue of *Novine horvatzke* (The Croatian newspaper) in 1835, he appealed to readers who may be "Croatian, Slavonian, Dalmatian, Dubrovnikan, Serbian, Carniolan, Styrian, Istrian, Carinthian, Bosnian, and other Slavs," noting the Ottoman provinces but expressing no particularly strong claim regarding the areas across the Croatian border.[17] Yet by the 1840s, Gaj was not only seeking to publish materials from Bosnia in particular but was also introducing himself to potential diplomatic allies as "the head . . . of the society regarding Bosnia and Herzegovina," where he was working for Slavic "liberation from the Muhammedan yoke."[18] In fact, prompted by political agitations of Illyrian activists in these areas, the Ottoman governor Vecihi-pasha lodged a protest to the Habsburg authorities alleging that "a Catholic by the name of Gaj" was sending spies and revolutionaries from Croatia into Bosnia.[19]

To understand the rise of intense Serbian and Croatian interest in Bosnia-Herzegovina, it is first necessary to revisit a crucial intervention in the realm of national culture and language, an intervention that redefined not only linguistic debates but also broader understandings of how and where the key attributes of the nation could be discovered and publicized. In fact, what gave "Herzegovina" in particular a distinct populist ring during the nineteenth century was the work of Vuk Karadžić, whose career and stature afford insight into the process of the Serbian-Croatian discovery of Bosnia and Herzegovina.

Vuk Stefanović Karadžić (1787–1864)—in Yugoslav history simply called Vuk—remains best known as the linguistic reformer and philologist who standardized the Serbian language and thus helped lay the groundwork for the emergence of the shared South Slavic dialects, today called the Bosnian-Croatian-Serbian languages. As the ethnologist Dunja Rihtman-Auguštin described, "Karadžić's linguistic canon, and with it, the pattern of Serbian popular culture and folklore, enjoyed currency as the sole norm for the entire Croatian and Serbian language region, and for Serbian and Croatian popular culture" since the mid-nineteenth century.[20]

It is easy to see why Vuk was held up by both Serbian and Croatian intellectuals as the decisive figure in the history of South Slavic nationalities. As most accounts emphasize, Vuk was born to a peasant family in Tršić, a small village in Serbia near the Bosnian border, and was among the few local children to receive some education before the First Serbian Uprising swept through this region. This personal background—sketched in terms of village life, cattle herders, peasant customs, and folk songs—played a pivotal part in his scholarly work, which he embarked on shortly after leaving Serbia in the wake of the defeated uprising and arriving in Vienna in 1813. Settling in the Austrian capital, Vuk quickly formed deeply productive relationships with many Slavic and German intellectuals of his time, particularly with the Slovene scholar Jernej Kopitar, who gave Vuk crucial advice and support in the imperial capital.[21] Once established as an author, Vuk continued to publish, travel, assemble, and disseminate numerous works—collections of Serbian folk poetry, stories, riddles, proverbs, and customs—which were extraordinarily well received; writers like Goethe, Ranke, Pushkin, and the Grimm brothers wrote euphoric prefaces and promoted Vuk's work across Europe into German, English, French, Swedish, Italian, Russian, and so on.[22]

Perhaps the crowning and certainly the most cited of Vuk's achievements was the reform of the modern Serbian language, codified principally in his dictionary and demonstrated in his later writings. There was, as always, fierce opposition to the creation of the new national linguistic standard; particularly vehement objections to Vuk's Serb-centric argumentation came from Croatia, with philologists like Bogoslav Šulek emphasizing Croatian distinction and more aggressive nationalists like Ante Starčević, whose faction remained small until the late 1860s, vehemently opposing the Serbo-Croatian convergence.[23] Nonetheless, by 1847 (known as the year of "Vuk's victory"), his linguistic standard—what he called the "Herzegovinian" dialect—became the basis for the Serbian and Croatian languages that were formally linked by the Literary Agreement of 1850.[24]

My interest here, however, is not in the linguistic reform victories that Vuk achieved, impressive and partial as they were; much has already been written about them.[25] Vuk Karadžić's project, often referred to as a "war for vernacular language," was not a mere linguistic conflict over the imposition of one dialectical preference over another, but a struggle over the political understandings of "the people" (*narod*), challenging national activists to reconsider who comprises this formation and who generates knowledge about these matters. Vuk's work changed over the years, but amid the shifts in his canon it is possible to discern certain recurring operations and telling preoccupations with the elusive character of "the people." It was, in other words, a struggle to create new political subjects and their attendant practices, imperatives, and sentiments.

In the first instance, there is the problem of locating the exemplary population, region, and speech for the work of national revival. Vuk was fond of posing this question, as he did already in 1814: "Now, were someone to ask me, 'So in which region are the Serbs nowadays located, where they kept the most of its *Nacionalizmus* to this day? And where do they speak Serbian most purely?' I would answer him like this: The core of the Serbian kin and the purest language is located nowadays between the rivers Drina and Morava." In this rendering, the Serbian *Nacionalizmus* (the initial Germanism was soon replaced by expressions like *narodnost*) survived from the "old days" until "nowadays" in regions like Kragujevac, Kruševac, and the Resava area, extending partly across the Drina into Bosnia and "above Novi Pazar into Herzegovina proper"—but its "core" was basically said to be around Šumadija, the region at the heart of the emerging Serbian state.[26]

However, over the next several years that he spent working mostly in Vienna, Vuk adjusted the source of the purity of the Serbian speech toward what he called "Herzegovina." On the seminal occasion of publishing the first comprehensive *Serbian Dictionary* in 1818, Vuk explained that he "divided the Serbian language into three dialects (as it is itself divided)," naming each after the Herzegovina, Resava, and Srem regions, but explicitly insisting on the *Herzegovinian* as the most appropriate basis for any future national work. This idiom, Vuk argued, was the strongest in its eponymous area, but it was also spoken in a far larger geographic expanse by all "who live in Herzegovina, Bosnia (both Greek and Turkish confessions), Montenegro, Dalmatia, Croatia, and [parts of] Serbia."[27] His subsequent publications, including the second revised edition of the *Serbian Dictionary* (1852), continued to make the case for the superiority of a specifically Herzegovinian dialect and spirit. This campaign allowed Vuk to revisit in 1845 the recurring question about the proper location of the exemplary national attributes: "Now that I have shown where Serbian is spoken the worst, anyone can ask me: But where is it spoken the best? Here is the answer to that. Serbian is spoken in the purest and most correct way in *Herzegovina* and in *Bosnia*."[28] Crucially, Herzegovina and Bosnia—unlike the already "liberated" Šumadija—remained under Ottoman rule and were thus perceived by Serbian nation-builders as yet "unliberated" lands (that would remain such throughout the long nineteenth century). This move thus signaled not a simple change from one region to another, from Šumadija to Herzegovina, but rather a more fundamental transformation in the understanding of what constitutes the nation's "core" and its peripheries.

In this transition, Vuk outlined a series of dichotomies that allowed him
to elaborate several subject-positions, positioning and fashioning himself
as both a "man from the people" and as a "patriot-scholar" who expertly
mapped out the contours of national belonging. To establish these relations,
Vuk—who consciously adopted and capitalized on the common romantic attitudes of the time—invariably began by pointing to impurity at the
presumed periphery. Those who "spoke the worst" Serbian and who were
the least truly national were those whom Vuk derisively called "the upper class" (*viša klasa*)—those elite "gentlemen across the Austrian Empire,
especially in Hungary," those doctors, noblemen, lawyers, priests, teachers,
and village district scribes who have become, in various ways, "far from
the people," "as if alienated from their people and their customs" by learning foreign languages (namely, German and Hungarian) and abandoning
village traditions. "It is true that many of our gentlemen study and know
some sciences (*nauka*) that our simple people does not," wrote Vuk, but
their manner of learning only served to separate them further from the village folk.[29] The alienation of the "upper class" from the national body—so
many of "those [Serbs] in the enlightened and free [Austrian] Empire . . .
have become estranged from their kin (*odrodili*) in everything"—has raised
the distance from "the people" (*narod*), both physical and metaphorical, as
an essential consideration in this political imaginary.[30]

In opposition to "the upper class" (obsessed with foreign trends, forget-
ful of popular customs, negligent of older values), Vuk offered an argument for the primacy of the peasant—particularly the peasant out there in
Herzegovina—as the exemplary subject at the center of the nation. This
intertwined reorientation (toward the peasant and toward Herzegovina) is
especially evident in Vuk's introduction to the *Serbian Dictionary* in 1818.
The dictionary was supposed not only to present the first great collection of
Serbian words but also to offer "the literary figures and gentlemen across
Hungary" a lesson in the purest dialect, Herzegovinian, "so that the Srem
and Bačva and Banat people can see how *their brothers* speak over in those
lands, since nothing has been written about that up until now."[31] The dictionary bore out this argument for a vernacular reoriented toward the humble
"brothers in Herzegovina," incorporating many words from oral traditions
in the Ottoman provinces, Dubrovnik, and Montenegro alongside the lexicon
of South Slavic speakers and literatures from Serbian and Habsburg regions.

It is important to note that Vuk himself preemptively raised the charge
of elitist condescension: Serbia's elite "gentlemen" would find Herzegovinian to be "a language of *pig and cattle herders*," a vulgar speech of ignorant peasants.[32] Of course, Vuk did encounter tremendous opposition
to his work on many linguistic points—orthography, lexicon, selection of
material, etc.—but very few of his rivals actually argued against the notion
that the peasants were "honest, hardy folk" who embodied the national
spirit.[33] Vuk's charges of elitist belittlement of the peasantry were very useful

polemical tools, preemptively imputing pompous condescension to his opposition and also revealing an important aspect of his populist reorientation toward a new national center. Before Vuk, Dositej Obradović argued for simplicity in the vernacular-based literary language so that "learned men" and their wisdom "would not only remain among those who know the old [Church Slavonic or other elite] languages but would also extend and reach even the peasants."[34] Vuk's intervention affirmed the focus on the peasant but essentially reversed this direction of enlightenment. From "over in those lands," a place where "the core (*jezgra*) of the people is all *peasants* and *serfs*," genuine national treasures emanated outward and tutored "the upper class" in the ways of pure language, epic tales, beautiful songs, clever proverbs, and so on.[35]

Such an understanding of "the core" significantly differed from other contemporaneous understandings of what constitutes a nation's "center." As Vladimír Macura has shown, "the notion of the center as mediation and intermediary" remained the dominant conception among the Czech national revival thinkers, even for those who went beyond the earlier Herderian ideas to elaborate new convictions about the center as a place of broad cultural and political synthesis.[36] In fact, when the great Czech scholar Josef Dobrovský was asked to intervene in the fierce debate between Vuk and the Serbian writer Milovan Vidaković, he stated that he could not side with Vuk's *Dorfsprache* ("village language") and instead recommended a centrist "middle path" between the "vernacular" (common, oral) and "literary" (elite, written) variants.[37] Vuk categorically rejected this kind of mediating, even if "village language" did not have words for "anthropology or psychology or physics," and even if Vuk in practice used countless "literary" terms not found in "vernacular" speech.[38] Ignoring the appeals for moderation in embracing the folk, Vuk relentlessly promoted a reorientation toward a new center that was "over there" among peasants and cattle herders in areas like Herzegovina, thus continuing his national-populist project that unsettled even some of his own supporters.

Indeed, how could the treasures deep in "the core" even reach outward and make themselves known in the world? One needed "a man from the people." Vuk later recollected, "I first came to Vienna in the middle of the autumn of 1813," just in time to complete his first collection of folk poetry. As fortune would have it,

> my little book . . . came to Mr. Kopitar as the government censor official; and once in his hands, recognizing from it (like he said then and like he says now) that I am a man from the people (*čovjek iz naroda*), and that I am different from all the other Serbs whom he had seen and known before, he came to me to see me.[39]

To become recognized as a "man from the people," Vuk invoked several personal characteristics to establish his profile and authority. Already in

his first work, *The Little Songbook* (1814) that attracted Kopitar's attention, Vuk appealed to the unvarnished quality of his poetry—"here there
is not a single poem enriched by the spirit of education or the reading of books"—and especially to its direct collection straight from the
source: "I am not a singer, but I memorized all these songs twelve years
ago when, in the happiest moments of this mortal life, I lived tending sheep
and goats."[40] Moreover, Vuk's upbringing was apparently crucial to his ap-
preciation of the Herzegovinian dialect, for "that is how it is spoken where
I was born, and that is how I learned it first from my mother and father."[41]
But this appeal to childhood, encapsulated in toponyms like Tršić, Loznica,
and Jadar, "where I heard and without any intention memorized so many
poems," could only go so far since Vuk had to consult numerous other singers and methods of collection for his subsequent publications. Beyond the
repertoire of peasant childhood, then, Vuk also gestured toward his general
association with "the people . . . [including] Bosnians and Herzegovinians,
with whom I spent years," and toward his specific familial ancestry that
led back to "Herzegovina," from where his grandfather emigrated in the
mid-eighteenth century and settled in Serbia.[42]

It was recognition from others that cemented Vuk's status as the messen-
ger from and the pioneer into the land of the people. Jovan Subotić wrote
in an 1846 review of Vuk's work that it took a special "peasant, who did
not study in any great school, [to] establish Serbian as a literary language;
properly speaking, as if he were discovering an unknown land."[43] Vuk himself called attention to the praise heaped on his work by illustrious scholars
like Goethe, the Grimm brothers, Leopold von Ranke, and Sir John Bowring, among many others: "All of erudite Europe marvels and acclaims the
creations of our people, and because of them praises and compliments our
people," he wrote with pride.[44] Vuk was quite conscious of the importance
of the endorsements from prominent universities in Weimar, Jena, and Berlin: "You cannot imagine how other Serbian intellectuals envy him because
of his European fame," Kopitar (Vuk's crucial partner) told Jacob Grimm in
1824.[45] Other Eastern European colleagues took note of Vuk's peculiar profile, leading the Slovak philologist Pavel Šafarik to complain to the Czech
historian František Palacký that Vuk manages "to trumpet his work all over
Europe, which then stares at it, open-mouthed and goggle-eyed; isn't it our
duty to trumpet our own work like that too?"[46]

However, Vuk could not be just a "man from the people"—he was also
a *scholar*. Vuk claimed to be "different from all the other Serbs" because of
his status as a "man from the people," but this background alone was not
enough to propel his rise to international fame. Very few other contemporary
European folklorists, such as Jørgen Moe, Yuriy Venelin, or Elias Lönnrot,
also came from peasant or distinctly lower-class contexts; as Peter Burke
and many scholars have long established, this was in itself exceptional given
the overwhelming dominance of bourgeois, noble, and other "upper-class"

individuals in the nineteenth-century national movements.[47] In other words, Vuk was one of a small number of other "men from the people" who kindled the existing middle-class and aristocratic interests in the folk. It is his transformation of this populist background into a basis for a new body of knowledge—a new national science, complete with its own proper procedures and subjectivities—that marked one of his most significant political interventions.

For all his aversion to the sterile book learning of "the upper class," Vuk still found in his work a certain science that not only helped establish his own scholarly authority but also promoted exemplary new sentiments and practices for aspiring patriots. In polemics over the linguistic standard and debates over the character of folklore, Vuk insisted that his publications were not mere repetitions of things he had heard somewhere from "the people," but were products of careful research, studious travel, and overall serious work. Collection of folklore proved to be fertile grounds for demonstrating his growing expertise as a scholar. In preparing new folk poetry compilation publications from the 1820s onward, Vuk began to travel across the South Slavic regions and cite specific individual reciters that he had discovered as especially talented and illuminating (as opposed to rival singers whom he deemed "poor" or too artificial). Vuk's ability to survey the landscape, to organize exploratory journeys, to find the proper sources, to separate them from inferior figures, to explain the significance of their peasant backgrounds—Filip Višnjić was a blind singer with a gift for composing new epics, Tešan Podrugović was a brigand whose specialty was recitation, the old man Milija could sing well only when he drank enough (but not too much) brandy, etc.—advanced his Europe-wide reputation as a master collector of folklore.[48]

Moreover, Vuk was fond of creating new classification schemes that came to stand as marks of his scientific activity. Not only did he bitterly argue with rivals over the many controversial categorizations of Balkan dialects, but he also established a profoundly influential, if rather straightforward, gender-based taxonomy of South Slavic folk poetry. "All our folk poetry," Vuk announced in 1824, "is divided into *heroic* poems, which people sing with the *gusle* [a single-stringed instrument that became a symbol of South Slavic folklore], and into *women's* poems, which not just women and girls sing, but also men, especially younger ones." Heroic (*junačke*) songs were supposed to be longer epic tales (of conquests, battles, deeds) and women's (*ženske*) were shorter lyrical songs (of love, longing, nature, etc.). Both kinds of poetry existed across the South Slavic areas, but in the Habsburg regions, according to Vuk, they were neglected, disparaged, and badly sung, whereas the best examples and singers (both men and women) were to be found "further inland, especially toward Bosnia and Herzegovina."[49] In this repertoire, Vuk recognized that some songs are "on the border line between women's and heroic ones, so that one does not know how to sort them

Ерцеговац, пјева уз гусле.

out." He nonetheless proceeded to categorize and publish them mostly as gender-separate volumes, a pattern that other ethnographer-activists continued into the twentieth century.[50]

This was supposed to be a serious scholarly undertaking with little room for funny stuff; there were, of course, also "many humorous songs, but of them I now do not know any one in its entirety," Vuk claimed. His own writings, however, provided several examples that suggested how humorous poetic forms easily gave rise to the "heroic" depictions and thus disrupted the confidently asserted male-female, heroic-lyrical dichotomy.[51] Despite these genre- and gender-crossing affinities, it was paramount to keep the heroic register, considered to be the most significant for national awakening, in a properly somber and dominantly male element. One of Vuk's leading students later wrote in 1868: "I always wondered why [Vuk] never recommended that I collect for him humorous folk tales, asking only for those supernatural and serious ones" (an absence that several ethnographers later tried to address).[52] Even when describing one of his best singers, Tešan Podrugović, as a fellow "who very much liked to tell jolly and funny tales," Vuk immediately cautioned that "he never laughed, but always had a bit of a stern grimace."[53] If there were smiles in this cultural project, they were those of listeners' patriotic admiration and enchantment, as shown by the 1823 frontispiece illustration of the exemplary folk singer, composed according to Vuk's personal instructions: "*The Herzegovinian*, singing with the *gusle*" (see figure 1.1)[54]

The making of Vuk the scholar, then, entailed sustained cultivation of new sentiments and practices revolving around particular notions of "science" and "learning" (*nauka* in Serbo-Croatian, a term loosely meaning science, but also possessing a host of connotations of knowledge production). This was an absolutely crucial—and largely overlooked—development that reinvented a field that romantic nationalists had widely condemned and seemingly abandoned. What Herder himself called *Kultur der Gelehrten* (learned culture) was cast off as elitist, abstruse, and obscure, whereas the *Kultur des Folkes* (popular culture) was passionately celebrated and embraced. Yet despite their apparent banishment, science and learning had triumphantly reappeared to claim a central place in nationalism, emerging as practices of ethnography, linguistics, history, geography, and other "national sciences" and patriotic bodies of knowledge about "our people."[55]

Vuk's evolution from a "man from the people" into a "patriot-scholar" is reflected in his presentation of himself in the title pages of his pioneering grammar and folk poetry collections. Initially referring to himself only by

Figure 1.1 (**opposite**) "The Herzegovinian, singing with the *gusle*": Illustration for Vuk Karadžić's *Narodne srpske pjesme* (1823). Image courtesy of the Museum of Literature and Performing Arts, Sarajevo.

his name in 1814, Vuk subsequently added a number of clarifications in his books published in the 1820s and 1830s: "Vuk Karadžić, a Jadranian from Tršić, and by ancestry a Drobnjak from Petnica [village]"—that is, an invocation of his peasant childhood (innocence, sheep, memory) along with references to familial descent (heritage, socialization, Old Herzegovina). This bolded *man from the people* label was then followed by, in smaller letters, a longer list of his later credentials as a *scholar*: "Doctor of philosophy, member of the learned societies, academies, and research institutes in St. Petersburg, Cracow, Thuringia-Saxony, Göttingen, Belgrade, Moscow," Berlin, etc.[56] Early biographies appearing in German, Russian, and English editions of Vuk's works—such as this 1827 introduction by Sir John Bowring—stressed this trajectory: from a peasant child in "an obscure village in Turkish Serbia (Iadar)" to Vienna, Leipzig, and other European cities where he learned to direct "his inquiries to the hidden stories of popular literature which his country possessed. . . . He soon obtained high reputation there and received the diploma of doctor in philosophy and was elected to many literary distinctions."[57]

Vuk was keen to draw a distinction between what he saw as the artificial learning of "the upper class," dominated by seemingly esoteric subjects, and the healthy, even indispensable patriotic instruction that all proper nationals—even peasants—had to experience. When a fellow patriot wrote verses attacking "the grammaticians" for their petty regulations of the people's language, Vuk stood up against such criticisms and defended the learned work of "grammaticians" as indispensable, "like that of a historian of his time, or of a statistician who describes things as they are."[58] Writing in a major 1849 treatise, he stressed the role of sciences and learning in the formation of patriotic sentiments: "As Greeks and Romans have already taught us, the noble, pure, and real love for the people, by which a man loves his own people and its well-being and glory more than himself and his life, is not born with man, but is received through learning (*nauka*) and upbringing."[59]

These were pivotal interventions that outlined a new subject-position that Vuk and other ethnographer-populists came to promote: that of a "patriot-scholar," one who belonged neither to "the upper class" nor completely to "the people," but occupied a distinct third national figure. This form of ethnographic-populist conduct proved to be extraordinarily appealing over the course of the nineteenth century; it provided an accessible, widely adoptable, and easily imitable set of patriotic practices revolving around the collection, publication, and analysis of poetry and other material pertaining to "our people." The patriot-scholars that emerged with the romantic discoveries of the folk endured as role models of what one Serbian academic in 1908 called "a real *self-made-man*, just as Vuk himself was" (a phrase spelled out in English in the Serbian original).[60] Seen in this light, Vuk's publicly performed transformation—a trajectory that took this "man from the people" and remade him into a distinct "patriot-scholar" leader—illustrates how ethnographic activities worked as a medium of national self-fashioning, a way of establishing oneself as a proper national and of creating one's subject of political activity.

Vuk's significance in this regard definitely did not lie in any meaningful claim to intellectual originality; he openly adopted his key positions and terms—like the familiar opposition between "the culture of the learned class" and "the vitality of peasant life"—from renowned European thinkers like Herder, Schlegel, and Kopitar. It is precisely because Vuk came to embody these commonly held romantic ideals and act as a pivotal guide to and from the lands of "the people" that he was able to claim such a major role in the cultural life of his time. If Vuk was any "different" from other contemporaries, it was only insofar as he provided an especially compelling way of publicly performing and enacting the relationships that bound "the people" to the birth of new national-ethnographic "sciences" devoted to studying them.

The Discovery of Herzegovina

As Vuk established himself as a patriot-scholar, his central subject of study was a strangely elusive land: "Herzegovina." Throughout his work, Herzegovina remained a pivotal and recurring site of reference that stood for a number of interrelated matters: for purity of language, for profusion of folklore, for heroic poetry, for a notion of "the core" that happened to be—when viewed from the perspective of national awakeners in Serbia and the Habsburg Empire—out there, over among the villagers and cattle herders beyond the Ottoman border. A recurring and exemplary folk character in many of Vuk's collections of proverbs and folk tales was "Ero" or "Hero," a peasant man whose very name is derived from "Herzegovinian."[61] As Vuk once stated while explaining his preference for this site, "one should also know that the peasants in those lands over there [i.e., under Ottoman rule] do not yet have those worries or needs like they do in the Christian lands, so they live quite like in those times that are called *the golden age*."[62]

This site was multiconfessional, presenting a critical test case for the extent and the character of national belonging that seemed to be emerging along what Maria Todorova called "the double boundary of religion and language" in the Ottoman Balkans. During the nineteenth century, Serbia, Greece, and Bulgaria broke away from the Porte, forming new national communities that stressed confessional and linguistic dividing lines.[63] In practice, the new Serbian nation was most clearly defined in negative relation to the Ottoman rulers, stressing that the Serbs were overwhelmingly Orthodox Christians (not Muslims) who spoke the Serbian language (not the Ottoman Turkish of the viziers and janissaries who abused the *raya*, the

Christian subjects in Ottoman Bosnia). The Serbian statesmen of the early nineteenth century continued to push this differentiation even further after the end of the Serbian uprisings in 1817, officially confining and eventually expelling nearly all "Turks"—Slavic-speaking or not—from the emerging principality. The combination of these revolutionary measures thus made Serbia an effectively Orthodox Christian country that sustained tense relationships with other confessions.[64]

Vuk, a participant in the 1804–1813 Serbian Uprising, shared much of the anti-Turkish ethos of Balkan Christian liberation, often writing about the Turkish oppression of the *raya* and calling on his colleagues across Europe to help relieve their suffering by overthrowing Ottoman rule. An unsigned article that Vuk sent to the *Augsburger Allgemeine Zeitung* in 1833 described how "all the Turks" in Bosnia and Herzegovina "are almost unrestrained lords over the *raya*," using "every chance to vent their violence on them."[65] The heroic poetry that Vuk collected, particularly the collection of Kosovo poems and the epics depicting the First Serbian Uprising of 1804–1813, glorified the fight against the Turks as a political duty of Serbian patriots.[66] Similarly, Vuk's 1836 collections of proverbs contained a number of references comparing "the Turks" to predatory "wolves," depicting the cruelty of Turks who impaled *hajduk* outlaws and taunted them on the stake, and often casually mentioning Turks as "evildoers."[67] Moreover, in an 1854 letter to the Montenegrin prince Danilo Petrović Njegoš, Vuk stressed his family background as proof of his anti-Turkish credentials: "You know what the family house of Karadžićes in Herzegovina was and how it fought with and slaughtered the Turks just like anyone else . . . [My relative] duke Šujo, in addition to his heroism and constant war-making against the Turks, is a relative of your father."[68]

From the perspective of Vuk and other Serbian awakeners, the "Turkish yoke" clearly had to be overthrown, preferably by the expansion of Serbia, but the prospect of an emerging Serbian state raised still new questions. Who exactly were "the Turks" in Bosnia, given that Serbian and Croatian activists used the same term both for their "brothers of the Turkish faith" and for the hated Ottoman oppressors? Could any "Turk" be a Serbian brother?

Vuk dealt with these issues by articulating a broadly assimilationist stance that insisted on the primacy of language, not religion, as *the* national marker. In regard to the rather large Bosnian Muslim population, he insisted that these "Turks" are in fact "Serbs" because they spoke "Serbian," and spoke it "most purely" and "beautifully" at that. Regarding Herzegovina and Bosnia, Vuk explained, "It is true that over there in towns and cities there are a lot of Turkish words"—a constant cause of concern for Serbian and Croatian linguists—"but it could almost be said that, among other things, those brothers of ours of the Turkish faith speak Serbian more beautifully than the peasants of either the Greek or Roman [i.e., Orthodox and Catholic] faith! Their Turkish words we will easily replace with ours in the writing of books."[69] The Bosnian Muslims were thus acknowledged as an integral, even linguistically exemplary part of the national community, yet their incorporation—and the overarching vision of "our people" that this process entailed—came with several important stipulations and clarifications.

There was, for instance, Vuk's insistence on the proper national name, recognizing Bosnian Muslims as members of the South Slavic national community under the condition that they would eventually "realize and admit that they were not Turks, but Serbs."[70] Moreover, there was the expectation that Muslims would, in due course, also abandon their "Turkish" attributes. Among other things, conversion to Orthodoxy was suggested as a possible, if remote, option. Vuk's own vernacular translation of *The New Testament*, he wrote in 1831, might prove to be useful for "the Turks and other non-Christians (*nerišćanima*)"; in fact, "I would precisely like to print [it] for the Bosniacs" in "their own dialect."[71] In a reinterpretation of Obradović's plea, Vuk's new framework encompassed different confessional communities, proclaiming the unity of *Serbs of all three faiths*," Muslim, Orthodox, and Catholic; Jews were rarely, if at all, mentioned and were practically excluded. This blanket claim covered in his judgment "at least five million souls," though Vuk freely admitted that "only three million call themselves Serbs, and the rest do not accept the name."[72]

But confessional, imperial, and regional distinctions, Vuk stressed, ultimately mattered little at the moment as long as everyone—including "the Turks"—spoke the same language. "We must all make the effort that our literary language be so consistent so that every book can be exactly reproduced in Latin and Cyrillic letters," Vuk urged in 1845. "And when, in due time, we are joined by our brothers of the Turkish faith, our brothers by kin and by language—across Bosnia and across Herzegovina—then we will be united like the Germans of Catholic, Lutheran, and Calvin religions" and everyone will enjoy "honor and dignity."[73] This unifying power of language and folklore across South Slavic religious divides attracted the attention of observers like Leopold von Ranke, who wrote in 1829 with the help of Vuk's supplied notes: "Even those Serbs who converted to Islam could not, to this day, separate themselves from their love of folk poetry. There are identical, self-same poems on both sides; only each respectively sings of the deeds of his own hero. . . . Poetry overcomes difference in religion: it joins together an entire tribe with strong ties, it lives in the entire people." At the same time, both Ranke and Vuk continued to stress the alien, antagonistic, and "fanatical" qualities of "the Turks" and "the turned Turks," posing "the centuries-long struggle between Islam and Christianity" as the main theme of Serbian history and the ongoing struggle for independence.[74]

Vuk's famous *Serbian Dictionary*, widely upheld as "the mirror of the people," visually reflected this ambivalent relationship to Bosnian Muslims as national (br)others. In this massive assembly of terms, the only entries singled out by an asterisk were "Turkish words" for which Vuk could find no suitable replacement—*kičma* * (spine) or *jastuk* * (pillow)—leaving them highlighted as integral yet uneasily admitted parts of the Serbian language.[75] (See figure 1.2.) In fact, had Vuk's own last name appeared as an entry in the dictionary, it would have been marked with an asterisk on account of its obvious Turkish etymology: "*kara* *, indeclinable adjective, black."[76] To this day, the vast majority of these starred words have not been replaced by other coinages, remaining integral parts of the Serbo-Croatian language. The asterisks punctuating the great national text thus alerted the readers

КА́ПОТ   **264**   КАРА̀ШНИЦА

КА́ПОТ, m. (у Ц. г.) гуњ с кукуљицом.
КА́ПОТИНА, f. (у Ц. г.) augm. v. капот.
КА̂ПТА̂Р, m. од луба као капа што се меће на кошнице да их чува од кише.
КА́ПУЛА, f. (у Дубр.) die Zwiebel, caepa, cf. лук.
КА́ПУРА, f. (у Грбљу) vide капорка.
КАПУ́РИНА, f. augm. капа.
КА́ПУ̑Т, капу́та, m. 1) der Kaput (österr.), Kapot, genus togae. 2) (у Ц. г.) vide капот.
КА́ПЦА, f. dim. v. кап.
КА̂Р, m. 1) das Ausschelten, increpatio: Кар је Божји дар, али је мука кад бију па не даду плакати; Од *кара* глава не боли. 2)*, vide брига, Sorge, cura.
КА̀РА*, adj. indecl. vide црн:
  И метни му расток на обрве,
  Кара бóју на зулове —
  Синоћ мене *кара* хабер дође,
  Кара хабер, а у *кара* доба —
КА́РАБЕ, ка̀ра̂ба̂, f. pl. vide карабље.
КА́РАБНЦЕ, f. pl. dim. v. карабе.
КА́РАБЉЕ, f. pl. 1) eine Art Hirtenflöte, fistulae genus. 2) на гадљама, das Flötenstück am Dudelsack, fistula utriculi: гадљар у карабље удара прстима, а доље је на карабљама рог.
КА́РАБЉИЦЕ, f. pl. dim. v. карабље.
КА́РАБОГДА̀НСКА̂, f. adj. die Moldau, Moldavia: Дмитар узе земљу Каравлашку, Каравлашку и *Карабогданску* —
КАРА̀ВИДА, f. ein Frauenname, nomen feminae.
КАРА̀ВИЉЕ, в. die Nelke, dianthus caryophyllus Linn.
КА̀РАВЛА, влаа, m. vide Каравлах.
КА́РАВЛАХИНА, f. vide Каравлахиња.
КА̀РАВЛАХ*, влаха m. der Walache aus der Walachei, Valachus proprie u Valachia.
КА̀РАВЛАХИЊА, f. die Walachin, mulier Valacha.
КА̀РАВЛАШКА̂, f. adj. die Walachei, Valachia. cf. Влах.
КА̀РАВЛАШКИ̂, ка̂, ко̂, walachisch, valachus.

КА̀РАЊЕ, n. das Ausschelten, objurgatio.
КА̀РА̂Р*, кара́ра, m. das Gleichgewicht, aequilibrium: Сам је Бог на *карару*.
КА̀РАТИ, ка̀ра̂м, v. impf. ausschelten, objurgo.
КА̀РАТИ, m. pl. (у Ц. г.) плата кметовима или судијама од онијех којима суде, die Prozesskosten, litis summa.
КА̀РАТИ СЕ, ка̀ра̂м се, v. r. impf. 1) einander schelten, objurgare se invicem. 2) н. п. кара се отац, Бога, zürnen, irascor.
КАРА̀ТУНА, f. вода у Рјечкој нахији у Црној гори, Name eines Flusses, fluvii nomen: *Каратуну* воду пријеђоше —
КАРА̀УЛА*, f. der Wachtthurm, specula, turris excubitoria.
КА̀РАЧ, кара́ча, m. der Schelter, objurgator.
КАРА̀ЧИЦА, f. она која се кара, die Schelterin, quae increpat, objurgat:
  А јетрве *карачице* —
КА̀РАШ, кара́ша, m. die Karausche, cyprinus carassius Linn.
КАРА̀ШНИЦА, f. вода у Славонији, Name eines Flusses, fluvii nomen.
КАРА̀ШИНЧАНИН, m. човјек који живи покрај Карашнице, Einer der an der Карашница wohnt.
КАРА̀ШЉАМА, f. некаке ране трешње, eine Art Kirschen, cerasi genus:
  Карашламе у меду кухане —
КАРА̀ШЧИ̂Ћ, m. dim. v. караш.
КА́РБА, f. (у Боцн) das Ausschelten, increpatio, cf. кар.
КАРБО̀НА̂Р, карбона́ра, m. (у војводству по варошима) Art Mantel, pallium:
  У швалера *карбонара* нема —
КА̂РБА, f. (понајвише се говори pl. карве) пречаге у лотре, die Sprosse, gradus, cf. нглица.
КА̀РБА̂Н*, карва́на, m. die Karawane, commeatus, comitatus.
КА́РЕТ*, m. die Strafe beim прстен-Spiel, mulcta (poena) in ludo annuli.

Figure 1.2 The "mirror of the people," with an asterisk. The entries marked with an * in Vuk Karadžić's *Serbian Dictionary* (*Srpski rječnik*, 1852) signified Turkish-derived words, which "we will easily replace with ours."

to the presence of "Turks" even in the purest national language and raised unsettling questions. Were "the Turks" a part of "our people" or not? By what criteria could one come to identify (with) one's co-nationals? How could one discover and map out relations of belonging that constitute one's own people, the "our selves" of the nation?

Vuk's commentaries on such considerations continually returned to "Herzegovina" as the ideal site for clarifying and working out a number of exemplary national matters. Over the course of his career, Vuk forged and invoked a privileged relationship to this land, leading both his critics and supporters to debate his frequent appeals to Herzegovina in so many different contexts. For instance, after Vuk published yet another unrelenting broadside against rival linguistic projects, a colleague complained of Vuk's relentless vehemence: "But how strange are the Herzegovinian blows! It is terrible to fall to the hand of a Herzegovinian!"[77] Whereas some associated Vuk's Herzegovina with a new kind of populist criticism, other more sympathetic observers were willing to interpret Vuk's insistence on Herzegovina more generously, not as a place that he retreated to in polemics, but rather as a new direction of cross-confessional national revival, a direction described explicitly as a redrawing of borders. "And [Vuk] himself had long drawn his drafting compass and expanded on the other side the terrain (*zemljište*) of the people's language. No longer is Herzegovina his Paris, but now Herzegovina is everywhere where Serbian is spoken," the Serbian scholar Jovan Subotić approvingly noted in 1846.[78] However, at the same time, other national activists refused to accept that Herzegovina could be so easily dispersed and dispensed with as being "everywhere," since it clearly stood for a more specific place. Jovan Stejić, a prominent Serbian intellectual, complained in 1847: "Really! He [Vuk] says: '*in the people*' (*u narodu*). . . . We thought he directed us to our *entire* dear people; but these days we just figured out that this people of ours, which speaks Serbian so well, is only out there in *Herzegovina*."[79]

What makes Karadžić's dedication to Herzegovina and Bosnia remarkable—and significant for the forging of new understandings of nationhood—is that he never visited or traveled through this "land of the people." This obvious fact of Vuk's work has become strangely invisible and curiously forgotten in the subsequent assessments of his career. Indeed, it is not even mentioned in any English-language studies.[80] It is an obvious fact because Vuk himself acknowledged several times his lifelong absence from Herzegovina and Bosnia; and it is invisible because the authority of his knowledge, reinforced by his oft-repeated references to his family's lineage, made it unquestionable that Vuk was anything but a Serb originally from Herzegovina. Despite frequently expressing the desire to undertake a journey to Herzegovina and Bosnia, the lands he had written so much about, Vuk never quite managed to cross those borders, citing problems with funds, travel documents, and other pressing obligations. He stated numerous times his intention to step into what was, by his own account, a fascinating world, but, much to his regret, his hopes never materialized. As he put it in a note in the second edition of the *Serbian Dictionary* in 1852, "For this work, I have traveled all over, as for example, to Croatia, Dalmatia, Boka, and Montenegro. If I had, by some fortune, been able to go to Bosnia and Herzegovina and to Kosovo and Metohija, I would have surely found many more significant words, but despite my desire, it could not be."[81] Vuk's aspiration to "collect our nationality" (*kupiti našu narodnost*) across all areas—especially to visit "our people and Bosnia and Herzegovina"—turned into a lifelong endeavor that, as he predicted, "I will take with myself to the other world."[82]

At the heart of this project, then, was a curious gap. There, the scholar pointed, behind those hills or just further down the road, there is something we may not have yet seen, whose voice we may not immediately recognize, whose character we may not yet have fully verified—but whose true name the scholar already knew: "the people." The tentative ellipsis, the ambiguous space apparently waiting to be explored, thus turned out to be not a blank at all, for something well known was there all along. In Vuk's case, his peculiar relationship to "the people" is perhaps all the more noticeable thanks to the contrast between the conspicuous presence of Herzegovina and Bosnia in his work and his lifelong absence from these "core" lands of the Serbian nation. It is rather unlikely that forays into this land, whether quick excursions or long, studious journeys, would have done away with the foundational gap that sustained this endeavor of national awakening.

Despite Vuk's nonpresence in these lands, the emerging contributions regarding Bosnia had to be continually measured against his great authority. In the 1830s, an emigrant from Bosnia, the priest Pavle Karano-Tvrtković, approached Vuk with some "historic documents" that he apparently got from some monasteries, asking the great scholar to help him publish these and "other works about Bosnia."[83] Karano-Tvrtković posed similar queries to the Illyrian leader Ljudevit Gaj, with whom he spent some time in 1837 discussing the state of South Slavic literature.[84] For his part, Vuk cautioned that only an expert hand—his own would do—could actually pull it all together, but Karano-Tvrtković nonetheless proceeded alone, publishing *Srbski spomenici* (Serbian historical documents) in 1840 with a short preface on the geography and current affairs of Bosnia, "so that Serbs will now find out" more about their "brothers in my dear fatherland."[85] In a polemic that he initiated over the book's portrayal of the Bosnian "fatherland," Vuk recognized the well-intentioned effort but also disputed and firmly corrected the Bosnian priest's knowledge of Bosnia, which Vuk mastered through his own vicarious insight into the land: "I knew even earlier how [certain place names in Bosnia] were spoken in Serbian, and later I was confirmed and convinced anew in Vienna by Jovo Besara from Sarajevo (through which Miljacka flows and from which Mount Trebević is seen), and now here in Zemun by Toma Ćuković of Trebinje and two Turk Bosniacs from Ževče."[86]

Yet even in these moments of assertion of the authority of his knowledge, Vuk still conceded that "we have nothing decent printed about Bosnia."[87] There was much to be learned and authenticated, from geography to history to folklore to the ongoing events in the Ottoman provinces. The need for such accounts was pressing since Vuk often had to respond to European journalists' and historians' calls for materials about the uprisings, reforms, and other events in Bosnia and Herzegovina. When the great German historian Leopold von Ranke planned to write an essay on Bosnia in 1833, he asked Vuk to "describe the Bosnian affairs, which you without a doubt know well." Vuk naturally obliged, but also at the same time admitted that he found it quite difficult to assemble even a general report on Bosnia. Vuk finally sent these Bosnian materials to Ranke with a list of several qualifying notes: "(3) About the characteristics of the land I can tell you for now only that it is mountainous. (4) I also do not know reliably the population numbers. Bosniacs do not just live in the towns and fortresses (like they do in Serbia), but they (like the peasants) also live on the land, in the villages, where they do not have mosques, so they go to nearby towns to . . . on Fridays [*ellipsis in the original*]. Many of the richer Bosnian beys have their mansions in the villages and live there permanently."[88]

Ranke published his "Sketch on the Insurrection in Bosnia" in 1834 based almost entirely on the materials provided by Vuk, making a noted contribution to European studies of this curious Ottoman region.[89] But the underlying call to gain deeper knowledge of this peculiar province nonetheless remained insufficiently answered. To inform the various Serbian and Croatian patriots about their brothers, to convince the European public of the glory of South Slavic folklore, to learn about the land of the people, the ellipses had to be either omitted altogether or filled out in more detail.

Generating Knowledge about "the People"

The creation of new bodies of patriotic knowledge about Herzegovina and Bosnia became a driving preoccupation for Croatian and Serbian nationalists during—and well after—Vuk's discovery of these two lands. Vuk's death in 1864 only intensified the ongoing searches for the "core of the people" that supposedly remained untouched and uncollected somewhere "out there." Vuk's posthumous collection *Serbian Folk Poetry from Herzegovina* (1866) served as a testament to this unfinished project; as the preface clearly stated, the book was actually the work of another collector, Vuk Vrčević from Dalmatia, but it was Karadžić's name that ultimately appeared on the title page.[90] For his part, Vrčević was glad to cede authorship to his great mentor, whom he met in 1835 and whose guidance led him to the one land that the famed folklorist idealized—Herzegovina.[91] "When I came to [the Herzegovinian town of] Trebinje in 1861," Vrčević wrote, "I saw a miracle of miracles and witnessed with my own eyes that this here is the real seedbed of Serbian national poetry. I say a miracle, since in Herzegovina even under the [Muslim] crescent . . . fathers sang heroic songs to their sons with the *gusle*, while mothers sang lyrical love songs to their daughters by the weaving loom." Thanks to such writings, the reputation of Herzegovina as a land that embodied the fictional "purity" of the folk—in gender relations, language, customs, and so on—continued to thrive throughout the nineteenth century.[92]

Many aspiring patriots like Vrčević, however, struggled to improve on the pioneering work of "the father of Serbian nationality," who remained like "a ghost" in South Slavic patriotic literature.[93] Ognjeslav Utješenović-Ostrožinski similarly stressed that "there remained an immense amount of work" to be done for national culture after the passing of the great scholar: "Vuk labored in that field like a poor man who finds a rich golden ore in a great mountain, and striking randomly with his shovel in the ribs of that giant, he dug from his entrails as much as he could. . . . But there is no more Vuk. . . . It is our task to continue the effort."[94] A Serbian student society in Vienna also resolved to continue Vuk's mission in the 1870s: "For this work, 'Dawn' would name people who would travel as apostles among the people (*kao apostoli po narodu putovati*) and report on its inner position" for scholarly publication. Despite such ardent desires, it proved difficult to find a sufficient number of "trained men, who would not do it superficially, but who were actually capable of performing it in a scholarly-serious manner (*naučno-ozbiljno*)."[95]

In practice, generating knowledge about "the people"—especially "the people" in the core lands of Herzegovina and Bosnia—was a task made difficult by a number of issues. To begin with, there was the intimidating presence of Ottoman Bosnian authorities, who were hostile to any initiatives seen as nationalist and therefore damaging of the Porte's already weakened territorial integrity. Moreover, literary circumstances in the province itself proved inhibitive to the spread of new patriotic ideas. During Vuk's life, his publications and dictionaries found their way rather slowly to a very small number of subscribers in Sarajevo, Mostar, and other Bosnian towns.[96] From the outset of Vuk's work, it became apparent that finding local patriots in Bosnia itself was going to be a very long and difficult undertaking. As one Bosnian Franciscan student complained in 1839 in a letter to the Illyrian leader Ljudevit Gaj, "Of all the Slavic people, as far as learning is concerned, the Bosnians remain the deepest in the mud, so to say."[97] Three decades later, "it was naturally expected that with time an unimaginable multitude of the most beautiful Bosnian and Herzegovinian folk poems would appear" as numerous "works attempted to answer Vuk's longtime desire" to explore these lands, the renowned Croatian literary scholar Vatroslav Jagić wrote in 1868. "But unfortunately not much of substance has appeared."[98]

At the same time, there were a few small but encouraging signs of budding patriotic activity among some Bosnian writers from the 1830s onward. For instance, the young Bosnians who joined the Franciscan order and studied in Italy and the Habsburg regions were immensely excited by the work of the national awakening that they witnessed in the European metropoles, particularly by the opening of new societies, publications, and political prospects across Croatia, Serbia, Vojvodina, Slavonia, and Dalmatia. Even if stuck in "the Bosnian mud," they nonetheless enthusiastically responded to the proclamations of Gaj, Vuk, Stanko Vraz, Đuro Daničić, and other South Slavic intellectuals; aspiring Bosnian publicists like Martin Nedić, Blaž Josić, and Bono Perišić began to make their literary contributions, initiate correspondences, and collect books relevant for Bosnia's national revival, including "all newly published works of our tireless native Karadžić."[99] Several Orthodox merchants and teachers who left Bosnia to settle in the neighboring regions, like Sima Milutinović (originally from Sarajevo) or Dimitrije Milaković (originally from Mostar), became literary figures in Belgrade, Cetinje, and Novi Sad. Gaj encouraged such work in general and Vuk also appreciated the Bosnians' burgeoning dedication to patriotic learning (though he was critical of Milutinović and wary of his intentions to collect poetry in Montenegro and Herzegovina before he could get there first).[100]

In Bosnia itself, the work of Ivan Franjo Jukić (1818–1857), an enterprising activist who undertook the first sustained attempt to write new and comprehensive national textbooks on Bosnia, shows how the processes of creating, disseminating, and naming this knowledge easily crossed the supposedly distinct national movements and simultaneously engaged what are often seen as different stages of national work. Born and raised in Bosnia, where he spent the vast majority of his life, Jukić first came into contact with the Illyrian and Serbian national movements during his studies in Hungary, where he was educated after joining the Franciscan order in his early youth. In 1842, Jukić described the surprising discovery of his homeland in the works of Vuk and other Slavic intellectuals as a stunning revelation: "I was really amazed when I read in Šafárik's *Slavic Ethnography* that there is such a thing as the Herzegovinian dialect in Illyria!—This was news to me, I say to me, who has labored [for national revival] for two years in Bosnia and Herzegovina and who has grown up with Herzegovinians! . . . The learned Šafárik thus follows Vuk in this matter."[101] Though closely affiliated with Ljudevit Gaj's circles in Zagreb, Jukić continued to keenly admire Vuk, pointing out with considerable pride that the great Serbian intellectual was "by birth from Tršić in Serbia, but by ancestry a Herzegovinian from Drobnjak."[102]

By the 1850s, Jukić became the leading and best-known national activist in his native Bosnia. As his reputation grew among South Slavic patriotic circles, Jukić also attracted the attention of the Ottoman reformist governor Omer-pasha Latas, who cultivated a close relationship with Jukić before deciding in 1852 that the enterprising friar was too much of a political threat; jail and permanent expulsion from Bosnia followed.[103] Subsequently, many of Jukić's colleagues in Bosnia shied away from overt participation in Croatian-Serbian projects and media of the time.[104] His severe example was widely heeded—"be careful, do not have confidence in the promises of political powers, think of Jukić," one Bosnian Franciscan admonished another in 1867—leading Bosnian activists to remain acutely alert to Ottoman initiatives to suppress any suspected agitators.[105] Jukić's far-reaching influence in Bosnia itself was undeniable; even after his death, he remained a towering intellectual figure and a point of reference for subsequent patriotic work in this province.[106]

When Jukić embarked on his ambitious projects, aiming at establishing new publications and societies, one of the key concerns that vexed the Bosnian activist was the problem of "unity" (*sloga*) among the South Slavic patriots who were supposed to awaken, enlighten, and liberate the Ottoman provinces. Whereas regional centers like Zagreb, Novi Sad, and Belgrade had small but at least established societies, Jukić's attempt to create a similarly collaborative, unified activist front in Bosnia was frustrated by the apathy of the general populace and even among the few participants who expressed interest in patriotic matters.

Moreover, there were abiding concerns about whether the Serbian-Croatian character of these movements connoted national unity or division. The formative Serbian-Croatian explorations of Bosnia were undertaken in the spirit of brotherly contributions for the benefit of all South Slavs, but this process was also marked by increasing competition over the procedures, discoveries, and codification of knowledge gathered through these ethnographic-activist projects. The exploratory spirit of the early Serbian-Croatian undertakings in Bosnia is especially evident in the work of Stefan Herkalović, a former Habsburg officer from Lika who devoted his energy to serving both the Illyrian and the Serbian national causes. Already during a trip to Brod in Slavonia in 1837, Herkalović glimpsed Bosnia across the Sava River, noting that "a special feeling came over me at the sight of the Bosnian mountains, from where our forefathers came to the present place since the fifth or the sixth century."[107] Two years later, Herkalović sent to Ljudevit Gaj a brief but jubilant note, "which I know you were not expecting at this time from this place"—that is, from Travnik, Bosnia. Not having the time to elaborate on how he got there or "the philological progress" he made, Herkalović principally wanted to confirm certain convictions to the great Illyrian scholar: "As you and we all have already thought, and now by my own eyewitnessing—we have to consider it the pure truth that Dalmatia and even more Bosnia hold within them untold treasures for our language and our Slavicness. Vuk Stefanović collected the material for his dictionary only across Serbia and the Illyrian lands of our emperor, never daring to go to Bosnia, where his goal could be more fully realized than anywhere else. Bosnia can rightly be called the nest of the core of our Illyrian language."[108]

The sense of Illyrian competition with Vuk over who would be the first to explore Bosnia is evident here, but the character of this rivalry should not be overstated. After his brief trip to Bosnia, during which he was promptly expelled by the Ottoman authorities on allegations of spying, Herkalović returned not to Zagreb, but instead proceeded to the Serbian capital Belgrade, where he worked with the minister Ilija Garašanin to establish a network of national activists in Bosnia and Serbia's other neighboring regions.[109] Far from disavowing their Illyrian past or severing ties with their Croatian counterparts, such Belgrade "agents" intensified their contacts with possible local partners.[110] The creation of a common Serbo-Croatian linguistic standard built around Vuk's work furthered this spirit of mutuality and helped spur both movements' exploration of Bosnia-Herzegovina as the center of an emerging South Slavic national community in the 1840s and 1850s. Thus from the very outset of these patriotic movements, Serbo-Croatian convergence as well as competition marked knowledge produced about Bosnia.

Herkalović himself tried to assure Jukić in 1843 that national activists in both Serbia and Croatia were deeply committed to aiding Bosnia; Jukić, however, nonetheless remained concerned about the implications of nationalist competition over his homeland:

> I am very glad that many a native has taken up the cause of the happiness of the Bosnian people, but I am still torn by worry: Do they have an understanding among one another—is there a single plan? Or will the Serb want one [thing], and the Croat another? That would give rise to disunity (*nesloga*), and what is born of it is well known to us all. That is why I highly recommend that you work out an understanding with the Croats; I say with the Croats, because they are committed to it. If among the Croats and the Serbs, likewise among the Orthodox and the Catholics, there is no understanding, it could happen that the populace will be split into two parties: the Serbian and the Croatian.[111]

The specter of division and splintering of the fragile national cause in Bosnia remained a continuing concern among the South Slavic activists, but once again Jukić took the initiative to argue that committed nationalists could work through such obstacles. On the one hand, he did not shy away from criticism of his patriotic colleagues: "Our 'unity' is obviously receding, its former advocates obviously frozen," Jukić continued to complain throughout the 1840s.[112] His friend Bono Perišić shared this sentiment and went even further, lamenting the lack of response to Jukić's call for the establishment of the first patriotic society in Bosnia and stating that "the society has failed." Jukić, however, countered with a brilliant response: "What has never existed cannot fail."[113]

National unity understood in this way could more or less recede, be
thwarted, or radically fractured, but it could not altogether "fail"; instead
it appeared as a basic foundational premise enabling any sense of patriotic
activism and operating regardless of existing conditions like indifference,
disinterest, discord, or division among the activists themselves. "As long as
there are men, there will be [patriotic] societies" sooner or later; in practice
it was crucial to continue the exhortations to patriotism, casually assuming
its presence even where it was known not to exist.[114]

Faced with organizational difficulties, Jukić determined to proceed
largely on his own, conducting field trips and collecting much new material on the folklore, history, geography, and other features of his Bosnian
homeland. This was not a simple collection of folklore or existing literature;
prior works on Bosnia were "erroneous," "superficial," "insignificant,"
and overall unreliable, and Jukić therefore had to travel and research Bosnia anew.[115] Publication of these findings would be the first main result of
these projects, but Jukić also had bigger plans in mind. A new museum and
several academic societies were supposed to follow and serve the "patriotic
necessity" of collecting, displaying, and publicizing native Bosnian materials (an idea suggested already in the 1850s, but not realized until the 1880s
under imperial Habsburg auspices).[116] In the spirit of the time, finding pure
folk poetry was a clear priority. "I have heard that in Sebešić [a village near
Travnik] there is someone, a little *cattle herder* (*čobančić*) peasant, who
knows the most beautiful poems; won't you go get him if you can," Jukić
asked a fellow colleague in 1840.[117] No such peasant would appear in his
subsequent work. In the absence of a truly exemplary source, from Sebešić
or elsewhere, Jukić nonetheless pressed on with his quest and made great
use of synthesis and generalization as the underlying procedures for creating
new knowledge about Bosnia.

His groundbreaking publications, crowned by the appearance of *The
Bosnian Friend* (*Bosanski prijatelj*, 1850–1851), reflected Jukić's totalizing
ambitions in constantly combining different materials: cartographic descriptions, excepts from folk poetry, different statistics, Franciscan chronicles,
observations from his personal travels, local proverbs, taxation procedures,
new Ottoman decrees, village customs, and so on.[118] Unlike Vuk, who invoked the especially authoritative Herzegovinian and Bosnian singers as the
sources whom he had discovered (Višnjić, Podrugović, et al.), Jukić mostly
left out names of local informants, singers, and inhabitants whom he consulted: "The greater part of Bosnia I myself toured and saw; where I could
not reach, I asked experts of that locale, and some friends with their reports
did aid me, on which I thank them much."[119] Even though Jukić wrote
that "there is a mass of uncollected poems" in Bosnia simply awaiting its
scholars, he found it difficult to collect and give proper shape to this material. After amassing some material, Jukić printed numerous folk poems in
The Bosnian Friend and, "following the example of Mr. Vuk," prepared a

"heroic poetry" collection that appeared only posthumously (edited by Grga Martić, 1858) and without mention of any individual sources or specially talented peasants.[120] Later editions of *The Bosnian Friend* (1861 and 1870) followed the same pattern.[121] Apparently, it was still hard to find a good "man from the people" in the general picture of his land. This enterprise consequently presented a synthesized, broad picture of the land and "the people" in an effort to fill in the important bodies of knowledge that had eluded Vuk and other writers interested in Bosnia (characteristics of the terrain, population numbers, legal structures, village customs, etc.).

Like other South Slavic patriots, Jukić stressed the numerical dominance and the plight of the Bosnian Christian populations as the main themes of Bosnian history and politics. Regarding Bosnian Muslims, Jukić's nationalist narrative described them with deep ambivalence and anxiety. "Turks, numbering with Gypsies some 384,000, are the descendants of the lying prophet Muhammed," he wrote; "these were formed from wicked Christians who, wanting to keep their property by any means, became Turks" and sworn enemies of their own people. As Jukić claimed, "In their law, it is sin to kill an eagle or a dog, but to kill a Vlach [pejorative term for Christian] is a virtue."[122] Yet these "Turks" also spoke the same national language as their Christian counterparts; even Bosnian Christian folklore became inseparably fused with that of the Muslims.[123] Jukić's collection of Bosnian folk poetry in the 1850s warned its Slavic and European audiences that they might be startled by encountering "so many Turkish words; this is because our Christian generations live mixed with Muhammedans, who are of the same blood." This was an uneasy admission for Jukić, Martić, and other national activists because "Turkish words have blackened our poems" and national language, yet they still "became so common and liked by the people that without them a poem would be as pleasant as a meal without spices."[124] As such, Muslims were marked as both a disturbing and integral element of "the people" being discovered by Serbian and Croatian nationalists in Bosnia.

The circulation of this newly acquired and expertly verified knowledge about Bosnia shows just how inseparable Serbian-Croatian discoveries of "the people" were despite their respective claims to separate origins. Jukić was a declared "Illyrian" patriot generally supportive of Croatian currents in South Slavic debates, but he first published his work in the *Serbian-Dalmatian Magazine* (*Srbsko-Dalmatinski Magazin*, Zadar) in Cyrillic before the flagship Illyrian journals (like *Danica Ilirska* and *Kolo*, Zagreb) reprinted his work in the same year in the Latin script, thus simultaneously spanning a range of audiences interested in Bosnia in the 1840s.[125] Jukić structured his work with contemporary scholarly-patriotic expectations in mind, openly acknowledging emulation of Vuk's forms and carefully modeling his Bosnian contributions on related Slavic, Italian, and German ethno-geographic texts of the time. Many of these articles became the basis for Jukić's seminal *Geography and History of Bosnia* (1851). Published in Zagreb in Latin script, the book described in detail various regions of Bosnia-Herzegovina, its main rivers, mountains, and towns, as well as the histories and political circumstances that shaped the land and its inhabitants. As a text that provided information in response to so many Serbian and Croatian queries about Bosnia, Jukić's *Geography and History* was warmly received in both Belgrade and Zagreb. The journal of the Serbian learned society extolled it for helping "us get to know the lands where our people live, and that have been so little known among us until now,"[126] while the leading Croatian newspaper praised it as an "indispensable" collection that "the general public does not know as well as it should. . . . In his [work] the language is purely ours, with all its resilience, strength, and richness, a language difficult to find in any one of our recent books."[127]

At the same time in Belgrade, Jukić's former colleague Toma Kovačević appreciated *Geography and History of Bosnia* for a more practical reason. Once a Bosnian Franciscan student, Kovačević left the order in the 1840s after an unsuccessful attempt at a national uprising and emigrated from Bosnia to Serbia, where he converted to Orthodoxy and became an officer in the Serbian principality. Operating from Belgrade, Kovačević closely followed and consulted the work of his former colleague and friend Jukić. In 1851, Kovačević wrote a "topographic and statistical" guide to Bosnia based heavily on Jukić's information for internal Serbian state purposes, namely, to educate Serbian "agents" about the layout of the land and to prepare the ground for Serbian liberation of Bosnia.[128] Moreover, several years after Jukić's death in 1857, Kovačević prepared yet another similar document, this time presented as a Serbian scholarly publication illuminating the history and geography of Bosnia. In his Serbian edition, Kovačević was named as the author, but it soon became clear that Kovačević plagiarized and almost identically reproduced Jukić's text, this time in Cyrillic. The content overwhelmingly remained the same, often repeating Jukić's descriptions word for word, but the crucial revision was in the national adjectives: "Illyrian" was simply replaced with "Serbian."[129] The first South Slavic surveys of Bosnia—published in different cities and appearing in different scripts from the 1840s to the 1870s—thus bore interchangeable attributes and presented overwhelmingly identical content from both Croatian and Serbian perspectives.[130]

In exploring the spread of nationalism to areas like Bosnia, analytical focus on the generic qualities of this process is useful for several reasons. In addition to helping us trace the dissemination of major nationalist forms (like the national geographic, the national historic, and especially the national ethnographic literatures that Jukić closely studied and emulated), such an approach also sheds light on the recursive interactions and the extraordinarily productive relationships that South Slavic patriots mutually formed in their quest for "the people." Jukić's pioneering work—whose content was repeatedly appropriated as "Croatian" and/or "Serbian" and/or "Bosnian"—offers a valuable glimpse into the interconnected and rapidly expanding spaces of national revival. Far from being a peculiar aspect of South Slavic dynamics, the plagiarism and the interchangeability of national adjectives evident in the Jukić-Kovačević case can be productively read as manifestations of the broader generic and generative qualities of nationalism. I refer to this as a generic quality not in the sense of such attributes being nonspecific—they in fact appeal to national particularity—but rather as an extensible dimension of a *genre*, engaging in a broad set of conventions, practices, and repeatable activities that can accommodate an immense variety of adaptations. Genres are in that sense made to be broken, but that only highlights their generative power, their ability to produce new situations, subjectivities, and expressions.[131]

The Discrete Charm of Ethnographic Populism

There are, of course, a number of objections that can be raised against this reading of the generic and generative qualities of ethnographic populism. One could, for instance, characterize such sharing of political forms as a passing stage in the growth of nationalism, a feature of the "early" Croatian, Serbian, and other South Slavic patriotic movements that later sharpened their differences and developed distinct institutions by the beginning of the twentieth century. One could further develop this stageist view of nationalism, which depicts a progression from early reciprocity to later conflict, by claiming that the ethnographic explorations of Vuk, Jukić, or other intellectuals were romantic-era projects that fizzled out sometime after the mid-nineteenth century. By the 1890s, many South Slavic intellectuals had already criticized the work of romantic folklorists as "shoddy" and called for the establishment of more rigorous and professional national "sciences" like geography, anthropology, history, and sociology.

However, the impulse to confine the nationalist obsessions with "the people" to a passing romantic phase risks misunderstanding the enduring appeal and the larger significance of the kind of ethnographic populism that Vuk, Jukić, Kovačević, and other activists practiced and established. What should be especially noted here is the spirited affirmation of something like entry-level ethnographic populism throughout—and ever since—the nineteenth century. Despite the creation of new institutes, regulations, and departments that many later observers characterized as a shift from amateurish "ethnology" to the more professionalized schools of "anthropology," the late nineteenth century also witnessed a vigorous redevelopment of a peculiar kind of "science of the people," an ethnographic practice that was much more invested in the dissemination of patriotic forms and subjectivities rather than the establishment of rigorous scientific institutions.[132]

To understand these developments, it is first important to recognize the critical turn against romanticism at the end of the nineteenth century, when a number of emerging South Slavic scholars began to vehemently criticize ethnographic works that seemed to dabble indiscriminately in many areas under the guise of folklore and patriotic passion. Reports of blatant forgeries—like the discovery of the "ancient Slavic Veda" in Macedonia by Stefan Verković (a former Bosnian Franciscan activist) in the 1870s and 1880s—threatened to stigmatize folklore collections as the work of either unscrupulous propagandists or incompetent amateurs (or both).[133] Though countless volumes had been written about "the people," there was a sense among a growing number of Balkan intellectuals that this body of knowledge was not "scientific" enough, particularly when judged by the standardized disciplinary codes adopted by many German, French, and English learned academies. In the eyes of fin de siècle intellectuals like Matija Murko or Jovan Skerlić, the romantic-era pursuits of the folk were understandable and valuable projects, but they lacked the type of scientific rigor and reliability that only modern critical disciplines could provide.[134] In fact, in 1908, even Vuk's own work was subjected to vigorous critique, with some scholars disputing the origins and authenticity of particular parts of his oeuvre.[135]

The work of Jovan Cvijić—by far the most prominent South Slavic geographer and anthropologist to emerge at the turn of the century—appeared in the 1890s as one prominent departure from the earlier folkloristic ventures. While acknowledging the efforts of the first "followers of Vuk" as well intentioned and somewhat useful, Cvijić nonetheless found their work to be lacking "even the slightest bit of scientific perspective."[136] Other Serbian intellectuals agreed: "To analyze scientifically (*naučno obradivati*) means to study the conception and development of the people itself (including its respective parts) as well as its characteristics and culture." And folklorists like Milan Milićević, Vuk Vrčević, and others "did not do this, they only collected some material" for "the real, scientific, ethnological study of the Serbian people" that still had to be carried out.[137] Such challenges and criticisms successfully led to the establishment of new schools of sociological and nationalist thought at the turn of the century, among which Jovan Cvijić's "anthro-geographical" and "ethno-psychological" approaches became particularly influential.[138]

The elaboration of such new "scientific" projects, however, did not lessen the centrality of the *narod* or "the people" as a basic and enduring category of nationalist work. In fact, the polemics of the legacy of the romantic movement helped ignite several vehement and overwhelmingly positive assessments of amateur ethnography as a quintessentially patriotic pursuit. In the 1890s in particular, this development manifested itself not only in spirited defenses of Vuk's scientific credentials but also in articulations of ethnographic practice as an activity indispensable for nationalists' own self-fashioning.

Such fin de siècle reassertions of ethnographic populism came partly through the reaffirmation of Vuk himself, who was "resurrected" in 1897 when his bones were exhumed from Vienna and reburied in Belgrade in an impressive series of international ceremonies. In Sarajevo, Serbian journals extensively reported on the event, pointing out that "our proud Bosnia and Herzegovina were well represented" at events that included speeches by the Serbian king Alexander I and the Vienna mayor Karl Lueger, stopover commemorations in Ljubljana, and day-long final ceremonies in Belgrade.[139] The symbolic "return" of Vuk to his homeland occasioned many reflections on his enduring significance for South Slavic politics, not only in the field of linguistic reform but also as an unrivaled role model of a national scientist among the South Slavs. Once again, Vuk's standing as a "man from the people" was crucial to reiterating his authenticity and authority. "The time Vuk spent with the cattle, from a purely psychological-educational perspective, was very important" for his scientific work, noted one observer in 1897. Others also stressed that Vuk "was a child from the people" whose "parents came from Herzegovina to Loznica" in Serbia, bringing with them the purest Herzegovinian customs and language.[140] Vuk then brought out this lineage to Vienna and into the wider world, making a contribution "that was the most scientific, most straightforward, and most natural" even when judged by "the latest sciences."[141] In 1899, a leading Serbian ethnographer, Tihomir Đorđević, founded an academic journal for Serbian national life simply titled *Karadžić*.[142] The reorganization and republication of his work as a "collection of historical and ethnographic writings" further cemented Vuk's standing as a classic ethnographer *avant la lettre*.[143] Overall, by the turn of the twentieth century, Vuk's work was affirmed as unsurpassed and indispensable for any further development of national-scientific knowledge about "the people." (In 1937, when the 150th anniversary of Vuk's birth was marked, similar celebrations were organized in Bosnia and throughout Yugoslavia.)[144]

But beyond homages to Vuk as the exemplary national ethnographer, the crucial figure in the active reinvention of ethnographic populism was Antun Radić (1868–1919), widely considered the "father of Croatian ethnography." Along with his older brother Stjepan—who became the most prominent Croatian politician of the first half of the twentieth century—Antun Radić initially pursued political as well scholarly ambitions before dedicating himself largely to ethnographic work in the 1890s. Educated in Zagreb and Vienna and well-versed in Balkan and European (particularly French) social scientific debates, Radić, like many others of his generation, wanted to reinvigorate ethnography among the South Slavs, ridding it of forgeries and "bad practices," defending it from charges that it was an outdated romantic pursuit, and making it both more rigorous and more accessible to the wider public.

In taking up mission, Radić outlined and elaborated a field of knowledge that he preferred to call *narodoznanstvo*, a Croatian neologism that signified ethnographic science but could be translated more loosely as "peopleology" (a translation that also captures the fact that this term was eventually eclipsed by the more widespread *etnologija* and *etnografija*). As a prolific writer and tireless editor of *The Journal for Folk Life and Customs of the South Slavs*, Radić became an established and widely consulted authority on a variety of social scientific issues.

In his advocacy of ethnology or "peopleology," however, Radić viewed its status as a "science" with great ambivalence. To be sure, he was deeply invested in endowing folk studies with a clearer, more robust methodological apparatus, but at the same time Radić also insisted that proper ethnographic work should not be locked away in an ivory tower. "By my judgment, this is what ethnology must not be. Ethnological material . . . must not be a new addition to the enormous heap of tiny, most specialized, historic-literary studies . . . not to speak of the vast part of the intelligentsia to whom the less something is understandable the more it is appealing," Radić wrote in 1898. "Ethnological material is not collected with erudite modern ambitions to be a dead witness serving endless parallels and dead little theories. . . . Ethnology should become a *social* science, in the first place the *people's* science."[145] In another treatise, Radić stressed that since "ethnology, by its object of study, cannot be equated with any other science that holds an endowed chair," it represented a different kind of scholarly undertaking, one that was scientific but also popular and engaged with the uneducated masses. "So until the gates of courtly science are opened to it, let ethnology seek its admirers (amateurs) among the learned men of all fields of knowledge."[146]

In further developing this appeal to scholarly "amateurs," Radić composed a major and profoundly influential programmatic statement for conducting ethnographic work known simply as "The Foundation" (*Osnova*, 1897). In the first place, Radić consistently warned that elite "gentlemen" (*gospoda*), including "municipal officials, magistrates, lawyers, scribes, or landlords," usually make for bad ethnographers. Such aspiring students may have had considerable education, but they generally lacked proper ethnographic training and native understanding of the ways of folklore, a predicament that led to awkward situations: "Just imagine. . . . A man comes to a village, where he's never been before, bursts into a house, not knowing the customs of greeting or conversation, and immediately says: Bring some grandma over here! Now you, grandma, tell stories! . . . That's plain vulgarity," Radić wrote. Just as "you'd never stop a man in broad daylight and ask him: Hey, have you seen a werewolf?," even a beginner ethnographer would take the time to study his region, communities, circumstances, and relations before initiating any deeper conversations.[147] Having concluded that his middle-class, town-dwelling compatriots, well-educated as they may have been, were not the most suitable candidates to work as ethnographers, Radić emphasized the role of the more "amateur" local actors—preferably *peasants* themselves—as collectors and contributors to the ethnographic-populist project.

In fact, Radić's ideal ethnographer-subject remarkably resembled Vuk and his famed trajectory from Tršić to Vienna: "The most successful collectors of materials would be bright, literate peasants. . . . Men who are born among the people, and have among it kin, godparents, friends, would do equally well." Older teachers, local priests, and others who immersed themselves in their own home regions would do, though they also needed guidance to make sure that they did not misunderstand their sensitive task. Radić's "Foundation" was supposed to provide authoritative directions in this regard, furnishing an extraordinarily detailed handbook and questionnaire with an elaborate classification scheme containing hundreds of specific queries and subjects.[148] Knowledge gathered in this way would be both scientific and patriotic, increasing among its practitioners a "love of the homeland."[149] In other words, Radić's ideal beginning subject was a "man from the people," someone familiar with folkways, but also equipped with just enough literacy and education to file notes and reports that would—with the aid of ethnographic guides—lead to scholarly contributions, associations, and political projects. This process of encouraging peasants to make themselves into scholar-patriots (preferably of the nonprofessional kind) described an idealized trajectory of ethnographic self-fashioning, a way of shaping oneself into a conscious national.

Just as with earlier movements inspired by Vuk, Radić's initiatives did not spread among the peasants, whom he targeted and praised, but rather among the burgeoning, largely middle-class aspiring patriots whom he mistrusted and disdained. After 1904, Radić put his ethnographic projects on hold and devoted his considerable energies to political party organization, establishing with his brother Stjepan the Croatian Peasant Party. But the ethnographic projects themselves continued unabated without Radić's involvement. In the larger context of South Slavic politics, Radić's "Foundation" fanned the flames of already well-developed folkloristic interests, injecting new vigor and providing new templates that inspired hundreds of articles, local exhibits, monographs, and municipal archival collections in Croatia alone in the first decade of the twentieth century. Despite calls for "scientization" and more rigorous quality control, folkloristic activities of all kinds continued to thrive in Serbia, Bosnia, and across the Balkans.

Seen in this light, the larger significance of such work is not that it failed to enlist the peasants for particular causes or parties, but that it provided accessible, deliberately entry-level and amateur-appropriate practices—a set of strategies I have called "ethnographic populism"—that politically curious individuals could appropriate to make themselves into proper (Croatian, Serbian, Bosnian, etc.) patriots. Ethnographic populism thus had many charms and appeals for aspiring patriots. Its fieldwork operations were relatively easy to carry out, often requiring short trips to the countryside and experimentation with the collection of folklore, but also difficult and obscure enough to contain an element of adventure and mystery. It created a sense of rescuing highly endangered national resources; it produced publicly prized cultural artifacts like folk poems, puzzles, and customs; it opened up and covered an enormous array of topics that filled volume upon volume of nineteenth-century patriotic journals. Crucially, it was a practice capable of being constantly deferred and renewed, infinitely extensible into that elusive subject of nation-making: "the people."

Radić himself overtly spelled out this incompleteable dimension of his ethnographic-populist work in a research trip to—where else?—the famously rich folkloric terrain of Bosnia-Herzegovina. Having conducted several similar field trips and made extensive preparations for this special round of research, Radić was ready to tackle a number of difficulties that arise in ethnographic work; yet careful planning and comprehensive questionnaires could only go so far. His 1899 *Report on the Trip to Bosnia and Herzegovina* is worth quoting at length:

> But the key is this. I want to, for example, see this or that man or woman from the people (*čovjeka, ili ženu iz naroda*), who told this thing or another; or one needs to find this or that piece of clothing, artifact, or thing; but it cannot be, because this man or woman is out there, working in the field. "Wait until Sunday, or until the market, or until this or that saint's [day]." That would, it is true, be best, but I cannot stay in every place on Sunday or on market day. Even if I were to stay until Sunday—the day passes and little is gathered, so again one must wait until another Sunday. And it has also happened that, having come to "the spot" itself, seeing it with my own eyes, I acquired an entirely different impression about the people's life than I got from reading the material. Moreover, I would find in the material terrifying absences. Asking about this or that which attracted my attention, I heard entirely new but interesting and worthwhile things, about which there is no mention in the material. I want to fill in and make note (in contributions published in the *Journal* one can already see these traces); but there is so much, all this collected material seems worth so little, that I lose the will for filling in and note taking and I already think of new material. I always think: it is destined that I must go on, here nothing will happen, and I don't know if the same waits for me elsewhere.[150]

The elipses, the absences that were discovered during these searches may have been terrifying, but they also operated as sources in themselves, compelling the scholar-patriot to take note with renewed effort, to fill in, to undertake more trips, to generate more knowledge, to authenticate the ever-new places of "the people."

Such searches for "the people," then, revolve around a certain principle of *alibi* in its Latin sense of *elsewhere, in another place:* One can come to know an exemplary "man from the people" (like Vuk), but not quite grasp or reach "the land of the people" or "the people" itself (in Vuk's case Herzegovina and Bosnia, which eluded him and remained elsewhere, beyond his reach). Conversely, one can exhaustively survey and come to know "the land of the people" in its broad, general outlines (recorded in books and journals), but it is the particular and essential "man of the people" that then remains elsewhere, out in the field (as in Jukić's and Radić's searches).[151]

An Impossible Subject

A key dimension of this kind of ethnographic populism was a pervading sense of distress about the unknowability of "the people." As Ivan Lorković (quoted at the beginning of this chapter) lamented in 1898, "the people" and its soul "remained unknown" even after a century of intense work dedicated precisely to discovering, exploring, and documenting this elusive subject. The unknown and unknowable dimension of "the people" was not some provincial Balkan idiom, but a more basic sentiment that pervaded the general discovery of "the people" as a political subject in nineteenth-century Europe. Jules Michelet, the author of the famous tome *The People* (*Le peuple*, 1846), pensively wrote in the second edition of 1869 that despite all his life's work on this topic, "the people's language . . . was inaccessible to me. I have not been able to make the people speak." As Roland Barthes commented, "Just as all Magicians since Moses have seen the Promised Land without being able to cross into it, so Michelet has seen the People and yet remained at the People's frontier. No matter how often he repeated, in each of his prefaces, that he was born of the People, that the People was his Father, there was always an obstacle to this magical incorporation." This "whole cosmology of redemption involves a distress," but it is crucial to note that this is not an alarming afterthought that arrives only at the end of one's work on "the people."[152] To the contrary, this peculiar distress was always there as a perpetually frustrating condition of national-populist projects that were founded on and driven by the impossibility of their fulfillment.

CHAPTER TWO

The Land of Suffering

In 1868, Velimir Gaj published a lengthy report in *Croato-Serbian Literary Leisure* "telling our readers about the evils suffered by our brothers in Bosnia and Herzegovina." The news about the continuing suffering of the *raya*, the Bosnian peasants under the Turks, Gaj noted, "comes not from their mouths; the real truth is sounded to our soul by a sad trumpet's wail" and is often related by outside observers. His search for a more immediate witness to suffering proved to be disappointing:

> Few are the Bosnians or Herzegovinians who come [to Zagreb] who are willing to speak of their dark misfortune. Innate pride prevents them. When you just ask one of them, "How is it?" — "Oh, good, sir," he says, squirming. "How is it at home?" — "Oh, good, sir!" "And what are the Turks doing?" — "Oh, good, sir!," squirming a bit at every answer. What kind of good, then, when you are hungry and tattered; what kind of good when your impoverished wife and family are naked, barefoot, hungry; what kind of good when the Turks, the masters, are impaling your own kin on the stake? But who can interpret the *raya*'s replies that issue from under that little, tattered, sweat-soaked red cap? No one knows who holds what in their heart. So who could guess what this slave, this martyr of four hundred years ponders in his head and heart?

What emerges from Velimir Gaj's account is not only the evident frustration with the peasant's dissatisfying replies but also a driving demand for a certain voice of suffering, a certain kind of subject ready to speak his pain to the world. In the face of the Bosnian peasant's apparent reluctance to embody the subject he was thought to be— "this slave, this martyr" — Velimir Gaj strove to translate the opaque content of the *raya*'s heart into intelligible and patriotic speech. "As far as we are concerned," he wrote, "let the truth spread, either in songs, or in simple sayings, though it is hard to represent" the suffering in the Balkans to "such a manifold readership," especially to those enjoying the sheltered "privileges of Western Europe." To that end, Velimir Gaj (the son of the famed Croatian leader Ljudevit Gaj) urged, "Let us strive to make even a small sacrificing contribution for better recognition of our miserable homeland!"[1]

Why were activists like Velimir Gaj so intensely invested in locating, documenting, and reproducing the voice of national suffering? In the wake of

52

Herderian romanticism, early nationalist projects proclaimed a new age of happiness and glory of the folk, yet by the middle of the nineteenth century national activists were busily chronicling the harrowing pain of their "miserable homelands." How did these new literatures dedicated to national wounds come about? What can we as historians do with the vast archives of national suffering that patriotic activists across Europe—from the Balkans to Poland to Ireland and beyond—produced over the course of the nineteenth and twentieth centuries?

On the one hand, scholars of nationalism have long noted the prominence of suffering in nation-building projects. Ernest Renan observed that "suffering in common unifies more than joy does. Where national memories are concerned, griefs are of more value than triumphs, for they impose duties and require a common effort."[2] Benedict Anderson too pointed to the capacity of national imaginings to "generate such colossal sacrifices."[3] Yet on the other hand, these valuable insights have suggested the centrality of suffering for nationalist projects without delving deeper into this concern or its attendant histories and implications. While some scholars have thus outlined this subject, other writers—philosophers, psychologists, doctors, sociologists—have extensively explored suffering as a crucial problem of modern politics and morality. From Nietzsche and Foucault to the more recent reinterpretations by Elaine Scarry, Susan Sontag, and Veena Das, an immense critical literature has contributed brilliant insights, yet little of it has been written with nationalism in mind despite the fact that nationalism has been a key force in producing modern discourses of collective suffering.[4] Historians in particular have had little to say about matters of suffering. For many, depictions of hardships elicit reactions of recognition and at least some sympathy for the expressed pain; at other times, historians have responded to some stridently politicized accounts of victimization with notions of "cultural construction" and even "myth." In either case, such reactions have tended to effectively sidestep an enormous body of nationalist production that few scholars have taken seriously and explored in depth.

My first goal here is simple: it is to raise questions about the nationalist investment in depictions of suffering. How does one write about the narratives of suffering that appear so central to the constitution of national movements? What explains not only the interest in but also the persistent nationalist *demand for* certain voices of suffering? What do the archives of suffering that nationalists have produced over the last two centuries say about nationalism as a political project?

My second goal is to advance my arguments regarding these questions by delineating a historically specific genealogy of what I call an aggrieved nationalist subjectivity, a pervasive political outlook that arose over the course of the nineteenth century. In an important recent discussion, Dipesh Chakrabarty argued that "the capacity to notice and document suffering (even if it be one's own suffering) from the position of a generalized and necessarily disembodied observer is what marks the beginnings of the modern self." In showing the rise of new political interest in the suffering of the upper-caste Hindu widow in colonial India, Chakrabarty emphasized the impact of the European Enlightenment theories of sympathy, like those of Hume and Smith, on molding "the cast of the citizen of a modernizing nation-state."[5] Yet there are some critical elisions in arguments for the centrality of sympathy, which in the natural theory of sentiments was general and universally extendable to almost *any* feeling, idea, or sensibility, not just pain. Then why is it, in the words of Oscar Wilde, that "it is much more easy to have sympathy with suffering than it is to have sympathy with thought"?[6]

To engage this thorny issue, we must depart from the natural theories of sympathy (positing a timeless human nature) and seek more historically specific explanations for the intensely modern political concerns with suffering.[7] Wendy Brown has argued that a sense of "wounded attachments" is indispensable to modern liberal identity politics wherein injury emerges as the foundational grounds of a kind of *ressentiment*-driven identity, seeking "to avenge the hurt even while it reaffirms it, discursively codifies it."[8] Moreover, as Asma Abbas has shown, liberalism not only "assigns undisputed value to a form of expressed suffering as fitting with recognition, inclusion, and empowerment," but also privileges specific notions of "voice" as the proper form of that expression; "such voice becomes an index of [the sufferers'] democratic desire" and potential for political agency.[9] Although often suffused with Christian religious imagery, such discussions of suffering—especially its political significance—are clearly rooted in what is usually described as "secular" liberal thought. Approached in these ways, the key issues are not just ones of representation, as in who speaks for whom and for what injuries, but of moral imperatives that shape modern subjectivities as well—who demands certain voices, presences, and why?

Building on this critical scholarship as well as the burgeoning field of the history of emotions, I trace a fragment of the Balkan archive of national suffering in order to make a broader argument about the emergence of an aggrieved nationalist subjectivity since the nineteenth century.[10] Because Bosnia was the subject of so much South Slavic patriotic outrage over the suffering of the *raya* since the 1840s, it presents exemplary grounds for exploring the discovery and sustenance of national wounds on this site from the Ottoman through the Habsburg era ending in 1914. The monumental body of literature on the tribulations of "sad Bosnia" carried great political significance as it underpinned the mobilization of nationalist sentiments and the organization of patriotic societies among the South Slavs throughout the nineteenth century. The notion of collective suffering was not a simple rhetorical device embellishing various programs, but constituted the very ground from which nineteenth-century nationalists began to speak to their co-nationals and to the world. This ground, what I call an aggrieved national subjectivity, had to be produced, made known, and sustained, a task that proved frustrating and impossible to complete; yet like Velimir Gaj's frustration with the reticent Bosnian peasant, this apparent obstacle only breathed new life into the underlying demand for ever more voices of national suffering.

Such an approach differs from investigations of socioeconomic causes of the blatant political injustices in the Balkans, including the very real and unquestionably dire plight of Bosnian peasants. These levels of analysis, focusing on agrarian policies, taxation ledgers, organized repressions, and abusive practices are well documented, firmly established, and familiar to historians today.[11] Less familiar are the political forces that produced the distinct voice rather than the procedural verification of specific griev-ances. The following discussion explores the political significance of suf-fering, bringing together different registers—from diplomacy to poetry, from newspaper offices to painting exhibitions—that had a lasting trans-national resonance.[12] The emergence of new nationalist subjectivities was a part of the larger growth of activist politics and humanitarian sensibili-ties in many parts of the world; the agonies of the Greek, Polish, and Irish struggles played especially important roles in the internationalization of patriotic concerns with suffering.[13] Across starkly disparate fields, various rights-activists elaborated a shared set of moral sensibilities, equating their struggles as parts of a universal movement of humanity toward progress. "You are full of sympathy with nations that rise against the domination of the Turk," Emmeline Pankhurst told the New York women's suffrage supporters in a famous 1913 speech. "How is it, then, that some of you have nothing but ridicule and contempt . . . for women who are fighting for exactly the same thing?"[14] When seen as an integral part of this growing web of liberal causes—abolition of slavery, women's rights, penal reform, humane treatment of animals, religious freedom—the globally prominent rise of the Balkan nations raises important questions about the relationship between nationalism, liberalism, and the voices of suffering that echoed well beyond the nineteenth century.

"Sad Bosnia": From Captivity to National Slavery

In 1835, the Illyrian writer Mate Topalović published "Sad Bosnia" (*Tužna Bosna*), a short patriotic poem that became a surprisingly popu-lar point of reference for South Slavic national discourses. The poem—the first text about Bosnia to appear in the flagship Illyrian journal *Danica Ilirska*—contemplated the agony of this noble province. Ever since the ar-rival of the Ottomans at "dreadful Kosovo," devastating "disunity" set the South Slavic "brothers quarreling" and "made them slaves / buried in dark graves"; the "bright nobility of my mighty people," Topalović lamented, was shackled in iron and destroyed, leading the poet to wonder whether the Turkish conquest of Bosnia was imposed by blind fate or whether the land was simply abandoned by God. Only the final stanza departs briefly from the tone of despair to assert a more hopeful vision of Bosnia's future: "still the sun will rise / still the evil will extinguish."[15]

"Sad Bosnia" elicited a range of responses, some of them coming immediately from Bosnia itself. In 1835 Martin Nedić, a young Bosnian Franciscan, contributed his *Conversation of Illyrian Spirits in Springtime*.[16] The work depicted a gathering of the Illyrian female spirits (*vilas*) in a spring dance to mark the end of a long winter, each representing a major South Slavic region (Dalmatia, Srem, Buda, Dubrovnik, Belgrade, and Croatia). From this joyous awakening, however, only the *vila* of Bosnia was missing; stranded and left to contemplate her tragic fate atop a cliff, she cried and wondered when "will happiness dawn on you, Bosnia / When will you cast off the Turkish yoke from your neck?" Only later do the other Illyrian spirits notice their inconsolable sister, but nothing can make her forget the oppression by "the damned Turkish faith" — "I've never been more sorrowful / I, the slave Bosnian *vila*."[17] Another young Bosnian Franciscan, Ivan Franjo Jukić, also responded passionately to Topalović, arguing that "Illyrian brothers and sisters" would surely set this land free "as soon as we get to know each other better / And spread love among one another." But this day remained a distant hope, Jukić wrote in 1838, for "Sad Bosnia is still grieving / And, they say, sadly sighing."[18]

Yet it was the subsequent adaptations outside of Bosnia, primarily by national activists in Croatia and Serbia, that ensured the longevity of the "sad Bosnia" motifs. By the 1850s, the Croatian painter Vjekoslav Karas composed music to Topalović's lyrics — "the piano introduction is melancholy" — and the song remained fashionable among South Slavic singing groups into the 1890s.[19] The Zagreb dramatist Mirko Bogović adapted parts of Topalović's imagery to the theater stage; in his 1857 play on the fall of the medieval Bosnian kingdom to the Turks, the last Slavic king tells sultan Mehmed Fatih that "as far as my sad Bosnia is concerned," hundreds of years may pass in "the dark night," but someday, the sun will surely rise.[20] In Serbia, too, there were numerous stagings of Bosnia's sorrow. In the first issue of *Greater Serbia* (1888), Stevan Kaćanski published his "Poor Bosnia" poem, retaining Topalović's frame of reference but adding more strident pronouncements of pending "salvation for our miserable Bosnia!"[21] A newspaper in Serbia began to appear under the title *Bosnia: The Herald of Subjugated Serbdom*.[22] Tavern bands, student groups, and state orchestras in early twentieth-century Serbia frequently performed "Oh Bosnia, You Cursed Wretch," a popular song with motifs of slavery, darkness, and suffering.[23] Ljudevit Pivko, the Slovene officer in charge of pro-South Slav Allied propaganda during the First World War, enlisted the song in his repertoire of music "that has the best effect on non-Slavic guests."[24] Debating in the Yugoslav parliament in the 1930s, Vojislav Lazić was among several delegates who intoned this song from the podium (to applause from the Left and the Right) and wistfully recalled: "Already as children, it was impressed on our souls that out there exists a land of ours, where the foreigner rules, where there is no sunshine, no light, and no freedom."[25]

How did one particular place become the object of so much sustained reflection over national sadness? What made the tropes of slavery such popular subjects for early national movements in the first place? A critical clue to the emergence of the tropes of "sad Bosnia" comes from Topalović's 1835 poem itself, which bears an epigraph from Pavao Ritter Vitezović, a well-known early modern Croatian writer and author of *Bossna captiva* (1712). In this treatise, Vitezović described the fall of the medieval Balkan provinces to Ottoman rule in the fifteenth and sixteenth centuries; Croatia eventually emerged "revived" (*rediviva*) after the Habsburg reconquest of the region (1683–1699) and Bosnia remained "captive" (*captiva*) to the Turks.[26] Mapping national sadness onto this geopolitical landscape in the early nineteenth century largely followed the long-established contours of Turkish captivity. Because the Habsburg-Ottoman borders had remained almost unchanged since Vitezović's time, the emerging Illyrian patriots of the 1820s and 1830s—stimulated not only by romanticism but also more directly by the Serbian and Greek uprisings—repurposed the early modern tropes of "captivity" and "revival" for their projects of national awakening. As in the earlier Christian Slavic literatures, the divide between the captive and the free, the sad and the happy, often carried religious connotations, with Islam mostly associated with captivity, darkness, and ruin, and Christianity with liberty, light, and morality.[27] Similar associations linking "plague, sodomy, and Islam" were also present across France, England, and central Europe since at least the seventeenth century.[28] These themes persisted into the nineteenth century, appearing in Orthodox and Catholic theological polemics against Islam, its "false prophet Muhammed," and "the Turkish menace."[29]

It is worth noting that prior to the nineteenth century, however, captivity was only one of many ways of conceptualizing Muslim-Christian relations and did not necessarily spell unmitigated doom for the captive in most Mediterranean, Slavic, or central European literatures. As recent scholarship has made clear, early modern writers (European and Ottoman) understood the Muslim-Christian-Jewish communal relations in a very broad array of terms—not only of captivity and slavery but also of conversion, translation, and exchange—reflecting the inequalities, economies, and customs of Mediterranean and Balkan societies.[30] Moreover, captivity itself cut both ways on the Muslim-Christian spectrum; Muslims were captured and enslaved by Christians and vice versa.[31] Finally, early modern captivity narratives were multifaceted genre templates, encompassing tragic enslavement as well as dramatic and even apparently comic aspects of imprisonment and custody.

Numerous plays, such as Gjuro Palmotić's adaptation of *Happy Captivity* (*Suxanjstvo srechno*, ca. 1680), told stories of Bosnian and Croatian nobility whose strange encounters and fates stake their drama on the reversal of the expectations of disaster for the captured.[32]

By the middle of the nineteenth century, however, any scenario for a "happy captivity" of Christians under Ottoman rule was unimaginable as the trope of captivity became a cornerstone of liberal-democratic debates within the literatures on national suffering. In the first place, discussions of Bosnia's captivity gradually shifted away from lamentations over fallen medieval nobility—kings, queens, and princes—and shifted toward explorations of a generalized suffering of "the people" (*narod*), especially emphasizing the subjugation of the *raya*. In a related move, South Slavic patriots increasingly turned to "Europe" as a crucial witness to these injustices, which they compared with outrages—namely, chattel slavery—that attracted the attention of the growing liberal nineteenth-century publics. In other words, conceiving of a generalized suffering of an entire nation entailed a sustained development of new frames of references appropriate for this important subject.

On the one hand, it is easy to see why nineteenth-century national activists continued to be drawn to histories depicting glorious medieval ages cut short by brutal invaders. In elaborating such accounts, the emerging South Slavic patriots drew on early modern depictions of several prominent historical events and individuals. According to Miodrag Popović, for example, different retellings of the 1389 Battle of Kosovo before the nineteenth century revolved around a handful of core protagonists who shared similarly elite lineages (Prince Marko, Prince Lazar, Miloš Obilić).[33] Chronicles about the fall of the Bosnian kingdom to the Ottomans in 1463 likewise focused on a small number of highborn individuals like the Bosnian king Stjepan and queen Katarina. In nineteenth-century nationalist reinterpretations, the tragic fate of the medieval royalty and related personages provided a useful metonym for the defiance and the eventual defeat of an entire people (Serbs, Croats, Bulgarians, etc.).[34] Thanks to these qualities, many historical depictions of fallen kingdoms and protagonists appeared in the nineteenth century, as several works about the medieval Bosnian kingdom by Antun Knežević, Mirko Bogović, and Mita Popović readily demonstrate.[35] Such histories overtly appealed to the patriotic conscience of the regional—and thus fairly limited—audiences who could relate to the presumed noble ancestors and emblems of their nation.

On the other hand, a new kind of discourse quickly eclipsed this historical literature, ushering in a strikingly novel emphasis on the ongoing slavery of the *raya* that unfolded before European liberal publics. Instead of locating the source of injury in the medieval past, writers of the mid-nineteenth century began to stress the ongoing suffering of their co-nationals, particularly in regions like Bosnia that remained under Ottoman rule. Viewed in this context, Croatia, Slavonia, and Vojvodina appeared freed from the Ottomans by Austria since the 1690s, Montenegro had preserved its self-rule in the remote highlands for centuries, and by the 1820s Serbia had won its autonomy from the Porte thanks to the aid of the Great Powers. As the renowned Illyrian-Bosnian activist Ivan Franjo Jukić wrote concerning Serbia and Bosnia-Herzegovina, "the former managed to rid itself of that [Turkish] plague, but the latter remain afflicted up to this very day!"[36] A young Serbian poet in 1849 agreed: "All our world celebrates the rising of Christ / While Bosnia drowns in tears. / Shackles fall from all the Slavic peoples / But Bosnia alone groans under the yoke."[37] In other words, while national activists in most South Slavic regions could invoke memorable injustices in both the recent and remote past, it was Bosnia that conspicuously remained under the Ottomans in its *present*, continuing to languish in captivity and in plain sight of the more liberated neighbors.

Echoes from the Balkans, an 1842 poem by the young Serbo-Croatian intellectual Ognjeslav Utješenović (Ostrožinski), broke new ground on several emerging themes of patriotic literature. Prior to this piece, Utješenović did not, by his own account, have much literary success; *Echoes from the Balkans* was his "first poem to see the light of day." Much to his "huge surprise," then, the poem instantly became a transnational hit, published both in the original Croatian (*Jeka od Balkana*) and in German in 1842 in the *Augsburger Allgemeine Zeitung* (one of the most prestigious European newspapers of the time), with a French translation and editorial following in the Parisian *Le Correspondant* a year later and in Italian by 1848—a rare feat for South Slavic authors at that point.[38]

Subtitled *The Tears of the Bulgarian, Herzegovinian, and Bosnian Christians*, the poem unfolded an echoing soundscape of mourning over the "burning, bitter wound / inflicted by slavery." As it depicts Balkan sorrow under the Turks, the poem brings out a recurring, structuring imperative to "Listen!"—to the "the jangling chains of slavery / that bind the Christian," to the "mournful wails of Mostar," and to the final call for a new "Alexander, the conqueror of Persia," to "grab the sword" and free "the sad slaves." In managing this proliferation of voices ("howling children," "weeping mothers," "crushed elders"), the poem occasionally cautions that "this is no fable," a gesture that establishes its claim to realism and furthers its emphatic plea for recognition. While the work obviously calls on South Slavic peoples as one audience listening to these cries, Utješenović also explicitly situated the Balkan "echoes" in a larger global framework. "Even in the far reaches of the globe / Truth's and freedom's day arrives / Even the Negros of wild stock / The shield of holy justice now guards," Utješenović wrote in a novel juxtaposition of chattel slavery of the Americas and the suffering of the Balkan Christians. The plight of the latter, however, Utješenović deemed less widely recognized: "All the world is lit by dawn / Only in the Balkans there's no daylight!"[39]

Both German (1842) and French (1843) editorials accompanying the poem positioned the listeners of "the echoes" as an explicitly "European" audience cultivating liberal sympathies. The French editorial openly addressed its audience as such: "O you Europeans! . . . Listen to the groaning of the children and maidens, cast a glance of compassion." Comparisons to other liberal causes drove home the editorial point that Europeans, particularly "diplomats," unjustly ignored the suffering of the *raya*: "You boast, Europeans, that you have arrived at such a civilization that you even shield animals from the cruelty of their masters, yet you do not notice the thousands of your hapless co-religionists who moan under the yoke of barbarity. They are Bosnians, they are Christians."[40] The German commentary likewise framed "the echoes" as an outrage to liberal conscience, but described "Europe" as an already informed party that "empathizes with the nameless sufferings that, in European Turkey, shackle in lowest bondage the groaning Christians. From all sides we hear expressions of Europe's sympathy."[41]

Attending to the imperative "Listen!" presupposed two new and modern subject positions: that of the outside observer able to hear, recognize, and act on the observed suffering, and that of the sufferer, whose voice and expressions of pain here appeared as groans, sighs, and pleas emanating out into the world as "echoes from the Balkans." Writing about the inspiration for his work, Utješenović clearly placed himself in the position of the external sympathetic observer, recalling that in his youth he was "always lovingly gazing from my hills of Ostrožin over there across the Turkish boundary," a process of imagination that led him to "seek out on the literary field the traces of Turkish oppression, reading with great interest all the news from the other side, with the fate of my co-nationals (*sunarodnika*) in Turkey constantly occupying my mind and heart."[42] Looking across the Bosnian border and observing "the sighs," "the chains," and "the bitter, bitter tears" was an important experience for Mato Topalović as well: "Oh! You blue horizon over there / Oh Bosnian mountains! / Can my song express you this . . . / That I have no peace / On this side here / While my mind is over there!"[43]

It is crucial to note that the results of this scrutiny appeared as a generalized suffering borne not by some elite individuals but by the *raya* as a whole, by the ordinary Balkan Christian peasants whose humble lives were wrecked by the Turks. While the captivity of the nobility had been a long-established trope, new comparisons served to underscore precisely the collective—and, as the *Augsburger* editorial put it, "nameless"—suffering of the *raya* that unfolded before "Europe." In this regard, it was important for national activists to draw clear lines between the masters and the slaves, as Jukić did in his 1850 survey of Bosnia: "Only the Turks, that is, the followers of Muhammed, enjoy legal and policing power, while the Christians are just *raya*, that is, slaves (*robovi*)!"[44] After reporting this situation, however, Jukić was still troubled about the broader appeal of his description of the *raya*'s suffering: "Whoever is outside of Bosnia . . . cannot even conceive of what we here bear and endure, and we do not know how to express our grief! The English and the French manumit African slaves, forbidding the slave trade, and with that seek some kind of admiration from enlightened Europe; yet they will not get to know about us, the sad slaves, Christians in Turkey."[45] Despite the shift in tone, the continuing concern with reaching audiences "outside Bosnia" links Jukić's thoughts, moving from a lament over the inadequacy of his descriptions of the *raya*'s suffering to an invocation of "enlightened Europe" and chattel slavery as apposite moral frameworks for Bosnian reports.

Utješenović and Jukić were not the only ones issuing comparisons to slavery, particularly to its American dimensions. After the German American writer Therese Luise-Robinson (Talvi) wrote to Vuk Karadžić in 1853 to tell him about *Uncle Tom's Cabin*, Vuk replied, "The Christians in Turkey, the poor *raya*, especially our Serbs in Bosnia and Herzegovina, are in no better position than the blacks in North America."[46] In a memorandum on the Eastern Question, a high-ranking Serbian official similarly wrote, "Are not the sufferings and trials that the [Ottoman] Christians experience equal to those of the slaves of America? This is truly an epoch of exceptional humiliation for humanity!"[47] These appeals, as Jukić himself stated, relied on the ability to subsume the reported injuries "everywhere under the name '*raya*,'" thus establishing a new, collective, and easily recognizable subject of suffering.[48]

The growing invocations of slavery were not simple figures of speech, but conspicuous marks of a new liberal outlook among aspiring patriots in the Balkans. As Michel-Rolph Trouillot, Susan Buck-Morss, and other historians have observed, "slavery" had become for Enlightenment and liberal thinkers "the root metaphor of Western political philosophy," opposed by the ideal of "freedom" as its counterpart. Moreover, it was an "an easy metaphor, accessible to a large public"—including American, Italian, German, and increasingly South Slavic writers—"who knew that the word stood for a number of evils, except perhaps the evil of itself."[49] It is precisely this sense of slavery as a metaphor for "a number of evils" that Ničifor Dučić invoked in 1871 when he wrote of "the myriad sufferings, miseries, and tribulations that the glorious Americans in the eighteenth century bore for their independence," concluding from the American Revolution that "no Serb, just like no American, will ever consent to being a slave."[50]

Thus Utješenović's pioneering invocation of "Negroes," "chains," and the *raya* are important precisely as the markers of a generic liberal conscience that emerged among the Slavic national movements from the 1840s onward. Far from being a mere figure of speech, the trope of slavery was a conspicuous sign of the transnational popularity of these particular moral-political conceptions, which greatly appealed to Balkan patriots seeking to highlight their own national activism. An understanding of political struggles in the Ottoman Empire as a variation on the theme of slavery and liberation became an integral part of nineteenth-century liberal platforms. John Stuart Mill, a central figure in liberal thought, wrote in 1864 of the necessity of revising British foreign policy toward the Ottoman Empire, "with a view ultimately to the substitution of the Christian Gospel for the Koran in Turkey in Europe." "Bosnia and Bulgaria, as well as Syria and the Lebanon," were exposed to "the feeble, capricious, and corrupt dominion of the Turks," a "cruel wrong" that was, as Mill suggested, a kind of slavery for the Christians:

> It is not to be expected that the instincts and habits of twelve centuries [of Islam] will be eradicated by the lectures of European Statesman, or by the liberal manifestoes of the Sublime Porte. . . . As long as two populations, Mussulman and Christian, are intermingled, with the one essentially dominant over the other, the idea of equal justice or social equality is but a dream. Equality between the whites and the blacks of America is not more impossible than between the conquering religion and these who are tributaries to it.[51]

In addition to a favorable reception in the Western European press, works like Utješenović's *Echoes* encountered a broad array of responses in the Habsburg Monarchy and the Balkans, ranging from enthusiasm to indifference to hostile rejections. By September 1842, Illyrian politicians like Ivan Kukuljević Sakcinski appeared inspired by *Echoes*, writing about the "deep-seated" and possibly "dangerous" tendencies that led "some patriots among us [to] gaze with great longing across the Kordun [border region] to those lands where the Christians live, . . . where the Muslims are the masters."[52] Kukuljević Sakcinski's story "Brothers" (1842) largely took place in Herzegovina, where a "slave supervisor" named Mujo not only guarded "black slaves" tending lavish gardens in Mostar but also pondered how his "Turkish" nature overpowered his "Illyrian" roots.[53] For his part, Utješenović proudly noted that the eminent Slovak intellectual Ján Kollár had personally endorsed *Echoes* and that the poem "caused such a sensation that the public officials in Croatia . . . went on to address the imperial chancellor Count Metternich with a petition urging him to take a stance for the hapless Christians in Turkey."[54] This apparently desired effect, however, raised many suspicions precisely among Habsburg imperial officials intent on keeping order in the possibly volatile Balkan border provinces. In 1845, the Habsburg censors, not wanting to fuel further Croatian interest in the neighboring Ottoman lands, suppressed the second reprint of *Echoes* in Utješenović's publication.[55] In other words, gazing into "sad Bosnia" appeared unsettling and politically hazardous to some politicians, but also rewarding, thrilling, and vital for many other activists in the making.

Not all suffering was recognized as belonging to this new genre or deserving of political attention. Alongside impassioned depictions of the *raya's* suffering, for instance, Jukić cheerily wrote "The Suffering of a Man with His Wife." In this "humorous" folk story, the suffering (*patnja*) in question relates to the problems that "an insane wife" causes her husband, who has to mend her many misdeeds (a killed cow, a ruined garden, spilt wine, etc.); the husband tries to correct her behavior by "beating her into the ground" several times—"but it was all in vain." The woman's insanity eventually becomes a boon for the man after she finds a pot of gold and escapes the Turkish officials precisely because she is judged to be unbelievably crazy; the suffering man thus "got to keep the treasure." Jukić's telling of the story is lighthearted, unconcerned with implications about its casual violence, and contrasts sharply with the somber, outraged tone of his writings about the plight of the *raya* in Bosnia.[56] Utješenović too tried his hand at many other topics—the tragedies of medieval Serbian history, aesthetics, the pains of love—but none encountered the passionate reception granted to his poem about the Balkan *raya*.

Echoes from the Balkans thus signaled more broadly the arrival of a new kind of liberal patriotic discourse, one intensely invested in observing, generalizing, and publicizing the ongoing suffering of one's co-nationals. The editors of *Le Correspondant* already pointed to the political novelty of this literature produced by "Illyrian poets steps ahead of diplomacy," in tune with the spirit of the time and marked by "elevated feeling, enthusiastic tone, and real patriotism."[57] In the wider context of the nineteenth century, this growing concern with the slavery of the *raya* dovetailed with the earlier romantic-populist imaginings of the folk to create an image of the Bosnian Christian peasants as the bearers of both national culture and national suffering. The national past told in this genre went beyond chronicling royal deeds to explore the plight of the downtrodden masses; "the history of the *raya*," wrote Tadija Smičiklas in 1891, "is the history of misery, suffering, and bitter torments"—a new kind of national history.[58]

For all its subjugation, the *raya* was simultaneously recognized as possessing a special political power and world-historical mission. Leopold von Ranke, an engaged observer of the dissolution of the Ottoman Empire and an extraordinarily influential historian, discerned in the Balkans—especially in "Servia . . . and the other Servian tribes in Bosnia and Herzegovina"—a process of major significance for "the Western spirit." As Ranke wrote in the late 1830s, the new Balkan principality of Serbia embodied "the spirit of modern times" that came about through "the liberation of a people" from the Turks, a struggle that illuminated the inevitable "progress of the West towards the East."[59] The peculiarly "Christian" marking of the *raya*'s potential and of "modern progress" was elucidated several years later: "The Ottoman Empire is overpowered and penetrated in all directions by the Christian system. We do not mean by that expression the Christian religion; nor would the words 'culture,' 'civilization,' fully convey our idea; it is being enlightened by the genius of the West: by that spirit which transforms nations into disciplined armies, that traces roads, cuts canals, covers all the seas with fleets and converts them into its own property, which fills remote continents with colonies, that has taken possession of the domains of knowledge and cultivates them with unflagging industry."[60] In this momentous struggle, the forces of progress faced many obstacles—janissaries, viziers, and "the most inflexible adversary . . . Islamism" itself—yet in the end, "the Western spirit" prevailed in the newly independent principalities of Serbia and Greece: "The *Rayah* have become a nation." What made this process so troubling was that it was grievously incomplete; the *raya* remained subjugated in places like "sad Bosnia," making the *raya*'s torments an issue of national slavery and thus a matter of modern conscience for thinkers ranging from Leopold von Ranke to John Stuart Mill. These, then, were the factors inciting deep European interest in Ottoman Christians' "emancipation, an interest which extends far beyond the boundaries" of the small Balkan provinces.[61]

Searching for the Voice of Suffering

These emerging discourses were beset from the beginning by troubling concerns over proper representation of the subject of suffering. Already in 1841, Jukić outlined an intractable problem regarding the activists' attempts to document and publicize certain topics. At the end of a report on tax extortions and widespread Ottoman abuses facing the Bosnian Christian peasants, Jukić expressed reservations about his own position as a "reporter" and an "insider":

> Here I write about what people outside of Bosnia already know; but to describe what people inside of Bosnia know, to *describe from within* what those who know, who suffer—including myself, who have seen it so many times—indeed, my description could be more a distraction than an aid in this regard. I thus abstain from this task, leaving it to others.[62]

Jukić's doubts pointed to recurring national concerns: What constituted an appropriate description of national suffering? Where should such a description come from? How could activists "describe from within" and still be able to report the interiority of suffering to diverse publics?

Contrary to the expectations of our own "era of the witness"—where the prevailing documentary form for expressing suffering is first-person eyewitness testimony—nineteenth-century national activists did not consider it self-evident that those "from within," like those with an immediate experience of the *raya*'s plight, made the best reporters on the subject.[63] In fact, as Jukić suggested, a too close description of pain could "be more a distraction than an aid" in properly expressing the gist of the matter. In grappling with this problem, national activists eventually elaborated a new vision of poetic-political "fantasy" as the preferred mode of distilling the authentic condition of national suffering and managing its expression through careful management of speaking roles and voices. This major development, however, occurred in a context where other approaches also attempted to address the problem of documenting and publicizing national suffering. Writers like Matija Mažuranić in his 1842 account *A Glimpse into Bosnia*, for instance, provided reports that focused on regional circumstances and major news as occasions for publicizing the *raya*'s plight. This realist-documentary mode was sensationalist since it highlighted shocking stories for its repertoire, but it still retained reporting as its defining activity, be it in form of newspaper articles, diplomatic bulletins, or travel accounts.

To contextualize these developments, it is important to remember that obtaining detailed reports about local events inside Ottoman Bosnia was a difficult task for Serbian and Croatian activists. Travel to and through the Ottoman provinces was possible, but various merchants or officials who went or resided there made very few contributions to the emerging nationalist literature for a variety of reasons: lack of close ties between different groups, indifference toward patriotic projects, or fear of political consequences for nationalist engagement. When committed South Slavic patriots actually traveled to Ottoman Bosnia (like Stefan Herkalović did in 1839), their declared activities—writing down folk tales, inquiring about local events, getting to know "our people"—raised suspicions among the Porte's officials who tracked nationalist societies agitating against Ottoman rule.[64] Imperial vigilance against nationalist agitation continued to be a major obstacle for aspiring patriots throughout the nineteenth century.

In these circumstances, journalistic reports by regional residents or by outside travelers proved to be valuable sources for constructing the realist-documentary narratives of national suffering. A few major themes mark this body of writing. For a start, most patriotic news or travel reports from Ottoman Bosnia were published anonymously or under pseudonyms precisely because of the imperial pressures against this literature. Second, the realist-documentary literature generally focused on describing the conditions in Bosnia and other Ottoman provinces, allotting a significant amount of space to covering major news from these areas and commenting on them with consistent outrage. A look at Bosnia-related reporting in the Croatian and Serbian newspapers of the 1850s and 1860s illustrates both of these features, showing that most such articles were signed by simple initials or phrases like "a patriotic native"; the content of these articles, often titled "From across the Bosnian Border," repeatedly stressed that the plight of the "unfortunate Bosnian Christians" remained the same or worsened despite the Tanzimat reforms. One author in 1868 summed up this attitude in his opening sentence: "From sad Bosnia do not hope for any good news, but expect only misery and grief."[65]

However, translating peasant grievances—especially taxation abuses and agrarian exploitation—into marks of national suffering turned out to be quite difficult within the bounds of the realist-documentary narratives. Already in the 1840s, Serbian and Illyrian national activists were keenly aware of the potential of peasant grievances, which they hoped to steer into a full-fledged uprising against Ottoman rule and use for a variety of purposes. Leading Pan-Slavist activists like František Zach were interested in publicizing reports from Ottoman Bosnia in the regional press and were confident that they would attract the attention of European newspapers as well.[66] Officials working under the minister Ilija Garašanin urged the Serbian government in 1848 "to file grievances [from Bosnia] in a special dossier, from which we would compose a memorandum to Europe in case of war and thus justify the cause of the war."[67] The Serbian cabinet collected numerous reports highlighting the exploitative conduct of the Ottoman tax collectors, who mercilessly "take from the peasant every third egg, every third head of cabbage, and of everything a third, so how will [the peasant] live?"[68] Activists like Risto Bogdanović often ended their reports with a reminder to the Belgrade officials to "put this in the newspapers."[69]

Articles on Bosnian peasant grievances did appear in the Serbo-Croatian press of the time, but they paled in scope and in popularity with the much more widely read exposés stressing religious dimensions of the Turkish oppression of Balkan Christians. *The Christians in Bosnia*, an anonymous feuilleton in *Augsburger Allgemeine Zeitung* also published as a separate booklet in Vienna in 1853 and then translated into Serbian in the same year, billed itself as a "contribution to the closer knowledge of the condition of the Bosnian *raya*," but was in effect a fusion of already published reports and Orientalist formulas.[70] "No less dangerous than the wild Kurdistan," Bosnia was a land "where intolerance and hatred against Christians is more striking and more real than in the environs of the ancient-fanatical Damascus." After explaining that "the primary source" of all such abuses lies in "the Islamic order . . . rooted in the Qur'an," the account discussed village structures and land regulations in Ottoman Bosnia. The staging of local peasant grievances concerning land plots, labor, and payment of specific taxes in kind or cash, however, remained tied to the overarching emphasis on Muslims' religiously motivated, "raw, horrific, fanatical, greedy, and reckless" persecution against the "impoverished, despised, terrified, despairing" Christians. This condition can be "expressed in one word—the poor *raya*."[71] The focus on Muslim "religious fanaticism" remained a ubiquitous trope for introducing and incorporating local peasant grievances into broader patriotic projects.

One of the accounts that best exemplifies the realist-documentary literature on national suffering is Matija Mažuranić's travelogue *A Glimpse into Bosnia*. Published anonymously in Zagreb in 1842 ("by a certain patriot"), this work was based on Matija Mažuranić's firsthand travels and notes he had collected in 1839. It strove to present both a stirring patriotic story and a detached travel account of this Ottoman province. Aided by his brothers Antun and Ivan, Matija Mažuranić styled his narrative as a daring foray into the strange land between the Croatian and Serbian borders: there "the Turks" ruled, "hating horribly every unbeliever" and obeying religious customs that allowed "each Mahomedan . . . to kill his wife when he wishes, and any master his servant, especially if he is a Christian." The Christians had "nothing under the sun, neither house nor shelter nor cat"; dispossessed, browbeaten, and constantly threatened with violent punishment—including impalement for arbitrary infractions—they could only crouch before the malice of the Muslim lords. Like *The Christians in Bosnia*, Matija Mažuranić's work devoted considerable attention to taxation abuses and peasant poverty, but only insofar as these subjects were framed by stark contrasts with "European" society and by the gripping narrative of Muslim "fanaticism" against Christians.[72]

The realist-documentary credentials of *A Glimpse into Bosnia* are most emphatically borne out by its repeated references to on-the-spot observation and first-person reporting of Bosnian Christian suffering. In his introduction, Matija Mažuranić stressed the documentary purpose of the trip: "to head personally" to a virtually unknown Turkish province in order to collect new information and then "present these reports" to "our educated countrymen" who might "know more about America, China, India, etc. than about Bosnia."[73] The conspicuous use of the Bosnian-Turkish vocabulary immerses the reader in local character and is elucidated by a "glossary of Turkish barbarisms." Its fast-paced travel narrative in the first part is constantly interrupted by situations personally dangerous for the author—"the Turks thought I was a spy," for example—who then synthesizes his impressions in the second part to make broader observations about the cruelty of life under "the Turkish yoke."[74] (It should be noted, however, that Matija Mažuranić returned and lived in Ottoman Bosnia for almost two years in 1847–1848, working as an engineer for the Ottoman governor and sending more private letters, but no public reports, from Sarajevo, Travnik, and Istanbul.)[75] As the first major account by an Illyrian activist traveling to Bosnia, the book garnered considerable attention in South Slavic circles and parts of it were translated into German in 1843 and most recently into English in 2007, when its prose was noted for its "documentary, direct, and moving fashion."[76]

At the same time, such accounts clearly showed some crucial limitations of the realist-documentary literature concerning national suffering. The anonymity, brevity, and ephemerality of the press reports from Ottoman Bosnia made it difficult to create a canon of national literature in this largely journalistic genre. Most important, while realist-documentary narratives successfully presented general circumstances—Muslim fanaticism, Christian poverty, and so on—they struggled to "describe from within" and convey the fuller significance of national suffering. The voice of the sufferer proved to be especially intractable. A telling instance comes from a 1868 Serbian story styled as "a report from a French officer" about his travels in the Balkans; the foreign officer's encounters compel him to relate scenes of Turkish violence to a broader audience that he identifies as "you, free Christians" in Europe. At a few crucial junctures in the story, however, the narrative shifts from "I," "a French officer" observing the *raya*'s suffering, to "we, the miserable *raya*" experiencing the suffering, as in the following passage: "Here *I* could clearly see what you free Christians cannot even imagine or see: that in this land rules the law of the victor over the vanquished, that the only law for the poor Bulgarian Christians is the law of the Turks." Without stopping, the "I" voice of outside witnessing shifts into the "we" voice of the *raya*'s testimony: "To us, slavery would be better; for if they beat and harness a slave like a dog, at least his master feeds him. A free man lives under the protection of the law that shields him, but *we*, the miserable *raya*, live in fear as neither slaves nor free. . . . We are the children robbed of our inheritance in the family of Christian peoples." Narration in this manner could be sensational, but staging and alternating the distinct voices of reporting and experiencing suffering proved difficult to sustain in the realist-documentary accounts.[77]

The Power of Poetic-Political Fantasy

Certain kinds of poetry, on the other hand, provided ways of overcoming these limitations and opened new realms of political expression. To begin with, poetry had a privileged place in the romantic conception of the nation. As elsewhere in Europe, emerging Croatian, Slovene, Serbian, and other national activists saw folk poetry as "the mirror of the people," documenting its past for historians and "tremendously rousing all senses from heart to heart," particularly the senses of patriotic pride and sorrow.[78] Moreover, national activists attributed specific political significance to poetic expression as such. In an important treatise titled "The Serb and His Poetry" (1860), Jakov Ignjatović further developed these views, which located the source of nationality "in the inner being (*unutarnjem bitju*) of our spiritual forces," to explicitly argue that poetry constitutes a separate political domain that first emerged under imperial subjugation.[79] "When the Turk completed the conquest of the Serbian land," Ignjatović wrote, "the Serb, in his sadness and misery, took the *gusle* in his hands and began to sing his famed past and to mourn the dismal fate that befell him." This withdrawal—first into "the mountains, the Serb hugging, kissing trees as his brothers," and then into "the patriarchal family" of peasant society—was absolutely critical to the formation of a new moral realm. "Sad poetry" (*žalosne pjesme*) overshadowed the earlier, "more cheerful" epics and thus emerged as the defining mark of Serbian national character, which Ignjatović cast in psychological, emotional, and even physiological features. In this particular structure, national activists faced on the outer, worldly side "the violence and the physical dominance of the Turk, and the moral dominance of the Serb" in the inner, ever-expanding national realm.[80]

As Partha Chatterjee argued, such normative assumptions about the "inner" domain of the nation had far-reaching consequences, providing nationalists with powerful moral positions for articulating the cultural outlooks, gender dynamics, and state-building programs of the national community.[81] Croatian and Serbian activists openly encouraged such interpretations of nation-formation, structuring their historical narrative as an evolution of cultural—overwhelmingly poetic and "sad"—sentiments into the more prosaic state-building agendas of the twentieth century. Citing English abolitionist writings on Africa, the Croatian writer Franjo Rački wrote in 1867 that "besides physical slavery, there is also a spiritual slavery" that afflicts the Croats and the Serbs, "the martyrs in the struggle against Muhammadanism, who with not yet healed wounds now realize that only the spiritual deeds of the people can erect unconquerable monuments."[82] In mapping out these emotionally charged realms, South Slavic activists located Bosnia as a site of specially concentrated national suffering; Ignjatović wrote that while walking through Belgrade in the 1850s, he sometimes "heard the wind from the Drina River carry the wails of the ill-fated Bosniac tortured relentlessly by inhumanity. Then a burden falls on my soul, and I ask myself, as in a dream, 'Are you a Serb, can you have a calm soul and be happy as long as this wailing reaches your soul?' "[83]

Certain authors could acquire special insight into national suffering through the piercing force of creative imagination or, to use the illuminating term of the time, "fantasy" (*fantazija*). Among the many meanings of this important concept, which ranged from perceptive intuition to unrestrained invention, fantasy stood out for most nineteenth-century national activists as an agency enabling political imagination; it is this specific sense that was crucial for a new kind of national activism.[84] August Šenoa, the doyen of nineteenth-century Croatian literature, had no doubts about the cultural value or the political significance of this faculty. "Fantasy is the mother of poetry," Šenoa wrote. "Fantasy" is the "creative force" that elevates the poetic above the more prosaic forms relying on "sheer imitation of nature, sheer narration of past events, [which] is not poetry" even if put into verse form, he wrote in an renowned literary treatise in 1876. This is not to say that poetry and fantasy were released from documentary burdens. In fact, Šenoa stressed that fantasy in this sense faced major documentary limitations that ensured its basic "authenticity." "To what extent must the poet strictly adhere to history, to what extent can he depart from it?" Šenoa wondered and offered this argument as the literary consensus on the issue: "Poetic fantasy should not distort the main, generally known events. [The poet] should not narrate against history, so that . . . King Lazar defeated the Turks at Kosovo, but he can alter freely any accompanying events" or invent new characters. Unlike "the historian" (or an ideal objective reporter) who is bound exclusively to "his sources and the events themselves," "the poet is much freer" in his work as long as he grasps not the exact historical but rather "some psychological truth" of an occurrence, some deeply rooted "authentic" essence. The only imperative for poetry in this sense is "fantasy itself," for it alone transforms ordinary factual description into a variety of "compelling, creative expressions," be they "idealistic," "realistic," "lyrical," "epic," or otherwise.[85]

At the heart of this authentic fantasy that claimed to document the nation's character, Šenoa emphasized, was an enduring concern with political values borne out by national struggles and sufferings. According to the stalwart of Croatian literature, the South Slavic national canon concerned not so much the grace of peasant folklore, but rather

> that enormous cultural struggle, the beautiful vision that puts to shame the entire diplomatic, cultural world. . . . Islam and the cross, slavery and freedom, culture and darkness struggle on our own battlefield; for this idea our blood flows. . . . Our people has transferred the virtues and flaws of our model heroes to every hero, which is why the epic folk poem has become stereotypical; that is why its stereotypicality appears even where there is no battle with the Turk.[86]

The kind of suffering born under the sign of Turkish oppression, then, was already in the 1870s understood as a "stereotypical" template, a flexible framework and transferable narrative script that shaped political outlooks "even where there is no battle with the Turk." In addition to presaging the extensibility of this concern well after the end of Ottoman rule, this understanding of South Slavic nationhood fostered intense interest in national wounds, encouraging activists to cultivate their fantasy and convey matters of national suffering to their compatriots and to the world.

The work that was widely held up as the consummate achievement of poetic-political fantasy was *The Death of Smail-aga Čengić* (*Smrt Smail-age Čengića*, 1846) by Ivan Mažuranić (1814–1890), who went on to become one of Croatia's most famous writers and governors.[87] In the epic poem, Mažuranić cultivated the authenticity of his fantastic insight by reinterpreting an actual historical event: the 1840 skirmish in Herzegovina during which a group of Montenegrin fighters killed Smail-aga (Ismail) Čengić, the local notable from a well-known Bosnian Muslim family.[88] Revisiting this incident several years later for a solicited literary piece, Ivan Mažuranić collected a variety of sources, ranging from newspaper articles to regional rumors to his brother Matija's reports from the Ottoman province (including *A Glimpse into Bosnia*).[89] In basic terms, the emplotment of this work is fairly straightforward; it presents a series of scenes leading from Smail-aga's torture of his captives in Herzegovina to Montenegrin mobilization and final victory over the Muslim lord. The clearly signaled religious dimensions of the struggle follow a well-established pattern: the Turkish retinue is "vicious"; the *raya* are "poor," "beaten," and derided by the Turks as "dogs and Christlings"; the Montenegrins are "defiant" and "victorious."[90] In themselves, these are not major departures from the established literary directions traced by Utješenović, Jukić, or Petar Petrović Njegoš and developed by many other writers.

The work's greatest contribution thus lies not, as some scholars have suggested, in its appropriation of the Montenegrin fighting ethos (Njegoš's *locus classicus*) or in its religious coloring of the conflict (already prefigured), but in Mažuranić's innovative and extraordinarily influential staging of the voices of *raya*'s suffering.[91] Indeed, to nineteenth-century writers like Šenoa, the sensibility and the very sound of suffering was clearly a dominant theme of *The Death of Smail-aga Čengić*: "Here you see in live words the horrible image, you sense by the sound of the words the terrifying suffering of the poor *raya*."[92] The poem abounds with examples, but two specific acts out of the poem's five parts stand out: the first act, "The Aga's Lording" (*Agovanje*) and the fourth and the longest act, "The Tribute Collection" (*Harač*).

The "Aga's Lording" opens the epic in Herzegovina (Stolac), where Smail-aga commands his servants to prepare and execute the captured Montenegrin "highlanders" through meticulously organized impalement. Thus instantly framed by Turkish malice, the third-person narration relates at considerable length the physical torture and the impalement accompanied by an eerily silent soundscape of suffering:

> The stake creaked a few times,
> The sword slashed a few times,
> Flimsy gallows swayed,
> But the Montenegrins made no sound,
> Made no sound, not even gnashing of teeth.
> Through the fields dark blood flowed,
> Made no sound, not even gnashing of teeth,
> The fields grew full of corpses,
> Made no sound, not even gnashing of teeth.[93]

Contrary to the usual associations of impalement with agonizingly vocal punishment—"Curses like a Vlach on a stake," went the South Slavic proverb—Mažuranić's staging repeatedly stills the scene marked only by creaking stakes and "occasional" cries to God.[94] In part, the Montenegrins' silent bearing signals their unshakeable pride, which instills fear into Smail-aga's heart, but Mažuranić's managing of the sounds and the "mute speech" of suffering also serves more important purposes evident throughout the epic.[95] The victims' virtual silence opens up new fields of expression,

notably foregrounding the visual register of the narrative marked by scru-
pulous observation of the tortured body: the dark blood flows in the fields,
the bodies shudder and writhe, the bodies pile up and hang from trees—but
these bodies are mute, emitting no sound save for a few moans that resonate throughout the setting. This careful management of visual and aural
registers calls attention to the conspicuous—and physically stifled—spaces
of suffering dominated by other voices, like that of Smail-aga as he orders
and ponders the torture that unfolds before him. Crucially, it is the voice
of poetic fantasy itself that is able to present both the stillness of the impaled bodies and Smail-aga's inner thoughts, that calls attention to the overwhelming silence and brings out the faint but echoing sounds of suffering.
The 1876 illustration accompanying a major reissue of the epic poem shows
a similar dynamic at work (see figure 2.1). In this scene, the victims' bodies,
depicted as headless torsos and amorphous hanging corpses at the margins
of the image, effectively frame Smail-aga and focus on his act of ordering the
impalement that is about to unfold.

Figure 2.1 "The Aga's Lording," illustration for Mažuranić's *The Death of Smail-Aga*
(1876). Smail-aga presides over the torture of the Montenegrin captives and the
Herzegovinian *raya*, with headless corpses mounting before the Turkish torturer. With
permission from the Museum of Literature and Performing Arts, Sarajevo.

The staging of the *raya*'s torment in "The Tribute Collection" (*Harač*) demonstrates Mažuranić's meticulous management of voices, echoes, and speaking parts in his work. In a succession of graphic scenes, the act begins with a depiction of Smail-aga's attempt to collect the *harač*, the poll tax paid by non-Muslims in the Ottoman Empire, and his failure to extort money from the absolutely impoverished *raya*. Enraged, Smail-aga undertakes new cruelties described in excruciating detail; his retinue shackles the *raya*, hitches the chains to horses who then pull and trample "the moaning *raya*" while the Turks watch, "laughing loudly" and eagerly awaiting more "blood-letting," "lashing," and "slaying." The omniscient narration brings into focus particular details, again stressing the Turkish torture, orders "that resonate across the field" and the groans, pleas, and screams that followed. At other times, the victims' bodies come to the fore of the description as the *raya* are dragged, slashed, and hung, but for all the chaos and terror, their bodies make a limited range of sounds. Throughout the epic, the *raya* indistinctly "whimpers," "wails," and "begs," managing only to make terse utterances like "Bread, bread, master!" Even in the few occasions when the possibility of the *raya*'s more extensive expression is raised, Mažuranić carefully shifts witnessing and speech away from it—"The *raya* alone is not the only witness / The *raya* alone has no eyes or mouths"—retaining those activities for other voices, namely, for the voice of poetic fantasy.[96]

Nineteenth-century literary critics like Franjo Marković already noted in 1876 that "for all its significance, the *raya* is characterized very generally, not a single person standing out." In Mažuranić's staging, even gender attributes of the *raya*'s suffering tilt toward depictions of the sufferers as a collective and almost androgynous mass of bodies. This is not to say that the sexual dimension is absent; in fact, Smail-aga's penchant for impaling his "slaves" and his fleeting "thoughts of girls" upon his arrival to collect the *harač* tax clearly signal his sadistic sexual desire. Yet these remain passing references, as most of the torture scenes are remarkably void of explicit gender attributes concerning the *raya*'s bodies or conduct—even personal names are absent—reinforcing Marković's point about the *raya*'s generalized, collective character. "Robbed of its human consciousness and will by horrific slavery," the *raya* could present "an aesthetically unpleasant" problem for the poet, Marković admitted; nonetheless, Mažuranić skillfully avoided it by alternating "calm, vivid imagery" with "exalted and always aesthetically measured fantasy-ness (*fantastičnost*)."[97]

Moreover, the voice of narration not only stages this "sad theater lit by a sad candle" but also insists on dispelling its theatrical, "illusory" character and affirming its authenticity. Direct appeals often exhort the reader to consider "is this wailing an illusion," "is this clanging an illusion," only for a first-person voice to dispel such doubts—"Ah, it is no illusion / For I see where your pain's so deep"—and anticipate the readers' tears: "For you, I deem, would not cry from an illusion!" Even when the text rhetorically questions the adequacy of its description, wondering, "Who will faithfully describe / The most wretched heavy wails?," it immediately prefigures the desired emotional reactions: "And who will with a calm heart listen / Just how vast this bitter sorrow is?"[98] In these ways, for the *raya*'s plight to be made known, its voice had to be represented as the stifled, almost incomprehensible cries of pain whose sound the patriotic poet—gifted with fantasy—heard, translated, and conveyed to "the peoples of the world" in the form of a recurring imperative: "Listen, listen."[99]

This manner of fantasy-driven narration proved incredibly popular among nineteenth-century activists, who elevated Mažuranić's work to the status of an absolute national classic. The book itself was published in dozens of often sold-out editions, translated in several foreign languages (including German and English), and assigned as mandatory school reading in both Serbian and Croatian schools by the First World War.[100] Within three decades of its publication, it established what Vjekoslav Klaić called in 1875 "the technique of Smail-aga," a way of deploying narrative interventions, rhetorical tropes, and linguistic devices that Ivan Mažuranić presented so compellingly in his "classical epic."[101] Among its key achievements, *The Death of Smail-aga* successfully transformed the Ottoman peasant grievances over tax collection abuses into clear symbols of collective suffering borne by the *raya* yet observed and expressed by the patriotic poet. Moreover, such expressions enabled the poet to steer the *raya*'s pleas toward ever-wider "European" audiences, imploring them to recognize and potentially intervene on behalf of the emerging nations. Ivan and Matija Mažuranić had originally prepared alongside the poem a tract on the Bosnian *raya*'s suffering, written in German and addressed "To the monarchs of Europe" (*An die Monarchen Europas*); they did not publish it, apparently preferring to reframe such appeals within the epic itself.[102] Other Serbian and Croatian writers of the 1860s and 1870s, including August Šenoa, Stevan Kaćanski, and Đura Jakšić, wrote literary works directly addressed to "Europe," explicitly accusing "the West" of hypocrisy and lack of compassion in light of the *raya*'s ongoing torment.[103] Here it is important not to read these references to "Europe" narrowly or assume that they are only appeals for Great Power intervention, though such (highly improbable) effects would have been welcome by the national activists. Rather, "Europe" in these patriotic discourses occupies first and foremost the place of the outside observer who may or may not be moved to action by the spectacle of national suffering, but who is supposed to observe and recognize it nonetheless.[104] In other words, it was important to know and to show the awareness that "Europe" or "the world" is watching, an outlook that propelled national activists to continually position their writings with the growing European liberal publics in mind.

Crucially, the authenticity of poetic fantasy could withstand a number of documentary challenges. In the late nineteenth century, a number of critical challenges to the veracity and the authorship of *The Death of Smail-aga*

Čengić surfaced in South Slavic literary and political debates. Why should one author's particular account overshadow the local folk poetry appearing immediately after the event? Did Mažuranić stray too far from the historical record? On what grounds did his authority rest? By the 1890s, Ivan Mažuranić's son Vladimir undertook research to examine these mounting critical concerns.[105] After reexamining the original drafts of the torture scenes in "The Tribute Collection," Vladimir Mažuranić sought the expert commentary of Grga Martić, a leading Bosnian Franciscan friar, poet, and chronicler deeply familiar with the historical context of the Smail-aga poem. Having examined Mažuranić's works, friar Martić replied in 1893, invoking his own eyewitness experiences in Ottoman Bosnia since the 1840s: "The confrontation with the poll-tax collector in Žepče is a complete poetic fabrication that in the poem aggravates the cruelty of the Turks and makes the scene horrific, just as it did in Mažuranić's *Čengićiad*. Besides, it has not been known in Bosnia and Herzegovina that the dragging of the *raya* by the tails ever happened."[106]

Such documentary challenges, however, appeared largely irrelevant to most commentators fascinated by the epic's "authentic" spirit.[107] After listing many discrepancies in Mažuranić's work, the twentieth-century commentator Milorad Živančević stated that these "inventions" do not undermine the epic's overwhelming "authenticity."[108] Such statements built on a long line of thinking about the relationship between history and fantasy. Franjo Marković, introducing the poem in the 1870s, similarly deemed Mažuranić's work more authentic than folk poetry commemorating the same event because folk retellings, valuable as they were, still remained "sheer prose in its makeup, without any poetic expression." Mažuranić, on the other hand, had to put aside the descriptive limits of folk poetry and imbue the event with "ethical pathos" in order to show "the suffering of the *raya* in its exalted pain," thus establishing "an idealistic yet still naturalistic" expression for this matter.[109] In other words, the documentary record was valuable as given material, but it alone was incapable of developing a new set of interests and practices needed to make national suffering widely known. Only poetic-political fantasy could go beyond these limitations and provide ways of adequately expressing and reproducing certain narrative scripts, subjects, and sensibilities.

Inspired by this "idealistic yet naturalistic" style, a new wave of depictions of the *raya*'s torment thrived in the mid- and late nineteenth century. Šenoa himself updated Utješenović's 1842 classic, composing "New Echoes from the Balkans" after reading reports of Turkish repression in Bulgaria in 1861.[110] In Serbia, the writer and painter Đura Jakšić studied Mažuranić's work and produced a number of works describing Turkish cruelty in Bosnia; his poem *The Martyress* (*Mučenica*, 1862) occupied a noteworthy place in this growing literature.[111] The work is immediately framed by the image of a martyr engraving "in one word the outrage of the world, . . . The dark injustice of his kin: *Bosnia!*" The poem then abruptly shifts to an Ottoman court where the vizier (unnamed), smitten with a Serbian girl, tries to tempt her into his embrace, demanding her "supple body" and her submission to Islam. Enraged by Danica's stubborn refusal, the vizier vents his fury through "miserable, Qur'anic torture" and murder of the martyress, who dies "praying for Bosnia" just as her "Serbian lover" carries out a fatal revenge attack against the Turkish master (for "a Serbian woman loves only a Serbian man").[112] On the one hand, Jakšić's work retained much of the framing of Mažuranić's epic, even reproducing the soundscape of suffering dominated by jangling chains, piercing cries, and the fragile, clipped speech of the tormented Danica, who rejects the vizier. On the other hand, however, works like Jakšić's *Martyress* also notably reshaped the collective, nameless, nearly androgynous *raya* into a female character whose body— "beautiful," "shackled," and "whiter than a mound of snow"—the Turkish brutes desire and torture. This sexual-sadistic dimension, already suggested in the earlier depictions of impalement, here explicitly attributed a feminine form to national suffering, with the principal female victim and her male avengers resisting Turkish penetration. Despite highlighting elements of heroic resistance, this manner of depiction remained tragic and focused on Turkish violence, "psychological" as well as sexual, that possessed the national body.[113]

The paintings of Jaroslav Čermák (1831–1878), a well-known Czech French artist, provided striking visual counterparts to these writings. Long fascinated with South Slavic nationalist imagery, Čermák created in the 1860s and 1870s a series of paintings depicting Montenegrin, Herzegovinian, and Bosnian events and personalities. *The Abduction of a Herzegovinian Woman*, painted in 1861, closely dovetails with Jakšić's *Martyress* written roughly around the same time (see figure 2.2). Both works depict the principal victim as a Christian Bosnian-Herzegovinian woman, the sensational "whiteness of the victim" contrasted with the "swarthy Satanic ravager," as one unimpressed Belgian reviewer of the time noted regarding Čermák's work.[114] The sexualized and racialized dimensions of the unrelenting Turkish violence are foregrounded in both Jakšić's and Čermák's creations; the viziers and the Ottoman soldiers, the French poet and art critic Théophile Gautier observed, desire the Christian woman, "taking care to avoid blemishing this prized object" so as to enjoy the "spirited luxuriance of her flesh" after her capture.[115]

Čermák's work, despite some critics' reservations about the brutality displayed in *The Abduction*, was enthusiastically received across Europe, winning a medal at the Paris Salon of 1861 and touring exhibits in Berlin, Rouen, and Munich in the late 1860s. Its subject—a Balkan Christian woman about to be brutally enslaved by the Turks—was familiar, appearing several decades after Eugène Delacroix's famed paintings of Greek massacres, but also novel and relevant enough to merit renewed attention from French, German, and eventually American audiences.[116]

Figure 2.2 *The Abduction of a Herzegovinian Woman by Bashi-Bozuks* by Jaroslav Čermák. The painting was awarded a medal at Salon de Paris in 1861. With permission from the Dahesh Museum of Art, New York.

Croatian authors like August Šenoa and Serbian painters like Uroš Predić wrote about their fascination with Čermák's images, crediting him as inspiration for their own works. Ognjeslav Utješenović, the author of *Echoes from the Balkans*, saw Čermák's "wonderful paintings" in Vienna and "wept before them," composing a poem ("The Slaves," 1870) in their honor alongside paeans in Serbian and Croatian newspapers: "What a magnificent and noble representation of the beauty of the body and the elation and the fullness of spiritual pain, of the greatness of suffering!" South Slavic patriots who could not visit the exhibit, Utješenović urged, should at least acquire the widely available reproductions and postcards of Čermák's work—"it will be a great satisfaction" to own and gift "reminders of that great question, which cannot slip away from the minds of any one of us."[117]

Artistic expressions of the 1870s thus amplified and gave new shape to *Echoes from the Balkans* that Utješenović had discerned almost three decades earlier. In their works, the Mažuranić brothers, Jakšić, Šenoa, Čermák, and other contributors endowed the nameless "sad slaves" of Utješenović's 1842 poem with novel, striking emotional forms, vividly depicting the physical torment and the Turkish violence inflicted on wretched peasants' and virtuous women's bodies. For all their innovations, however, these writers also retained and emphasized the soundscape of "echoes:" the wails, groans, pleas, whimpers, prayers, shrieks, moans, and cries of the victims of Turkish brutality. In their quest to make these resounding voices more widely recognizable, the national activists elaborated a particular faculty—that of poetic-political fantasy—that could both depict the physical infliction of pain and lay claim to a "spiritual," "psychological" dimension of national suffering.

The Aggrieved National Subject

Key features of this literature of national suffering—particularly the demand for the victim's voice as the expression of an aggrieved national subjectivity—proved remarkably adaptable to changing circumstances, continuing well after the disappearance of the Turkish threat. In 1875, an uprising in the Herzegovinan countryside surprised both the Serbo-Croatian national activists and the Ottoman officials who struggled to assert control over the peasant insurrection. The ensuing conflagration, which involved Russia, Serbia, Montenegro, related revolts in Bulgaria, and massive Ottoman reprisals across the region, became a major international crisis that marked a high point of Western coverage of atrocities in the Balkans, particularly the massacres in Bulgaria. William E. Gladstone, the Liberal politician and later prime minister of England, provided the most influential examples of this growing Western European literature with his *Bulgarian Horrors* (1876) and *Lessons in Massacre* (1877).[118] Regarding Bosnia specifically, the Ottoman atrocities, the outpouring of thousands of refugees, and the diplomatic discussions of the province's eventual fate enflamed the earlier depictions of "sad Bosnia," inspiring South Slavic patriots to new cries of pain—as well as joy—over the prospect of liberation from the

Turkish yoke.[119] At the Congress of Berlin in 1878, the Ottoman rule was officially withdrawn from Bosnia and replaced by a new Habsburg administration, bringing an abrupt end to some four hundred years of Turkish rule in this province.

The arrival of a new Habsburg government, many observers speculated, could perhaps improve this "sad" Balkan province, but committed nationalists doubted that such a sudden change was easily possible. Whereas some Croatian and Slovenian writers celebrated the arrival of Habsburg troops to Sarajevo in 1878, others remained cautious and many Serbian activists became actively hostile to this turn of events.[120] The Serbian schoolteacher Mita Živković, for one, viewed the end of Turkish rule with ambivalence. In 1880, he accepted a new job in Sarajevo that inspired him to revisit verses from Jakšić's 1862 *The Martyress*: "In one word the outrage of the world, . . . The dark injustice of his kin: *Bosnia!*" As Živković explained, "These words came to my mind when, in the month of September, I went on my journey to Sarajevo to work as a professor in the former Serb Orthodox Gymnasium."[121] Teachers like Živković learned about Bosnia as a national wound from an abundant literature of suffering to which they also contributed. Živković spent about a year in the now-Habsburg province. "A new time has arrived," he wrote, noting the introduction of railways, factories, schools, and laws while also positing certain continuities in the imperial rule of the province. "Whereas the Turks severed heads and threw men into jails from which one did not leave, the Austrians do not let the Serb call himself as his grandfather called himself," Živković wrote before concluding with an almost Foucauldian flourish: "The Turks killed the body, but the Austrians kill the soul."[122]

The new political constellations of the late nineteenth century, then, brought about several changes that intensified the emphasis on the interiority of suffering, on the wounds borne by the national "soul" and voiced by an aggrieved national subject speaking to the world. To bring out such a subject, South Slavic nationalist activists had to recalibrate their outlook in changing circumstances. In the first place, they had to shift away from the long-standing Turkish threat to confront a new "enemy" — the Habsburg administration in Bosnia-Herzegovina. Leading Serbian activists, such as Vaso Pelagić and Stevan Kaćanski, pioneered this shift by simply equating the new Austrian rule with the hated "Turkish yoke" already in 1878; many patriots leaning to Croatian, Bosnian Muslim, and generally Yugoslav causes were more cautious, but by the beginning of the twentieth century they similarly came to see the Austro-Hungarian rule as an opponent preventing the spread of nationalist sentiments. This was not a simple shift from one enemy to another, however. In moving from "the Turkish yoke" (Muslim, violent, physical) to "the Austrian prison" (Christian, legalistic, administrative), many Yugoslav patriots also affirmed the basic positioning of the already established map of national suffering, one framed by an alien, externalized oppressor and oriented toward an inner and ever-expanding domain of national grievance.

Nationalist responses to the establishment of Habsburg rule in Bosnia thus had profound consequences for defining the incipient Yugoslav community. The formative Croatian-Serbian patriotic discourses worked hard to expel the source of the suffering to the outside, to establish clear differences between the Muslim master and the Christian slave, but this task required sustained effort precisely because Bosnian Muslims could be, however tentatively, seen as belonging within the South Slavic national community. Even the classics of the literature of national suffering were ambivalent on this matter. On the one hand, the noted Smail-aga Čengić clearly stood out as the embodiment of Turkish violence, so fanatical, vicious, and sadistic, that this "popular" poem was widely known as "the Epos of Hate" for "stimulating their [Serbian-Croatian] hatred of the Turk," as the *Encyclopedia Britannica* put it in the 1890s.[123] On the other hand, many South Slavic writers viewed Muslim villains like Smail-aga in terms that fused hatred and externalization of "the Other" with existential questions about the place of "the Turks" *within* the suffering national being. The literary critic Franjo Marković, for example, was troubled by Smail-aga, who "is a general type of violent brute, but he is at the same time a type of violent brute of the Bosnian Turkish nobility, whose grandfathers were the heroes of *our* kin." Contemplating this uneasy relationship in the 1870s, Marković concluded that "the Turkified nobility, having abandoned their faith and become a sworn oppressor to *its own kin*, still retained the wooden *gusle* [as a symbol of its Slavic belonging]. What bitter irony in the development of our history."[124]

Bosnian Muslims thus embodied the liminal figure of the (br)other in the emerging Yugoslav national imaginary, a figure that could appear both as a fanatical, relentless oppressor and a strayed but redeemable co-national. Precisely because Bosnian Muslims could inhabit both roles, those South Slavic patriots who tried to do the work of othering not only stressed fanatical Muslim violence against the *raya* but also emphatically sexualized and racialized the Turkish threat, much like Jakšić, Čermák, and other artists did in their depictions during the Ottoman period.

With Turkish rule gone from Bosnia after 1878, new interpretations tried to soften the tone of the earlier literature in an effort to incorporate Muslims into the South Slavic community. The Croatian nationalist theologian Cherubin Šegvić, for example, argued in 1894 that Mažuranić's epic is "not the bitter spilling of hatred against the Muhammedans, whom [Mažuranić] considered his born brothers, but rather a vivid image of . . . cruel tyranny" as a general phenomenon. As such, the epic held out the hope of "unity and love among the sons of the land. The Turk will still remain under his veil, will retain his characteristics, but will recognize in the *raya* his brothers."[125] By 1914, Vladimir Lunaček similarly argued that in *The Death of Smail-aga*, Mažuranić wanted to show what happens "when one part of the people exploits another part of the selfsame people."[126] Other narratives were similarly reinterpreted. Laza Kostić, for instance, rewrote the end of Jakšić's *Martyress* in the 1880s; whereas the vizier is killed by the avenging Serb in the original, in Kostić's version the vizier survives thanks to a moral epiphany that leads him to convert to the Christian "faith of his ancestors."[127] Stories about "generational change" also helped promote the view that the Turks, once known "only for their savagery and bloodthirstiness," were actually noble, "elegant" Bosnian Muslim individuals who, roused by the arrival of Habsburg rule, finally began to grapple with "the demands of a new civilization" and realize that "they are the same, brotherly people with those across the Sava River."[128] After the end of Turkish rule, many Serbian, Croatian, and Slovene patriots hoped to approach the Bosnian Muslims not as the dreaded "Others" but rather as long-lost and rediscovered brothers.

These attempts met with rather mixed results—persuading Bosnian Muslims to join Serbian-Croatian movements proved difficult—but the initiatives themselves demonstrated important aspects of the narratives of national suffering: their flexibility and their underlying discursive structures. On the one hand, it became possible to refigure the place of the Turks in the national imaginary, downplaying Islamic fanaticism and emphasizing patriotic brotherhood with the Bosnian Muslims. On the other hand, the basic imperative of externalizing the source of suffering still remained at work after the end of Turkish rule in Bosnia, though now it labored to reorient itself toward a new enemy—the Habsburgs. Serbian patriots in particular, later followed by some Croatian and Bosnian Muslim activists, depicted the establishment of the Austro-Hungarian administration as an insidious foreign occupation hiding behind a veneer of "enlightenment" and "progress"— a shrewdly disguised continuation of Turkish repression—as Vaso Pelagić charged already in 1878.[129] The fact that many of the new officials came from different Habsburg regions and spoke German as the main (but not the only) language of the administration became for nationalists a crucial sign of the government's "alien" character. Nationalist writings often referred to the varied Habsburg-era newcomers, immigrants, and officials alike as *Švabe*, a disparaging label (literally, "Swabian") that ascribed a Germanic character to the new figures in Bosnia. "The people call these expensively paid supporters of the Austrians '*švaba*,' which means the same as 'turned Turk' (*poturica*)," claimed one Serbian newspaper in 1889.[130]

In the absence of overt violence and physical suppression, which the Habsburg government avoided in favor of extensive monitoring and isolation of potential "agitators," South Slavic nationalists seized on the Austro-Hungarian "rule of law" as the key weapon inflicting pain on "sad Bosnia." Nationalists charged that instead of being an actual "rule of law" enabling liberties and rights—particularly collective national rights— Austro-Hungarian "justice" was an enormous ruse whose secret aim was to strangle the national spirit and subdue the Bosnian *raya*. Nationalist comparisons to the Turkish period were frequent and unfavorable to the Habsburgs. Villains like Čengić-aga may have been gone, but according to Serbian organizers like Vaso Pelagić and Petar Kočić, the Habsburg taxation policies and land regulations were just as bad since they impoverished the peasant not violently but under the seemingly peaceful cover of bureaucracy. The Austro-Hungarian censorship of the press came under especially vocal criticism for suppressing public expressions of Serbian and Croatian nationalist sentiment while encouraging the seemingly anational Pan-Bosnian or *Bošnjak* outlook. Complaints about language use rapidly escalated by 1900, leading to an outpouring of nationalist outrage of the proper adjectives (Serbian, Croatian, Bosnian, Serbo-Croatian, etc.) for the dialect spoken in Bosnia. In a related vein, the Austro-Hungarian school system (as elsewhere in the Dual Monarchy) became a major target of nationalist attacks alleging that the Habsburg government actively denied children their proper national identity and freedom of national expression.[131] "All this is to say," a Serbian nationalist wrote after presenting a number of anti-Habsburg and anti-German grievances in 1894, "that we now have an even greater enemy than the Turks once were to us."[132]

To understand the significance of these developments, it is important to go beyond the individual charges, ranging from agrarian policies to language naming, in order to ask what was being violated here — more precisely, what was being produced here — and why it mattered. In other words, it is important to resist the temptation to investigate each grievance as a self-contained problem without its moral context. Historians often use procedures of verification to (dis)confirm particular claims (assessing, for example, whether Habsburg policies were actually productive when nationalists claimed that they were ruinous), but in doing so they miss the larger purpose of the sustained nationalist activity that elaborated new political positions.[133] First, there is the simple but significant matter that the end of Turkish rule did not bring about an abatement of discussions of national pain in Bosnia. The acute political investment in national suffering was not a temporary response occasioned only by acts of Turkish cruelty, but an enduring and foundational patriotic concern that thrived long after the lifting of the Turkish threat, thus showing the remarkable adaptability of this subject to starkly different circumstances. Second, this lasting investment began to explicate with greater clarity certain underlying demands, apparent much earlier but congealed by the late nineteenth century into what I call the "scripts of national suffering," narratives of citable and reproducible attitudes, voices, and gestures characteristic of an aggrieved national subject.[134]

Literary forms provided the most concise and most influential articulations of these nationalist positions, as amply shown by the career of Petar Kočić (1877–1916), one of the most prominent Bosnian Serb politicians of the Austro-Hungarian era. After attending school in his native Bosnia, Kočić left as a gymnasium student for Belgrade and Vienna, where he helped organize South Slavic nationalist youth clubs and began to write a number of literary works. His energetic activism placed the figure of the downtrodden Bosnian peasant at the center of his political and literary stage, particularly after his return to the province in 1905. Alternatively censored, released, and jailed by the Habsburg authorities for his "subversive" activities—which included a charge for a militant 1908 article declaring, "Brother to a brother, War to the *Švabo*!"—Kočić became the key anti-Habsburg nationalist figure in the regional press and in the Bosnian parliament. Widely known for his vehement criticism of virtually every aspect of Austro-Hungarian rule (language use, education, forestry management, press regulations, court conduct, landholding laws, etc.), he founded the "Fatherland" (*Otadžbina*) party group and attempted to organize, unsuccessfully, a peasant movement in the Krajina region in 1910.[135]

Kočić's writings, particularly *The Badger before the Court* (1904) and *The Wailing from Zmijanje* (1910), enabled him to encapsulate a wide array of grievances in an accessible and entertaining literary form. In *The Badger before the Court* especially, Kočić goes to great lengths to present an ideal type of the oppressed Bosnian peasant in the figure of David Štrbac, an impoverished farmer who turns the tables on the Habsburg "rule of law." Suing a badger who had eaten his cornfield, Štrbac arrives before an Austro-Hungarian judge (unnamed) to seek a legal remedy, since such a lofty court surely "has laws for every thing." The Habsburg judge struggles to understand the Bosnian peasant's complaint, which unfolds as a series of misunderstandings and satirical praises of Austro-Hungarian rule. "This glorious court had freed me of much trouble and misery," Štrbac says, and presents a litany of Habsburg "accomplishments": his son was conscripted into the imperial army and died in Graz; his cows, goats, and pigs were appropriated by the imperial administration; all local goods were similarly rendered "quiet, miraculous, smart, albeit a bit thin and weak." Making extensive use of unflattering comparisons to the Ottoman era—"No longer do strong oxen dash across fences and furrows like in that old, silly Turkish time"—Štrbac lavishes mocking praise on Habsburg "achievements" that devastated the Bosnian peasant more than "the old Turkish court."[136]

These features alone—the satirical tone, the complaints about the government, the comparisons to the Turkish yoke—do not stand out as particularly exceptional, suggesting in fact rather narrow targets of Kočić's critique. Like much preceding literature, *The Badger* couched a list of familiar nationalist grievances as a drama played out by the protagonist Štrbac. If anything, some contemporary commentators worried that Kočić's caricature could make the peasant Štrbac appear, however inadvertently, "superficial," "stupid," and unremarkable.[137] Moreover, Kočić's objections seemed directed not against political oppression as such, but rather specifically against the "foreign" character of the Habsburg administration; the nameless judge and the court doctor conspiringly whisper in German and broken "Slavic" throughout the drama as they frustrate the Bosnian peasant's quest for justice. A story later told in Kočić's own biography further illuminates this point about his ethnocentric framing. As a penniless student in Belgrade, Kočić was once rudely wakened by a boot to his side; he had fallen asleep in the street only to be confronted by a Serbian policeman: "'What the hell's this? Where the hell are you from?' Kočić, dreaming, shaken, answered, 'I am from sad Bosnia.' Kicking him in the ribs, the policeman threatened" arrest and chased him away. "But this cop, by Kočić's own telling, is forgiven—for Kočić knew that this was done by the same soldier who will, sooner or later, carry victorious banners into his sad Bosnia."[138] In other words, some roughness from one's own co-nationals was understandable, but an "alien" rule of law was intolerable since it violated, by default, the "native" national sentiment that Kočić claimed as his position.

Such features, however, do not convey the overall effect of Kočić's work, which cultivated the aggrieved national subject as its ideal political figure and aimed to furnish an accessible script of national suffering for broad audiences. It is in this regard that the protagonist David Štrbac is exemplary. Throughout the trial, Štrbac remains both effusively energetic and "so oppressed he can barely breathe"; he summons his righteous anger at the end of the ordeal, his eyes "gleaming with tears of immeasurable hatred and abhorrence," to deliver a speech against the Habsburg court perplexed by his demands: "I am strange to you because within me there are a million hearts and a million tongues, for I wept here today before this court on behalf of a million souls so deadened by this mighty good and joy that they can hardly breathe. (All stare at him in shock.)"[139]

The aggrieved national subject, in speaking for "a million tongues"— muted, subjugated, deadened—speaks in fact of an insatiable demand for the voice of suffering. Revisiting the instance at the beginning of this chapter, where Velimir Gaj expressed his frustration at the Bosnian peasant unwilling or unable to talk about torment or impalement, David Štrbac emerges here as a model interlocutor; when asked how he is doing, he is immediately ready to display his pain and wounds, to clearly identify and damn the oppressor, and—crucially—to reproduce the demand for ever more voices of national suffering.[140] The preparation for the impulsive outbursts of pent-up patriotic feelings is not hidden, but is openly laid out so that the delivered gestures are formalized as repeatable situations, scripts with anticipated expressions and prefigured responses ("all stare at him in shock").

Impressed critics in the first decade of the twentieth century observed that the kind of subject valorized by Kočić was "not the conventional, holiday-type peasant, with a flute in his hand and with love-sighs on his lips," but something different and startling, a peasant depicted with an emphasis on "his small and great pains . . . , bent over his plot of land, wily, untrusting, sharp-witted, acrimonious, stubborn," and thus "the representative of an entire grievous nation!"[141] (See figure 2.3 for an artist's illustration of

Figure 2.3 Petar Kočić's peasant "David Štrbac," illustration for *Spomenica Petra Kočića* (1928). Kočić described his peasant thus: "I am strange to you because within me there are a million hearts and a million tongues. . . . (All stare at him in shock.)" With permission from the Museum of Literature and Performing Arts, Sarajevo.

Štrbac.) As the pairing with the analogous image of the jolly peasant suggests, this subject too was an ideal type, albeit a dystopian one.

Bosnia itself was the ideal national dystopia in this regard, a quintessential space of national sadness that South Slavic activists first discerned in the early nineteenth century and mapped out in sharp relief throughout the subsequent decades. Bosnia was, in the words of the writer Radovan Perović-Tunguz in 1906, "the land of wailing" (*zemlja plača*) where "the foreigner" ruled and everything was thus violated, wounded, and weeping: "and the forests in the hills, and the birds in the forests, . . . and the fish in the stream, and the ox in the plough, and the seed in the furrow, and the wheat in its ear, and the shepherd with his flock, and the flute in his mouth, and the wind in the caves . . . and the entire shackled Bosnia and sad Herzegovina" under Habsburg rule. Perović's direct plea to "Listen!" and attend to this soundscape entailed not only an exercise of poetic-national "fantasy" but also a way of sustaining the new protagonist—the moaning, suffering national—so that, as he wrote, "whenever you lie down and get up you remember the Serbian peasant!"[142]

As Kočić's political work demonstrates, repetition was key to establishing certain sensibilities voiced by the aggrieved national subject. In the first issue of his newspaper *Otadžbina* (1907), Kočić "emphasized first and foremost" his role as a spokesperson "bringing out all the defects and all the injustices suffered by our people under this government," such as those concerning schooling, the agrarian economy, and the protection of the "Serbian national sentiment."[143] Alongside this programmatic statement, he also published an essay simply titled "The Peasant," opening in first-person with the words: "I hurt and I wither in bitter misery and awful poverty ever since I've known myself. I am hurt, immeasurably hurt, my dear, sweet brother, though I don't know exactly what ails me. I just know that my pain is great."[144] Similar templates rehearsed Štrbac-like gestures, like those about the Austrian court contrasted with the "freer" and "more tolerable" Turkish laws and viziers. Even before and especially after *The Badger*, Kočić's parliamentary speeches, newspaper articles, and literary writings continually staged scenes of patriotic outrage on behalf of "the oppressed nation" that itself cannot properly speak; in the words of his "peasant," "sometimes we try to get up, to cry out a little, but our strength and tongue always betray us, and deep darkness and silence engulf us again."[145] Similarly styled writings kept coming from Serbian, Croatian, and incipient Bosnian Muslim national movements. Rather than inventing a genre, in other words, Kočić condensed the already available scripts and political positions into his particularly vocal outcries.

The Austro-Hungarian officials monitoring the anti-Habsburg expressions meticulously archived the insistent repetition of certain nationalist tropes. Internal Habsburg reports in 1907 identified Kočić as the most prominent writer among the Bosnian opposition. His "prolific incendiary writings" were assessed as "chauvinistic" and "not having enduring value, but for their purpose they are very much skillfully written and rather popular because he knows like no one else how to turn a phrase for every sort of people."[146] The nationalist press in Belgrade and Sarajevo, another Habsburg clerk reported in 1911, praises Kočić as "a profound expert of the sad circumstances in which local Serbdom languishes, a valiant champion of the '*oppressed people*,' as this hounded-to-death phrase goes" (*Vorkämpfer des* 'potišteni narod', *wie diese zu Tode gehetzte Phrase lautet*); indeed, it was a phrase without which national activists could not do their political work.[147] Other Austro-Hungarian reports on Bosnian politics in the 1900s characterized nationalist writings as "innumerable . . . day after day" distortions "giving a most lugubrious and totally untrue picture of the alleged misery of the people in the two provinces."[148] Such remarks, however, missed the larger point of this vast body of patriotic literature: national suffering was not a mere legalistic claim waiting to be verified or refuted by documentary evidence and thus brought to a definitive conclusion, but a new form of political subjectivity, an enduring moral domain where the sentiments, meanings, and imperatives of patriotism were to be discovered, worked out, and brought out into the world.

The implications of this labor were evident to nationalists themselves. To be a truly modern patriot, wrote Ljudevit Dvorniković in 1903, means to immerse oneself "not in patriotic tirades, but in deep pain over the past of one's own people, which cries out to the sons to right the wrongs of the fathers and heal the suffering resulting from their sins. . . . This sentiment of national history is indeed a general one and applies to any upstanding member of any nation, for everyone has something to weep over in their past." According to Dvorniković, the work of the Croatian Bosnian poet Tugomir Alaupović was a striking example of this modern patriotic literature that was flourishing around 1900:

> His entire collection is, so to say, an elegy — it is the tear of pain that formed in the soul of the poet's people over centuries, and now it flows from his breast. Precisely the feeling of patriotic pain makes Alaupović a modern poet, for his understanding of the tragedy, which gave birth to the pain, has distanced itself from the old traditions based in our folk poetry and older artful poems. Alaupović does not write of the fate of his people merely as one of its members — with his perspective he rises over the entirety of his people, and from this perspective he cannot feel hatred, but only heavy sadness. That is why in his work we will not find a celebration of the victory of "the cross over the crescent," nor lamentation over the "suffering of the *raya* and the Turkish crimes" — but we shall still hear the desolate sad song over the luckless fate that separated the people of one blood and tribe, casting it mutilated into a centuries-long struggle. This understanding of patriotism is the one and only kind appropriate for a modern poet.[149]

Dvorniković not only concisely outlined the key themes that appeared since the nineteenth century — the power of poetic fantasy, the conflict between brothers, the centuries-long swelling of tears — but also made it clear that attention to suffering was a general sentiment of modern nationalism, one that went far beyond simple hatred and instead fostered an abiding patriotic sadness, a subjectivity deeply invested in matters of suffering. In this constellation, "the Turks" were no longer the ruthless inflictors of violence, but rather Bosnian Muslim (br)others whose very presence appeared to Serbian-Croatian activists as a permanent mutilation on the South Slavic national body.

Echoes from the Balkans

The impalement scene in *The Bridge on the Drina* (1945), the most famous work in Ivo Andrić's Nobel Prize-winning oeuvre, has attracted much attention. It has been routinely described as "the most gruesome death scene ever in Yugoslav literature" and "one of the most excruciating in all of world literature."[150] There is indeed much to ponder in this scene. In the very beginning of the book, the narrative describes how on the orders of the vizier Mehmed Pasha Sokolović, the Turkish commanders forced the local Christian *raya* to construct a bridge across the Drina River. The peasant Radisav defied the Turkish imposition, subverting the bridge's construction at night until he was caught and impaled by the Turks for his resistance. It is here, as one Yugoslav observer noted, that the pace of the narrative slows down, "as if it wants to hold the scene before our eyes as long as possible and engrave it into our consciousness in an enduring way."[151] The text sets the impalement stage in meticulous detail, lingering over the methodical infliction of pain on Radisav, describing the growing pools of blood as the stake is slowly driven through his anus and into his shuddering, silent body, finally "upholding" the impaled peasant, still alive, into full view so that everyone can witness this spectacle. The text's studied attention to the soundscape is remarkable: "The silence from both banks of the river was such that not only every blow but even its echo from somewhere along the steep bank could be clearly heard." The narration modulates this stillness, however, focusing at times on the victim's "wide open mouth" that emits clipped, damning speech: "'Turks, Turks,' . . . moaned the man on the stake, 'Turks on the bridge . . . may you die like dogs.'" Above all, certain sounds loom larger than any utterance—"another and unusual sound, that was neither a scream, nor a wail, nor a groan, nor anything human," the sound of the stake itself—and suffuse the peasant's suffering into the emerging bridge, resounding throughout and beyond the book.[152]

In the beginning, then, was the wound. There are a number of different interpretations of Andrić's impalement scene, from reflections on rape and the fear of male impalement to an assessment of Andrić's "silence" as a metaphor for "Bosnia as a land of paralysis and tension."[153] My intervention here is different. It is to situate this particular and particularly famous staging of torment in a much longer genealogy of national suffering that I analyzed in the preceding pages. To see *The Bridge* impalement scene in the light of Mažuranić, Ignjatović, Šenoa, and related "sad Bosnia" writings is not to describe Andrić as a nationalist writer—a flawed view that mischaracterizes his work—but to appreciate his text in a historically critical way and to acknowledge the power of the imperative "Listen!" that emerged alongside the formative "echoes from the Balkans" in the nineteenth century.

The liberal-patriotic demand for the voice of suffering summoned forth new stages and introduced new subjects capable of making their injury known to the world. The scripts of national suffering, from Muslim fanaticism to Austrian rule of law, from *Sad Bosnia* to *The Badger before the Court*, were essential tools in the patriotic activity that gave birth to and sustained the aggrieved national subject. The sensibilities cultivated by South Slavic national activism permeated even the writings of authors like Andrić, who disavowed associations with any nationalist cause but whose texts on Bosnia nonetheless explicitly drew on the monumental archive of national suffering.[154] *The Bridge* impalement scene is representative of the narrative conventions established to both satisfy and reproduce the demand for the voice of national pain. The omniscient narrator relies on poetic fantasy to manage and relay distinct sounds, voices, and echoes from all corners of his authentic stage; its straightforward script—a defiant slave impaled by a ruthless master—quotes the already established stagings while also furnishing its own citable affects and histories.

Echoes are strangely conspicuous figures in these discourses of national suffering. Their incomplete returns can be insidiously destabilizing. Gayatri C. Spivak, John Hollander, and Joan W. Scott have written about echoes precisely as unsettling phenomena that have the power to alter, contradict, and mangle the initial prompts that set them off.[155]

Why were national activists, often presumed to be invested in hiding such disruptions for the sake of stable national narratives, so encouraging of echoes in their search for voices of suffering? This national echophilia is an open-ended question to which I offer a few concluding thoughts. Echoes can travel far and wide, easily reaching new audiences; they can attract attention and prompt questions, especially since their delayed resoundings are often ambiguous and not completely intelligible. Echoes are also replies; like the mythic figure of Echo, they are condemned only to repeat, however dimly, the originary noises, be they words or screams. Echoes are thus partial replies, but it is precisely their inherent incompleteness that makes them so appealing to—and necessary for—the work of national activists. Their very partiality provides the grounds for nationalists to restate their outcries ever more forcefully, entering into a kind of dialogical relation with their own echoes as they try to make them say the right things, even when they know they cannot have the last word.

CHAPTER THREE

Nationalization and Its Discontents

One winter day in 1840, a small group of revolutionaries crossed the river Sava on their return to Bosnia. It was a homecoming of sorts, as each one of them was born and raised in the Ottoman province. As boys, they had joined the Bosnian Franciscan order that later sent them away to the Habsburg Monarchy and Italy for higher education. After spending several years in central European seminaries, these students were set to revisit Bosnia in drastically different circumstances, vowing to "liberate the *raya*" and rid Bosnia of Turkish rule. In Veszprém, "we befriended a Serb family . . . whose hearts were very anguished by the fact that the Bosniacs suffer in such hard slavery under the Turk," recalled Jako Baltić, one of the participants.[1] Promising guns, teachers, and masses, various patriots from Serbia, Hungary, and Croatia pledged to help make the hard-pressed Bosnian peasants into proper nationals.

The work of rousing and nationalizing the people, of course, was always accompanied by foundational disappointments and failures. The would-be revolutionaries, "dressed as peasants" themselves, discovered many difficulties in mobilizing Bosnian villagers against the Turks.[2] The small activist group found little response in the countryside and triggered a chain of reactions ranging from the local Franciscan elders to the Ottoman and Habsburg authorities who sought to punish the "rabble-rousers." As the project rapidly fizzled out, the four or five Bosnian students parted ways. After laying low for a while, Jako Baltić and Blaž Josić returned to Bosnia and remained supportive of the Illyrian movement, while Ivan Franjo Jukić rose to great prominence as a tireless activist, teacher, and collector of folklore.[3] According to some accounts, there was also a certain companion named "Jurić," who may or may not have existed; it was reported that the local Ottoman authorities, upon learning of the insurrectionary plans, arrested and executed him.[4] Finally, there was Toma (Bartol) Kovačević, who after the failed uprising fled to Serbia, converted to Orthodoxy, and joined the Serbian state administration. Within a few years, Kovačević became known in Belgrade as the "old conspirator of 1840" and a leading state organizer of nationalist networks, planning "liberation and uprisings" across the Balkans in the subsequent decades.[5]

Kovačević's career neatly captures the key considerations that shaped the work of national activism throughout the nineteenth century. To begin with,

there was the nationalist belief that "the people" (*narod*) were a readily mo-
bilizable resource, a political asset that could be promptly deployed in uprisings, wars, and other projects of state formation and expansion. Kovačević's
reports in the 1840s and 1850s, for example, assured Serbian state ministers
that across Herzegovina and Bosnia, "the people will eagerly rise against the
Turks" when "given the sign."[6] Like Kovačević's own trajectory—which
spanned service to a Catholic monastic order and to the Serbian Orthodox state—this national awakening was envisioned as cross-confessional
and capable of uniting Catholics, Orthodox, and even Muslims under the
same national banner. Revisiting his 1840 experience, Kovačević continued to hope that monitoring "the borders of the region" would help "our
confidants . . . to cross the Bosnian border and begin the war, given that
Bosnians are ready join them."[7] Indeed, throughout the long nineteenth
century, revolutionarily minded activists frequently sought to capitalize on
unrest in Bosnia-Herzegovina, which flared up in peasant rebellions several
times—1859, 1875, 1882, to name the most conspicuous instances—and
which appeared as ripe targets for national liberation. As Kovačević put it,
"fire and patriotism" appeared abundant; there was "this awe, this divine
idea of our kin Bosniacs and Herzegovinians, the ever-present love of country" and "eagerness to rise up" against the Turks.

Yet at the same time, this patriotic fire was a fragile thing: activists
had to "kindle and stimulate" it, shielding it from "fatal influences" lest
it unpredictably vanish or fail to materialize, Kovačević wrote in 1848.[8]
Bosnia appeared to be an ideal site for the success of Serbia's expansionist
project—a land unified by common folklore and suffering—but also a site
where the nationalizing mission could unravel when confronted with peasants' indifference, interconfessional tensions, and imperial opposition. In
1862, Kovačević explicated such grievances, ruefully writing that the Bosnian Christian population "does not have the foundation, the ability, or the
means" to start uprisings, particularly "in the middle regions [of Bosnia]
that we would like to conquer." (The easy slippage between "liberation"
and "conquest" is telling of the character of this nationalizing project.) Regardless of circumstances, Kovačević concluded, it was not "the people" but
professional nationalist activists who had to bear the burden of "rescuing
dear Serbdom" from Ottoman rule.[9]

In other words, national activists nurtured two simultaneous and com-
plementary visions of "the people" (*narod*). On the one hand, the people
were the embodiment of the nation-state and the stated object of the activists' mobilization efforts. As such, the people already possessed the necessary attributes to become full-fledged nationals; just a sign would suffice
to activate their potential. On the other hand, however, national activists
also perceived the people as incapable of understanding the signs that the
nationalists gave them, let alone the diplomatic intrigues, the historic mission, and the institutional projects that they were supposed to carry out

according to plan. For all their promise, the people appeared to lack certain qualities, especially consciousness and organizational ability, that prevented them from realizing their national potential on their own. It is the latter conviction—that the people were disappointingly defective in the ways of proper patriotism—that endured as the basic operating assumption of nationalist work, which focused more on the instruction rather than insurrection of the people in Bosnia-Herzegovina.

A sustained exploration of these issues helps show that self-proclaimed agitators in the nineteenth-century Balkans, such as the young patriots of 1840, are best understood not as "social bandits" or representatives of a "Balkan revolutionary tradition" (in the vein of influential studies by Eric Hobsbawm and Dimitrije Djordjević).[10] Despite their invocation of peasant customs and "primitive rebellion," men like Toma Kovačević were new political figures who were primarily preoccupied with the imperatives of nation-building. The establishment of Serbia as a nation-state, autonomous by the 1830s and independent after 1878, was a seminal process in modern Balkan and European history. The rise of Serbia introduced new considerations into Great Power diplomacy and radically transformed political relations in the region, spurring attempts at nationalization of peasants and disparate co-nationals, including efforts to turn "our Turks" or Bosnian Muslims into nationally conscious Serbs. Seen first and foremost as an issue of state-formation, the task of liberating Bosnia entailed not only anti-imperial agitation but also deeper problems of identification of potential co-nationals, diffusion of patriotic sentiments, and creation of new political subjectivities. To study national activism with these issues in mind is to read "failure" differently, not simply as the conclusion of or obstacle to certain projects, but rather as the chronic condition of the work of nationalization.

How to Make a Nation (State): Serbia's Nationalizing Mission

"The ways in which nationality can be preserved even among subjugated peoples," one Slavic patriot wrote in 1839, concern mainly "the forces of spirit"—language, poetry, folklore. "The path toward that invisible sanctity is not cleared by the sword; it will remain unspoiled as long as you yourself prize it."[11] The distancing from the more immediate means of power—"the Slavs of the nineteenth century do not base their existence on the bloody sword, they do not sigh after the loot of other states," Miroslav Hurban declared in 1842—constituted key strategies for the establishment of many patriotic movements that embraced "the weapons of spirit, of cultivation, intelligence, literature."[12] Historians of nationalism, including Eric Hobsbawm and Rogers Brubaker, have similarly written that linguistic and cultural constructions of nationhood were at the heart of the "early" national projects; Czech and Slovak cases were most often cited as the normative examples of the situation in which "independent nationhood was unthinkable."[13]

At the same time, it is also evident that some "early" patriots understood the attainment of nationhood quite differently. "Get the sword, get the knife / The sabre, the flintlock, the rifle / Anything that cuts, anything that sears / For the people believe in us," wrote Medo Pucić, a young Dubrovnik-based Serbian activist, in his militant poem "The Bosnian Marches" (1841), which urged patriots "to seize their guns" and "strike against the enemy."[14] "What are weapons for, other than for him who molests us? And for our freedom? . . . [Ypsilantes] and Kara-Djordje made their glory, long live their genius! . . . Brothers, let us be men who do not fear, who know what weapons are and what they are for."[15] This 1862 Croatian call to arms by Fran Kurelac, much like Pucić's plaudit to the liberation of Bosnia, explicitly referenced the Serbian and Greek uprisings that had resulted—already by the 1830s—in a political triumph: the establishment of national principalities, or de facto states with their own leaders, laws, courts, ministers, schools, and incipient resources for the "liberation" of neighboring territories. Even the Slavic patriot who stressed the primacy of "the national spirit" in 1839 wrote in the same breath that "political independence (*nezavisnost*) is, in truth, the first and greatest good of any nation."[16]

In this context, the specter of state-formation cut across moderate and revolutionary, philological and institutional, early and late nationalisms.[17] The rise of Serbia, Greece, and other new Balkan states amid the disintegration of the Ottoman Empire was a process deeply familiar to nineteenth-century political figures, from Metternich to Mazzinni to Marx.[18] Throughout the countless speculations over the conduct of the Eastern Question, a process that had already produced new states, "still greater changes in the map of Europe" seemed certain to editors and readers of *The New York Daily Times* in 1854.[19] To be sure, this kind of border drawing was on the one hand a preserve of Great Power diplomacy, a matter overwhelmingly arbitrated among imperial cabinets, less so in the Balkan capitals. But on the other hand, the intertwining of the Eastern Question with a number of national questions had another major consequence: that of introducing the prospects of statehood into the emerging patriotic programs.[20] Put simply, notions of statehood—even when declared unattainable or rejected by many patriots—were nonetheless present as organizational templates that helped generate in the early nineteenth century new political positions and relations across eastern Europe.

Building a nation with the state in mind, then, entailed a number of practical considerations for Serbian and related Slavic national activists during the unraveling of the Eastern Question. Three issues—secrecy, insurrection, and expansion to potential co-nationals—profoundly shaped the formative visions of state-building in the modern Balkans.

In the first place, planning for state-formation required developing a secret politics of nationalism. This notion is often associated with secret societies like Filiki Eteria (the transnational underground network seeking the liberation of Greece from Ottoman rule in the 1810s and 1820s) and other similar groups crucial to the formation of Italian, Polish, and German national movements in the first half of the nineteenth century. Freemasonry and Carbonarism have served as major models for understanding this kind of secrecy, marked by small cells and clandestine rituals, codes, symbols, and loyalty oaths.[21] But in addition to this Masonic-type confidentiality, which was influential in many parts of Europe, there is another dimension of secrecy that nationalist organizations claimed at this time. As Michel Foucault wrote, "the problem of the secret" was widely recognized as essential to modern state-making already by the eighteenth century; keeping certain resources, statistics, and plans known only to highest state authorities was "an explicit part of *raison d'État* called the *arcana imperii*, the secrets of power."[22] This understanding of secrecy as an aspect of state sovereignty sheds light on the ambitions of early South Slavic nationalists. When Ljudevit Gaj in 1840 introduced himself to a Russian diplomat not only as an Illyrian scholar but also as the head of a liberation movement in Ottoman Bosnia and the author of a memorandum titled *Secreta arcana*—containing the keys to the Eastern Question—he tried to present himself, among other things, as a holder of statelike attributes.[23] Gaj's failure in this diplomatic endeavor should not blind us to the appeal of such aspirations during the nineteenth century.[24] The more sustained efforts in this vein came from Serbia, where high-ranking officials like Ilija Garašanin, Matija Ban, and Jovan Ristić continually prepared secret plans, agents, and resources for acting like a state.

Second, this kind of national activism linked mass insurrections to state formation in the Ottoman Balkans. With the Serbian and Greek revolutions as precedents (in which regional revolts led to the internationally sanctioned creation of new principalities), nationalist work after the 1830s introduced new elements of activist planning of popular uprisings for state-building purposes. In the eyes of many South Slavic patriots, uprisings could lead to the further "liberation" (*oslobođenje*) of Bosnia, Bulgaria, and Macedonia from Turkish rule, enabling either the expansion of the existing Serbian and Greek areas or the creation of still new Balkan states. From the 1840s through the 1870s, many South Slavic nationalists busily drew up plans, proposals, and blueprints for the "liberation" of Balkan peoples. Despite differing points of emphasis, nearly all the plans called for massive insurrections—namely, the overwhelming participation of the peasantry in actions planned by nationalist leaders—in order to assure swift successes against the Ottomans. In Serbia's case, these operations had to be executed rapidly because the small principality wanted to present the Great Powers with the fait accompli of its victories, thus avoiding protracted diplomatic negotiations that could negate any gains.[25] Choosing the right time to "put the plan quickly into operation" and then "controlling the local populace," as one Serbian blueprint stated in 1850, became important elements in calculations for national liberation during Ottoman rule.[26] As one Serbian official wrote, "revolution and constitution" were not opposites, but were intertwined forces of liberal social change.[27]

The third crucial consideration dealt precisely with the future incorporation of new populations into the emergent national states, particularly incorporation across confessional lines. In order to appeal to peoples outside of the confines of the Serbian principality, for example, aspirant state-builders centered in Belgrade repeatedly tried to revise the message of Serbian nationalism so that other neighboring populations—especially Catholics and Muslims in Bosnia, Dalmatia, Croatia, and so on—could support (or at least not resist) Serbian leadership. Crafting such a broad and interconfessional outreach program, however, was at odds with Serbia's already established anti-Turkish and staunchly Orthodox outlook. As a principality that defined itself against Ottoman rule, Serbia was from its outset an overwhelmingly Orthodox Christian nation, both in population and official symbolism; moreover, its liberal constitutions defined its citizens in explicitly national terms—"all Serbs are equal before the law"—leaving those potentially identified as "non-Serbs" outside the national community.[28] Muslims were particularly targeted, facing expulsion from the province by the 1870s, while other possible "non-Serbs," especially Jews, Vlachs, Roma, and "others," found themselves in a precarious position within Serbia.[29] But outside of Serbia, the messages of interconfessional unity emphatically proclaimed "all three faiths"—Orthodoxy as well as Catholicism and Islam—to be essential to Serbian nationalism, at least in the writings of folklorists like Vuk Karadžić and liberal politicians like Vladimir Jovanović. A practical consideration drove this balancing act: expanding the state of Serbia entailed the incorporation of ethnically and religiously diverse populations in areas like Bosnia, Dalmatia, Macedonia, Kosovo, and Croatia.[30] Blueprints for state-building thus had to be sensitive to the prospect of future co-nationals, whose foreshadowed presence posed challenges to the existing practices and political programs.

The *Načertanije* (*Plan*)—the first extensive articulation of Serbia's state-building strategies proposed in 1844—embodies the nexus of the above concerns. Drafted in secrecy by a group of Polish, Croatian, and Serbian activists and championed by the influential Serbian prime minister Ilija Garašanin (1812–1874), the *Načertanije* remained a highly classified document throughout the nineteenth century, verified first by Austro-Hungarian operatives in 1883 and acknowledged publicly only in 1906.[31] Since then, it has been cited as "proof" of aggressive Serbian expansionism, but its content is much more revealing of the nineteenth-century practices that produced it than of the twentieth-century Yugoslav polemics that made it infamous in the last three decades. While Ilija Garašanin is rightly credited with implementing this plan as a long-lasting Serbian policy, the initial drafts came from František Zach, a close ally of Prince Czartoryski and an advocate of independence for the Poles and the South Slavs who remained in the service of the Serbian principality until the 1870s.[32] Direct and sustained involvement of Polish and Pan-Slavic leaders in this Balkan endeavor is noteworthy because it makes explicit a common nationalist strategy: that of linking national questions, including Polish and Balkan ones, to the Eastern Question and Great Power diplomacy.[33] This was a strategy that enabled various patriots, from Toma Kovačević to František Zach, to claim for themselves new roles as planners, negotiators, and advisers vying for limelight on the European stage.[34]

In this context, Garašanin and many related activists articulated the view that Serbia had a special calling, a kind of a "nationalizing mission" in the Balkans and Europe at large. The *Načertanije* put the case thus: "Serbs were the first among all the Slavs in Turkey to fight with their own means and strength for their freedom; consequently they have the first and full right to manage this work in the future. Already in many places and in some cabinets they foresee and anticipate that a great future stands before the Serbs; this is what has attracted the attention of all of Europe to Serbia." Though admittedly — even troublingly — "small," Serbia had both "a historical foundation" in the lost medieval kingdom and "the present resources" for prosperous future statehood, namely: "the geographic position of the country, its land, the richness of its natural production, the martial spirit of its inhabitants, then its exalted and fiery character of nationality, its origins, one language — all this indicates its stability and great future." The state's destiny was manifest: "to win over all the Serbian people that surround it." In fulfilling this "task" (*zadatak*), it could "gain untold importance and high value before the eyes of all peoples as well as cabinets, . . . giving Europe all guarantees that it would be a capable and effective state." The *Načertanije* anticipated even more immediate success in the Balkans, where "other South Slavs will very easily understand this idea and embrace it with joy" and hope for independence. "That is why one can almost certainly count on the favorable reception of this work among the people, knowing that decades of activism in the people (*dejstvovanja u narodu*) are not necessary for it to comprehend the use and benefit of independent government."[35]

Among the key issues facing this activism was the need for broad cross-confessional work that would attract patriots from heterogeneous backgrounds. For its part, the *Načertanije* stressed "the principle of full religious equality" as the basis for harmony between "the two Christian peoples" (Orthodox and Catholic) — "though Muhammedans too might like and be satisfied with this [principle]." The purpose of such broad appeals was to prepare the ground for the incorporation of future co-nationals, even "Muhammedan" ones, whose inclusion in new national narratives would be encouraged ("the glory and names of some converts to the Muhammedan faith should not be left out of the general history book of Bosnia" planned by the Serbian officials in the 1840s).[36] Whereas Catholic Slavs were addressed directly and even implicitly acknowledged as rival bearers of national activism, Bosnian Muslims stood at the outer limits of the Serbian and other South Slavic nationalizing missions, a position they would continue to occupy well into the twentieth century.

The *Načertanije* and Garašanin's post-1840s policies charged new political actors—called "agents" (*agenti*) in the political terminology of the time—with the responsibility of putting these varied considerations into practice. Appointed to state positions as "sharp-minded" and "loyal men," nationalist agents would collaborate in secrecy, shielding their work from foreign influences; they would attend to the "political" and "military condition of the people" to prepare mass insurrections at the opportune moment; and they would be sensitive to the possibility of diverse co-nationals accepting or joining the national cause. The Serbian principality, though strapped for financial resources, vowed to "give these agents directives and means by which they will travel" and perform their work. Before taking action, however, their first task was studious and detached; agents needed to collect information about "Bosnia, Herzegovina, Montenegro, and northern Albania, . . . getting to know the people better and the character of its heart, its secret desires," its "expectations and fears regarding Serbia."[37]

Under Zach's and Garašanin's leadership, new officials from Bosnia, Dalmatia, Croatia, and Montenegro were drawn into Serbia's growing administration. Garašanin, for example, made the Dubrovnik-born Catholic writer Matija Ban (1818–1903) his confidant and high-ranking officer in the Serbian army, while Atanasije Nikolić and Antonije Orešković (both from Croatia), and Bosnia-born Jovan Marinović, Stjepan Verković, and Toma Kovačević were also given important positions as operatives reporting to Belgrade.[38] Combining philology with revolution, fusing discoveries of folklore with dreams of massive confrontation, mixing songs of love for the people with fantasies of revenge against the Turks, such "agents" advanced different strategies aiming at the liberation of Bosnia from Ottoman rule and its incorporation into a larger South Slavic state in the following decades.

But even at the outset of their project, the activists' fact-gathering missions already had the character of national instruction—agents were reminded "to make Serbian politics known," to "awaken certain hopes and direct some attention and interest" toward national sentiment.[39] In other words, state-building blueprints charged agents with "propaganda," a branch of nationalist activity named as such in plans by Garašanin, Ristić, and many others throughout the nineteenth century (the 1850 "Constitution of Political Propaganda to be Conducted in Slavic-Turkish Lands" by Matija Ban being a prominent example).[40] This set of relations, with agents at the center of nationalist work, remained a foundational nation-building strategy that Serbian nationalists continually reconsidered and revised until the First World War.

Are "the People" Ready for the Nation?

In the eyes of many South Slavic activists, Bosnians were a model people, possessing qualities that were highly prized in nineteenth-century nation-making. Ever since Vuk's seminal publications of Serbian folklore, scholars as well as revolutionaries expressed intense interest in the language, songs, and customs of Herzegovinian shepherds and Bosnian peasants, inspiring a wave of ethnographic activism aimed toward these esteemed provinces. Moreover, the population of Bosnia-Herzegovina was also conspicuously multiconfessional, with Muslims, Orthodox, and Catholics living side by side and presenting both Serbian and Croatian activists with the possibility of broadening their base beyond a single ethnoreligious community. Toma Kovačević's work is again telling here. As early as 1843, the Garašanin cabinet compiled a list of fifty-seven Bosnian Franciscans and divided it into categories of "real patriots," "those inclined to Germans [Habsburgs]," and "those vacillating."[41] As a former Bosnian friar turned Serbian official, Kovačević maintained links with his Franciscan colleagues (namely, Blaž Josić and Ivan Franjo Jukić) and created valuable recruitment contacts that Serbian ministers pursued among Bosnian Catholics into the 1870s.[42] In general, Bosnia's interconfessional character opened many opportunities for expansion of Serbian and Croatian nationalist mobilization in new directions, a prospect that different activists continued to explore even in the early twentieth century, particularly among the seemingly nationally elusive Bosnian Muslims.

Crucially, Bosnia was also the land where impoverished Christian peasants suffered and called out to their brothers to take action against the Turks (and later the Austrians). Graphic scenes of Bosnian peasants' torment inspired many proclamations of sacrifice for the national cause, including the support promised for the failed uprising of 1840 that launched Kovačević's political career. From this standpoint, the people of Bosnia were a tinderbox, driven to despair by Turkish oppression and ready to explode when the activists "gave the sign"—a common phrase in many agents' reports.

At the same time, the Ottoman and Habsburg authorities kept a very close watch on any nationalist-sounding activity in precisely these areas. Garašanin himself was dismayed by the intensification of Austrian influence and Ottoman policing along the Drina and Sava Rivers in the 1860s, recommending to agents new measures to counter the influence of both Istanbul and Vienna governments.[43] The archival documentation compiled by the Habsburg government is notable in this regard, beginning as reports on Ottoman-Habsburg border relations in the 1830s and developing into a full-fledged surveillance apparatus after the occupation of Bosnia in 1878.[44]

At the outset of Habsburg rule in Bosnia in 1879, imperial officials already observed that the turmoil of the past uprisings made "the population warlike, in recent years often forced to . . . protect their interests by arms, [and] easily accessible to foreign agitators" and "agents."[45] In 1881, Habsburg pressure compelled Serbia's Prince Milan Obrenović to sign a secret treaty pledging that "Serbia will not tolerate political, religious, or other intrigues which, taking her territory as a point of departure, might be directed against" Austro-Hungarian rule, particularly in Bosnia-Herzegovina.[46] Although this period thus ended Garašanin's strategy of directly sponsoring "agent networks," the specter of revolutionary action returned in 1903 when the Karađorđević dynasty toppled the Obrenovićes and fueled rumors of a more active Serbian policy in Bosnia. A 1903 report by the Austro-Hungarian minister Hugo Kutschera characteristically described the situation in Herzegovinian border districts as one in which "certain rumors spread, and the more fantastic they are, the more excited a mood they generate among the population"; the minister suspected "secret agents' agitations" (*geheime Agenten Agitationen*) were destabilizing "our position in the province."[47] Subsequent investigations noted local dissatisfaction, but found few "agents," excepting some declared opponents of the Habsburg administration.[48] Thus even when "agents"—often described as nationalist agitators and ethnographers—were not verifiably present on the ground, assumptions about their existence and influence lasted into the first decade of the twentieth century.

While attracting significant attention from activists in Zagreb, Zadar, Dubrovnik, and other areas in Croatia throughout the nineteenth century, it was Serbian nationalists who often seized the leading role by stressing the political resources and material sacrifices that the Serbian state offered. The 1867 "Plan for the Preparation of Action in Bosnia" illustrates this dynamic. The plan was a joint project—supported by both Serbian and Croatian leaders of the 1860s and the 1870s, including Ilija Garašanin and Josip Strossmayer—but it also bore a pronounced imprint of Serbian sponsorship. Not only was it drafted and finally amended by Serbian officials, but it also clearly specified that Belgrade, "having its own independent government and military resources . . . will manage this work, which Zagreb will help along." Other "Yugoslav tribes" too "must contribute sacrifices in blood and in money."[49] Once the means were provided, however, the assumed course of events would take place—the people would rise up and form "a broad and strong basis for the national cause in Turkey":

> The goal remains unchanging and eternal; the means naturally change according to the momentary political circumstances. . . . The goal is the liberation of the Christians groaning under the Turkish yoke, in order to create a field for the unification of all the Yugoslav groups into one state. . . . Belgrade and Zagreb stand at the forefront of the entire movement. . . . Religion will not meddle into

the national matters in the least; for the state, the only foundation is nationality (*državi je jedini osnov narodnost*).[50]

However, doubts about the people's patriotic readiness were present from the outset of national work in Bosnia. The reports by the agent Hristifor (Risto) Bogdanović, sent to Serbian ministers in the 1840s and 1850s, exemplify the twin nationalist concerns over the (lack of) popular resonance of their mission. Bogdanović, on the one hand, repeatedly assured the Serbian officials that "the people's spirit is in the best state" in Bosnia and that "the poor *raya*" places its faith in "no one else but God, then in you [the Serbian government], and in Europe."[51] Yet even in these confident assessments, warnings about the people's patriotic qualifications abounded. On several occasions, Bogdanović reported that the inhabitants of Bosnia were for the most part "fearful," "confused," and "pressed by obligations"; in fact, if "the Bosnian Turks" were to "slay the town-dwelling Christians," then the Turks "could very easily do with the peasants what they like, because they are simple, and the town-dwellers guide them anyhow."[52] When Bogdanović heard "news that an uprising of the Christian people in Bosnia against the Turks will happen on the ninth or the tenth" of September 1850, he asserted his expert activist knowledge over popular rumors: "this seems ridiculous to me—but people will talk to make the time pass faster."[53] Having laid out a portrait of a proud, tormented, yet unfortunately pliant and confused people, Bogdanović also reminded his superiors in Belgrade of his superior credentials: "I am a real Serb (*pravi Srbin*) and I will continue to perform my duty to help my Serbian brothers," just like other agents who understood the intricacies of national work.[54]

In fact, the attributes praised as model marks of national spirit—the profound suffering under the Turks, the folkloric imagination, the interconfessional population—were also perceived as severe obstacles to the practical fulfillment of the nationalizing mission in Bosnia. Antonije Orešković, the Croatia-born officer who left the Austrian military for a high-ranking position in the Belgrade government, openly stated this sentiment after a clandestine trip to Bosnia in 1863:

> He who knows Bosnia and its inhabitants the way I do . . . will know that a general uprising in Bosnia . . . can never come through the Bosnians themselves. . . . [Locally] the uprising can never be organized. For such organizing, outside elements are necessary since the Bosniacs are neither able nor do they have any patriotism, resolve, or real will for this. Through four hundred years of pressure, these inhabitants have lost all soldierly capacity and are only in a position to be disunited and mistrustful. If any one of them dares to raise his head proudly, even that is out of personal egoism; he thinks not of serving the collectivity but hopes that he too will be some kind of a master and does not want to listen to anybody.[55]

Orešković then generously offered "to organize outside of Bosnia [i.e., in Serbia] the necessary forces, at certain points break into the Bosnian land, and there at an agreed-upon spot and under one general direction" lead the local inhabitants to successful liberation.[56]

"The liberation of Bosnia," another plan from 1869 stated, cannot come through the people because "the people has no leaders, has no weapons, because it is split into three religions, and because it has no consciousness of itself." Niko Okan, the plan's author and former Sarajevan trader who joined the Serbian government in the 1850s, invoked reports of other agents and personal experience as basis for such judgments: "Since I have by practical experience witnessed that the people in Bosnia cannot be rendered conscious (*osvěstiti ne može*), not even in half a century, and cannot liberate itself by itself," then Serbian agents would have to act on behalf of their incapable brothers.[57] Lists of men "to be deployed exclusively in Bosnian action," all of them residing in Serbia, were kept by Serbian officials for emergency purposes.[58] Other Serbian officers agreed: "There are no elements for a revolution. Even if we speak of the border region of Podrinje, I affirm that . . . the revolution cannot be born of the people itself (*ne može se poroditi revolucija iz samoga naroda*)."[59]

In the context of Ottoman Bosnia, this set of relations enabled agents to develop several kinds of strategies for engaging and nationalizing the people. Though Serbian officials continually revised their proposals and added new considerations, the militarization of activism and increase of propaganda remained the favored nationalist approaches in Bosnia for several reasons. First, proposals to militarize the process of national mobilization promised to solve the problem of popular indifference by injecting discipline and action into the process of nation-building. Already in the *Načertanije*, Garašanin stressed the formation of an independent Serbian army that would not only provide protection but also enable the expansion of Serbia in the future. Whereas Ilija Garašanin and Jovan Ristić took great pains to keep Serbia out of any potentially disastrous wars, others in the Serbian government, particularly Antonije Nikolić and Antonije Orešković, voiced the opinion that combative action could be undertaken even in less than favorable diplomatic circumstances.[60] Although the option of outright war against the Ottoman Empire was constantly postponed, the desire for more militant discipline in national activism nonetheless remained an attractive prospect. In fact, nearly all plans for the liberation of Bosnia from the 1850s to the 1870s urged activists to secretly form *čete*, small military brigades composed of Bosnian peasants and town dwellers, usually of all religions. Ideally agents would smuggle and distribute firearms, but even in the absence of hard-to-procure weapons, the practice of *čete* formation was a clear priority.[61] However, keeping this kind of militant organization entirely secret proved impossible beyond the short run; Ottoman officials regularly policed the countryside and several times expelled any activists who were suspected of organizing *čete* in Bosnia. Militarization thus remained a very appealing prospect, though one rendered unfeasible in practice.

Second, national activists proposed to increase propaganda to raise national consciousness among both the people and potential agents. Serbian state officials like Garašanin, Kovačević, and Ban initially used "propaganda" as a term for the practical organization of agent networks, correspondences, and codes; Ban's reports on "the development of propaganda" in the 1850s, for example, overwhelmingly concern the delineation of agents' positions in a strict hierarchy ranging from the "ringleaders" (*kolovođe*) to the "serfs" (*kmeti*). Calls for increased "propaganda" in this sense entailed the fine-tuning of the assigned roles, instructions, and resources given out to agents. Activist training was especially important; greater care needed to be taken in preparing local figures for political work, one Serbian officer noted in 1866: "I know of several agents and conspirators who are almost always the most developed men in Bosnia, that is, the least stupid. Still, when one hears them speak, one would take them for children. . . . To questions about how many troops would it take to mount a revolution, they answered with childish confusion" and inability to articulate a clear plan of action.[62]

Other directives from Belgrade made similar points about the need to increase the numbers and to improve the training of agents.[63] New books, symbols, and folk stories praising Serbia's heroic accomplishments (starting with its recent overthrow of the Turks) were to be made widely available, either by smuggling or through popular retellings. Several proposals in the 1860s reinforced this impulse, instructing agents to guide aspiring patriots—especially the literate classes like merchants, priests, and teachers—toward more active involvement in secret societies.[64] Most local Bosnian elites, however, proved to be reluctant and unlikely to support the violent toppling of Ottoman rule, into which they were firmly integrated.[65] Moreover, even these plans for the recruitment of priests and teachers saw such elites mainly as stepping stones toward more direct engagement with the peasantry, deemed to be crucial for the mobilization of national forces. The spread of propaganda, like the impulse toward militarization, thus returned to the problem of "the people" and its ambiguous consciousness, which remained the prime targets of national work.

The career of Bogoljub Teofilo Petranović (1830–1887) offers a prime example of the different kinds of work that national agents practically carried out in Ottoman Bosnia. An Orthodox priest from the hinterland of Dalmatia (Drniš near Šibenik), Petranović entered into contact with Serbian nationalists, became interested in activism, and managed to obtain a position in an Orthodox school in Sarajevo, a task that he "enthusiastically embraced" in 1863.[66] He stayed in Sarajevo for six years until the local Serbian elites and Ottoman authorities expelled him for subversive activity in 1869. Bogoljub Petranović was not the only teacher to arrive in Ottoman Bosnia from abroad. His relative Stevo Petranović, for example, left

Montenegro also for a teaching career in the northern Bosnian town of Tešanj, and Jakov Vučković made a similar journey from Dalmatia to Sarajevo.[67] After establishing themselves as educators and respectable members of their adopted towns, these activists initially concentrated on the already existing networks of Orthodox teachers, many of whom had successfully lobbied the Ottoman government to open a new seminary in Banja Luka in 1863.[68] Judging from Bogoljub Petranović's account of his activities, his occupation as a teacher was useful primarily for establishing his local reputation and for entering into contact with other potential national agents, twenty of whom he recommended to the Belgrade government. Most of those were other teachers and priests; none were Petranović's own students.[69] Overall, Petranović wrote about his teaching career in Sarajevo mostly as a poorly paid side career from which he saved bits and pieces to "buy and sow the seeds for the general fruit that we will reap in due time." Overall, "the whole purpose of my arrival in Bosnia was to collect folklore and to awaken national consciousness (*narodnu svijest*)."[70]

Petranović's work as an ethnographer was in many ways his most prominent and most profitable occupation. According to his writings, Petranović had used his stay in Sarajevo to seek out and converse with local peasants during his trips to the Jahorina, Bijelašnica, and other mountains, where he wrote down numerous notes about the customs and attitudes of Bosnian Muslims, Orthodox, and Catholics alike. Petranović shrewdly utilized his ethnographic material. To the local Ottoman authorities, including the governor Osman Topal-pasha, Petranović offered his friendship, reputation, and cooperation, as evident in his substantial contributions to the newly established Ottoman-Bosnian publications. In 1867, Petranović submitted a sizeable volume of "lyrical" or "female" *Serbian Folk Poems* to the Ottoman printing press, which published the collection as a contribution by one of its outstanding citizens.[71] At the same time, Petranović sent similar materials, this time of the "epic" or "heroic" variety, to Serbia's highest-ranking learned society. In Belgrade too, the reception of Petranović's work was very positive; scholars and politicians alike publicly praised and handsomely rewarded the collection for documenting the proud customs of "our suffering Serb brothers in Bosnia."[72] Some Serbian officials were particularly anxious to publish Petranović's poetry collection quickly "before it could fall into Croatian hands" and appear in print in Zagreb.[73] This sense of competition reveals an important nationalist anxiety: that this kind of ethnographic-activist work—valued as the expression of passionate patriotism and national consciousness throughout the nineteenth century—was actually rather mutable and capable of crossing Serbian, Croatian, and Ottoman lines.

"Having finished the folklore creations," Petranović devoted himself entirely to the "noble work" of "waking the national and political consciousness (*narodnu i političku svijest*) in Bosnia." Despite the importance of this

mission, there is relatively little documentation as to what this work actually entailed. Petranović's descriptions of consciousness-raising activity were
scattered, short, and focused on the recruitment of high-ranking "national
awakeners," mainly teachers and priests, rather than "peasants from many
areas." In fact, encounters with many villagers were problematic: "At first
only [the Bosnian priest] Savo Kosanović could hold relations with" the
peasants since "they did not have trust in the other [activists]." Subsequent
engagements in the countryside were also obliquely mentioned in his reports to the Serbian government. Contemporaries remembered Petranović's
interactions with the peasants as being sporadic and instructional in nature;
a Sarajevan resident later said that "Petranović's committee" was fond of
"standing at the city gates" and urging the peasants on their way to the mar-
ket to abandon "names like 'Vlah,' 'Rišćanin,' 'Rkač,'" and instead adopt
proper national attributes, calling themselves "Serbs."[74]
    Petranović's own report, written shortly after his expulsion from Bosnia
in 1869, outlined his career as a leading national awakener in Ottoman Bosnia in terms that reiterated the priorities of Serbia's nationalizing mission:

> Much success has been achieved. In the decisive moment, the people will take
> up arms, occupy the most important points, contribute much to the liberation,
> and save much blood of the regular army. Whoever could buy weapons and
> gunpowder has done so, and is hiding it well from the Turks. The key ideas
> about Serbian nationality are realized. Now a Serb is a Serb, and is no more:
> a provincialist, a countryman, a 'Bosniac.' He knows with whom he needs
> to work and in what kind of community will he get rid of the heaviest of the
> Turkish chains.[75]

This confident statement claiming the final "realization" of the nationalizing mission was greeted with both praise and skepticism in Belgrade.
A number of high-ranking Serbian state officials evaluated Petranović's services favorably. The Belgrade-based government adviser Niko Okan, for
instance, characterized Petranović as "the most capable agent" in Ottoman
Bosnia, a pivotal figure who would be very difficult to replace after his
expulsion.[76] The Serbian state official (and Herzegovinian Orthodox priest
and writer) Nićifor Dučić also praised him, recommending that Petranović
continue his agent work in Dalmatia while drawing important cautionary
lessons from his time in Bosnia.[77] In fact, the harshest commentaries criticized not Petranović as an agent-awakener, but rather as an unreliable ethnographer whose countless and patent forgeries marred his prolific folklore
collections.[78]
    In reviewing Petranović's work, the wide range of his activities stands
out as especially remarkable. Having assumed the roles of an ethnographer,
arms dealer, teacher, agent recruiter, and general purpose national awakener, Petranović often conducted these activities not in a gradual procession

from one stage to another, but as political tasks that coexisted alongside one another, often overlapping and blurring presumed distinctions between scholars and revolutionaries. The work of nation-building demanded engagements on multiple fronts, converging on the overarching goal of rendering peasants conscious of their part in actualizing the projected nation-state. In this regard, however, most observers remained somewhat pessimistic. Even Petranović himself admitted that, despite his claims of having successfully made peasants into Serbs, national work was far from finished: the Serbian government, he urged after his expulsion, would have to deploy twenty or more teachers to Ottoman areas to continue its costly mission (at least 200 ducats a year), including the organization of *čete* and the raising of popular consciousness.[79]

Thus from the 1840s through the 1870s, South Slavic nationalists strove to stage a massive uprising that would liberate Bosnia from Ottoman rule. Yet despite three decades of planning and working in Ottoman Bosnia, even the most fervent agents of national politics came to believe that the circumstances were not favorable. The Serbian government was too indecisive, the agents too timid, the people too weak. As Mićo Ljubibratić, the leading national agent for Herzegovina, complained to his fellow activists in 1873, "I could never imagine that the Herzegovinians could be so deeply mired. If I were certain that [Serbia] would wage war in two, four, or even six years, I would gladly wait. But I see that it will not." It would thus be in vain to wait for Serbia to take action, or to link this "sacred matter" with the flow of Serbian aid: "We Herzegovinians say, how can we fight when we have no weapons, no gunpowder, and no money; but did the Šumadija [Serbs] have that at first [in the Serbian uprising of 1804]? . . . It would be even more glorious for us if we would achieve all those goals through unity, skill, and heroic effort."[80]

Productive Failures: Uprisings, Consciousness, and the Ambiguities of Patriotism

The single greatest opportunity for insurrectionary-nationalist action came in 1875. That summer, many village elders in Herzegovina refused to pay their taxes, while brigands and peasants in some areas quickly and successfully struck against the local officials and large landowners. Within a few months, Ottoman authorities lost control over many regions now dominated by rapidly growing peasant crowds and brigand groups. In response to the peasant refusal to pay taxes, the Ottoman government immediately assembled irregular troops whose brutal repression and pillaging only drove more villagers to rebellion. In northwestern Bosnian villages, for example, men "from almost every house [joined in], with wheelbarrows, axes, and only rarely armed with a small gun."[81] The long-awaited uprising of "the people," then, finally seemed to erupt—yet from the perspective of the national activists, this movement was also intractable and deeply frustrating. The activist plans made few provisions for such a sudden flood of popular rage against the Ottoman authorities, a flood they desperately tried to steer toward the overarching aims of patriotic awakening and liberation.[82] In February 1875, Ljubibratić himself called on other Serbian activists with news that "conditions for an uprising are favorable" for implementation of long-laid plans.[83] But by November of the same year, Ljubibratić, now a prominent insurgent leader, was paralyzed by the events. As he told a journalist, "The whole thing has been entirely different in its course from our original design. [National activists had] . . . been at work two years on a plan that we have not been able to follow out. All our work was in vain and we found ourselves compelled to begin anew."[84]

Instead of long-awaited liberation, what unfolded was a series of international confrontations that dwarfed the local struggles in Bosnia. At first characterized by skirmishes and Ottoman reprisals mainly in Herzegovina and Krajina, the 1875 uprising quickly assumed much wider international dimensions, involving Serbia (which declared war on the Ottoman Empire in hopes of gaining territory), Russia (which also entered the fray), Bulgaria, Austria-Hungary, England, and other Great Powers. The Porte's deployment of its irregular troops (*başıbozuk*) to crush the unrest resulted in many massacres of the local population, particularly in Bulgaria, where the Ottoman forces killed and displaced tens of thousands of people in 1876. By then, the Bosnian uprisings were only small parts of a larger Balkan conflagration that forced the Great Powers to debate a number of solutions to the conflict, the final settlement being reached at the Congress of Berlin in 1878.[85]

If the outbreak of the uprisings in 1875 offered a chance for a demonstration of patriotic strength and spirit, then that opportunity passed by quickly, bringing only distressing news for the national vanguard in Bosnia. Activists from both Serbia and Croatia did try to use the uprising for their aims. Small brigades of volunteers, for instance, crossed from Serbia into Bosnia across the Drina and the Sava Rivers, local agents proposed the formation of interim governments, some proclaimed the unification of Bosnia with Serbia.[86] Nonetheless, in the three years of wars, riots, and negotiations (1875–1878), no great national movement took root in Bosnia itself. No patriotic society emerged as a distinct political force; moreover, there were no recognizable "heroes" who could embody the spirit of national activism the way Vasil Levski or Hristo Botev, for example, did in Bulgaria. Mićo Ljubibratić started out as one of the best-known nationalist insurgents, only to be sidelined and thereafter arrested by the Austrians in 1876. In the meantime, other local rebel leaders appeared in different parts of the country; the Sarajevo-based Hadži Lojo (Salih Vilajetović), a Muslim bandit with no interest in patriotic movements, seized the anti-Ottoman and anti-Habsburg momentum in 1878. The final diplomatic arbitration in Berlin transferred

Bosnia from Ottoman to Habsburg rule—replacing one imperial structure with another—and thus shut the door on the remaining hopes of the national liberation of Bosnia.

Since then, nationalists as well as later historians have viewed the 1875–1878 uprising—and the three decades of national activism that preceded it—as something of a failure. Serbian leadership, for example, was deeply disturbed by the perceived loss of Bosnia, fueling a fierce debate over policy and personal blunders of previous administrations (at the same time that the Serbian government decisively turned to southern Ottoman areas for future expansion, namely, to Macedonia and Kosovo).[87] A similar sense of disappointment pervaded the work of many Yugoslav historians, from Vaso Čubrilović to Milorad Ekmečić, who interpreted the rather anemic national mobilization in Ottoman Bosnia as a manifestation of multiple failures: the failure of the agent networks ("these organizations were not in a position to mount a national uprising"), the failure of adequate planning ("the unsuccessful actions of minister Ban"), and even the failure of the peasantry to capitalize on its potential (it being the only "revolutionary force for the destruction of the Turkish state from the inside").[88] Failure, then, does a great deal of narrative work in activist as well as scholarly accounts of nationalism; it provides, among other things, an assumed starting point for different explanations and assessments of some ultimate "lack" (of national consciousness, preparation, institutions, compromises, etc.). It is in these varied senses that the history of Yugoslavia can be generally depicted, in the terms of a recent work, as the history of "a failed idea."[89]

This understandable focus on failure, however, can often act as a kind of interpretive closure that prevents further exploration of the character of nationalism that developed in activist practice. In other words, instead of reading histories of emergent nationalisms as being primarily about various absences and related failures, we can attend to what nationalist work created and made possible. Explorations of the productive aspects of nation-making and state-building projects—even failed ones—can reveal a great deal about the dynamics of nationalization themselves and about what the notion of a lack enables activists to do; in other words, to inquire what doors failure can open. We can disaggregate several strands of nationalist activism premised on the notion of lack and failure, all of them revolving around the idea of an incomplete national consciousness among "the people."

In the first place, the work of agents in Ottoman Bosnia exposed certain "idealist-materialist" fault lines of activist approaches to generating national consciousness. This was a set of problems already announced in the *Načertanije*, which made provisions both for giving agents the means to realize Serbia's mission and for attracting other South Slavic patriots by supporting favorable books, schools, and societies. Minister Garašanin began to dispense funds to several individuals for precisely such purposes already in the 1840s.[90] Shipments of publications, church donations, monetary aid, and other expressions of support were periodically sent by activists from Zagreb, Đakovo, Zadar, Cetinje, and especially Belgrade to "our brothers under the Turkish yoke."[91] But as the number of official agents and prospective patriots grew in the 1850s and 1860s, including well-paid activists like Bogoljub Petranović, the Serbian government had to widen the scope of material support for its growing but still secret activist network. It was amid the expansion of this state-building project that its leading figures most clearly articulated competing logics of national consciousness development. In the words of Niko Okan, a prominent Serbian official who wrote an important plan for the liberation of Ottoman Bosnia in 1869, the emergent state had to balance "Serbia's sacred mission—and *at the same time its tight financial situation*" (emphasis in the original).[92]

Okan explained the tension between the "sacred mission" and its fiscal constraints as a problem revolving around insufficient national consciousness. Beginning with the premise that "the uprising of the people itself is very uncertain" since "the people . . . has no consciousness of itself," Okan concluded that the most effective approach to creating a proper national sentiment would be the deployment of even more alert activists in Ottoman Bosnia. Okan stressed the affordability of his approach; at most 500 ducats would be spent that year on sponsorship of agents and their work (mainly the organization of *čete* "without any difference in religion" and the general cultivation of "patriotic awareness").[93] These goals in themselves were nothing new, but the linkage of rising costs of state-building to the mobilization of "consciousness" was now fully explicated—and elicited a brusque response from Jovan Ristić, Serbia's minister of foreign affairs and a leading statesman of the 1860s and 1870s: "If we are going to buy off the Bosniacs with ducats for their patriotism and their liberation—then you can have such a Bosnia!"[94]

This nationalist debate is illustrative of certain fault lines within activist understandings of their own work. On the one hand, as Ristić's response bluntly stated, real national conscience stood for something that could not be bought with money; it was a "sacred," lofty sentiment with a mission removed from the fickle considerations of sponsorship and funding; it was, in other words, nationalism in its generic sense: ideals, passion, selfless sacrifice, all for the love of country. On the other hand, the organization and recruitment of patriotic activists fostered an understanding of national consciousness as a rather volatile matter that had to be provisioned, even paid for, in order to take root among "the people" not yet under the control of the state apparatus, namely, among the inhabitants of Ottoman Bosnia. Approached from this angle, patriotic ideals and convictions, no matter how passionately asserted or promoted, were inescapably variable, vulnerable, unstable—and thus subject to further nationalist work. In fact, it was this latter sense of patriotic conscience—a susceptible and partial conscience—that nationalists themselves established as the foundational operating assumption of their projects.

Despite objections to a patriotism "bought off with ducats," then, state-building officials in Belgrade, from Garašanin to Ban to Ristić, in practice always managed Serbia's national task alongside "its tight financial situation," a framework that only encouraged national agents to account for consciousness in terms of costs. At the level of diplomacy, speculations over international "trading" or "buying" of provinces—rumors in 1866 suggested elaborate transactions between Austria, Italy, and the Ottoman Empire over the respective territorial losses and gains of Venice and Herzegovina, for example—heightened the sense that nation-building entailed intricate calculations involving Great Power interests and micromanagement of local affairs.[95] Nationalist agents occupied a pivotal position in this framework. Many of them (Kovačević and Petranović, for instance) worked as professional activists, that is, as political figures paid by the incipient Serbian state to fulfill its nationalizing mission and promote Serbian national sentiment.[96] This political dynamic—paying agents to render conscious the wavering provincials—quickly became known as a venue where potential local supporters could make (and earn) their own patriotic contribution, perhaps even a new political career as well.

The case of Stevo Petković, an Orthodox priest from the northern Bosnian town of Brčko, helps shed light on this development. Petković, unlike earlier agents, did not enter into contact with Belgrade officials through an intermediary operative who usually recommended specific persons to the Belgrade government. Instead, Petković personally approached the Serbian government in March 1872, persuading officials that he would be its ideal advocate in Bosnia. "Even if full and clear relations do not exist between me and the Serbian government," Petković wrote, a remarkable coincidence of interests nonetheless linked them:

The liberation of the vanquished in the east, which stands in the plans of the Serbian government, stands in my head too; and I hope to move the same [ideas] into the heads of all those who are directly and indirectly within my reach. Thus in this liberation, the Serbian government, with its own part of the people, will be in the first place an active fact. . . . But it should be considered that some areas, where no sign of consciousness (*nikakav znak osveštenja*) has arrived, will often be against us (obviously, not of their own true will). . . . Thus before the Serbian government risks its independence for the liberation of its yoked brothers, it should be made certain that it is the holy duty of every activist (*radenik*) to work and contribute as much as possible to the achievement of national liberation. . . . This is at least what my six-year experience, which was gained in constant dealings with the people of many districts, tells me. There is no day, gentlemen, in which we could not awaken in my neighborhood alone at least one, sometimes fives, tens of weeping Serbs, without difference in religion, whether of Orthodox or Western confession.[97]

So far, so good. In a short letter, Petković thus highlighted all the key national issues—Serbia's mission, the people's insufficient consciousness, the need for tireless activism—and pledged himself to promote the cause. Only one obstacle remained—the lack of "material means":

> All this, respected gentlemen, should I have so much daring, is to seek from you a certain sum of money, which will help me in the realization of these goals, and which will be available to me only insofar as it is necessary. When you wish to have successful work yourself, please do so, taking care to not surprise us with any [unannounced] visit, which could be dangerous.[98]

Petković's continuing involvement with Serbian officials indicates that he found his way into the project of national liberation as a low-profile activist and political observer in the town of Brčko.[99]

We should be careful not to read Petković's entry into national activism as an act of mere opportunism. As Petković indicated, being a Serbian activist was actually dangerous; just three years earlier, the Ottoman authorities expelled nationalist teachers like Vaso Pelagić to Austria, and other suspected "agitators" like Serafim Perović and Gavro Vučković were banished to jails in North Africa and the Middle East.[100] Furthermore, there is no discernible evidence to doubt the sincerity of the expressed nationalist sentiments or the requests for material aid and money. Most important, there is no analytical advantage to considering sponsorship-aware or even sponsorship-obtained patriotism as somehow less "valid" or "real" than other nationalist convictions, which are often presumed to be deeply held ideals and essences. Nationalists themselves, of course, always raised moral objections to a "patriotism bought with ducats," but they were the same ones who encouraged officials, recruits, and the local populace to think of the national cause as a matter of plans, budgets, and costs. In this framework, Petković's initiation as a national activist speaks not so much of opportunistic dealings as of a major practical venue of creating—and distributing—patriotic consciousness through its material means.

The flow of activist materials, ranging from money to revolvers to books to shoes, revolved around a similar understanding of national consciousness as a resource susceptible to a variety of influences. For example, Vaso Pelagić, a leading Serbian national activist in Bosnia, was attentive to the impact of teachers, wages, and gifts on cultivating proper national identifications. Many patriots, Pelagić warned in 1867 in a manual for elementary school teachers in Bosnia and "Turkish Serbia," were too passive and too negligent, justifying their laxity by complaining about the inadequate compensation they received for their work. They would say, "Let things go how they will; as is the wage, so is the work, etc."[101] Pelagić criticized such attitudes, urging teachers to be more energetic and self-sacrificing in their activism on the one hand, while on the other, he suggested that material enticements be passed to children in patriotic classrooms: "Every teacher should teach first his students and then all the local children who can speak. When someone asks them, 'What are you, young man?,' the young man should immediately answer: 'I am a Serb' (*ja sam Srbin*). It would be beneficial if some good men could be found who would reward the children with a few pence for that; by doing so, an even greater earnestness would be awakened toward that answer."[102]

Enticements toward the right national answer also came in other forms. Nićifor Dučić, the official in charge of dispensing Serbian state aid to a variety of causes in the 1860s and 1870s, often wrote about his patriotic-budgetary rationale. When a village school near the Bosnian town of Kupres requested monetary aid for hiring a new teacher, Dučić allocated 30 ducats, "but only for a teacher who knows how to awaken national consciousness and how to work shrewdly for the national cause."[103] Dučić not only distributed money but also arranged for more symbolic gifts. In 1872, he requested the purchase of "three revolvers" for "Jevto Bjelobrk and his crew, which is currently the strongest in Mostar." After banishing a rival Montenegrin agitator and proving their patriotic credentials, "the Mostar crew" asked for guns as gifts from "Serbia or Prince Milan. If Serbian factories do not make revolvers, they could be bought from Mr. Trifković, and Serbian symbols could be affixed to them before sending. This would not cost more than 12–15 ducats, while for them, this will be more precious than anything else, binding them ever more to the work that Serbia will begin in Bosnia-Herzegovina one day."[104] Preparations for uprisings and other national involvements did not involve only wages and guns. An Ottoman official in Herzegovina in 1870 described a surprising discovery during a search for suspicious agitators in the Trebinje countryside. The local Orthodox school had not only "books calling people to an uprising" but also other requisites: "I went with soldiers to all the villages that have over forty houses and found over seven thousand peasant shoes (*opanci*), which they were distributing to the people for the uprising. After that, I arrested those [responsible] and brought them to Ali-bey . . . and then I mounted the same peasant shoes on horses and with the soldiers went to Mostar."[105]

In interpreting these relations, it is important to remember the key question: not whether the activists failed or achieved the desired aims (liberation, mobilization, etc.), not whether a well-paid teacher, well-decorated revolver, or a well-heeled pair of shoes was too little or just enough to win over the local populace—but what these relations signified and made possible in the first place. The spread of patriotic ideas and incentives in Ottoman Bosnia reveals a great deal about the kind of national consciousness that nationalists themselves tried to cultivate. Going beyond the notion of consciousness as a dormant sentiment "awakened" by some prompt, activists put a different notion of consciousness into currency, conceiving of it as a susceptible, variable matter that is subject to countless influences, including kinship relations, local rivalries, education, wages, peer pressures, rhetoric, symbols, gifts, and so on. Nationalists often bemoaned the pliability of this kind of national consciousness, usually expressing disappointment in the lack of firm patriotic commitments among "the people"; in practice, however, the activists precisely sought to encourage and capitalize on such ambiguous patriotic sentiment, which they saw as a crucial precondition for the growth of their national movements. After all, working with those who had promising or loose political inclinations was much easier than overturning already deeply held commitments and ties. (Dučić's work again provides a good example. When the Bosnian Franciscan monastery in Kreševo expressed interest in Serbian aid, Dučić commented that he saw "little benefit for our national cause" in sponsoring "a wealthy Catholic community, already helped by Austria"; but if this monastery appeared not very persuadable and "difficult for us," then at least individual Franciscans from other monasteries, like the friars Grga Škarić and Nikola Šokčević, proved to be "more open" to Serbian influence and worthy of sustained state interest and sponsorship.)[106] For their project to spread, activists worked to make access to patriotic consciousness significantly open, enticing, even formulaic and vague enough so that potential co-nationals could easily join the cause—all while extolling national conviction as unique, unbreakable, immortal.

This balancing act shaped the nationalist message itself. Details from a Serbian patriotic gathering in 1873 in Tuzla illustrate this dynamic. By the 1870s, there were fledgling signs of nationalist activity in this northern Bosnian town where aspiring Serbian agents, Orthodox priests, and Franciscan friars became interested in developing patriotic societies.[107] Thanks to a hastily arranged photograph that later elicited a number of locals' comments, we get a glimpse into what this manner of nationalist organization looked like in practice (see figure 3.1).[108] Isailo Mićić, an activist and participant in the gathering, later wrote that a traveling photographer from Dalmatia "one day showed up in Tuzla; it was, as far as I remember, a Sunday, and we all quickly agreed to have our picture taken, so we met by the old Serbian church."[109] The arrangement of the photograph itself is fairly straightforward, showing five rows of thirty-six men, including the town's Orthodox priests, Bosnian Franciscan friars, and local teachers, thus illustrating cross-confessional solidarity at work. It is the national symbols, however, that stood out, prompting a journalist who came across the photo in 1921 to single out these details: "In the background on the wall, the words *Only Unity Saves the Serb* are written out; while in front of the group, one youth holds in his lap a white piece of paper on which a word is nicely written out: *Flag*." Mićić himself commented on the prominent insignia: "I don't remember who wrote out those words on the church wall, but

Figure 3.1 The flag that says "*Flag*": A gathering of Serbian patriots in Tuzla, 1873. One participant wrote, "I remember that sign *Flag* on the piece of paper in front . . . we wanted to have our picture with the flag, but we could not get one at the moment. So we wrote out our desire on a piece of paper." With permission from the Archive of the Tuzla Canton, Tuzla.

I do remember the sign *Flag* on the piece of paper in front, it means the national tricolor; we wanted to have our picture with a flag, but we could not get one at the moment. So we wrote out our desire onto a piece of paper."[110]

This image—a society around a flag that says "*Flag*"—forms a kind of a patriotic metapicture, "a picture that shows what a picture is" and thus reveals the underlying nationalist practices of organization and representation.[111] On the one hand, there are strong assertions of passionate national conviction: praise of Serbian unity, pride in organized displays, rallying around a flag. Yet on the other hand, all of these declarations also reveal the nationalist proclivity toward formulaic expressions and referents that are ambiguous despite their proclaimed national specificity. Take, for example, the assumed reference of the word "flag" to the "tricolor" in Tuzla—which tricolor? As Đorđe Popović pointed out already in 1881, the national tricolors of Serbian, Croatian, and Slovene (as well as Czech, Slovak, and other) causes all shared the same colors (red, white, and blue), with the exact color order and the heraldic emblems subject to much dispute and confusion throughout the nineteenth century.[112] In the company of budding South Slavic patriots, abstracting and writing out the word itself thus helps both signify the desired national form ("flag") and defer its precise content (Serbian, Croatian, Bosnian, Yugoslav) to some future point. What comes across is the significance of the gesture itself: rallying around the sign "flag" and affirmation of patriotic expression as such. In many ways, appeals to a national "essence" demonstrate a desire not so much to be unique but precisely to be like any other nation, possessing a flag, patriotic organizations, slogans, gestures, and other nation-like attributes.

On the other hand, does not the slogan in the background reassert some national specificity? According to the vast majority of scholars, "Only Unity Saves the Serb" is the most famous Serbian nationalist motto, attributed either to the medieval Serbian saint Sava or simply to Serbian folklore. Yet even this ur-Serbian proclamation was very new, dating back only to 1859; thereafter, it was rapidly relieved of its authorship. Its originator was Jovan Dragašević, a military professor and not very successful writer; his most notable poem was *Echoes of the Gusle*, which first featured the now-legendary alliterative slogan *Samo sloga Srbina spašava*.[113] Some three decades later in 1891, Dragašević personally complained to a friend that he saw his increasingly ubiquitous motto "attributed in [newspapers] to 'Serbian folk lore.' I cannot tell you the meaning of my laughter when I saw that. . . . I was glad that my expression is being taken on as a creation of the folk itself — but I was also dejected that my expression is being wrested away from me during my own lifetime. . . . That just went too far." Dragašević added, "The Serbian intelligentsia knows that every expression of Schiller or Goethe is properly theirs, whereas the expression of one of its own activists, it does not know whose is it?"[114] Here it is important to consider the implication of this case of nationalization: not that the national public "does not know," but perhaps that it prefers the other, more ambiguous story of the immaculate conception of its key motto. Divorced from its otherwise undistinguished author, the slogan could then be ennobled (by forging links to older symbols like the medieval *ocilo* emblem) and popularized as a quick, formulaic expression of nationalism — fitting background graffiti for a hastily arranged patriotic gathering in late nineteenth-century Tuzla.

Nationalizing Bosnian Muslims: A Study in National Disappointment

An important objection should be raised here: Are there not concrete limits to these valences of nationalist activism? In this case, is not "the unity of the Serbs," however formulaic or partially accessible to potential co-nationals (like the Catholics of Tuzla), also defined negatively against the hated enemies of the Serbian nation — the Turks, for example? The answer clearly must be yes, of course, there are exclusionary limits to national communities; yet a careful consideration of the case of "the Turks" also helps demonstrate the ambiguities and abiding discontents of nation-making.

The emergence of politics of patriotism among Bosnian Muslims, though surprisingly little researched, is nonetheless often cited as an example of the "lateness" of nationalism or even "confusion" over national identity.[115] Robert Donia, the author of an outstanding study of the Bosnian Muslim movement for religious autonomy under Austria-Hungary, summarized the developments thus: Since the late nineteenth century, "the vast majority of Bosnian Muslims ultimately rejected both Serb and Croat identity, but not until the 1960s did they assert themselves as a separate nation distinguished from both Serbs and Croats by their culture, history, and religious heritage. Until then, the national identity and loyalty of Bosnia's Muslims hung in the balance in the fierce debate between Serbs and Croats staking claims in Bosnia."[116] Such accounts rightly point to the uncertainties within these processes, but also remove the underlying tensions by stressing what happens "ultimately." For all the uncertainty, surely some Bosnian Muslims, even if it took them decades, ended up with what we and they recognize as a nation of their own—after two world wars and a devastating conflict in the 1990s, of course. Until then, they "hung in the balance."

My approach takes a different route: it does not assume that certain historical actors are delayed, unfinished, or waiting for a proper denouement—but rather asks how nationalization developed as a project and what it enabled. To get at these issues, we need to go beyond the usual focus on the emergence of a distinct national identity, in this case a Bosnian Muslim identity. Narratives written in this vein usually seek to explain how was it that Bosnian Muslims developed "their own" sense of nationhood; not surprisingly, such retrospectives focus on those Bosnian Muslims who "resisted" the Serbian and Croatian nationalizing advances, eventually elaborating a sense of communal distinction and patriotic pride.[117] This is not a new approach. Articles from *Bošnjak* (*Bosniac*), a prominent fin de siècle journal advancing similar arguments, described in 1900 how "we Muhammedans remain in the middle, and we are the tipping weight that would slide the scale's gauges to any side that we cross to. The Serbs and the Croats know this too well, so they constantly court us, pressing their thoughts and ideas on us"; advances were to no avail, however, since "we are neither Serbs nor Croats" but "Muhammedans," "Bosniacs," or "Bosnian Muslims."[118] Those Muslims who, in rather significant numbers and ways, actually took up the Serbian and Croatian causes were defined as "exceptional" and "controversial" figures deviating from the "middle" course endorsed as the norm by later histories.[119]

Stepping back from such assessments and teleologies, however, let us consider different kinds of questions: How did Serbian nationalists, self-proclaimed enemies of "the Turks," come to court Muslims as "their own people" in the first place? How were programs of nationalization of

Muslims organized and pursued in practice? What emerged from such encounters? What can this history tell us about nationalization as a historical process?

On the one hand, "the Turks"—a broad label conflating Islamic, Ottoman, and "Oriental" connotations—clearly came to constitute the threatening "Other" of Serbian, Greek, and Bulgarian nationalisms of the nineteenth century. Uprisings, wars, and massive violence that swept through the Balkans in the early decades of the century rapidly drove dividing lines between "the Turks" and "the Serbs," for example; subsequent developments, including further wars, Ottoman retributions, and expansion of the Serbian state, only deepened these divisions. In the eyes of the Balkan nation-builders, continuing Ottoman rule over the "unliberated" parts of southeast Europe could only spell doom for the local Christians. Even Ottoman reforms, one Serbian official wrote in the 1860s, could never secure justice or "equality of citizens" because the character of Muslim rule—its "medieval barbarity" and "blind adherence to Muhammed"—remained the same, causing only "tyranny and suffering."[120] The Serbian official Nićifor Dučić filed a state document in the 1860s, written in the form of a newspaper editorial, that similarly described Bosnia as a place of Ottoman torment and "injustice unlike anywhere else in the world."[121] The only solution would be Serbia's liberation of Ottoman regions.

But on the other hand, Dučić's file continued, "here someone might ask, what kind of fate will befall the Bosnian and Herzegovinian Turks once these areas are joined with Serbia?" A passionate reply followed: "Well, the same fate as for us Christians of both confessions—we will have equal rights together. . . . In Serbia, freedom of religion stands on mighty foundations. It is guaranteed, patriotic, liberal, tolerant in the highest sense." The "Bosnian Turks" thus had nothing to fear from Serbia, since this was a nation that protected and even supported a single mosque in the Serbian capital itself (the text, of course, omitted the planned destruction of some thirty mosques in Belgrade during the nineteenth century). All states would have to uphold the liberal principles of justice, and Muslims will surely thrive when they embrace them, Dučić's document concluded—only to add: "a people that is not in step with the spirit and progress of its time must either submit to another, more progressive nation, or vanish."[122]

This argumentative thread, easily slipping between visions of "thriving" and "vanishing" Muslims, ran throughout nineteenth-century Serbian and Croatian political programs, which conceived of Bosnian Muslims as liminal yet integral parts of their nations for several reasons. The fact that Bosnian Muslims spoke the same South Slavic dialects as their Christian counterparts, for example, already presented strong grounds for many Serbian and Croatian patriots to proclaim Slavic-speaking Muslims as their co-nationals (views famously championed by both the Serbian folklorist Vuk Karadžić and his Croatian opponent Ante Starčević). Moreover, not only did Muslims make up a rather substantial part of the population—around a third by most accounts—but they also constituted the key landowning and governing elites in Bosnia, with many families long established as provincial Ottoman nobility. This position made Bosnian Muslims a target of anti-Turkish agitation, though Serbian and Croatian nationalists also realized that a great deal could be gained by winning over rather than entirely rejecting the Ottoman Bosnian elites. Finally, religious difference posed a crucial obstacle, challenging Serbian and Croatian nationalists to include or at least acknowledge the faith of "the Turkish oppressor" as constitutive of South Slavic nationality.

All this made for a very tough balancing act, but also a promising one—if Serbian and Croatian patriots were to find a way to cross deeply entrenched religious, class, and political boundaries, then perhaps their national programs could demonstrate the kind of resilience necessary for their emergent nations to grow and thrive in the future. It is high time, urged one Serbian historian in 1894, to leave behind "the shameful relics" of a bygone era "when people persecuted and killed one another because of religious difference. Today that is a disgrace, nonsense, and inhumanity, for Serbs espouse several faiths"—quoting a well-known South Slavic proverb: " 'Cherish your brother, his faith be yours or other' (*brat je mio koje vjere bio*)."[123] Through these various considerations, Bosnian Muslims came to embody the promise of national resilience and growth in the eyes of many South Slavic patriots, making at least some "Turks" desirable targets of nineteenth-century nationalist work.[124]

The Serbian state expressed interest in reaching out to Bosnian Muslims as early as the 1840s, a concern reflected in the *Načertanije* and pursued by national agents in the subsequent decades. As the Serbian cabinet adviser František Zach wrote in 1844, "I have yet to find anyone who has a trusted friend among the Turks in Bosnia, and that is what we need today."[125] To Zach and Minister Garašanin, enlisting some Bosnian Muslim *beys* seemed possible because such elites already opposed the reformist governors from Istanbul. Kovačević followed up in 1848 with a motion to "wholeheartedly and seriously kindle the bitterness of the Bosnian Turks toward the imperial [Ottoman] officers, bringing them to such a degree that the two sides will fight and the Turks will weaken."[126] Reports that "the Bosnian Turks . . . are in a fatalistic mood," fearful of both Ottoman reforms and Austrian spies, kept similar hopes alive well into the 1860s.[127] One Serbian agent, Petar Uzelac, assured his superiors in Belgrade in 1871 that "as a Serb, I only want to be useful for Serbdom," so "believe me, if you don't reach an agreement with Bosnian Turks, nothing will be accomplished anywhere."[128] Winning the sympathy—or at least securing the neutrality—of the leading *beys* thus seemed to most Serbian activists crucial for their success; if the Muslim elites could be convinced of Serbia's good intentions, mobilization in Bosnia would be assured of a favorable outcome.

Initial strategies for reaching out to Bosnian Muslims, however, were very limited. For a start, Serbian officials saw it necessary to distinguish between "the Turks," depicted as the depraved oppressors of the Balkan Christians, and "our Turks," the Bosnian Muslims. The Serbian official Matija Ban pursued this theme in several works. His best-known play, *Mejrima, or the Bosniacs* (1849), staged a tragic Christian-Muslim conflict, with a violent ending cautiously bringing some Bosnian Turks into the fold of the triumphant Serbs.[129] In another unpublished dramatization, Ban presented three fictional "conversations between a Serb and a Frenchman" (1866) about "the Turks" in Bosnia. In the opening salvo, the Serb explained: "There is a great difference between the Turk (*Turčin*) and the Ottoman (*Osmanlia*) in Bosnia. The Ottoman came from Anatolia, whereas the Turk was born in Bosnia, where our own great-grandfathers were also born. The Ottoman doesn't know a word of our language, whereas the Turk speaks only our language." Not entirely convinced, the Frenchman insisted on the difference between the Turks and other Balkan peoples, with the Serbs poised, in one way or another, to take Bosnia:

> *The Frenchman*: Well, you know, something occurs to me now. You Serbs have no other option but to make an agreement with the Catholics, and then strike in unison against the Turks. Then you will be three against one, so when you exterminate your Turks, then the Ottoman too is done.
>
> *The Serb*: I must express shock to you for saying that! Whom should we slay? Our own Turks? To spill our blood and weaken our national strength? No way. Were we to exterminate the Turks, wouldn't thousands of us die as well? And then what? If they disappear, and if we're halved, wouldn't we come again under the rule of the Ottomans or the Austrians? So what would we gain then? It's a bad deal, my friend. . . .
>
> *The Frenchman*: Very well. I was just testing you with those words, but now I see you are a wise man.[130]

Another Serbian correspondent filed in 1869 a similar Bulgarian "conversation with a Pomak [Muslim] villager in regard to nationality," presenting a kind of activist catechism designed to show Balkan Muslims the benefit and the pride of proper national belonging.[131] The attempts to distinguish Bosnian and Slavic Muslims—"our own Turks," "our brothers"—from the Ottomans as the real enemies succeeded mainly in showing that the dividing lines between brother and Other were subject to repeated revisions, reversals, and anxieties about the foundational categories of national belonging. In fact, recurring movements across these categories reveal the extensive spaces of undecidability within the national imagination, spaces conspicuously occupied in the South Slavic context by the Bosnian Muslim (br)others.

Demonstrating the appeal of brotherly Serbian patriotism to Bosnian Muslims, however, proved to be extremely difficult during the Ottoman period. The Serbian state steadily worked to overthrow Ottoman rule and expel Muslims from its own territory, particularly from towns like Užice and Belgrade in the 1860s. Many Muslim refugees settled in eastern Bosnia and brought with them eyewitness accounts of Serbian repression. When presenting the image of Serbia to future co-nationals, however, Belgrade-based activists framed legal equality, freedom of religion, and liberal tenets of justice as "patriotic principles" inherent to Serbia's nationalizing mission.[132] The Ottoman Empire was doomed anyway, the Serbian nationalists constantly stressed, but even this argument was hard to make on the ground. A certain Petar Vasić, for instance, traveled in 1868 with the aim of "visiting prominent Turks" in northern Bosnia, but he cut his trip short after conversations with just two Bosnian Muslim notables. They and "the Turks of the lower classes" were, he reported encouragingly, "cursing Osman-pasha" and "the heinous Ottomans," but Vasić felt that he "could not raise" the sensitive issue of mounting a massive uprising against the very system that provided Muslims with a basic sense of authority and familiarity. Similarly, the qualified attempts to craft a nuanced message about the different kinds of "Turks" (the good and the bad) also failed to make an impression in Ottoman Bosnia.[133]

However, the sudden arrival of Habsburg rule in 1878 altered this situation radically. With the removal of Ottoman rule, one of the key Serbian nationalist aims was, in a way, fulfilled (even if Serbia failed to capture the contested province). Relieved of the need to make fine distinctions among "Turks" any longer, Serbian and increasingly Croatian nationalists found Bosnian Muslims to be suitable targets for their revitalized activism. A number of novel issues—especially the growing Muslim emigration from Bosnia and the open discontent with Habsburg management of religious affairs—appeared to many Serbian observers as fertile grounds for increased nationalization efforts.[134] Two areas in particular stood out: political alliances and education.

In terms of political alliances, Serb Orthodox and Muslim movements for religious autonomy found several areas of convergence during the Habsburg period. Amid Austro-Hungarian attempts to regulate religious affairs in Bosnia, both the Orthodox and Muslim clergy began to organize in the 1890s and demand a significant degree of autonomy in their institutional, educational, and communal affairs. Thus positioned against a common Habsburg opponent (perceived as a Catholic power), many Serbian Orthodox and Muslim political figures formed working alliances; these primarily included local intellectuals, teachers, merchants, and community leaders like Gligorije Jeftanović and Šerif Arnautović rather than the small number of clergy initially involved in the movements. Arnautović, who had previously espoused pro-Croatian views, was to remain largely inclined to the Serbian cause for much of his subsequent political career, though without embracing the Serbian label explicitly.[135]

Though such alignments appeared intriguing and useful to both parties, they were perceived precisely as temporary and unlikely to bridge deeper differences between Serbian and Muslim politicians on issues like statehood and agrarian relations. One Sarajevan Serbian leader, Gligorije Jeftanović, summed up this view in 1905: "Now that the Muslims are beside us, we have an easier struggle for the church question, and it is in their interest too. But I believe, as do all our leaders, that in larger undertakings we cannot confide in them even a little bit. We're with them together now, but later we will surely must break with them" in pursuit of land redistribution and union with the Serbian state.[136] Muslim leaders themselves harbored major doubts about Serbia; clergy like Ali Džabić, once open to the idea of Serbian alliances, denounced in 1903 "the Serbs [as] the worst spoilers of the Ottoman and Islamic faith."[137] Indeed, after both Orthodox and Muslim denominations received imperial charters granting religious autonomy, the tenuous alliance largely unraveled and more strident nationalist arguments (voiced by Serbian figures like Petar Kočić) gained force by 1908. Shared political struggles against the Habsburg government, then, could bring Serbs and Muslims together, inspiring paeans to "the same blood and kinship" that united the two peoples; but the alignments were themselves perceived as fragile and unlikely to inspire lasting national convergences.[138]

Education, on the other hand, held out a more ambitious prospect—the hope of not only attracting Bosnian students to Serbian schools but of also producing the desired outcome, the nationally conscious Muslim. In pursuit of this goal, Serbian as well as Croatian activists discovered that they had very limited venues and resources. The Austro-Hungarian government tightly controlled schools in the province, inspecting and removing materials and teachers deemed to be inflammatory; the chances of overtly nationalist appeals reaching Muslim children in Bosnian schools were thus minimal. Moreover, neither the Serbian state nor the Croatian institutions had developed separate materials catering specifically to Muslim audiences, even though they promised such programs to receptive Bosnian Muslims students.

Translation and publication of the Qur'an in Serbo-Croatian was one initiative that Serbian activists pursued in this regard since the late Ottoman period. In fact, Jovan Dragašević, the author of the famed motto "Only Unity Saves the Serbs," crucially contributed "to the great idea, which is envisioned in the translation of the Koran," by suggesting a "well-known personality in Herzegovina" to take up this serious patriotic matter in 1873.[139] Thus encouraged, the prominent activist Mićo Ljubibratić embarked on this project, albeit with a major constraint: Ljubibratić could translate only from the French, but not at all from the original Arabic.[140] Though started in the 1870s, the translation was finally completed in 1895, appearing as the first print publication of the Qur'an in any non-Arabic language in the

Balkans.[141] Because of its awkward translation process and heightened Serbian national character, the book encountered unfavorable reception among the Bosnian Muslim ulema and most established intellectuals, some of whom had by 1910s undertaken their own translation initiatives. The Serbian Qur'an was quite useful, however, to Serbian activists themselves, who announced to their Muslim contacts in 1901 that "Qur'ans translated in Cyrillic are coming [to Sarajevo] to be distributed to Muslim youth."[142]

Around the same time, outreach to secondary schools began to involve at least some promising Bosnian Muslim students. Rumors that Serbia would sponsor stipends and perhaps open some kind of Muslim school were common; in 1905, for example, a Muslim promoter of the Serbian cause in Sarajevo excitedly told his acquaintances that "the Serbian government has issued 100,000 forints as subsidy for impoverished Muslim students in Bosnia, with the aim of attracting more followers, since it was not possible for the government to open a Muslim school in Serbia this year."[143] Offering monetary aid, usually in the form of stipends, was easier than establishing a new Islamic school in Serbia, where Muslim students and teachers were few and far between.[144]

The contrasting careers of Osman Đikić and Musa Ćazim Ćatić are telling examples of the uncertainty of the educational-nationalizing venues in Serbia. In the late 1890s, both Đikić and Ćatić were aspiring Bosnian Muslim writers who sought higher education in Istanbul, where they came into contact with well-connected Serbian activists. Osman Đikić quickly distinguished himself as an especially committed "Serbian Muhammedan." After putting together a collection of "Serbian Muhammedan" folk poetry, Đikić and his supporters in Mostar managed to sell it in 1899 to the Serbian Academy of Sciences in Belgrade "for a decent sum."[145] Though the collection was never actually published, Đikić continued his patriotic work, enrolling in a Belgrade gymnasium (1900–1903) on the "advice of friends" and pledging to Serbian officials to "help his brothers and his subjugated homeland Bosnia."[146] Along with S. A. Karabegović and Omer-beg Sulejmanpašić, Đikić published collections of Serbian Muslim poetry in Belgrade and tried to recruit others for similar literary-nationalist programs. Jusuf Pečenković later wrote that as Serbian nationalists eagerly sought out Muslim students in Bosnia around 1900, "my Serbian national declaration became stronger day after day, filling out almost my entire consciousness. Such was the case with other Muslim nationalists who did away entirely with the notion of 'the Turk' (*s pojmom 'Turčin'*) and consciously accepted the name Serb."[147] After eventually returning to Mostar, Đikić was very active in nationalist politics as a publicist with a pronounced interest in taking over the editorial boards of Muslim-oriented journals like *Gajret* and especially *Musavat*, work that was vigorously opposed by other Muslim organizations. Osman Đikić, however, persisted in his efforts, remaining one of the most conspicuous role models for the Serbian Muslim program well after his death in 1912.[148]

On the other hand, the experiences of Musa Ćazim Ćatić and other Muslim students produced far more frustration than satisfaction with Serbian nationalism. Much like Đikić, Ćatić became involved with Serbian activists in Istanbul and from there followed nationalist advice to enroll in a Belgrade high school in 1899. Once there, however, Ćatić became outraged at the hostility toward Muslims that he encountered. In less than a semester, he abandoned his school, his Serbian affiliation, and returned to Bosnia.[149] Ćatić thereafter became a very active and renowned literary contributor with explicitly pro-Croatian national views. Another local patriotic aspirant, Mehmed Spahić, described a similar trajectory, beginning with curiosity about Serbian nationalism, developing into confidence in Serbia's mission, only to be followed by disavowal of Belgrade programs. Back in Mostar, Spahić spitefully embraced the Croatian cause and wrote diatribes against Serbian nationalism. That, as he wrote in 1899, was "the history of my Serbing around" (*historija moga srbovanja*).[150]

What is especially remarkable here is that some individuals seized on certain logics of nation-making without attending either Serbian or Croatian schools. Consider, for instance, the case of Mehmed Dželaludin Kurt, a restive student attending the Sarajevo Sharia Law School, an institution that was a far cry from Serbian nationalist schools.[151] When the ambitious Kurt first wanted to make a name for himself as a popular writer in 1899, he actively sought out a Mostar Serbian politician and asked for help in publishing a patriotic collection of "Serbian folk poetry" from Herzegovina.[152] After his discussions with Serbian academics faltered, Kurt then passionately threw in his lot with Croatian societies a few years later, replacing the adjective "Serbian" with "Croatian" in his work and publishing the same folk poetry collection under the new "Croatian Muslim" label in 1903.[153] By 1905, however, when Mostar Muslim leaders solidified an alliance with Bosnian Serb leaders, Kurt abandoned his Croatian appellation, stating publicly that he had "mixed so long with Catholics and Croats and collected poetry for them only to see and check out what Catholicism intends; but when he gained insight, he left them, because he saw that the Serbian party thinks more honestly and joined [its cause]."[154]

With such a range of initiatives, pressures, actors, and actions, how is nationalization to be conceptualized and interpreted? Kurt's career suggests an entry point. What nationalist work made available were certain forms of professional-political engagement, forms that potential co-nationals not only "received" as directed but also sought out, appropriated, and managed in a variety of ways and for a variety of purposes. To be a patriot in the sense that Kurt and some other Bosnian Muslims enacted was to promote and write a certain formulaic kind of poetry, to passionately declare one's allegiances, to vow to spread the national idea, to malign the opposing sides, to gain the backing of a political project in one's midst. Serbian and Croatian movements certainly had their respective differences, histories, and profiles, but in terms of entry-level political engagement, they worked as largely inter-changeable projects, extending many generic, ambiguously delineated ven-ues and practices to actors like Ćatić, Kurt, Spahić, and many others. In fact, once they were posed as objectives that national activism should "achieve" and "spread," particular matters—such as national consciousness, national organization, national poetry—quickly became popular conventions, though their precise content and use were difficult to determine and sustain.

Here Mehmed Kurt's back-and-forth shifts could be alternatively inter-preted as an instance of "national indifference" enabling some subjects to cross sides, or as an example of "political opportunism" where individuals simply followed the prevailing winds. To be sure, his rapid changes were remarkable even to his contemporaries, who became wary of his "affairs" and "fiascos." But to close the case with labels like "indifferent" or "op-portunist" is to misunderstand the matter by assuming that true nationalists have an authentic, deep, and essential attachment to their national cause, implicitly contrasted with seemingly superficial or fickle sentiments of fig-ures like Kurt. What Kurt's actions instead reveal is precisely the durability and accessibility of certain patriotic conventions and forms. Viewed from this perspective, Kurt was very much working in the tradition of earlier Serbian Orthodox activists like Bogoljub Petranović and Stevo Petković of the 1860s and 1870s: he initiated contact with national movements, pas-sionately offering his services as an ethnographer-activist, publishing same folk poetry on different sides, all the while requesting appropriate sponsor-ship for his contributions to the nation (whose exact attributes could be ascertained and updated later).

What the history of Serbian-Muslim dynamics allows us to trace are the workings of nationalization as a process rather than a finite outcome (an end presumably either achieved or not achieved). Instead of reading Bosnian Muslim figures like Đikić or Ćatić as failures or exceptions to the report-edly "fully formed" nationals, my interpretation attends to the productive aspects of their subject formation, stressing the relation between the nation-alizers and their targeted populations and objectives. In the development of Serbia's nationalizing mission, Bosnian Muslims were on the one hand praised as the readily available keys to the success of the patriotic project in Bosnia, and condemned on the other hand as strange, unmanageable, and almost unteachable "provincials": backward, superstitious, uncooperative, opportunistic, divisive, and confused co-nationals who needed the activists to firmly lead them to a better, more national future.[155]

In this sense, Bosnian Muslim experiences of nationalization ran paral-lel to those of peasants, immigrants, Orthodox, Roma, Catholics, Vlachs, Šokci, Cincars, and many other populations who were to become—and not necessarily remain—"Serbs" (or other kinds of nationals). After Osman Đi-kić passed away in 1912, Đorđe Pejanović wrote that "it was a great rar-ity, even among the intelligentsia, to find a proven and well-nationalized

Muslim (*dobro nacionalizovanog muslimana*)." Of course, Pejanović wrote that further renewed efforts were required to rectify this situation, "approaching this work with exceptionally great sensitivity." Pejanović outlined a series of problems "among Muslims" that particularly thwarted this work—yet the complaints themselves are exemplary. Far from being unique to Muslims, they read like a compilation of nationalizers' generic frustrations with the process of turning peasants (or other populations) into nationals:

> Among them there are . . . far too great and strongly rooted general prejudices, particularly in regard to other confessional groups; weak cultural conditions, especially among the broader swaths of the population; a very poor state of education; a lack of wider organization; a weakly developed social life; medieval divisions of people by religion, enacted at great length and applied to the entire life, work, thoughts, inclinations, and upbringing; insufficient knowledge of one's position and rights; a weakly developed feeling of higher needs; excessively stubborn personal interests, elevated most often to the level of utmost life goals; and above all, the absence of higher ideals and aims.[156]

The seemingly strange case of Bosnian Muslims forms one distinct—and for that reason useful and telling—segment of a much larger spectrum of concurrent processes of nationalization that unfolded over the course of the long nineteenth century. The research presented here is possible precisely because Serbian activists wrote extensively about their programs of nationalization, documenting in depth their engagements with Bosnian Muslims as well as with various other "provincials," especially peasants. For all their embedded silences and elisions, the archives of these nation-making practices show just how inextricable—and in many cases indistinguishable—were the projects of liberation and conquest, empowerment and discipline.

Vojo Vasiljević, a Serbian activist who vigorously led patriotic missions to organize Bosnian Christian peasants—campaigns that very much echoed Pejanović's complaints about the impossible yet thoroughly "our" Muslims—left us in 1913 a concise glimpse into the demanding work of nationalizing "one's own people":

> There is very little sense of cooperation and discipline among our people. I remember at the beginning of work on the Sokol [society] by Staniša's [place], at the drill command "Attention!," the peasant would say, "Hey man, wait, let me finish my smoke." Or when he stands in line with a cigarette and smokes during the exercises until you reprimand him. Generally, there was no discipline, and only a bit more was imposed when they got used to it. There is also very little sense of cooperation. Our peasant directs all his work and all his thought toward an easy life, only to gain something, even if it were dishonest and dishonorable. Our peasant has no developed inner life, he has no ideas that could guide him, which is why he is such an enormous materialist. We must

impose the idea of "Serbdom" on the peasant, the idea of unity, of elevation cultural and material. Ceaselessly we must parade before his eyes Serbs and other cultured peoples, we must show him our miseries and troubles, show him all that injures him, yet which he cannot feel.[157]

In 1907, almost seventy years after the appearance of the first nationalist organizations in Bosnia, Risto Radulović similarly urged his fellow activists and "political agents" to take up, once again, the "crucial task of politically instructing the people, to bring the people to political maturity," a prospect long awaited and continually deferred because of the people's seemingly ineradicable "immaturity, credulity, and volatile temperament."[158]

"Everywhere I Go I End Up Disappointed"

Over the course of the long nineteenth century, the process of nation-making around the emergent state of Serbia brought into being a set of relations organized around a few foundational dichotomies: nationalizer—co-national; conscious—unconscious; idealist—materialist. In political practice, the figure of the co-national came to bear a double burden in the projects of nationalization. Self-proclaimed nation-builders both exalted their co-nationals as future patriots who were destined to realize the nation's sacred mission and, at the same time, condemned them as alarmingly ignorant, provincial, superstitious, obsessed with petty affairs, insufficiently patriotic, appearing always a bit disappointing. As one Serbian activist noted after conducting many consciousness-raising forays into Bosnian villages in 1912, "It's funny that everywhere I go I end up disappointed."[159]

In this sense, the Serbian project of nationalizing "our people" actively produced "our strangers": not just Muslims and peasants, but the Serbs (and other nationals) themselves. The recurring disappointments in one's (br)others were not a minor side effect of patriotic activism, but its basic prerequisite. In this national order, just as in the pedagogical order of modern mass education that emerged alongside it during the nineteenth century, teachers and activists continually depicted their target audiences (peasants, students, co-nationals) as incapable, lacking proper knowledge, and thus requiring careful instruction and supervision. As Jacques Rancière has written, "that very incapacity provides the structuring fiction" around which instructional (and nationalizing) practices are established and reinstated: "it is the explicator [or the nationalist] who needs the incapable and not the other way round; it is he who constitutes the incapable as such."[160] For nation-builders, co-nationals thus came to represent the indispensable site of some uneliminatable difference, a remainder that troubles and spurs nationalists to close the gap, to renew the push for nationalization, to instill a stronger sense of patriotism.

Many of these persisting anxieties are certainly brought about by the reality that all people have diverse social allegiances, political priorities, or economic interests that stand besides—and sometimes at odds with—declared nationalist programs. But beyond these conflicts that nation-states constantly negotiate, nationalization also continually produces its own anxieties and uncertain subjects: children and youth. Eugen Weber's assessment that nineteenth-century French peasants' patriotism, "far from instinctive, had to be learned," remains the core premise of national education to this day.[161] Though peasants have faded from the political scene as a distinct social factor, children and youth are always there as uneasy reminders of the impermanent, unfinished nature of nationalization and the discontents it produces.

CHAPTER FOUR

Year X, or 1914?

Throughout the first decade of the twentieth century, nationalist youth activists passionately debated ways to solve the long-simmering political frustrations in Habsburg Bosnia. Many believed that political circumstances in this province were not quite right for revolutionary undertakings, but Miloš Pjanić, a prominent nationalist organizer in Sarajevo high schools, thought otherwise. As he wrote to a colleague in August 1913, Pjanić believed that the people in Bosnia were in "an unfavorable socioeconomic position," but their suffering and "hard life" could also offer important advantages. Comparing the histories of Bohemia and Bosnia, he acknowledged that "it is the Czechs who are in a favorable economic position. They can produce good artists of any kind, good merchants and industrialists." Bosnia lacked comparably renowned figures, Pjanić wrote, but it held a different field of distinction: producing young assassins. The Czechs could not have "produced one Bogdan, or one Luka," he wrote, referring to the Bosnian students who had tried to assassinate the Habsburg governors of Bosnia and Croatia (Žerajić in 1910 and Jukić in 1912, respectively). Situating the Bosnian youth at the forefront of a yet unredeemed national history, Pjanić emphasized the mounting pressures that would worsen the situation and bring about more nationalistic youth in the future: "And then what? Then year X will be born!"[1]

With the benefit of hindsight, it is hard not to read year X as 1914, given the string of assassination attempts and Pjanić's own indirect involvement in the Young Bosnia circles that organized Gavrilo Princip's attack on Franz Ferdinand some ten months later. As Pjanić himself had written in the same letter, "we want either to die in life or to live in death!"[2] In explaining these events many scholars have stressed the radicalization of nationalist sentiments at the turn of the twentieth century; from Italy to Poland to the Ottoman Empire, new political groups extolled struggle, clamored for immediate action, and advocated the primacy of the deed. To account for the rise of Young Bosnia and its 1914 assassination, historians have similarly emphasized political radicalization generated primarily by diplomatic events, especially the 1908 annexation crisis and the 1912–1913 crises accompanying the Balkan Wars. International influences of anarchism usually round out the picture. All this makes for a familiar, self-evident story of mounting radicalization driven by decisive events, pervasive influences, and shadowy conspiracies like the Black Hand society. Leo Pfeffer, the presiding judge-investigator in the trial of Gavrilo Princip, narrated much the same story in his book *The Investigation of the Sarajevo Assassination*, written some two decades after the event. "Starting in 1895, the South Slavic university youth . . . embraced small step-by-step work," the former judge wrote; "but this struggle, which was legal, did not have success. . . . [Events] after the Annexation crisis [of 1908] produced among the youth the belief that they cannot succeed solely through peaceful political action, but that through terrorism they must alert the whole world about the oppressed people" in Habsburg Bosnia. This sequence of radicalization, often framed within the familiar "reformers versus revolutionaries" dichotomy, has been rehearsed and variously retold many times since.[3]

Yet how did this sense of youth radicalization become legible in the first place, appearing so natural and even obvious in narrating "the road to Sarajevo"?[4] What kind of visions of youth and time made the notion of year X possible at all? To explore such issues seriously, we cannot simply resort to one of the favorite charges of historians—anachronism—to show how later actors merely projected their own notions back onto the past, constructing neat teleologies leading to the Sarajevo assassination. Pjanić's fervent prophecies of youth-heroes and year Xs projected into the future, not the past, raise different kinds of issues. Rather than contributing to a narrative culminating in June 28, 1914, Pjanić's focus on "year X" is useful because it poses more troubling questions about the notions of temporality and youth in national histories. How and when did youth in particular come to be linked with violent ruptures in the national future? What kinds of action promised to resolve the mounting tensions—between suffering and liberation, between the activists and the people, between unity and division—that had plagued South Slavic national movements since the early nineteenth century?

These questions are parts of a broader history of youth, nationalism, and modernity, terms that, as Eric Hobsbawm observed, "sometimes became almost interchangeable" in the late nineteenth century.[5] The nationalist attention to "the young"—attention that was conspicuously gendered and heavily directed toward budding male patriots—is well known, with an enormous array of young nationalist organizations (Young Italy, Young Ireland, Young Java, Young Turks, Young Czechs) appearing across different political spectrums in the past two centuries.[6] For Benedict Anderson, youth in the context of European nationalisms had "little in the way of definable sociological contours," standing as a symbol of "dynamism, progress, self-sacrificing idealism, and revolutionary will." Thanks to its obvious associations with the future—"the young are the future of the nation" may well be the generic slogan of every nationalism—youth became a common trope of nation-making. But in colonial contexts outside of Europe, the notion of "youth" also had another, more specific meaning, according to

Anderson; it stood for "the *first* generation in any significant numbers to have acquired a European education, marking them off linguistically and culturally from their parents' generation."[7]

As an Ottoman and then Habsburg imperial province claimed by South Slavic national movements, Bosnia blurs this distinction between colonial and European "types" of nationalist youth. It offers the possibility to chart an alternate genealogy of youth as a central subject of nation-building movements, a subject that exceeds the familiar sociological definitions (e.g., youth as a specific age, class, or educational group) and instead points to recurring nationalist pressures that created a sense of youth as a distinct—and distinctly *heroic*—political element, one capable of violently rupturing and redeeming national history.

The centrality of violence in such understandings of youth perhaps seems unsurprising for a good reason. As Claudia Verhoeven wrote of the rise of terrorism in imperial Russia, the potential for unprecedented action, especially shockingly violent action, pervades modernity; such "violence is promptly communicated to everyone everywhere, and . . . this message guarantees meaning: the act will have happened, and the world will not be the same."[8] To speak of "radicalization" in this context sheds little light on the problem because the possibility of far-reaching, radical violence already prefigures and shapes the modern subject, including the figure of the youth. Indeed, insofar as we can speak of radicalization, perhaps the only genuinely radical development in this history is the naturalization of the assumption that youth and political violence are inseparable.

"It Takes a Very Long Time to Become Young"

Throughout the nineteenth century, nationalists struggled to define "youth" as a category and subject of political work. On the one hand, certain connotations of youth may appear obvious, implying regeneration, energy, dynamism, and other qualities prized by emerging national movements like Young Germany or Young Poland.[9] At the same time, major questions abounded about exactly who was young, what youth as a collectivity stood for, and how was it best expressed and made politically useful to the nation.

It took nineteenth-century Serbian and Croatian national activists decades to develop new terms and ideologies to address youth-related issues; to use Picasso's illuminating turn of phrase, the history of nationalist youth shows that "it takes a very long time to become young."[10] In Serbo-Croatian, the now-ubiquitous term for "youth"—*omladina*—is itself a nineteenth-century nationalist coinage that came to be widely used only since the 1860s. Before then, *omladina* had a different meaning; it was used mostly in the sense of one's progeny and household descendants (what Vuk Karadžić translated as *Nachwuchs* and *suboles* in his 1818 dictionary), whereas the word *mladež* referred to "younger people" in general (something closest to but not quite capturing *die Jugend* and *juventus* in Vuk's translation).[11] Given the lack of a direct, widely adopted term for politically conscious, educated youth, it is thus not surprising that the student nationalist organizations in the 1840s often referred to themselves, for example, as "Young Serbs of the Learned Class." As Teodor Mandić recalled in 1900, "The word '*omladina*' no one knew back then."[12]

This situation changed in the 1860s with the rise of the "United Serbian Youth" (*Ujedinjena omladina srpska*), a union of small literary, student, and singing clubs that rapidly evolved into the most prominent South Slavic youth organization of the nineteenth century. The society was overtly modeled on earlier movements like "Young Italy," but finding appropriate categories for the new collective body of "youth" among the South Slavs took considerable effort and creativity. Several Serbian writers in Vienna, Budapest, and Novi Sad began in the early 1860s to use *omladina* (rather than a variant on the older *mladež*) as a distinct unifying term for their collective patriotic movement; the name was adopted in 1866 by the inaugural assembly that included participants from many Balkan regions, including Bosnia.[13] The attempts to distinguish the nationalist youth as a collectivity that required a distinctive new term raised some bristles. "Using *omladina* instead of *mladež* is incorrect; for when we say *omladina*, we mean all those persons who are under the authority of the household head . . . meaning his sons, daughters-in-law, male and female servants, some of whom are sixty or seventy years old," one Serbian linguist and opponent of neologisms complained in 1863.[14]

The cries for linguistic correctness, however, were already overwhelmed by proliferating references to the more nationalist-tinged concept of the *omladina* collectivity—though these also provoked further questions about what this particular kind of young people meant. (It is important to note that to this day, *omladina* remains a much more widely used term in Serbo-Croatian political discussions of youth than *mladež*.) In an 1862 editorial, the Serbian writer Stanoje Bošković tried to explain the meaning of the *omladina*-type youth as a "moral solidarity," a "life force" that channels the energy of the society, only to pause and consider an objection: "But then you'd ask me again, 'Say, by God, when did this first youth (*prva omladina*) appear, how did it come into being?'" His response offered a brief genealogy that stressed the evolution of education and patriotism—two inseparable fields—into a social force that went well beyond schools and universities. In the 1840s, so the story goes, male Serbian students in gymnasia in the Habsburg Monarchy slowly formed small literary clubs in which "the youth" initially meant "students in higher-level schools, beginning from the first year of taking philosophy." Then within a decade, "the youth" grew and encompassed students from technical schools, eventually encompassing wider "generational" and "genetic nationality." "The youth" in this sense thus finally came to mean any "child of the people," irrespective of education—though still clearly gendered as male: "the sons" of the nation. This collective body was charged with the future task of resolving the many tensions inherent to nation-building: "The youth awakens national consciousness—it mediates between the people and its leaders—it guards the female sex from harmful foreign influences . . . it prepares independently for future work, for the time when it steps onto the public citizenly stage."[15]

Debates over the temporal and political valences of youth continued throughout the 1860s and 1870s, dominating the writings of the *Ujedinjena srpska omladina* movement. The society itself was short lived, officially operating from 1866 to 1872, but historians have long recognized its far-reaching influence. One of its most prominent advocates, the liberal politician Vladimir Jovanović, described in 1866 the many reactions to "the first question [facing the inaugural assembly]: Who is understood by the "entire Serbian youth" (*celokupnom omladinom Srbskom*)? Some participants argued that the quality of youth "belongs to anyone 'who feels young in their heart and soul.'" Another group characterized youth as a "temperament," but others countered that it was a matter of political principles. More commentators joined in, arguing that "one cannot set limits to youth, for youth is eternal," though dependent on active patriotic work. A few were puzzled by these protracted arguments, Jovanović wrote, whereas more participants insisted that "anyone who wants to work [for the national cause] belongs to the youth." As Jovanović reported, "The assembly listened to all this, but it still did not determine *who is meant by the youth.*"

As a leading spokesperson for the movement, Jovanović then proceeded to offer his assessment designed to give direction to this new and yet undetermined force: "Nations, like faces, have their age and development, their young and old days. Today the Serbian people is politically regenerating; *all* of it is young. I think that the Serbian youth, in its desire for national progress, represents the youth of the nation, not the youth of the individual faces. If that is the case, then all of today's Serbdom belongs to the Serbian youth. . . . As I understand it, 'the entire Serbian youth' means the Serbian nationality itself, which is young."[16]

Having fused nation and youth, Vladimir Jovanović laid out a set of tasks for young Serbia to tackle in the near future. Addressing the youth as an explicitly male political force, he urged Serbs "not to be mere admirers of our women, but to be brothers and educators to them. Our women . . . are the future fellow travelers of our lives, the mothers of future Serbs." The task of raising and uplifting the nation as a whole thus fell into the domain of budding "brotherly consciousness" that remained elusive and insufficiently developed. If any single factor was needed for youth to flourish, Jovanović concluded, "Learning and knowledge (*nauka*) is the only means to that end." In other words, only progressive education could guarantee the evolution away from ignorance and insecurity, pointing the way toward freedom and prosperity. "The Serbian youth begins to establish itself on that very foundation! . . . Today from different regions, even from Bosnia itself, reverberate the vehement responses of young Serbian voices: for knowledge and eternal truth."[17] In this interpretation, the youth stood for a general spread of enlightenment, for growth and progress through education and knowledge. "The Serb will finally come out in glorious victory from his battle against the enemies of freedom and progress," Jovanović wrote, only through the transformative power of enlightenment.[18]

However, concurrent with this understanding—in which youth signaled growth through education—another argument cast the battle cries more literally, invoking the youth as an element of decisive and violent action. "In the nineteenth century, a strong fist enables political rights," wrote a contributor to *Young Serbs* (*Mlada Srbadija*) in 1871. In his treatise on "military issues," the author identified "two approaches to preparing for liberation: with intellectual and with physical-material weapons." In the intellectual arsenal, freedom of expression and "education formed weapons as mighty as the gun and cannon, in some circumstances education being even stronger than gunpowder." Serbia's mission, however, went beyond education; its commitment to its "unliberated brothers groaning under the foreigner's yoke . . . requires a military force, a physical arming" capable of "moving the borders of current Serbia to encompass all of our nationality."[19] In the same year, the writer and priest Ničifor Dučić wrote that "young Serbs"—men as well as women—bore an especially heavy responsibility in preparing this future liberatory endeavor. One day "when the Serbian war trumpet sounds," Dučić wrote, "the Balkan peninsula will shake and burst into flames like gunpowder." Serbian women would aid the effort, he wrote; they would keep the household together or, alternatively, they would die fighting alongside Serbian young men destined to become "heroes" (*junaci*) "at the decisive moment."[20]

The long history of national suffering was crucial in inspiring visions of violence and revenge against the Turks, ultimately leading to the complete liberation of the Balkans from Ottoman rule. For all the emphasis on education, the emerging South Slavic youth activism had already been tied to the possibility of massive liberatory violence, first clearly articulated (and later much commemorated) in the 1848 revolutions that captured the imaginations of young poets like Jovan Ilić and Jovan Jovanović Zmaj. Poems about "blood and tears," paeans to "the old Serbian sword," reflections on "the angels of revenge"—all these were common themes filling the volumes of the prominent youth writers of the 1860s.[21] Dedicating a poem to the so-called Serbian Student Legion in 1867, Sima Popović cried out that the "time has arrived for Serbian salvation": "Let inhumanity feel / How the Serb takes revenge on the enemy! / Serbian revenge is wonderful, men!"[22] While the Montenegrin highlanders carried the banner of freedom against the Turks, Bosnia became the *locus classicus* for these dreams of uprising, revenge, and liberation, a terrain saturated with visions of redemptive violence. Laza Kostić, one of the leading poets of the United Serbian Youth, issued a typical 1860s refrain addressing "sad Bosnia": "*Raya*, sad *raya*, when I think of you, / I would not sing songs to you, I would take revenge for you."[23]

Striking even more militant tones in an 1862 poem, the esteemed and well-established poet Đura Jakšić imposed a mission of patriotic sacrifice on the younger Serbian generations: "Fall, brothers! Vanish in blood! / Leave the villages, let the fires burn! / Throw your own children into the flames! / Shake from yourselves your shame and slavery! / Die, brothers! Heroes! Men! / All the world will know of your catastrophe."[24] To be clear, such violent rhetoric—shared by many national movements of the time—cannot be read as a harbinger of violent actions. Instead of providing some simplistic correlation between word and deed, what these languages of violence and youth offer is insight into the prevalent conceptualization of the national struggle as a liberatory and necessarily violent project that would be carried out by extraordinary generations in the future. In context of the 1860s and 1870s, the key targets of such liberatory violence remained "the Turks," who were marked as enemies standing in the way of South Slavic brotherhood.

Taking stock of these developments around the trailblazing United Serbian Youth movement, it becomes apparent that violence was an integral part of the nationalist image of youth and its projected role in achieving South Slavic liberation. The argumentative strands that invoked revenge against the Turks conceived of the youth in an openly revolutionary way, charging them with a generational responsibility for actualizing the future national state in which all co-nationals would be united, liberated, and victorious. It is important to note that for all the differences from Jovanović's education-oriented program, the vision of youth as a revolutionary factor was part and parcel of the same *Omladina* movement that emerged as a distinct political force in the 1860s and 1870s. Vladimir Jovanović himself wrote that Serbia, surrounded "by bayonets and diplomatic intrigues that tear apart our national limbs," desperately needed "cannons and guns as the pillars that uphold" Serbian statehood—as long as such weapons are directed by independent, educated minds. In a state "besieged by enemy armies," he counseled, young Serbs had to enlighten themselves and "seize their task like a man (*muški*), like descendants of a heroic and glorious people!"[25] In other words, reform and revolution, education and heroism, were not competing opposites but were concurrent and mutually related strands of youth activism from the moment of their emergence on the Balkan political scene.

Even when the chance presented itself, however, there was no significant mobilization among the South Slavic youth for action in Ottoman Bosnia. When the Herzegovinian Uprising erupted in 1875 and ushered in three long years of regional conflicts, activists gathered around the United Serbian Youth were caught off guard by the suddenly escalating events. Aside from a few volunteers from Croatia and Serbia in 1876, very few youth leaders from those provinces participated in military actions raging in Bosnia.[26] To be sure, political observers—particularly the Ottoman and Habsburg authorities—suspected and named *Omladina* as a force behind the uprisings, but such assessments were based on the reputation rather than the conduct of the United Serbian Youth, which remained sidelined in the international conflicts (the organization had formally disbanded already by 1872).[27] Even Vaso Pelagić, the principal youth activist in Ottoman Bosnia of the 1860s and 1870s, exercised little influence in his home province after his expulsion from Sarajevo in 1869.[28] Similar lack of militant youth action characterized the entire late Ottoman period in Bosnia. In other words, despite the soaring rhetoric of patriotic sacrifice, there were no major nationalist battles, no youth heroes, and certainly no assassinations of Ottoman governors in Sarajevo.

While many lamented the absence of decisive heroic deeds—"Battles are not fought / No hero can look up to another hero" in "terrible peace" that reigned, complained the poet Zmaj in 1875—this deferral of violence also served a productive purpose in generating new demands for further organization of South Slavic youth.[29] Even as "reality came to kill off all these reveries [of the 1870s] with sad brutality," the imperative of future action remained present thanks to the formative failures of groups like the United Serbian Youth. If the wars of 1875–1878 "could not shake up the numb nerves of the Serbian youth," leading to "the loss of our most beautiful lands, Bosnia and Herzegovina," other kinds of work would have to "save the nation from threatening failure."[30] Once again, ideas of educational associations predominated in the 1880s, envisioning student alliances between Serbia, Croatia, and Bosnia—but a very basic problem remained: there were no comparable European educational institutions in Ottoman Bosnia. To speak of liberal nationalist generations in Bosnia once again returned to the formative problem of defining who exactly was a "young nationalist" and why—or whether at all—"youth" mattered politically.

In that sense, the different *omladina* strategies shared a common understanding of youth as a collective national subject that was both already present and not yet fully actualized. This ambiguous temporal register of youth, a topic of much debate since the middle of the nineteenth century, was crucial in creating a sense of suspense in national history, with youth simultaneously propelling the nation forward toward its destiny but also deferring its fulfillment to other times to come.

Is Youth a Political Factor?: Discovering Liberal-Nationalist Activism in Bosnia

As in neighboring central European and Balkan regions, the early groups of European-educated young men in Bosnia often assumed the role of the nationalist youth—but it is far from obvious which cohorts constituted the "first" generation. Some Bosnian young men, such as Ivan Franjo Jukić, Martin Nedić, and Sima Milutinović Sarajlija, had received secondary levels of European education already by the 1840s. Bosnian Franciscan students in particular formed conspicuous cohorts in schools in Hungary, Croatia, and Italy, and the Đakovo seminary under bishop Strossmayer became a beacon of nationalist activity in the 1860s. Many of these student groups claimed to be trailblazers who sought to bring back to Bosnia the education and passion necessary for a national revival.[31] By the 1890s, however, new student generations that had made their way through the Habsburg education systems seized—yet again—the mantle of being the "first" generation of educated young Bosnians to fulfill their patriotic duty. This is not to mention the various youth organizations in Croatia and Serbia that, at various points since the 1840s, made similar claims to having pioneered educational missions into Bosnia.

In addition to problematizing the notion of the "first" generation, the succession of various youth interests in Bosnia calls attention to the changing political and educational conditions in this province. Imperial officials, both Ottoman and Habsburg, keenly monitored the nationalist activities in Bosnia, paying special attention to schools and publications. The Ottoman Tanzimat reforms kept in place the separate confessional school systems (Muslim, Catholic, Jewish, and Orthodox), but also instructed regional officials to suppress nationalist organizations in Bosnia. In education, this meant an attempt (never fully realized) to introduce new Ottoman high schools and a sustained effort to oversee teacher appointments and publications in the province in the 1860s. These policies resulted mainly in the confiscation of "inappropriate" publications and expulsion of anti-Ottoman, nationalist teachers like Vaso Pelagić.[32]

However, after the Ottoman collapse and the establishment of Habsburg authority in 1878, Austro-Hungarian officials went to even greater lengths to reform educational venues in the province. The earliest assessments of the political situation in Bosnia already called attention to *omladina* and young men in general as an especially volatile political factor. One prominent Habsburg diplomat wrote in 1878 to Minister Andrássy that, given the influence of the United Serbian Youth in Serbia itself, "We can never allow that a similar path is trod in Bosnia. . . . We must ensure that the *Omladina* with its Pan-Slavist and radical rabble-rousing has no ground in Bosnia and Herzegovina."[33] Austro-Hungarian authorities were thus primed not only to prevent *Omladina*-type organizations from appearing in Bosnia but also to view any kind of political agitation among the regional youth with considerable caution.

The Habsburg development of an extensive educational system in Bosnia proceeded steadily in the late nineteenth century with two key aims in mind: first, to tightly integrate the newly acquired region into the Habsburg state as a whole; and second, to foster in the long term an element of stability and loyalty in a province rocked by uprisings in the past, especially in the 1870s and early 1880s. This Austro-Hungarian project brought the older confessional educational realms under governmental supervision, leaving Orthodox, Catholic, Muslim, and Jewish schools in place while asserting the state as the final arbiter of any educational disputes (especially over the selection of teachers and curricula). Moreover, new state-sponsored schools began to provide all levels of primary and secondary education; the first gymnasium was established in Sarajevo already in 1879, followed by different kinds of high schools throughout the province. This system of extending new government-sponsored schools enabled a close surveillance of both teacher and student activities. When it came to university-level education, however, the Habsburg authorities decided not to open a university in Bosnia itself. This constraint, aiming at integrating Bosnian education into the Habsburg state as a whole, thus ensured that local youth would have to leave their home province for the highest levels of education, departing to other cities within the Monarchy (Prague, Zagreb, Vienna, Graz, and Innsbrück), or often to Istanbul and Belgrade outside of it.[34]

By 1900, this systematic investment in education produced mixed results in Bosnia. As the high-ranking official Lajos Thallóczy wrote in a major governmental report on education in Bosnia (1903–1904), many structural changes had rendered the once wild "Turkish Bosnia" into a typical Habsburg province by 1900. Cities, railroads, and industries grew tremendously; the capital Sarajevo developed visibly. Alongside fashionable stores and cafés, new "bookshops appear where the youth, just as in Vienna and Budapest, can buy tasteful reading as well as French pornographic writings translated into a corrupted Croatian." Education was especially important in this "epoch of tutelage (*Bevormundung*), in which the [Bosnian] population willingly follows its foreign administration and acquiesces itself to its destiny." According to Thallóczy, this kind of integration meant that "those boys who experienced the occupation as children . . . got used to relations with the monarchy and . . . discovered themselves as native intelligentsia, which received Western European ideas in the raw and began to think in its own way."[35] Among those born during the Habsburg period, a small but steadily increasing number of Bosnian youth completed education in new gymnasia (the most elite of the provincial high schools), enrolling over 2,300 students annually by the 1910s.[36] Budding and usually short-lived student associations appeared in Sarajevo, Tuzla, Banja Luka, and Mostar.[37] University education, however, still remained a rarity pursued largely by those who either earned scholarships or were funded by their families, often from merchant, artisan, and other commercial backgrounds.

If the paths of these Bosnian students followed certain patterns, their political engagements are far more complicated to explain. In rapidly expanding cities across Europe, they were likely to encounter a wide array of fin de siècle movements, including socialist, pacifist, authoritarian, anarchist, and feminist. But among these, nationally inflected views were increasingly permeating all sorts of cultural and political commitments, especially ones held by schoolteachers themselves. The Croatian and Serbian movements had already laid their claims on the province, developing networks and literatures well before the Habsburg occupation, the dedicated Habsburg official Thallóczy admitted in 1904. It was thus not surprising that many middle schools after 1878 were staffed by teachers mostly from Croatia, who "spread the neo-Croatian historical views" to "hitherto completely impartial" Bosnians, particularly Muslims; teachers with Serbian nationalist leanings acted similarly. Education in that context served to expose Bosnian students to nationalist views rather than shield them from such polemics. Students who were not swayed in Bosnia often went on to regional cities like Zagreb, Graz, and Prague, where divisive "hypernational turmoil" initiated them into nationalist arguments.[38] For all the official Habsburg optimism about progress in Bosnia, troubling signs of youth discontent appeared conspicuous. In Thallóczy's words, some among "this young generation started to perceive a barrier to their own progress in the very order constructed by us. This has been the psychological motive of the estrangement in the cities between the locals and the representatives of our administration since 1900."[39]

In fact, several events at the beginning of the twentieth century propelled the small number of university-educated Bosnian youth into the political spotlight. The controversy around the so-called Academic Youth Memorandum of 1901 illustrates how certain nationalist strands of youth activism became topics of major public debates. In May that year, some twenty university students in Vienna, calling themselves the "Serbian Academic Youth of Bosnia and Herzegovina," published an open letter to the Austro-Hungarian delegations. Its members were mostly aged eighteen to twenty-five and included the budding writer Petar Kočić and the aspiring politicians Vasilj Grđić and Milan Srškić. The statement sharply criticized Habsburg rule in Bosnia, lambasting Governor Kállay and restrictions on the press, the curtailing of religious autonomy for Orthodox and Muslim Bosnians, the management of the agrarian tensions, and the suppression of nationalist sentiments among the youth. Printed in both Serbo-Croatian and German, the statement made extensive comparisons to the Ottoman period, when "unbridled Turkish officials and thugs were brutal, but at least chivalrous and valiant at that, whereas the current [Habsburg government] is deceitful and lacks the latter qualities." In demanding immediate representation, the Academic Youth Memorandum wanted "the Austro-Hungarian politicians to take note of the historical fact that the almighty Ottoman Empire . . . lost most of its prestige because it did not satisfy the Serbian people, especially in Bosnia."[40]

The issuing of the Memorandum raised a number of debates in Bosnia. Was this dramatic statement just another expression of the existing nationalist factions, or was there something genuinely new in the announcement of the Academic Youth? Was it worthwhile, for either Habsburg authorities or South Slavic nation-builders, to engage with usually short-lived student groups? Was youth a political factor at all? Answers were far from clear. Among the Bosnian Serb politicians, reactions to the Youth Memorandum were initially critical. "They don't care much here for the student movement," wrote one Serbian observer in Sarajevo in 1901. "People say: these are young people who still cannot have any significance in diplomacy and in the governing of Bosnia." Others were more blunt, saying, "I do not like that these pupils are writing memoranda. . . . These youth cannot be independent in any way," as they were completely reliant on their parents or the Habsburg government for their scholarships.[41] This was not an isolated view. Articles in the Serbian newspaper *Naš život* in 1906 similarly lamented the inadequacies of student activists, who were reportedly prone to "rambling and foolish speeches, causing noise and division among the people." Faced with tavern incidents in Banja Luka, where a certain *omladinac* and lawyer "enjoyed the ruckus he caused," the newspaper wrote: "We lay our hopes in the youth, but if youth should turn out like this, our hoping is in vain."[42] Even members of the revolutionarily minded societies in Belgrade were skeptical about the potential of Bosnian youth. In 1908, the Belgrade-based organizer Božo Marković commented that these "are young, inexperienced people who cannot judge and assess everything correctly. When it becomes necessary to show that they are Serbs, then we will see what they are like."[43]

Doubts over the political potential of youth were also consuming the South Slavic student societies themselves. An extensive review of South Slavic student organizations in Vienna appeared in the Prague-based youth journal *Novo Doba* in 1898. For too many students, the author complained, "the 'oppositional perspectives' of our studentdom" are "mere stepping stones that some politicians skillfully use to climb to popularity." The students "usually had either stipends or wealth" and formed patriotic clubs so that they could socialize or pass their days in Vienna. In this context, the real "center of gravity for most students" was "in pubs, in day and nighttime taverns." It was no wonder, the nationalist writer charged, "that [Habsburg governors] Khuens and Kállays send hundreds of Croatian youth each year into such circumstances, for they know very well what they are doing."[44] A Serbian commentator similarly charged that "almost all Bosnian youth are educated in higher German schools in Vienna and Graz . . . , where they grow distant from their nationality."[45]

But as the 1901 Memorandum affair demonstrated, some Bosnian youth in Vienna were in fact passionately nationalistic and eager to get involved in political debates. The Habsburg administration was keen to determine whether these students acted on their own or according to instructions of older opposition leaders like Gliša Jeftanović. Although some Serbian politicians in Sarajevo apparently knew of the intent, they were still surprised by the students' sudden actions.[46] Habsburg officials took a longer view, placing the Memorandum in a series of events, like the congress of young journalists in Dubrovnik in 1900, that showed the independent political ambitions of the regional youth. "This 'success' has impressed the young people and may have strengthened in them the flattering idea that they are, or could become, an important factor in the national movement."[47]

The most significant outcome of the 1901 Memorandum affair was the consolidation of certain liberal-nationalist understandings of youth as a distinct political force in its own right, a crystallization of direction that occurred amid debates over the meanings of "youth." In 1902, several groups of Bosnian university students from Prague, Zagreb, Vienna, and Graz—including a few of the signatories of the first Memorandum, namely, Vasilj Grđić and Petar Kočić—convened a series of meetings in Zagreb to discuss "the role of the youth in contemporary social questions: Can youth, by its own nature, participate in work of any practical political and social meaning? Can the immature and unfinished factors operate in undertakings where reliable results are demanded?" The unsigned statement then presented two contrasting answers. One approach, labeled "the materialistic, conservative view," argued that youth is a "reservoir of strength" that will only "in mature years" be useful to actual social progress. From this perspective, it followed that "youth has no right to engage in social, practical work until accumulated years and strength authorize it. But there is another view," the statement continued, founded on "the ideal life of youth":

> In this theory, youth is all-powerful. It has the right to meddle into everything, to give tone to everything, to criticize everything, to correct everything, to re-touch everything, to dispute everything. It has the right to give to all forms of life their ideal shape. In the form of youth the human race spends its most idealistic age. Human ideals: absolute freedom, equality, equal rights, sympathy, forgiveness, self-sacrifice, etc., like pride and dignity of the human race; these are by rule a manifestation of the life of youth. Undoubtedly, humanity without these ideals would be just a bunch of savages.[48]

In the practical circumstances of Habsburg Bosnia, this "ideal life of youth" required educational preparation—young men first had to "pass through various fires" of provincial schooling—and entailed a kind of liberal-nationalist activism. Like the *omladina* organizations of the late nineteenth century, these calls for action combined references to "dignity of the human race" and "forgiveness" with commitment to "struggle" and "self-sacrifice" on behalf of the Serbian nation. After more debates, the students' 1902 vision of "ideal youth" in Bosnia boiled to a few key principles.[49] In short: "As progressive, young [men], they want greater freedoms: of speech, press, and association. Convinced in the moral strength and natural brightness of their people, they want to preserve the language, national characteristics, tradition, Serbian schools." Finally, "they want to organize the people economically, to develop and elevate it. As long as the [Habsburg] government stands as an obstacle against the work and progress of the Serbian people, we will carry on our struggle."[50]

This was a fairly standard liberal-nationalist platform, combining appeals for liberalization of the public sphere (especially by lifting Habsburg censorship) with assertions of national superiority of one's own particular nation. Insofar as it was an "ideal," this program could be described as an idealized condensation of some basic values of nineteenth-century liberal nationalism: the importance of education, the primacy of national culture over local arguments, the need for patient organization, and so on. When it came to the ambitious vision of youth building a new nation-state, almost all members of the gathered Bosnian students agreed, "Let's be courageous and admit to ourselves that we should disband until another, better, readier generation comes, which will lead this cause differently." In the meantime, "the youth will be an element of work and only work, and not of the little projects of noise-makers and 'memorandumers.'"[51]

This was a common fin de siècle sentiment shared by other South Slavic youth organizations. "We little [nations] love to complain that might is always stronger than right," a Croatian youth journal editorial wrote in 1898. In a world ruled as much by ideas as by weapons, it continued, "we younger people must go forth on a new path, creating a new age for the people" through knowledge, organization, and steady work.[52] Report from a 1903 regional convention of Serbian youth held in Karlovci noted that unlike in earlier meetings, where discussions of active intervention predominated, "the ruling principle among Serbs now is: not to concern oneself with politics, but to strengthen the economic" and "literary fields."[53] Since its founding in 1906, the motto of the prominent Bosnian Serb society *Prosvjeta* (*Education*) expressed concisely this gradualist sentiment: "Grain by grain, bread is made; stone by stone, a palace."[54] The support of prominent Young Czech leaders like Tomáš Masaryk greatly strengthened the commitment to this steady, gradualist, liberal-nationalist work among broad swaths of university-educated youth from Bosnia, Croatia, and Serbia.[55]

In Bosnia, Muslims were marked as outsiders in the emergence of this kind of nationalist youth in several ways. As most Bosnian Muslims initially avoided attending Habsburg schools, which were seen as "Christian," the growing provincial cohorts in secondary and higher education tended to be composed mostly of Catholic and Orthodox students. This institutional disparity, which meant that educated Muslims often attended different schools than their Serbian and Croatian counterparts, posed a great obstacle for Serbian and Croatian efforts to mobilize this potential constituency in Bosnia.[56] Moreover, the liberal-nationalist commitment to gradualist accomplishment also meant that there was no need for sudden campaigns to incorporate Muslim students into Serbian-Croatian circles immediately. When some

Serbian patriots expressed the desire for a "Muslim representative" to sign the Youth Memoranda of 1901–1902, a discussion ensued about the lack of qualified Bosnian Muslim nationalists. Even when some suitable candidates were found in Vienna ("Šefkija Gluhić and a few others"), the more insistent Serbian nationalists were put off by their reluctance to openly declare themselves "Serbs" and not simply "youth from Bosnia-Herzegovina." The general opinion was that there was no need to rush; as one Serbian patriot stated in 1902, "One should be patient, there will eventually come a time in our circles when there will be honest Serb Muslims."[57] By the time that Young Bosnia emerged as a movement some ten years later, it included several Bosnian Muslim members in its ranks.[58]

Thus the question that emerged at the turn of the century in Bosnia—is the educated youth (*omladina*) a factor of any political relevance?—was answered by a consensus that youth was in fact a new formation with a decidedly liberal-nationalist valence. A large part of the significance of this youth came precisely from its educational background; in a society where over 85 percent of the total population did not attend any kind of school around 1900, the relatively rapid appearance of native, young, and highly-educated men signaled the emergence of a new constituency with a great amount of cultural—if not yet political—capital.[59] In this light, it is not surprising that the more established Serbian and Croatian opposition leaders (usually from merchant or religious backgrounds) viewed the return of Bosnian university cohorts from central European cities with both approbation and suspicion. These young men, the likes of Vasilj Grđić, were eager to prove their nationalist credentials, but their activism envisioned a national future built through steady liberalization and nationalization of the public sphere.[60] The vision of a full-fledged, united, and powerful nation-state (though certainly present as a guiding idea) was seemingly deferred to other, "better, readier generations" that would be up to the task of actualizing the national future.

Habsburg Anxieties over Bosnian Youth

In the first four decades of Habsburg rule in Bosnia, imperial officials tracked all kinds of provincial political actors, including students, ranging from "Croatian radicals" to Serbian academic organizers to budding "Muslim *Omladinsten*." In general, they did so because of a long-standing imperial commitment to monitoring "state-threatening" (*staatsgefährlich*) elements, which included socialist, nationalist, anarchist, and other revolutionary causes; similar governmental practices existed in France, Germany, and Russia.[61] The provincial officials registered various disturbances, in most cases preferring not to take immediate action unless the incidents were severe or criminal; instead, they usually filed away the reports and generated references for later investigations. The archives of the Habsburg administration, filled with thousands of reports on local "agitations" and "agitators," bear witness to the intertwined nationalist and imperial anxieties over youth in Bosnia.

Political concerns and suspicions, however, were not uniformly acted on in the Austro-Hungarian governmental apparatus. At certain times, particularly after major regional conflicts or diplomatic crises, the Austro-Hungarian administration attempted to tighten its control over provincial politics, often encouraging repressive measures against the most outspoken nationalist critics. At other times, however, the imperative of reform and liberalization officially mandated more permissive policies and significantly scaled down the surveillance apparatus in Bosnia, especially after the death of minister Kállay in 1903 and again after the formal annexation of Bosnia in 1908. As the Habsburg government loosened or eliminated numerous restrictions in the first decade and a half of the twentieth century, there was generally much less censorship and many more venues for political and cultural organization in the province. Nonetheless, some basic attitudes—ranging from intense alarm over nationalist agitation to indifference and nonintervention—persisted. In other words, Habsburg attitudes toward Bosnian youth politics are not a simple story of mounting imperial repressions, or an equally straightforward story of decreasing anxieties. Instead, different attitudes toward youth kept reappearing, shaped by a variety of factors—especially by the kind of information obtained by government surveillance and a network of local informants—and based on a foundational underlying premise: that youth in Bosnia were a volatile element with the potential for violent, state-threatening action.

In a way, aspects of this premise were already present in policies implemented immediately after the 1878 occupation. In the 1880s and the 1890s, heavy policing of anti-Habsburg expressions went on in the provincial press, classrooms, and even bars and coffeehouses. Serbian nationalism was singled out as an especially important issue. The Austro-Hungarian government considered Serbian nationalist movements, particularly their irredentist claims on Bosnia and Herzegovina, to be "state-threatening" forces possibly inciting regional uprisings and wars (even in periods when the Serbian government was officially conciliatory toward Austria-Hungary).[62] In terms of youth politics, this general vigilance entailed "strict control" over Muslim and Orthodox schools in order to prevent "public agitation" among students as well as teachers.[63]

But the government's initial reactions to student incidents—like the singing of nationalist songs in school—often overstated their case, a fact that Thallóczy observed in his formal assessment of Bosnian education in 1904. As he bluntly wrote to his Habsburg government colleagues: "We did not need to fear the state-threatening intention of our high schools' first generation of political children." When it came to the liberal-nationalist politics of student groups, Thallóczy wrote, the government should recognize such arguments as brash expressions of Bosnian youth's "immaturity" and "childishness," but should *not* view them as a sign of some "state-threatening" activity.[64]

In fact, Habsburg policies gradually allowed for more formal recognition of youth patriotic organizations after Kallay's departure in 1903. Cultural journals and new social clubs dedicated to the youth appeared across Bosnia. The *Sokol* organizations—combining group physical exercises with patriotic instruction for boys and later girls—became prominent, with Serbian, Croatian, and Muslim chapters opening across Bosnia by 1910s. Established originally in the Czech context in the 1890s, the *Sokol* movement emphasized discipline and training of youth collectivities, thus opening new possibilities for group action and physical expression of patriotism. Habsburg officials in Bosnia were willing to recognize such movements as long as they stayed within the accepted frame of Austro-Hungarian politics.[65] By 1914, even clubs like the Serbo-Croatian Nationalist Youth were not repressed, but were officially registered as civil associations in Sarajevo.[66]

However, if some Habsburg administrators took a broad view of youth as a benign political element, other government officials remained alert to surveillance reports they continued to receive throughout 1900s. Following the growth of irredentist forces in Serbia after 1903 — when the Karađorđevićes toppled the Obrenović dynasty and opened the doors for a much more nationalistic public sphere—surveillance reports began to state that some Bosnian students sought out connections with new Serbian revolutionary groups. Moreover, certain individuals associated with this rise of militant projects in Serbia were the same student leaders who featured as the signatories of the liberal-nationalist Academic Youth Memorandum or as participants in other liberal organizations. Thanks to the disparate reports they received and the stories they made out of them, many Habsburg officials found themselves immersed in a political landscape in which it was difficult, even impossible, to distinguish between liberal (supposedly harmless) and extremist (supposedly state-threatening) youth.

The case of Petar Kočić is telling in this regard. Kočić was one of the more prominent contributors to student societies in Vienna, a signatory of the 1901 Youth Memorandum who was deeply committed to organizing what appeared to be the liberal-nationalist youth societies. In 1905, however, Habsburg surveillance following him stated that Kočić began to secretly meet with militarily minded nationalist organizations in Belgrade. According to Austro-Hungarian intelligence, a so-called Bosnian-Herzegovinian Committee had already been clandestinely organized in Belgrade, apparently without the Serbian government's direct knowledge, for the purpose of "liberating Bosnia" and "uniting it with Serbia." The self-appointed committee was composed of more than forty members, mostly either active or former Serbian military officers and some Bosnian university students, including Kočić. Their initial plans revolved around the possibility of a strategic uprising in Bosnia or in Sandžak, with the committee discussing how to best offer training and weapons. According to informant notes, proposals by Petar Kočić and by Major Paunović specifically called for greater recruitment of the "academic youth from Bosnia" in actions that included "armed attacks" and "killing of some [government] advisers and chiefs."[67] In another meeting, Kočić was said to have emphatically stressed the primacy of students in such revolutionary undertakings since "they would be our strongest pillar": "It is my view that we must gain for our movement first our students, then the artisans in towns, and only then the peasants in villages. With the peasants it will be easy. Their discontent is known to you. You just have to say, there won't be any agrarian taxes, and done." Kočić's experience with peasants proved otherwise (in 1910 he found it very difficult to lead their movement), but his new political direction remained oriented primarily toward youth as an "element that will spare neither effort nor cost" for openly violent patriotic action.[68]

The Habsburg officials' responses are revealing of the imperial procedures, assumptions, and actions regarding Bosnian youth and the possibility of its organized violent action. Before passing on the report to authorities in Vienna, the Sarajevo official Wenzel Černy qualified the reports with cautionary remarks about the informants' notes. Government services ensured that the two principal sources (nicknamed Pobrić and Klein) worked independently and did not know each other; their reports on the "Bosnian Committee" in fact diverged on certain points, "giving different names" and details in some instances. In light of the serious claims and apparent discrepancies, Černy wrote, "I confess that I accepted the messages with a certain reserve," noting the limited, subjective perspectives of the informers and "finding it necessary to research such an important issue even further." The overall investigation, which included at least five separate sources, confirmed the overall report concerning Serbian plans and Kočić's increasingly vocal advocacy of violence. In Černy's assessment, there were some disconcerting developments here, though in general, the government had no great reason to seriously fear the "Bosnian Committee"; its actions were seen as unlikely and, even if carried out, would undoubtedly amount to "a fiasco" (the nationalist forces were deemed to be too weak and the Habsburg position was assessed as very strong). Moreover, unless the government obtained "more accurate information and something tangible in its hands," there was "hardly anything that could be done against" Kočić and his associates.[69]

Yet this qualified 1905 report, which made its way to high-ranking authorities, was also peppered with dramatic claims illustrating a crucial Habsburg assumption: that Bosnian youth was to be linked, sooner or later, with violent anti-imperial action. For instance, though Černy dismissed conflict as practically impossible at that point, he added that "the possibility of success of individual assassinations should not be disregarded." When it came to Kočić, the government was not only able to construct a detailed profile based on prior surveillance—nationalist since high school, likes to play demagogue, passionate card player, taught in Macedonia, recently married, etc. — but to also issue specific recommendations for further supervision of his activities and "conspirators" (*Verschwörer*). Most important, reports after 1905 increasingly wrote about youth in Bosnia as a volatile and easily radicalized collective subject. In Černy's words, "The turbulent, so inclined-to-conspiracies element of the local intelligence, *especially among the university students* . . . will be difficult to contain within the limits of a natural, peaceful evolution if the violent and subversive ideas should once pass into their flesh and blood."[70]

The fact that Kočić subsequently intensified his rhetoric and remained active in Belgrade revolutionary circles only deepened the government's suspicion that "criminal" conspiracies were afoot in Bosnia. In fact, Kočić held up his reputation as one of the most incendiary politicians of his time, continuing to publicly defy Habsburg restriction with his newspaper *Homeland (Otadžbina)*. In 1908, he went to even greater lengths, publishing a front-page article that urged Serbs to declare *War on the Austrians* [*Švabe*] and bring down the Habsburg state in a massive conflict "between the Yugoslav tribe and the conquering German element." Bosnia, where "the air smells mightily like gunpowder," was singled out as the epicenter of this struggle. The fact that Kočić's invocation of war occurred several months before the official proclamation of the Habsburg annexation of Bosnia in 1908 contributed to the tense political atmosphere of the time. Charged with incitement to violence, Kočić was tried, jailed, and released by the end of 1909 (there were no physically violent incidents and the newspaper issue was confiscated before public distribution).[71] Seen in a broader context, what this case reveals is not just Kočić's escalating rhetoric, but also the growing fears of youth and violence in the Habsburg administration's circles.

On the one hand, the imperial officials often assumed that "extremist" nationalists were a very small minority on the Bosnian political landscape. In 1906, for example, Kočić was one of four publicists (the "ultra-Croatian" Šegvić and Barbić alongside the "ultra-Serbian" Kočić and Kobasica) that the government wanted to exile from Bosnia because they had a "pronounced tendency to cause political putsches" and "sought to infuse the poison of aggressive incitement among the population and the students." But the report also noted that "the majority of the public, especially the Muslims, the quiet Croats, and the conservative Serbs had little to do with [their] affairs," a situation that the imperial government found reassuring.[72] Yet only a year later, a high-ranking Habsburg official filed another report about Kočić, now asserting that "the chauvinistic intrigues" of his publications could "have actually dangerous consequences, stemming in particular from their aggressive agitation and terrorism" (*die Hetzereien und der Terrorismus*) aimed at mobilizing "the uncomprehending, blindly following local people."[73] In reality, Kočić (like other militant nationalists) was never so popular as to merit such sweeping descriptions — his publications and his runs at political office always fell short of the more moderate nationalist rivals—but in the eyes of the imperial government, "radical" elements loomed as an insidious force threatening to quickly consume much of Bosnia's youth.

The case of Vasilj Grđić illustrates just how broadly the imperial officials interpreted—and often criminalized—some nationalist activities in Bosnia. Born in 1875, Vasilj Grđić grew up in Bosnia-Herzegovina during the Habsburg period, graduating from a Sarajevo gymnasium in 1898 and then going on to university studies in Vienna and Graz. It was there that his name featured as one of the signatories of the 1901 Academic Youth Memorandum, though Habsburg authorities already registered his "political intolerance" in high school; in fact, imperial officials continued to cite throughout his adult life an incident in which Grđić publicly "sang forbidden [nationalist] songs" as a teenage gymnasium student. Later acting as the head editors of the main liberal-opposition newspaper *The Serbian Word* (*Srpska riječ*), Vasilj and his brother Stjepan frequently got into arguments with imperial censors keen to curb their rhetoric, usually by imposing various restrictions on public speech. In a series of heated disputes over unpaid fines and detained contributors in 1905, Grđić became very agitated in the commissar's office, finally "shaking his clenched fist against the commissar and shouting as loud as he could—'Maxim Gorky ignited all of Russia!'—and then stormed out." The commissar gathered witnesses and charged Grđić with disturbing the peace, resulting in a jail sentence of eight days.

Most important, following "the Gorky incident" the commissar's report concluded that Grđić's "repeat offenses" demonstrated "a terrorist tendency (*terroristische Tendenz*) of the editorial staff members . . . that passes into brutal excesses against the authorities."[74] In turn, Grđić and fellow Serbian journalists wrote scathing condemnations of the Habsburg government, repeatedly calling Grđić's arrest "an assassination attempt (*atentat*) on the honor of the Serbian people."[75] The escalating charges, increasingly invoking "terrorist tendencies" and "assassination attempts" during and after 1905, bound the imperial and nationalist opponents into a kind of mutually exacerbating antagonism. The imperial officials continued to depict Grđić as a danger to peace—especially to youth—while Grđić persevered in his blistering rhetorical attacks on the Habsburg government as a publicist and, a few years later, as an elected member of the Bosnian provincial parliament. Grđić, however, still participated squarely within the Habsburg political spectrum, generally following the liberal political and electoral procedures during his career. Far from acting as a fin de siècle "terrorist" in practice—his commitment to Serbian nationalism showed little interest in causes like anarchism—Grđić was nonetheless often treated by Habsburg officials as a subject suspiciously close to revolutionary activities.[76] Amid attempts to co-opt rather than antagonize the Serbian nationalist leadership after 1908, the Austro-Hungarian administration largely ceased its open harassment of Grđić, but more files on his activities were still amassed in the subsequent years. After the 1914 assassination, the unbridled wartime Habsburg prosecution resurrected his entire case in 1915–1916, initially seeking the death penalty for Vasilj Grđić on charges of highest treason despite no evidence that Grđić was involved in the assassination.[77]

The broader and crucial point of these developments was that the Habsburg administration played a pivotal role in constructing Bosnian youth as an unstable — and possibly violent — political subject. In policy directives, the Austro-Hungarian authorities remained most concerned about the already established political factors: the known opposition leaders as well as the Serbian state, its diplomacy and its army. Youth was often declared to be too immature to be effective politically, yet in administrative practice, the surveillance of student societies took up substantial Habsburg energy and generated considerable anxiety. "The spirit and mind of school youth everywhere is a delicate plant that must be protected from pernicious influences," wrote a government official in 1905 in response to nationalist complaints about the lack of patriotic education. This was the standard Habsburg advice in Bosnia, stressing the importance of comprehensive schooling that would create cultural uplift, ward off "excessive" tendencies, and thus produce "loyal citizens of the land."[78]

But as these terms themselves already suggested, the other side of this coin fearfully anticipated that proper education could fail and that subversive tendencies could run wild, producing a harmful and far-reaching political element within Bosnia. Harsher measures like summary arrests seemed useless practically and difficult to justify legally; as one government informant wrote about conspiracy networks in 1908, "I have to tell you that in Belgrade, as in Zagreb, the same intention and aim of propaganda holds steady . . . for it should not be forgotten that the arrested ones are just tails, while the heads work freely in Belgrade and Zagreb."[79] In these projections, the ebbing and flowing Habsburg anxieties coincided with the Serbian (and increasingly Yugoslav) visions of Bosnian youth as agents central to the ruination of the Austro-Hungarian state and the emergence of a new South Slavic political formation.

The Heroic Youth: Violence, Time, and the National Future

For all the concern over nationalist agitation among Bosnian youth, Habsburg authorities were nonetheless never so consumed with anxiety as to see conspiracies in any incidents — even violent ones — among the provincial students. In fact, it was not the Austro-Hungarian officials but the emerging nationalist spokesmen who began to interpret instances of youth violence in a novel way: as foreshadowings of future heroism.

Divergent interpretations of the Žerajić case illustrate the rise of new visions of violence carried out by the Bosnian youth. On June 15, 1910,

Bogdan Žerajić, a twenty-four-year-old law student from Herzegovina, tried to assassinate the Habsburg governor of Bosnia, Marijan Varešanin. Waiting for the governor to emerge after an official public reception, Žerajić fired several gunshots at Varešanin, missed his target, and then killed himself. The event, needless to say, caused enormous commotion. Amid swirling rumors of conspiracies, the Habsburg government carried out an extensive undercover investigation, conducting interviews, excavating local police records, and gathering lengthy reports from several Bosnian towns as well as regional cities.

Remarkably for an administration concerned with the threat of youth violence, the official Habsburg investigation concluded that there was no great conspiracy. The investigators' verdicts, made in a series of reports in the fall of 1910, stated their case clearly: "According to the results of the investigation, conducted through research and confiscations in Sarajevo, Slavonski Brod, Zagreb, Vienna, Zemun, Nevesinje, as well as the known anarchist centers in Europe, [confirmed] lastly by the declarations of informants in Croatia and Serbia, it can be assumed with all probability that Žerajić had no accomplices." With no evidence of advanced planning, the assassination was found to have "resulted from the perverse disposition and anarchist outlook of the perpetrator."[80]

This is not to say that the Austro-Hungarian investigators saw the 1910 assassination attempt as apolitical or unimportant. To the contrary, the investigation uncovered many worrisome developments that connected Žerajić to several overlapping political networks. The Habsburg officials deeply researched the contents of Žerajić's pockets and apartment belongings, focusing on a few brief, partly illegible letters, train ticket stubs, books, and puzzling insignia. Constructing several stories out of this tortuous, disjointed set of clues, the Austrian authorities arrested the Graz university student Dušan Todović, a self-declared anarchist who knew Žerajić, possessed the same books and insignia (copied from a Kropotkin book cover), and was known to have connections with Belgrade groups like "Slovenski jug."[81] Most disturbingly, there was the possibility that Žerajić—or another person—could have considered an attempt on the life of the emperor Franz Joseph himself during his tour of Bosnia earlier in 1910. The visit passed without incidents, but fears of possible attacks remained. Žerajić personally knew several nationalist figures, reportedly meeting with the prominent leader Vasilj Grđić within two weeks before the Varešanin assassination. Government intelligence raised an unconfirmed possibility that several individuals may have known of planned attacks, but the speculative, unsubstantiated informant reports were taken only as signs that such persons—including Grđić—should be "under constant and inconspicuous surveillance."[82]

Overall, then, the Habsburg investigation of the Žerajić case resulted primarily in heightened government scrutiny of both the emerging anarchist individuals and the already noted nationalist leaders. In that sense, for all the alarming rumors and threats of violence that linked Bosnia to anarchist activity across Europe, the investigation's conclusions were somewhat comforting for the provincial administration: here was a marginal, extremist individual whose life and act were largely isolated and condemned by the Bosnian public.[83] Just months before the assassination attempt, one district report from Nevesinje (Žerajić's hometown) stated: "His influence is negligible, as he has no leading role here."[84] By the end of 1910, the Habsburg authorities considered the Žerajić case closed. Two years later, government reports noted "with disgust" some attempts at the glorification of Žerajić, but Habsburg officials described such efforts as aberrations and stressed that "youth gatherings and assemblies should not be feared"; most student societies were not involved in violent causes and many appeared to be not interested in politics at all.[85]

In retrospect, how Žerajić became the pivotal figure for the nationalist youth seems obvious: other nationalists made him a "hero" (*junak* or *heroj* in Serbo-Croatian parlance). In most interpretations, this notion of "hero" principally connotes an example, a model from the past to be emulated and revered. There is no shortage of such canonization of heroes in South Slavic history. In the twentieth century, many folkloric characters—especially the *hajduk*s and *uskok*s (outlaws and bandits) often memorialized as freedom fighters—became archetypal figures for later political actors seeking to position themselves as inheritors of hallowed national traditions.[86] Assassinations were not only inserted into such lineages but also became inspirations for more assassinations. In the 1960s, the historian Vladimir Dedijer made an especially influential argument about the folk "tradition of tyrannicide" that allegedly led Bogdan Žerajić, Gavrilo Princip, and other Bosnian activists to carry out assassinations at the turn of the century.[87]

Yet the idiom of heroism among fin de siècle nationalist youth was more peculiar and more interesting than the relatively straightforward notion of archetypal precedent. This is the case for two basic reasons. In the first place, the folkloric repertoire of heroism, long viewed as a repository of overwhelmingly positive images of heroes (*junaci*), is far more ambivalent than usually acknowledged. Instead of assuming that heroes were uniformly associated with great deeds, it is worth remembering that there was a wide range of popular critical attitudes toward such figures. "A hero is a shit whom everyone avoids" (*junak je govno, koje svak obilazi*), for instance, was a nineteenth-century folk proverb first registered by Vuk Karadžić and later published by Friedrich Salomo Krauss in 1907.[88] Other folkloric materials similarly indicate that the concept of the "hero" had numerous ironic connotations that mocked the kind of masculinity and sexual prowess associated with heroes, who were almost exclusively gendered as male characters.[89] Second—and most important for this discussion—the specific notion of "heroism" surrounding youth like Žerajić was different from both popular folkloric uses and from notions of archetypal precedent. It outlined a sense of a futuristic breakthrough in national time, a rupture that could mark an end to the frustrations of prior history and make new national visions possible.

Vladimir Gaćinović (1890–1917), one of the key organizers of the Young Bosnia movement, forcefully explicated the latter senses of futuristic heroism in his work, particularly in his reinterpretation of Žerajić's 1910 act. Born in eastern Herzegovina and educated in Mostar and Belgrade before going on to universities in Vienna and Lausanne, Gaćinović (like many others) aspired to be the new voice of nationalist literature among the South Slavs. Socializing with other modernist Serbian and Croatian writers like Dimitrije Mitrinović and Tin Ujević, Gaćinović was not only an important figure on the regional literary scene but also a key organizer in underground militant societies.[90] Before 1910, his principal role model had been Petar Kočić, whose dramatic characters, such as the exemplary national subject David Štrbac, inspired the young Gaćinović to his first literary compositions. Rooted in a long-standing literature on "sad Bosnia," Gaćinović wrote about this province as a land of endless suffering inflicted by the merciless Habsburgs and born by grieving peasants.[91] "While parts of our people in other regions experienced cultural uplift, ridding themselves of barbaric slavery, we continued to be whipped, remaining primitive, undeveloped, and naked," Gaćinović wrote in 1911. But there were encouraging signs of change: "Dark silhouettes of a new type hover before our eyes. . . . The awakening of our land will give birth to a new soul, which will separate itself from the present chaos and which will be humane, warm, and distant." Gaćinović's short but influential text also gave a name to this aspiration toward new souls: "Young Bosnia" (*Mlada Bosna*).[92]

The would-be assassin Žerajić came to embody this "new type" among the activists, poets, and organizers associated with the Young Bosnia movement. In his 1912 pamphlet *The Death of a Hero* (*Smrt jednog heroja*, published anonymously in Belgrade), Gaćinović sought to rescue Žerajić from encroaching oblivion by casting the 1910 assassination attempt as the arrival of a "deeply moral and unbreakable" political force. The essay was pathbreaking and extremely influential in Young Bosnian circles, which were loosely organized around a few secret clubs and reading societies.[93] Whereas Habsburg investigators saw anarchist influences and personal problems at the root of the Žerajić case, Gaćinović outlined a sweeping narrative arc posited on Bosnia's "tradition, rich in suffering, conspiracies, and uprisings." In the two years since the assassination attempt, "Žerajić remained without influence on the youth," Gaćinović opined; "Serbian fathers and children almost competed in forgetting his name and deed." Despite this indifference, Žerajić's life and death pointed to a new vision of the national future. "Full of innocence, moral beauty, and honesty," new nationalist types "advocated not small work, but struggle; not peace, but war and victory." The youth of the unawakened peoples must have a broad heart, Žerajić preached, "through which the pain of those who cannot speak will ring out." This capacity for concentrating diffuse suffering and sublimating it into "moral action" was to distinguish Young Bosnia from liberal movements dedicated to gradualist work. "The present Serbian generation must make the words of [Jean-Marie] Guyau a living reality: *We have more tears than we need for our suffering*." In Gaćinović's narrative, Žerajić had an especially deep understanding of "this psychology of tears," teaching that it took "soul, love, and empathy for the misery of his immediate homeland to become a terrorist."[94]

Insofar as Žerajić was a hero for the Young Bosnia movement, however, he was not a derivative of some past model, but rather the foreshadowing of an immanent nationalist future, one realized through forward-looking violence. Gaćinović's narrative, even while it referenced a tradition of "conspiracies," in fact depicted Žerajić as a singularly sensitive, even distant "soul," a characterization that in important ways coincided with Habsburg assessments of Žerajić as the lone perpetrator of the 1910 attack. By sublimating and transcending past suffering, the would-be assassin gave the youth an inkling of their historic mission, wrote Gaćinović: "We, the youngest, must begin to create new history" and produce "new types who will break open epochs."[95] Taken by itself, the proclamation of a "new type" was an old trope; the nineteenth and twentieth centuries abounded with claims about the new: new age, new woman, new society, and so on. Gaćinović drew on these modernist emphases, citing a wide range of French, English, and Russian thinkers.[96] What made Gaćinović's intervention so pivotal was his forceful articulation of the role of youth and heroism in shaping historical time. Fusing the idioms of nationalist and anarchist thought of the 1910s, Gaćinović argued that the assassin's significance lay principally in his vision of national future achieved through youth's sacrifice and rebirth.[97] "So many times Žerajić said, 'It's nothing. There will be men among the youth of the indestructible and invincible Serbian people. When we die, others will come.'"[98] Gaćinović produced a quote for his hero in another text praising Žerajić's last days: "The youth must get ready for sacrifices. Tell them!"[99] Like the aloof and sentimental Žerajić, youth was a distinct, exalted political element, one "that is separate from the masses by the virtue of its task."[100]

These, in short, were *heroic* qualities: heroic in the sense of being extraordinary, different from everyday occurrences, belonging to another temporal realm altogether, capable of rupturing and giving new shape to national history. This notion of "avant-garde heroism," which deliberately fostered feverish anticipation of an imminent revolutionary future, drew on and contributed to several strands of political thought popular at the turn of the century. These included not only anarchist writings from Russia and France, for example, but a very broad array of fin de siècle ideological forces and political developments as well.[101] Already in the 1890s, texts in a secret student journal in Sarajevo (*Srpska svijest*, 1896) discussed how the centuries-long suffering of the Serbian people ultimately "awakened in it a great physical force, rising to the greatest morality over time." The concentrated expression of this process "were men of tremendous heroism (*junaštvo*). . . . Endowed by nature with a greater spiritual and physical strength from others, they rescued their brothers" from oppression. To be sure, "they had to spill much blood and pay with their own heads" for "carrying out deeds that ordinary people were not capable of doing." According to the anonymous student author, youth played a crucial role in both preserving the memory and advancing the tradition of such heroism. Familiar with distant deeds of Serbian medieval princes, the nationalist youth should know that "folk epics and the *gusle* will one day glorify and revere them too."[102] Certain hallmarks of nationalist heroization—the sublimation of suffering and the rise of extraordinary men—were lyrically sketched in these fin de siècle narratives.

Writing around 1910, Young Bosnian thinkers built on these themes, but also sharpened the stress on youth's heroic agency and reoriented the nationalist narratives toward a future breakthrough produced by violence. One of the more prominent references in this line of thinking was the work of the Scottish thinker Thomas Carlyle. Though initially little known in the Balkans, Carlyle and his famous work *On Heroes, Hero-Worship, and the Heroic in History* (originally published in 1841) became popular at the turn of the century in Serbo-Croatian journals, with a complete translation appearing in Belgrade in 1903.[103] A commentator in the leading Bosnian journal enthusiastically recommended the work, pointing out its relevance in the era of "modern demagoguery that wants to equate all people—but this English thinker" preached otherwise. "The greatest majority of people live superficially, devoted to their jobs and entertainment, not even realizing that they are themselves the symbols of some secret, invisible reality," wrote a noted Serbian critic in 1904. "But then there are those in life who perceive a very serious, actually tragic matter, . . . who are always concerned with the ideas of duty and responsibility. These are the real and legitimate *leaders* of the people, the guiding stars of humanity—Carlyle calls them *heroes*."[104]

The activists of Young Bosnia similarly condemned the masses around them and eagerly anticipated the rise of heroic action. Alongside references to Carlyle, Nietzsche, Kropotkin, and Jean-Marie Guyau, for example, Young Bosnian activists invoked the prolific literatures on "sad Bosnia" and the benighted Bosnian peasant. "Our peasant world is drowning in ignorance," Risto Radulović declared in 1912; "even if our peasant understands an idea (something we doubt), it cannot have the kind of stimulus [it would have on] an intelligent man."[105] In the same year, Gaćinović gave a similar gloss. "Mere slaves, [the Serbs] carry slavery in their hearts and chase away the spirit of freedom. . . . The key features of our days are a materialistic outlook, small individualism, and personal enjoyment," he wrote. And "this little [provincial] life of ours must be torn apart by the hands of its own body," he urged.[106]

Not everyone was as enthused with the exaltation of heroic action over the seemingly quiet everyday life. In his commentary, the Serbian political thinker Slobodan Jovanović acknowledged Carlyle's arguments as powerful, noting that "one of the most useful lessons for strengthening and steeling one's will is, without a doubt, Carlyle's work," which discussed divinely inspired poets, prophets, statesmen, and conquerors who "made history." Nonetheless, Jovanović was troubled by the deeper implications of Carlylian hero- and history-making. "Wanting to make God all the more active" in every aspect of life, Carlyle ultimately blurred the difference between the ideal and the real, between the divine and the human, Jovanović complained in 1904. "It seems in the end that there is no difference at all between God's will, usually taken as an unreachable ideal, and our miserable human history, with all its stupidity and criminality, with that unceasing river of blood that flows through it."[107]

To others, however, the specter of violence—even with its transgressive and criminal implications—seemed to prove rather than undermine the extraordinary, otherworldly, almost godlike character of heroism. Several intertwined developments gave renewed attention to the linkage of violence, heroism, and youth. For the nationalists associated with Young Bosnia, Žerajić certainly stood as an "apostolic figure" (Gaćinović's term), having been both an attempted perpetrator and a valorized martyr, but other events quickly contested his place in the national pantheon. In Sarajevo in February 1912, for example, Croatian nationalist student demonstrations against the Austro-Hungarian government were brutally suppressed by the local police, who fatally wounded one of the younger protesters.[108] Croatian nationalists quickly elevated the wounded Salih (Salko) Šahinagić, a Bosnian Muslim high school student once associated with their circles, into a victim who sacrificed his life for the nation. Enterprising activists published and distributed postcards of his image with the caption "Martyr for the Croatian Cause" (see figure 4.1).[109] Serbian student societies likewise claimed the fifteen-year-old Šahinagić as a symbol of their own victimhood.[110] The incidents in Sarajevo prompted more demonstrations across Croatia, "showing that the youth is in the mood for rallies," which in turn evolved into "street demonstrations with no relation to the student movement itself."[111] In June of the same year, another assassination attempt occurred; the Bosnian student Luka Jukić unsuccessfully targeted Croatia's governor Slavko Cuvaj in Zagreb. His attempt immediately inspired more commentary on heroism. The budding writer and Young Bosnia activist Ivo Andrić wrote in his diary, "Today Jukić tried to assassinate Cuvaj. . . . How joyfully I foresee days of great deeds. . . . Long live those who die on pavements, knocked unconscious from rage and gunpowder, pained by our common shame."[112] Luka Jukić himself wrote, "I'm teaching the world that we don't need saints, but criminals; I succeed, but people don't understand me."[113]

NAPREDKOVA
KULTURNO - HISTORIJSKA ZBIRKA

Inv. br. *1894* Odsj. *V.* br.

SALIH ŠAHINAGIĆ,
mučenik za hrvatsku misao (18./II. 1912.)

Figure 4.1 "Salih Šahinagić, martyr for the Croatian cause." Postcards like this one depicted Šahinagić, a fifteen-year-old Bosnian Muslim student once associated with Croatian nationalist circles, as a victim who sacrificed his life for the nation in clashes with the Habsburg police in 1912. With permission from the Archive of Bosnia-Herzegovina, Sarajevo.

Such visions, however, returned to the established terrain of assassinations; what profoundly changed the possibilities of heroic violence were the Balkan Wars of 1912–1913, events that one Young Bosnian saw as the proof of "Carlyle's deep words: national faith is great and life-affirming."[114] The alliance of Serbia, Bulgaria, and Greece against the Ottoman Empire resulted in tremendous expansion of the respective Balkan states, followed by more conflicts between the Balkan states over the disputed territories and populations. Gruesome mass atrocities and collective expulsions—with tens of thousands of deaths in Kosovo, Macedonia, and Thrace—accompanied the fighting, but the victorious Balkan states hailed the wars as a galvanizing development that, among other things, expanded the prospects of youth action far beyond individual assassinations.[115]

Even though Bosnia was not directly involved in the conflicts, nationalist youth across the province experienced the wars as their own, reading and writing profusely about Serbia's mobilization, attacks on enemy lines, capture of thousands of villagers, and so on.[116] The Habsburg government's introduction of "emergency measures" for two weeks in May 1913 only intensified the existing nationalist agitation while dealing a severe blow to the incipient socialist organizations.[117] In Bosnian Serbian circles, the march of the Serbian army into Kosovo specifically became a crucial symbol of revenge against the Turks and a reminder of "the holy task" that remained to be completed in future wars.[118] The Balkan Wars also boosted the popularity of already circulating theories of "race" and "racial struggle." Like many well-known European writers and politicians, Balkan nationalists had begun fusing languages of race and nation by the end of the nineteenth century. The Balkan Wars heightened the sense of "racial struggle" unfolding in Europe, furnishing artists like Ivan Meštrović and writers like Dimitrije Mitrinović with a repertoire of heroes and enemies cast in explicitly racial-national terms.[119] "Speaking honestly," the Young Bosnian ideologue Mitrinović lectured in 1913, "the bastardized Romanian and newly Greek races (*rase*) are not morally powerful, nor is the subhuman and animalistic Bulgarian will for life." Only "the Serbian army is the deepest in morality and the most human in its strength," making it the natural bearer of a "new Yugoslav culture."[120] There was a broad sense of triumphant victory of the Yugoslav nations in the Balkan Wars, not just in Kosovo but victory over the entirety of the frustrating national past, which was now made ready to yield to a different kind of future.

Gaćinović again provided exemplary images of this development among the Young Bosnians. Soon after the Serbian advances into Ottoman territory, he left Herzegovina for Montenegro and volunteered, joining the Serbian siege of Shkodra (in what was to become independent Albania). With much of the fighting already concluded, his time at the front was brief. Gaćinović grew frustrated with the lengthy siege of the well-fortified Ottoman city; by 1913, he had made his way back to his university term in

Switzerland. Gaćinović thus left the Balkan Wars with little frontline experience, but he made sure to document his martial efforts in a personal photograph. Standing in a photography studio, with vaguely classical arches as background, Gaćinović and his fellow Young Bosnian volunteers (Špiro Soldo and Veljko Simović) look toward the horizon in anticipation. Their carefully accented military gear—binoculars, bullet belts, bayonet rifles—indicates the object of their serious gaze, suggesting some enemy activity outside the frame (see figure 4.2). Gaćinović, already recognized as a leading ideologue by his peers, distributed the image as further proof of his trend-setting nationalist credentials to other activists in Bosnia.[121]

Most Young Bosnians did not experience the Balkan Wars directly, but they wrote effusively about Serbian victories. To be clear, assassinations remained the primary mode of struggle among the more revolutionary of the Young Bosnian activists, but the Balkan Wars clearly reshaped how "the struggle" itself was conceptualized and justified. There were countless Bosnian reports about the Serbian fronts, ranging from Shkodra to Kosovo to Macedonia, while university students sent in contributions from abroad; the esteemed Slovene poet Oton Župančič, for instance, contributed to the Sarajevan journal *Serbian Youth* (*Srpska omladina*) verses pondering the freshly

Figure 4.2 Posing for war: Bosnian youth volunteers during the Balkan Wars, 1912–1913. Standing in a photography studio, Vladimir Gaćinović (marked X in the archival photograph), Veljko Simović (XX), and Špiro Soldo (XXX) look toward the horizon in anticipation, suggesting some enemy activity outside the frame. With permission from the Archive of Bosnia-Herzegovina, Sarajevo.

dug graveyards in Kosovo that allegedly made Yugoslav unity finally possible.[122] The same journal, one of the major outlets associated with the Young Bosnia movement, also carried jubilant accounts of fighting in the Balkan Wars. Anonymous stories described long nights spent roaming across Macedonian hills, a terrain where chance encounters with "the Turks" caused great confusion and bloodletting. "Having recognized the Turk by his soft hat [of the Ottoman uniform], I immediately commanded, 'Slit his throat!' My friend said, 'Done.'" Following more such nights and battles, "glorious and terrifying visions" of hundreds of villagers in a state of ecstasy and terror appeared before the soldiers' eyes. Such mass "mirages," however, apparently passed as Serbian offensives continued.[123]

Going beyond frontline reports, other writers made more general proclamations about the sudden obsolescence of older politics and the arrival of a new kind of youth subject. The Balkan Wars signaled "the end of a generation," according to one assessment in *Serbian Youth*. Prior to 1913, South Slavic literature had been too pessimistic, too accustomed to "wallowing in misery for centuries," but the wars transcended this piteous outlook in a flash.[124] The Croatian poet Tin Ujević agreed, congratulating the kingdom of Serbia on its conquest of Kosovo and writing enthusiastically about "the new youth" that many expected to soon materialize. "In the thought of a young man under the age of twenty, we must create the clear idea that everyone must . . . endure in the struggle until death or until victory," he wrote during the 1912–1913 fighting. Some Young Bosnian activists certainly advocated for the greater involvement of women in social and political life of the time, but "the new youth" of the Balkan Wars was explicitly gendered as having "the glorious and manly duty" (*muška dužnost*) of liberating the nation, including its women. In this vision of national history, "manly" youth was charged with the special task of "renewing the nation, casting off so much of the old, the dreamy, and the weak among us." Tin Ujević wrote, "We must become the soldiers of a far-off ideal, which seems like a utopia today; we must be fighters and we must ready our souls for a general sacrifice, like our brothers in the [Serbian] kingdom."[125] As with assassinations, the imperative of heroic youth violence always combined self-sacrifice with the willingness to commit murder, but the scale and the character of the Balkan Wars transcended the parameters of individual attacks; the narratives of youth heroism clearly stressed this collective dimension of violence.

Involving protracted mass fighting, such violence was nation-forming, capable of "striking the foundations of the edifice of Yugoslav *culture* and of the future Serbo-Croatian *nation*," wrote the modernist youth poet Vladimir Čerina in Zagreb. Urging Croatian nationalists to take Serbia's conduct in the Balkan Wars as exemplary, he exclaimed, "Let us stand as Croats, but let's be Croats in a completely and truly contemporary way, alive to this era after Kosovo, and this is the era of energy and heroism, not of softness and reveries." Criticizing other Croatian youth journals for their uninspired coverage of the Balkan Wars, Čerina wanted to explicate what he saw as the basic principles of the recent events. "To carry out immense good deeds, it is often sorely necessary to carry out immense evil deeds (*velika zla djela*)," he wrote in March 1914. "The blood that streamed from the wounds of Serbian soldier-revolutionaries, and those smashed heads, and those severed limbs, and those corpses, corpses, and corpses—all that was ours, ours, Croatian" in a broader sense of collective South Slavic national achievement. Serbia's conquests "were a *miracle* for the whole world. An entire unseen and unheard-of people was suddenly seen and heard, like some awesome announcement from heaven." Otherworldly and futuristic, this kind of violence was no ordinary matter. As Čerina wrote, "Serbs murdered bodies, but they also created souls. This is a heroic people, and heroes are not criminals."[126]

The Young Bosnia organizer Borivoje Jevtić sketched a similarly heroic vision of youth in a series of exultant articles in 1912 and 1913. "It took the Balkan Wars to sober us up," Jevtić wrote. "We were once slaves," but thanks to "the lone outcry of our unforgotten comrade [Žerajić]," there were signs of a better future to come. "And then a miracle (*čudo*) happened." National prophecies had come true, and more great deeds were on the way. "Now we have seen how a great idea, heroically envisioned, is realized. . . . To work for the nation, to sacrifice for the nation can be the only meaning of someone's life" and the only "pledge for our beautiful future."[127] Jevtić's short fictional story patterned on reports from the Balkan Wars—"The Undefeated," 1913—described the nameless ideal youth who would break through to the national future:

> You should have seen him! He flew with his friends like mad, crying out and singing songs of victory. . . . He flew, elated by something warm and great, firing into the cloud of smoke where they said the enemy remained. O you should have seen him! The thought of freedom was stronger than the thoughts of his wretched mother, whose eyes were red and swollen with worry, whose hands were weak from work. He did not even think of the girl to whom he promised his return, nor of the happiness they dreamt of in their warm room. He did not feel sorrow for those who die, he did not feel fear. Pale, tall, and brave, he sang songs of greatness, songs formed in the days of humiliation and shame, songs full of hope and anticipation of a beautiful future. And when he died, he died heroically, with his friends, released from all pain and suffering.[128]

This image of the heroic youth became one of Young Bosnia's most conspicuous legacies: an elated young man, full of warmth and expectation, happy to die and kill like a hero. Unlike targeted attacks on particular authorities, which could arguably be contained within definitions of tyrannicide, the euphoria of the Balkan Wars brought forth a different, more diffuse conception of violence as well as enemy: shrouded and anonymized in "a cloud of smoke" in Jevtić's spectral rendition. Above all, the experience of the Balkan Wars heightened the sense of anticipation and intensified the already charged temporal registers of nationalist practice, providing decisive action that seemed to move national history along while prophesying that even more extraordinary deeds and heroes were about to emerge from the South Slavic youth.

Heroism before the Heroes

In the months following the June 28, 1914 assassination in Sarajevo, the Habsburg investigation of the event often focused on Young Bosnian invocations of heroism. The investigators' notes on Gavrilo Princip, who repeatedly invoked Gaćinović's work as his model, sketched a heroic vision of national history: "There were assassinations before, the assassins were heroes for our youth. He did not think of becoming a hero. He just wanted to die for his idea."[129]

Whatever his desires may have been, Princip certainly did become the emblematic hero for several twentieth-century movements, his name overshadowing Žerajić, Gaćinović, and other Young Bosnians who paved the way for his heroic image.[130] Beginning already during the First World War, the heroization of the Young Bosnian conspirators emerged in the 1920s and 1930s, with various commemorations paying homage to those who made the new Yugoslav state possible by firing the shots of June 28, 1914.[131] In the wake of the Second World War, it was the Yugoslav Communists who took up and retooled the cult of heroes. "I read once again Carlyle's book *On Heroes*, which someone said has no place in this era of broad democracy," the Croatian writer Vladimir Nazor wrote in 1947. "I deny this view. I deny this view because I say the cult of heroes still flowers today"—and it continued to flourish in subsequent socialist commemorations of Young Bosnia and, more broadly, of "youth heroes" (*heroji omladinci*).[132] The Sarajevo assassination stood as a watershed moment for the historical narratives of several different twentieth-century political projects. New histories—of nationalist as well as communist stripes—had to be written with a retrospective anticipation of 1914 as a great heroic rupture in time.

Yet in another way, for all the later projections onto the past, Young Bosnians themselves not only prefigured the avant-garde terms of the discourses that followed—heroes and criminals—but also shaped certain basic assumptions about youth as a distinct and extraordinary political formation. Well before the First World War, national activist practices had cultivated the sense that there already existed a time of heroism, a year X fatefully allotted to some pending point in the national future, a year different even from the glorious years of the past. At the turn of the twentieth century, Young Bosnians positioned themselves as their own future heroes whose violence, yet to be undertaken, was not simply "necessary for political change" — this kind of apology for violence is rarely found in their writings — but appeared redemptive and extraordinary, possessing a "miraculous" character that would usher the South Slavs into a new age of triumphant nationalism.[133]

Scholars have begun to take "the future" seriously as a historical problem; Reinhard Koselleck provided especially influential arguments for "expectation" as an important category of historical analysis.[134] Attentive to issues of temporality, such approaches help move us away from the all too familiar teleological views that see the Balkans as somehow ready to explode into a world war in 1914 (a perspective that is deeply flawed on a number of levels). Instead of presenting yet another "ticking time bomb" scenario, the broader history of Young Bosnia makes us better appreciate a crucial feature of nationalist imaginations of youth, something closer to "a ticking sound that simulates thought and measures out . . . hours which still do not exist, which have not yet begun," to quote Giorgio Manganelli.[135] The development of youth movements in the South Slavic context affords glimpses into the formation and the workings of patriotic imaginations marked by such senses of suspense and anticipation. Youth holds a special status in histories of nationalism; it constitutes a horizon of expectation that enables nationalists to articulate their visions, develop new strategies, and justify the renewal of their always unfinished projects.

CHAPTER FIVE

Another Problem

In 1895, a new, lavishly illustrated literary journal appeared in Sarajevo. Its opening statement situated the magazine squarely within the South Slavic cultural milieu. Lamenting that "our people is small and spiritually divided into even smaller parts" despite having one common language, the Sarajevan editorial board hoped that the new journal would overcome this situation by "inviting our Croatian and Serbian writers" to join their forces. "We want to stand in strength with united forces and show ourselves before the outside world as a unified, strong cultural element," the editors proclaimed. In becoming "a mirror of the entire spiritual culture of the South Slavic peoples before the world," the journal was "born in an auspicious place, . . . in the heart of Bosnia-Herzegovina and of our entire tribe, in that region where popular romanticism (*narodna romantika*) flourishes not only in stories and songs but also in groves and hillsides, where to this day the mountain fairy . . . bestows wreaths on those heroes who always stood at the vanguard of the national name and pride." Promising "a wealth of printed images" alongside literary matters, the journal was to feature many patriotic illustrations and photographs.[1] Its ornate masthead emphasized a crucial symbol of "popular romanticism": framed by tree branches and dawning skies appeared a *guslar*, a folk singer with a single-stringed instrument, an iconic image of South Slavic nationalisms since the early nineteenth century (see figure 5.1).

The founder of this journal, however, was not a Serbian or Croatian national society but the Habsburg government itself. Called *Nada* (meaning *Hope*), the publication was one of several "patriotic" projects established and promoted by the Austro-Hungarian administration in Bosnia in the late nineteenth century. This development was part of a momentous long-term change in imperial policy. During and after Metternich's reign, the Habsburg authorities had become infamous for their suppression of nationalist movements across eastern Europe; the crushing of the 1848 revolutions became a globally recognized symbol of the Habsburg commitment to what appeared to be conservative dynastic politics. Modern historiography too has reinforced this view of the Habsburg state as a staunch "antinational" force that countered new forces of nationalism by encouraging "supra-ethnic" loyalty to the Monarchy among its bureaucratic servants, military officials, and imperial subjects.[2] Yet in Bosnia, the Habsburg government both condemned

Figure 5.1 Imperially sponsored national romanticism: The front page of *Nada*, 3 June 1897. The masthead prominently featured a Bosnian-Herzegovinian *guslar*. Offering literature and "a wealth of printed images," the journal encouraged imperial patriotism. Image courtesy of the National Museum of Bosnia and Media Centar, Sarajevo.

nationalist movements and, at the same time, developed nation-oriented projects of its own, sponsoring collections of Bosnian Muslim folklore, establishing local museums, and publishing cultural journals like *Nada*. How did this purportedly "antinational" state come to embrace so many patriotic projects in Bosnia?

George Polya's advice for stumped mathematicians—"What is the best you can do for a problem? *Leave it alone and invent another problem*"— could well have been the motto of Habsburg as well as Ottoman imperial officials in Bosnia since the mid-nineteenth century.[3] Faced with mounting political pressures in their imperial domains, Ottoman and Habsburg state officials not only tried to repress the emerging forces of nationalism but also began to adopt many of the basic forms, idioms, and strategies of nationalist movements. Borrowing and improvising from the nineteenth-century repertoire of patriotism, imperial authorities fought nationalists on their own terrain by mobilizing practices of ethnographic activism and relying on newspapers and journals to convey their new imperial-patriotic messages to the Bosnian public. These developments are significant for what they tell us not only about the Ottoman and Habsburg states, but also about the more general discovery of patriotism as an immensely pliable, appealing—and problem-generating—form of modern politics.

Instead of posing some essential difference between "national" and "imperial" politics (often read as "ethnic" and "supra-ethnic," respectively), it may be more productive to attend to their deeply intertwined relationships, which were marked by antagonism as well as mutual and thoroughgoing influence. A number of recent works have posed questions about imperial politics of patriotism. In regard to Austria-Hungary, for example, scholars have shown how the Habsburg state found ways to foster popular "devotion to emperor and fatherland—a fatherland defined by its association with the long-ruling Habsburg dynasty" and publicly celebrated through imperial inspection tours and birthday celebrations of the emperor Franz Joseph.[4] In the Ottoman realms, historians have long noted that the Ottoman state became concerned with promoting a sense of supranational Ottoman belonging at the turn of the twentieth century, posing Ottomanism as something of an alternative to the rising tide of "nationalism in a non-national state," as some scholars have described the process.[5]

However, the development of imperial patriotism in the distinctive circumstances of nineteenth-century Bosnia required bolder approaches that called into question the difference between imperial and national state forms.[6] As a province ceded to Austria-Hungary by the Ottoman state in 1878, Bosnia occupied a special status in both empires; the Kaiser formally ruled it, yet sovereignty over the territory theoretically remained with the Sultan until 1908, when Austria-Hungary abrogated that right and officially annexed the province. During these three decades, neither Franz Joseph nor Abdul Hamid II could visit Bosnia without causing a major diplomatic crisis. With personal visits out of the question until 1908, cultivation of the emperor's image remained a marginal venue for the promotion of imperial patriotism in Bosnia. Instead of focusing on the cult of "our good old emperor," both Ottoman and Habsburg officials experimented with different ways to cultivate and manage patriotic sentiments in this province. In taking up the patriotic discourses already developed and claimed by Serbian and Croatian activists, Ottoman and Habsburg authorities found themselves in the roles of latecomers who, in a sense, had to outmaneuver and outdo the established national movements on their terms. This was a difficult situation, but it also had its advantages. Imperial patriots found that ready-made forms of nationalism in Bosnia, including already codified linguistic standards and ethnographic activist practices, were rather elastic and easily adaptable for a variety of political purposes.

Ottoman and Habsburg sponsorship of print media in Bosnia, especially journals like *Nada*, is indicative of the priorities and procedures of imperial patriotic projects. The centrality of the printing press in the rise of nationalism is well known; Benedict Anderson famously stressed newspapers as an indispensable factor in fostering new "imagined communities" across the world, from Latin America to the Middle East and Eastern Europe.[7] Similarly, in Jürgen Habermas's influential account, large-scale structural transformations since the eighteenth century gave rise to "the public sphere" as a social domain where public opinion is formed, debated, and contested. The nation and the newspaper, then, appear inextricably linked; both appealed to new publics that accessed shared materials usually in the same vernacular languages. In that sense, the general historical consensus has been that "the emergence of nationality (that is, the growth of a public for nationalist discourse) was simultaneously the emergence of a public sphere."[8]

In many parts of southeastern Europe, however, it was not the national movements but the Ottoman government that established the first printing presses, published local newspapers, and policed political expressions in provincial cities like Ruse, Prizren, and Sarajevo since the 1860s. After its takeover of Bosnia in 1878, the Austro-Hungarian administration continued to focus on print media as a venue crucial for the management of patriotic sentiments. Faced with increasing competition from Habsburg authorities, South Slavic nationalists also stepped up their efforts to shape public and international opinion through new media campaigns both in and outside of Bosnia. The Serbian national cause, a leading Sarajevo activist said in 1905, "must secure some of the more important mouthpieces in France and England, because today the press is mightier than active official diplomacy."[9] As a result of these increasingly competitive imperial and nationalist projects, a kind of a "propaganda war" developed well before the First World War, a struggle between imperial officials and aspirant nation-builders over Bosnia's proper political, moral, and, above all, patriotic qualities.[10]

The journal *Nada* played an important part in this history. It appeared in the wake of other government-sponsored publications, thus continuing imperial interest in the management of provincial politics through print media. At the same time, *Nada*'s strong emphasis on visual representation added a new dimension to these pursuits. A cover page of *Nada* from 1897 offers several key representations of imperial patriotism in Bosnia. In addition to the *guslar* and the Cyrillic typesetting, the June issue of the journal prominently highlighted the pavilion of Bosnia-Herzegovina at the Brussels International Exposition (see figure 5.1). Looking very much like a mosque built in pseudo-Moorish style, this Habsburg invention emphasized Bosnia's "Oriental"—more specifically, "Muhammedan"—character as an especially distinctive and defining aspect of the province's culture and politics. Such representations of Bosnia nicely dovetailed with abiding Habsburg interest in developing Bosnian Muslims into a potential "state-building element" for future Austro-Hungarian projects in this province.[11] These messages and representations were directed to the outside world as well, seeking to capture the attention of both provincial inhabitants and international observers. Sustained focus on these issues—print media, sponsorship of Bosnian Muslim culture, and cultivation of new images of empire—can illuminate how nation-building projects revolving around Bosnia proliferated precisely thanks to empires declared to be hostile to nationalism.[12]

"Representing and Improving the Thinking of the People"

In its very first issue—May 16, 1866—the Ottoman newspaper *Bosna* printed a lengthy programmatic statement celebrating the inauguration of the publication made possible by the first printing press established in Sarajevo. The mission statement in part read: "The [Ottoman] provincial government wants . . . to help educate the people in the knowledge necessary for progress. . . . The aim of this newspaper is to educate the people, to direct it toward progress, and to advise it in their civic duties. . . . [It is hoped] that the Bosnian people will be informed and led in making progress by its newspapers, . . . [whose] light may not be well seen at first, but whose results will be experienced later."[13]

Many Serbian and Croatian weeklies registered the appearance of *Bosna*, mocking the profuse praises to the sultan Abdülmecid, "who delights and makes joyous his subjects." Four year later, after the Ottoman printing press brought out a number of titles for a variety of audiences, the Serbian scholar and statesman Stojan Novaković claimed that it was "before their death that the Bosnian Turks, those unjust elders of the people of those regions, remembered to become permissive in a way"; they were "helping schools," "printing some textbooks," and "publishing Turcoman newspapers on red and yellow paper." What Novaković found most offensive was that all this was done by "the Turks, the most eternal enemies of the Serbs," who were only trying to deceive the people by giving them textbooks containing nothing "that I think today's child should learn," which would be issues like: "What is nationality, what is Serbian unity, what is pride and heroism of one's own people, what is nationality and its expanses?!"[14]

The nationalist doubts about Ottoman reforms were not new. When the Porte first announced its reforms in 1839, *Danica Ilirska* voiced skepticism that the Ottomans could do any good for the inhabitants of Bosnia because "that curious Muhammedan," Sultan Mahmud II, was unsuccessfully trying "to introduce some European customs into his empire so as to fuse his subjects of European blood with the Asiatic Turks."[15] In almost forty years of evolving imperial policies in this Balkan province (1839–1878), nationalist objections to these processes repeatedly protested what they saw as empty words of "the Turks" meant to deceive the European public and the local populace while the old yoke pressed ever harder. Reacting to the appearance of Ottoman Bosnian newspapers, the Serbian *Zastava* commented: "With this newspaper, [the Ottoman government] wants to wipe out our nationality, so instead of the Serbian language, they write 'Bosnian' language and 'Bosnian' people. . . . Now they want to destroy our nationality, our holiness, our pride and joy."[16]

Thus from the outset, the appearance of the print media in Bosnia was an issue highly charged with arguments over the proper place of newspapers in "national" life. Among these contentious debates, the demand for vernacular language publications was one of the most consistent aspirations voiced by a variety of figures. The Illyrian activists of the 1840s, mostly consisting of young Bosnian Franciscans who studied in the Habsburg Monarchy, appealed for the establishment of the printing press as an indispensable tool for the rise of learned societies, theaters, and museums in Ottoman Bosnia. Though friar Ivan Franjo Jukić published an important Bosnian publication in Zagreb in 1850–1852 (*Bosanski prijatelj*), the Ottoman government in Bosnia viewed such ventures with suspicion and did not allow or establish printing facilities in the province until 1866.[17]

In that year, the Tanzimat reformers in Istanbul finally approved the much-debated resources necessary for the formation of newspaper teams across Ottoman provinces, including Bosnia. Ignaz Soppron, a printer from Vojvodina, was paid to transport his machinery from Zemun to the Bosnian capital and acquire a number of scripts for the press (namely, Ottoman, Church Slavonic, and Hebrew in addition to reformed Cyrillic) for the Ottoman government. Soppron personally prepared the first publication runs, but a host of local figures quickly took over and charted a new course for the printing press. Mehmed Šaćir Kurtćehajić, Bogoljub Petranović, and Jozef Alkalaj distinguished themselves by their contributions, while Miloš Mandić, a native of Bihać schooled in Slavonia and Belgrade, became an enterprising editor who elicited contributions from other Bosnian teachers, priests, doctors, and officials. In fact, it was the growing demand for nongovernmental discussions that led in 1869 to the establishment of a "nonofficial" newspaper called *Sarajevski cvjetnik* or *Gülşen-i Saray* (The flower garden of Sarajevo).[18]

The issue of language use presents a telling example of the Ottoman embrace of the forms of nationalist cultural production for purposes of imperial reform. Instead of imposing Ottoman Turkish as the only common language, the Tanzimat reformers encouraged bi- and multilingual publications across the Balkans, with newspapers in Bosnia appearing in both Ottoman Turkish (printed in Arabic script) and in the local "Bosnian" or "Serbian" language (printed in Cyrillic; see figure 5.2). The Ottoman editors settled the matter of vernacular use — crucial for reaching out to the intended audiences across Bosnia and "subscribers in Austria and Serbia" — by adopting Vuk Karadžić's linguistic standard that was still being debated by South Slavic language reformers. Given Vuk's fraught relationship to Herzegovina and Bosnia, this Ottoman act served as a curious homecoming of a dialect that was codified in Vienna, Zagreb, and Belgrade as "the pure speech" of Bosnian-Herzegovinian peasants. Vuk's creation, explicitly modeled on and named after "Herzegovina," thus finally arrived to its purported land of "origin," not from Zagreb or Belgrade (which had yet to fully adopt the linguistic reforms in their entirety) but from the Ottoman governments in Sarajevo and Istanbul. Prominent Serbian patriots were soured by this rapid imperial embrace of the national standard; Stojan Novaković in Belgrade wrote in 1870 that "because Vuk's attempt remained just an attempt [in Serbia] so far, Bosnia is the first land where a Serbian elementary primer is printed in the new grammatical standard. And this was done by the Turks!!!"[19] The language of South Slavic unity — which was to serve as the common platform for the Serbo-Croatian national struggle against "the Turks and the Austrians" — was thus also the pioneering language of imperial reform in Ottoman Bosnia.[20]

The very appearance of such a thing as a local newspaper was taken as a momentous sign of "progress" by those who created these artifacts in Ottoman Bosnia. The mission statement of the first issue of *Bosna* (1866) hailed its own arrival as a "necessary step" in helping the inhabitants of Ottoman Bosnia "achieve progress," especially in terms of their "civic duties" and "learning."[21] Three years later, the first issue of *Sarajevski cvjetnik* called out to "all the provincial newspapers," urging them to seize their "role in our society" and illuminate paths to "education," "progress," and "good governance and laws . . . that apply equally to the rich and the poor, for the strong and the weak."[22] In 1876, when another Ottoman Bosnian paper called *Neretva* appeared in Mostar, it explicated its role even more emphatically: "It is generally well-known that newspapers are the organ that represents and improves the thinking of the people (*narod*) and of vast hu-

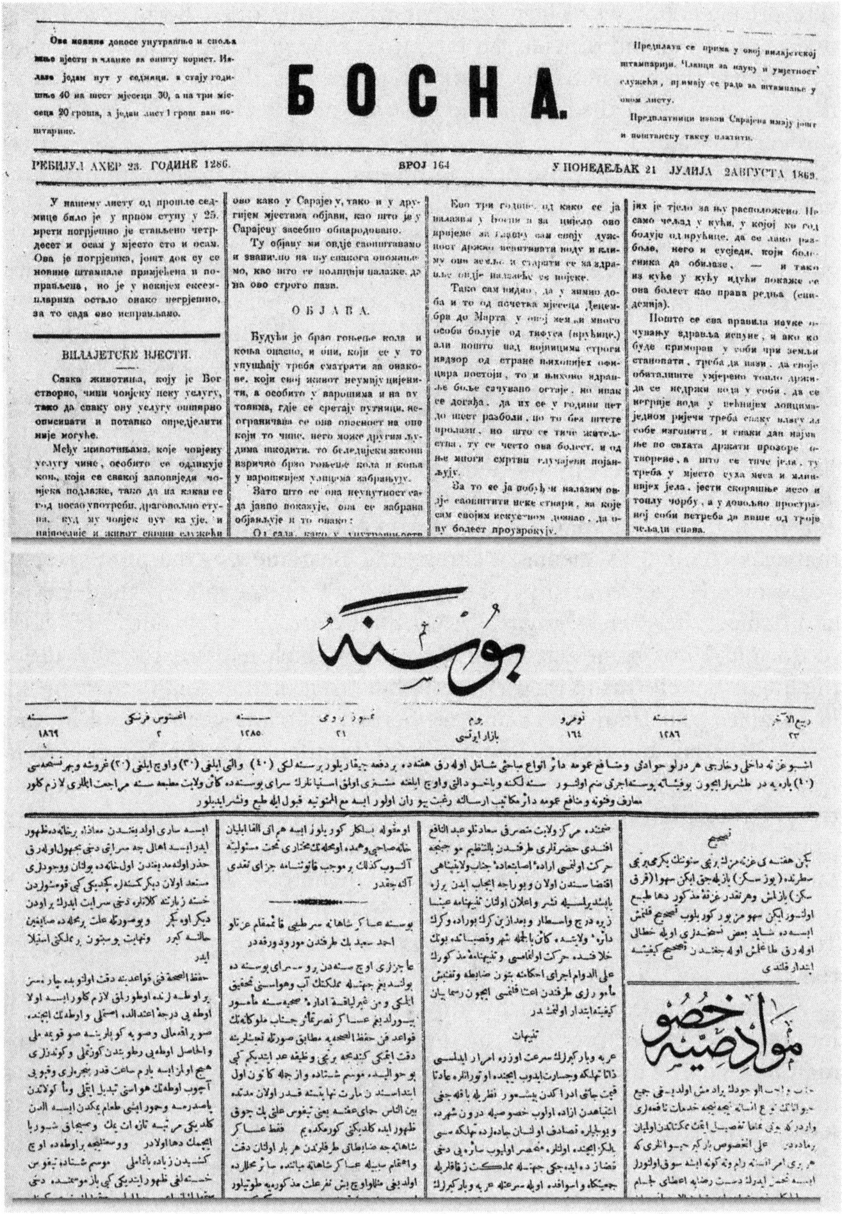

Figure 5.2 The first Bosnian newspapers: The mastheads of the *Bosna* newspaper, 21 July 1869. Typically, the Cyrillic-script Bosnian side was featured as the front page, while the Arabic-script Ottoman Turkish pages with identical content were on the inside of the paper. Image courtesy of the National Museum of Bosnia and Media Centar, Sarajevo.

mankind, that disseminates good things all around. Since . . . [newspapers] improve and advance the material and mental state of things everywhere, so it will be in Herzegovina itself with the establishment and dissemination of this lofty and decisive thing."[23]

The telling emphasis on the dual goal—"representing and improving the thinking of the people"—brings to light the underlying tensions that shaped the efforts of the Ottoman Bosnian press since the 1860s. In a way, newspapers and a growing number of publications would try to re-present Ottoman Bosnia to its own inhabitants; they featured many educational articles about Bosnia's history, its geography, its laws, its internal politics, its standing in international affairs, and about the idealized image of harmonious life of its four main confessional constituencies—Orthodox, Catholics, Jews, and Muslims.[24] Articles in *Sarajevski cvjetnik* followed with special interest the last set of concerns revolving around, as an 1870 piece put it, "the need to live and work together on educational enlightenment, setting our sights on our mutual love of the four confessions of [Bosnia's] inhabitants."[25]

It is important to note here that the task of "representing" the province entailed a twofold "improvement" of public opinion. On the one hand, there is the obvious attempt to cast Ottoman Bosnia, particularly the treatment of Christians under Ottoman rule, in a flattering light, one that would help refute many of the charges of Ottoman oppression and enhance the image of Ottoman rule. These polemical replies, however, were explicitly aimed at international audiences and critics of Ottoman rule in Bosnia; substantially different exhortations were directed toward the inhabitants of the province. Addressing this public, the publishers of the Ottoman newspapers sent a message of a different kind of "patriotic improvement," one that stressed the need for a more stringent effort to cast off "the old customs" and to work toward educational uplift in the province.

This latter approach to "improvement"—which entailed a struggle against "superstitious delusions" and for educational-social "progress"—was one of the key senses of reform that Ottoman Bosnian writers pursued in their undertakings. "To obtain knowledge," Mehmed Hulusi (1843–1907), the editor of *Neretva*, explained in 1876, "a teacher is needed; likewise, to learn crafts and agriculture, one needs masters and factories that are connected to capital and wealth." Ottoman newspapers, he claimed, could do the same for the people of the imperial provinces, but their mission was hampered by "material poverty" and "the love for old tools and customs, which are the reasons why we lag behind."[26] Such advocacy of society-wide improvements was a common theme among other Ottoman newspapers; the Istanbul-based *Terakki* (established in 1869) claimed *Progress* as its very name. The editors of these publications often reprinted and critiqued one another's articles and emphasized that their polemics were part of a self-proclaimed mission of "enlightenment" aimed at revitalizing the Ottoman state.[27]

No one championed this agenda of provincial enlightenment with more enthusiasm than Mehmed Šaćir Kurtćehajić (1844–1872). An energetic official and scholar living in Sarajevo, Kurtćehajić yearned to gain a better grasp of "Western learning," particularly of French language and literature, but these ambitions, he once ruefully complained, could not be met by his schooling in small Ottoman towns.[28] Kurtćehajić nonetheless demonstrated considerable political skill, becoming a member of the Sarajevo district council at a young age and the head editor of *Sarajevski cvjetnik* in 1869.[29] In the latter task, he showed great interest in following Ottoman, South Slavic, and Western European news and literature. The newspaper managed to cover a wide variety of topics (one unsigned piece even drew a comparison between the reforms in Japan and the reforms in the Ottoman Empire), but Kurtćehajić's writings repeatedly stressed themes of education, unfounded beliefs, history, backwardness, and, above all, the need for "progress" (*napredak*).[30]

Kurtćehajić's approaches tended to define the reform agenda—which called for changes in agricultural economy and the introduction of technologies like railways, roads, harvesting machines, and telegraph lines—against a background of "prejudice" and "ignorance" that hampered the new initiatives.[31] Already in the first year of *Sarajevski cvjetnik*, Kurtćehajić wrote a series of articles on "Superstition," which tried to demonstrate the following: "The inhabitants [of Bosnia] are marked among other peoples . . . by natural reason that cannot be denied. . . . But over time, the people came to have some delusions, in which many men, especially peasants, and all women are deeply mired. No one should think that we are here trying to rebuke the people or to ridicule it, but one should be convinced that we want to prove just how harmful the delusions and superstitions are . . . and to show that those who seek cure in such things often find poison in them."[32] In subsequent texts, Kurtćehajić listed various "superstitions," rebuking "the people" for trying to cure illnesses through "ineffective" home remedies and rituals instead of "trying to go to the doctor and telling him what's wrong." The serialized editorials repeatedly urged "those whose heart is committed to the happiness of the people" to pursue edification through schools, learned societies, and other hallmark institutions of education.[33] Such writings clearly indicated the gendered aspects of this reform program that explicitly addressed male audiences presumed to be not "mired in superstitions" and therefore presumably receptive to these exhortations.

A dose of "patriotism," which was necessary "for the revitalization and strengthening of our state," was central to this Ottoman mission of provincial revival.[34] While the influence of nationalist rhetoric may be evident in the appeals to the Ottoman "homeland," the kind of "patriotism" promoted by the Ottoman Bosnian publications nonetheless differed substantially from the Serbian-sponsored "awakening" of the 1860s, which stressed "consciousness of nationality" as a prerequisite for the rise of an armed national liberation struggle. Ottoman Bosnian patriots like Kurtćehajić, on the other hand, placed less emphasis on the notion of "consciousness" and expressed no comparable expansionist ambitions. Nonetheless, some common idioms and political commitments resonated across contemporaneous national and imperial movements despite their clear opposition to one another. After 1876, the Ottoman state would embark on a much larger and more systematic project of promoting "Ottomanism" among its citizens, but the notion of "patriotism" among Ottoman Bosnian intellectuals of the 1860s bore a distinctly provincial stamp that singled out Bosnia and its "special" standing, history, and sense of "nationality" (*narodnost*) as elements that bound its diverse inhabitants together.

Already the first issues of *Bosanski vjestnik* in 1866 called attention to the provinces' particular position in the empire, boldly asserting that Bosnia "kept its historical right throughout all changes of time, and its ancient nationality (*narodnost*) survived the storms of the past here. The Bosnian people expresses its nationality fully . . . and it has remained unharmed by the differentiation of confession."[35] In a related vein, *Sarajevski cvjetnik* carried in 1871 a curious notice "from Istanbul" addressed to "the Bosnian brothers": "You live in a province that is encircled by foreign borders, and you are therefore the real guardians of European Turkey; you have attained dignity that no one can deny to you. . . . You were praised in the imperial military decree with the words: my 'Bosnian people, brave and loyal.' Thus his highness, the sultan, looks on you as his moral sons."[36]

Articles on Ottoman Bosnian history and geography began to appear in support of this novel Ottoman contention, while Kurtćehajić linked these expressions to "civic duties toward the imperial government" in an 1870 editorial titled "Patriotism" (*Patriotizam*):

> This blessed word, which passed across the lips of all citizens with a certain satisfaction, is not just, as some believe, love toward the land and people . . . but is also the sentiment by which every individual subordinates his private interests to the general state interests and bears every sacrifice to the general needs. . . . The biggest mistake would be to consider oneself a patriot because of [one's] struggles and sacrifices to some political party . . . disconnected from the general state laws and structures. . . . We should liberate ourselves from old prejudices; lend each other a hand like brothers without considering who is of what confession; . . . and make the effort for everything that will serve the progress, wealth, and honor of the empire—if we want to be rightly called patriots, thus giving an example of reverence for the homeland and brotherly love to our descendants.[37]

The kind of "patriotism" being advanced here, then, appeared to be mostly concerned with furthering Ottoman reform initiatives, which increasingly invoked languages of "brotherhood" among Ottoman inhabitants to stress the underlying "reverence for the homeland." In fact, several other newspaper pieces signed "a patriot" (*Jedan patriot*) were not so much exhortations urging imperial pride as thinly veiled criticisms aimed at negligent Ottoman officials. Several such "patriotic" editorials, for example, blamed Ottoman authorities for their slow pace in building the planned railway lines, in improving the condition of the Bosnian roads, in opening new schools, and in removing bureaucratic restrictions in political affairs.[38] On the other hand, local contributions to the opening of new schools, such as the elite high school in Foča in 1870, were greeted with praise: "Patriotism and enthusiasm for the people's well-being is thus shown! These financial contributions of yours . . . will be remembered by your descendants."[39] In this sense, to be this kind of "patriot" in Ottoman Bosnia meant advocating comprehensive reform of the provincial institutions while also criticizing both "the officials" and "the people" whenever passion for this project was found to be lacking.

Schools, education, and the general spread of "knowledge" (along with the accompanying abandonment of "delusions" and "old customs") were cited as benchmarks by which reform was assessed, but this largely educational agenda also amplified the understanding of reform as improvement for Bosnian *Christians* within a revitalized Ottoman structure. In this regard, the Ottoman government not only aided the project of the construction of new churches but also printed textbooks for the growing number of Orthodox and Catholic schools in Bosnia.[40] In fact, the very first books published by the Ottoman Bosnian press were introductory teaching materials about the Gospel and other fundamentals of the Christian faith (both Orthodox and Catholic). As one might expect, many of these works were prefaced with profuse praises for "the most high sultan Abdülmecid . . . whose name is mentioned every day in gratitude in churches and especially schools," but their content suggested a number of different national lessons about geography, folklore, and history within this imperial framework.[41] In phrases resembling the Pan-Slavic rhetoric of the nineteenth century, an 1871 Ottoman geography textbook "for Catholic classrooms" emphasized that "the largest [group of] people in Europe are the Slavs, who number over eighty million souls . . . and are divided into five [*sic*] proud branches, Serbs, Croats, Russians, Bulgarians, Poles, and Czechs," further characterizing "their lands" as "illustrious and prosperous."[42] The expanding Franciscan and Orthodox schools were frequently visited by Ottoman officials; governors publicly attended ceremonies that lauded the "progress in education of all our citizens, regardless of class or religion."[43]

"Folk poetry" was singled out as a particularly valuable asset of the Ottoman "homeland" and, thanks to the efforts of Bogoljub Petranović (the Serbian activist and head teacher at Sarajevo's Orthodox secondary school), published in Sarajevo as a separate volume that complemented the "Muhammedan" and "Serbian" folklore collections that already appeared in the local newspapers.[44] Such accomplishments were also positively noted by the *Bosnian-Serbian Calendar* for the year 1869.[45] As long as such Serbian, Croatian, or other vaguely national claims on cultural artifacts remained within the imperial realm, the Ottoman government seemed content to incorporate them into its evolving reform program.

Some of the strongest Ottoman Bosnian statements about the meaning of these reforms were delivered as polemical replies to the Serbian and Croatian magazines published outside of Bosnia that attacked the Ottoman officials for oppressing and sowing disunity among their "brothers groaning under the Turkish yoke." Judging from the amount of commentary, it seems that many national activists in Zagreb, Novi Sad, and Belgrade closely followed the Ottoman publications coming out of Sarajevo and wrote many articles seeking to expose the Ottoman reforms as, in the words of one Belgrade newspaper, "pro forma" gestures that hid the "ongoing Turkish tyranny."[46] Kurtćehajić made it his task not only to refute such charges by publishing lengthy reports of "progress" and "enlightenment" in Bosnia but also to turn the tables on the nationalist critics and their self-proclaimed mission of upholding freedom and equality for all peoples. In a text characteristic of such efforts, Kurtćehajić set out the following justifications for Bosnia's precarious position during the Tanzimat:

If the Sublime Porte has been somewhat late in this century with its reforms, and could not immediately grant everything to the extent that the Western powers could, there were causes for that [delay]. But now we believe there will be few, excepting Serbia, who will venture to protest that the Ottoman government is unjust toward its peoples. Do not all confessions and nationalities enjoy equal rights? Are not Christians free to build churches for themselves, just as the Turks build mosques and the Jews synagogues? Are there too few officials in the lower and higher [governmental] services who are of Christian confession? Are Christian children forbidden anywhere from going to schools, and are they not gladly received there? ... Do Christians not have estates and goods all over Turkey just as other peoples do?[47]

The link between the reforms and the improving status of the Ottoman Christians, explicitly foregrounded in the above plea, appeared to be fleshed out by reports about more newly opened churches and new Christian officials, but the persistent challenges to this mission—from both within and outside of Ottoman Bosnia—revealed a great deal of political anxiety about this project, especially its "late" timing that was exasperated by "slow" improvements. "The people are able and the government desires it, yet still we do not progress," despaired Kurtćehajić in 1870, blaming the stagnating situation once again on the persistence of "old beliefs, ... prejudices, superstitions," and the lack of "educated" engagements with the evident "discord on so many political issues," implicitly referencing the confessional tensions that accompanied the changes in the social status of Bosnian Christians.[48]

On a few occasions, the Ottoman newspapers openly discussed the Muslim abuses of Bosnian Christians, but tended to treat them as "exceptions" that marred the usual peace and order. An incident in Bosanska Krupa in 1869, for instance, showed how the opposition of some Muslims to the Tanzimat programs often went hand in hand with hostility toward the Bosnian Christians, who were perceived as the primary beneficiaries of the reform process. In Krupa, a certain newly arrived *hafiz* Selimanović orchestrated a series of polarizing public declarations in his small town. "When we were celebrating the day of his highness the Sultan, a day celebrated in joy across the empire," a local reporter wrote, Selimanović interrupted the celebrations by insulting the Orthodox Christians: "He publicly shouted, 'What do you want, you Vlachs, your religion is sh— — [in original *g*— —], and you and your church and everything yours is sh— —, you have nothing.' Ever since this *hafiz* came to our town, he fostered negligence among us neighbors, Muslims and non-Muslims (*nas komšije, muslomane i nemuslomane*), giving advice to those who have no knowledge in their heads and who in their ignorance think: If such an effendi says this, why shouldn't I, who know nothing." Kurtćehajić urged punishment for Selimanović while commending local officials for keeping order, but incidents like this showed the fragility of the asserted bonds of Ottoman patriotism in Bosnia.[49] Indeed, such incidents and doubts about the actual situation in the province had to be repressed in polemical exchanges in which Kurtćehajić asserted "reforms" as already accomplished results, which were then favorably compared with the restrictive nationalist programs in Serbia and Croatia.

Ottoman Bosnian newspapers singled out Serbia's treatment of Jews, Romanians, and Greeks for especially sharp criticism. Kurtćehajić frequently denounced the Balkan principality for discriminating especially "against the Jews," calling attention to the fact that in Serbia "Jews [were] forbidden to conduct commerce freely," "settle in towns," and were taxed with "all those heavy dues and then [required] to give soldiers for the standing army."[50] This bleak situation in Serbia was made worse by the appearance of new anti-Jewish writings in several Serbian publications of the 1860s and the 1870s and the rise in threats and abuses against Serbian Jews.[51] When leading Belgrade newspapers refused to print a rebuttal from Alliance Israélite Universelle, the Ottoman Bosnian paper stepped in and published a text debunking the Serbian nationalist charges: "Alliance Israélite is not a conspiratorial society."[52] Scathing comments about persecution of Jews in Russia often included comments about Serbia's repression of its Jewish population, while Ottoman Tanzimat policies were highlighted as "progressive" and "beneficial" for all inhabitants of the Balkans.[53] The concern for the welfare of Serbian Jews and other minorities, as was amply clear from the framing of Kurtćehajić's polemics, primarily served as a means to establish a stark contrast between "oppressive Serbia" and "flourishing Bosnia," where one "will find hundreds of Christians and Jews in the service of the

[Ottoman] state . . . while non-Christians and non-Serbs [in Serbia] cannot have even civic rights."[54]

As these comments indicate, claims and counterclaims of national suffering became a recurring theme in polemics between imperial and nationalist print media. Ottoman newspapers like *Sarajevski cvjetnik* were keen to dispute the ubiquitous charges that Ottomans were repressing Christians in Bosnia, arguing that the nationalist press in Serbia and Croatia was exaggerating minor incidents. But in addition to defending the Ottoman reform record, Kurtćehajić and other Ottoman writers also sought to go on the offensive with charges that the real repression, censorship, and violations of basic rights came not from the Ottoman Empire but from Balkan nationalist governments and their supporters in Russia.[55] The Ottoman attempt to seize the moral high ground, to turn the tables on the Serbian and Croatian activists who had widely publicized their visions of "sad Bosnia," involved occasional championing of a variety of liberal-patriotic causes; Sarajevan newspapers, for instance, lamented the international injustices that faced Poles in Russia, whom "the Russian government cruelly deprived of rights" and "sent thousands . . . to Siberia, where many bright people will surely expire in terrible prisons."[56] Mirroring South Slavic discourses of national suffering, Kurtćehajić often issued appeals to "Europe" as a political observer and moral arbiter of competing claims of political injury in the Balkans. In 1871, he rhetorically asked: "Serbia . . . how long will you oppress, persecute, and mistreat your Greek, Vlach, and Jewish citizens? . . . You should know that because of your wrongdoings, all of Europe now must have a guilty conscience because it mediated in the establishment of such barbarians."[57] These early Ottoman responses to nationalist discourses of suffering never reached the kind of European popularity that nationalist writings of Mažuranić, Utješenović, or Jakšić already achieved. Nonetheless, the appeals are significant in themselves. They help indicate how rival imperial and nationalist claims over Bosnia's suffering or prosperity shaped Balkan provincial print media from their very establishment in the nineteenth century.

The eruption of the 1875 peasant uprising in Herzegovina and the escalation of conflict throughout the Balkans spelled an end to this Ottoman program of "patriotism."[58] The peasant-landlord tensions, routinely downplayed and ignored in the pages of the Ottoman Bosnian press, were impossible to disguise as mere "obstacles to reform" in the face of the massive revolts, atrocities, and crises that shook the Balkans from 1875 to 1878. Amid regional violence, most of the provincial newspapers stopped appearing in those years; at the same time, Sultan Abdülhamid's new government ramped up its efforts to counter reports on the infamous "Turkish atrocities" in Bulgaria with similar images of "Russian atrocities."[59] Finally, after the Congress of Berlin formally ended Ottoman rule in Bosnia and handed the administration of the province to Austria-Hungary in 1878, the bilingual provincial publication, *Bosna*, ceased publication after a thirteen-year run.[60]

Making Muslims Modern: New Patriotisms
in Habsburg Bosnia

When the Austro-Hungarian government acquired Bosnia following the Congress of Berlin in 1878, it already conceived of the province as a political space that required special treatment within the Monarchy. Since the addition of Bosnia to either Austrian or Hungarian domain would have disrupted the political balance within the Dual Monarchy, administration of the province was assigned to the joint Austro-Hungarian Ministry of Finance (*Gemeinsame Finanzministerium*). With a few years after the 1878 occupation, a new provincial government for Bosnia was established under the aegis of the finance ministry and run by officials from both halves of Austria-Hungary. The first generations of Habsburg officials, led by the enterprising minister Benjamin von Kállay (whose term ran from 1882 to 1903), openly spoke of their mission as being one of "Western" reform of a once-disorderly "Oriental" land. Not surprisingly, this undertaking situated itself alongside other "civilizing missions" of the time, such as the colonial ventures of the French, English, and Russian Empires.[61] A closer examination of the Habsburg political projects in Bosnia, however, shows not just the familiar imprint of empire but also of nationalism as a force that increasingly shaped the course of new imperial missions in the Balkans.

Entering a political field already claimed by neighboring Serbian and Croatian movements, Governor Kállay hoped to counter these established national programs with an overarching notion of "Bosnianness" (*Bošnjaštvo*). By cultivating identification with Bosnia as a distinct province, this Pan-Bosnian concept would, in Kállay's estimation, counter the potential spread of Serbian national sentiments and prevent close association with Croatian politics, a development that could disturb Croatian-Hungarian relations within the Monarchy. While the overarching Habsburg concept of "Bosnianness" was explicitly conceived of as cross-confessional, it became in practice most associated with the cultivation of modern *Muslim* sensibilities, especially through the sponsorship of print media and codification of Muslim folklore.[62]

When assessing the intense Austro-Hungarian focus on fostering cultures of patriotism—in new folklore collections, journals, schools, etc.—many politicians and scholars have often asked a simple question: Have these imperial projects accomplished their stated aims or not? Did they successfully establish their vision of *Bošnjaštvo* or not? When judged by a rigid pass-fail criterion, they obviously did not. No unified "Bosnian" nation emerged out of Kállay's policies.[63] But there are other questions that one could ask about these processes. What political meanings and consequences did these Habsburg activities produce in Bosnia? What can the entry of the Austro-Hungarian administration into the nationalist fray over this province tell us about the character of nationalism as a political force?

The Habsburg government's treatment of the Bosnian Muslims as a "state-building element" opens valuable insights into the intertwined histories of nation- and empire-building. On the one hand, the Habsburg administration directly acknowledged Bosnian Muslims as suitable political partners who could grow into a new patriotic force in the contested province. As several scholars have documented, this perception came in part through a process of elimination of alternative options—having Serbian or Croatian constituencies become the favored in-group for the Habsburg project—but also through positive Austro-Hungarian assessments of Muslim political potential. As the dominant confessional community under former Ottoman rule, Muslims appeared to the Habsburg administration as a distinct and valuable constituency. Moreover, Bosnian Muslim nobility in particular had important assets that officials like Kállay considered advantageous: they were a land-owning, privileged class well-versed in Ottoman imperial affairs. These qualities and experiences made Bosnian Muslims potential candidates for partnership with the Habsburg administration.[64]

On the other hand, for all the interest in cultivating local support, Habsburg officials also considered Muslims as the most "Oriental" element in a province itself seen as Turkish, unruly, and generally inhospitable to European influences. Not surprisingly, many Habsburg observers perceived Islam as a religion alien to the Christian heritage and "the modern spirit" of Austro-Hungarian politics. "Europe is the home of Christianity, a culture in a specifically European way," wrote the Austrian jurist Adolf Strausz after a visit to Bosnia shortly after the Habsburg occupation. "Islam is the insurmountable obstacle, as it has no real home in Europe any more. . . . There are only two paths: either Islam can be modified in the spirit of Western cultural work or it must cease to exist."[65] Armed resistance to the Habsburg occupation in 1878 only seemed to confirm the view that Muslims were deeply opposed to the new Monarchy. Austro-Hungarian assessments of Muslim education were particularly negative; as the supervisor of the education department put it in a formal review in 1894: "children in *mektebs* [elementary schools], where one only memorized mechanically, and where instruction had no moments of cultivation whatsoever, came out entirely ignorant and immature."[66] Seeing obstacles in Islamic religion, history, and education, many Habsburg officials feared that Bosnian Muslims would prove incapable of meeting the demands of European political life.

In trying to assess and manage Bosnian Muslim affairs, Austro-Hungarian administrators often compiled notes on how other empires—British, French, Russian, and American—dealt with Muslim subjects in their colonies. An Austro-Hungarian consular officer in Cairo filed a report in 1901 on the similarities between the Habsburg and British imperial missions in Bosnia and Egypt, respectively. "The many analogies in the political relations of the two lands, the similarity of governmental tasks," the Habsburg consul wrote, meant that the two colonial projects could learn from each other, just as "local politicians in Egypt are keen to draw useful lessons from this same situation."[67] In 1903, the Austro-Hungarian ambassador to the United States reported that his conversations with President Theodore Roosevelt often "returned to a favorite theme, namely, the success of our policies in Bosnia," and surmised: "I think he wonders whether and how the methods that we applied in our occupied provinces could be useful in the Philippines."[68] At other times, it was the Habsburg officials who sought to learn from other imperial counterparts, compiling detailed questionnaires about how the Russian Empire managed sharia law in its jurisdictions in the Caucasus and Central Asia.[69]

In 1900, an anonymous pamphlet on the "position of Muhammedans in Bosnia" (most likely written by Lajos Thallóczy and approved by Kállay) summed up the fears and hopes of the imperial government. "We do not know whether this administration, with its excessive confidence in the development of Muhammedanism," is deceiving itself about the potential of the Bosnian Muslims, the work proclaimed. Nonetheless, the pamphlet concluded, "the political weight is still with the [Muslim] large landowners" and "the policy of preserving the Muhammedans" as the state-building element in Bosnia appeared to stabilize the previously restless province.[70] In many ways, the Habsburg dilemmas in Bosnia were emergent imperial concerns shared by other European empires in the late nineteenth-century, projects that invoked the mission of European powers to "civilize" — or figure out how to rule — Muslim subjects in newly acquired colonial areas. In Bosnia's particular context, however, both Habsburg officials and Serbian-Croatian nationalists came to perceive Bosnian Muslims as a pivotal political group whose yet-to-be-determined national allegiances could make or break their respective projects. Because Muslims appeared as (br)others in these competing national visions, struggles over their ambiguous patriotic potential were especially loaded in Bosnian politics.

In their endeavor to remake Muslims into a viable patriotic constituency, the Austro-Hungarian authorities built on the enduring legacy of the Ottoman Bosnian press. This is especially evident in the work of intellectuals like Mehmed Hulusi, the former Ottoman official who continued his work as a journal editor under Habsburg rule, editing the journals *Vatan* and *Rehber* (1884–1897 and 1897–1902, respectively).[71] *Vatan*, meaning *Homeland*, continued to use Ottoman Turkish during the Habsburg period alongside the more prominent Serbo-Croatian dialects in Latin or Cyrillic alphabets. The choice of the Arabic script — whether to write Ottoman Turkish or Serbo-Croatian — became a significant issue in Habsburg Muslim politics, one that had major implications for engaging different audiences and promoting "modern" patriotic sentiments. When the first issue of *Vatan* appeared in 1884, a note in an official government publication commented that its Ottoman Turkish script showed the necessity of "this newspaper as an appropriate medium for the spread of enlightenment because many native Muhammedans do not know how to read modern letters (*moderna slova*)."[72] Though in subsequent decades other Muslim publications would overwhelmingly adopt Bosnian dialects in Latin or Cyrillic scripts, the use of Arabic remained a charged marker of the "old Turkish ways" that educational-religious publications continued to debate into the 1910s.[73]

If the 1884 comment about *Vatan* posited an underlying difference between "modern letters" and "old Turkish" ways, the pages of this journal sought precisely to stress the modern qualities of the Bosnian homeland. Alongside pages of poetry, prose, and literary criticism, *Vatan* carried many notes on the proud and increasingly scientific—archaeological, ethnological, historical—preservation of the cultural heritage of Bosnia since antiquity, especially emphasizing the importance of the newly opened Provincial Museum in Sarajevo.[74] In 1890, over a hundred German-language proverbs on the subject of "homeland" ("love of," "duties toward," etc.) were translated into Ottoman Turkish and serialized in the pages of *Vatan* to help teach and spread new patriotic sentiments among Bosnian Muslims.[75]

Whereas Hulusi's journals continued the Ottoman Tanzimat practices, literally using the same typesetting tools as the 1860s publications, the weekly *Bošnjak* tried to distinguish itself as a new publication for a new Habsburg age. Founded in 1891 and printed in Latin script, the newspaper worked initially with Kállay's administration to promote a broad Bosnian platform, stressing the need for education, reform, and economic progress in the province. Its main editor, Mehmed-beg Kapetanović Ljubušak (1839–1902), was a prominent landowner and a major political figure, becoming the mayor of Sarajevo in 1893 and using his prominence to facilitate the entry of new Bosnian Muslims intellectuals onto the literary-political scene (e.g., Edhem Mulabdić, Riza-beg Kapetanović, and Safvet-beg Bašagić). In terms of audience, one of the journal's first articles described its ideal reader thus: "Brother, I don't know Turkish that well, so I don't care much for *Vatan*. But I do know Latin and Cyrillic script, so I read foreign papers, though in the end, what good is that? . . . Everyone pulls to their side, and we [Muslims] remain, so to say, like a wolf between the hunting dogs and the hunter."[76] The pages of *Bošnjak* were supposed to provide a new environment where educated Muslims could discover and promote their national pride.[77] "We respect everyone's heritage, but we are proud of our own," was one of the publication's mottos in the 1890s. Polemics with Serbian and Croatian journals filled many pages with arguments over the proper national name for the province's inhabitants. Asserting that that Muslims were nationally neither Serbs nor Croats, the intellectuals gathered around *Bošnjak* proclaimed that "we will never deny that we are parts of the Yugoslav tribe, but we want to clearly show that we are Bosniacs first and foremost."[78] Discussions of Muslim folklore, proverbs, and poetry—the foundation of the romantic images of South Slavic unity—supplied much of the material for discovering Muslims as patriotic (br)others of Serbs and Croats. Once again, the key steps were undertaken by Mehmed-beg Kapetanović, who published his pioneering collection *Folk Treasures* in 1888 and who deftly fused various Ottoman ("Turkish, Arabic, and Persian") literatures with South Slavic folkloric repertoires.[79]

In the same year, it was Kosta Hörmann—a prominent Habsburg official in Bosnia—who contributed another major folklore collection characterized as specifically Muslim. Hörmann, born and raised in a Catholic family in Croatia, was one of the many Habsburg officials who arrived in Bosnia in the early 1880s to help establish the new administration. His enterprising spirit, knowledge of languages, and political tact earned him the trust of Kállay and other high-ranking Austro-Hungarian officials, who supported Hörmann's many initiatives in Bosnia. Having perceived the need to establish a greater Muslim cultural presence among South Slavic national literatures, Kállay and other Habsburg officials collaborated on Hörmann's proposal to gather and publish Bosnian Muslim epic poetry. The end result was a government-subsidized, impressively produced, and cheaply available volume titled *The Folk Poems of Muhammedans in Bosnia and Herzegovina* (1888). In the preface, Hörmann praised Mehmed-beg Kapetanović as a trailblazer, stressing the modern qualities of Kapetanović's work that Hörmann claimed to be merely enhancing: the Latin script, the love of homeland, "the spirit of the time" in which "Muhammedans join the circles" of Serbian and Croatian writers. Overall, Hörmann was eager to situate his—that is, Muslim—collection alongside the work of such South Slavic national luminaries as Vuk Karadžić, noting that they also praised Muslim folklore but never properly collected it.[80] In other words, imperial officials claimed to do what nationalists never quite managed: to reach the heart of the people, revel in its folkloric richness, celebrate its beautiful language (printed, of course, in Vuk's national standard).[81]

The sense of imperial and national competition over Muslim folklore—and implicitly over Muslims' political standing in the South Slavic national community—was clearly evident in several responses to Hörmann's collection. Serbian literary critics, for example, complained about Hörmann's choice of the Latin over the Cyrillic script and accused him of changing the allegedly "Serbian" character of this folklore with the "Muhammedan" label. Perhaps the sharpest rebuke came from Luka Marjanović, an established folklore collector at a prestigious institution in Zagreb, which had just published a few poems by some Bosnian Muslim folk singers in 1887. That Hörmann and the Habsburg administration were able to seize the mantle of Muslim Slavic authenticity infuriated the Croatian critic. The well-funded Habsburg government must have acted improperly in publishing Hörmann's "shoddy" work before Croatian ethnologists like himself could carry out the otherwise valuable projects in Bosnia, Marjanović charged in a lengthy article. "This competition (*takmenje*) could be very interesting," he acknowledged, and claimed that Croatian academics would prevail in best "presenting our people of the Muhammedan faith to the domestic and foreign learned world."[82]

The imperial folklorists, however, were not dissuaded; Hörmann responded in detail to nationalist charges in a second volume of Muslim poetry and reasserted the authenticity of the Habsburg-Muslim project in Bosnia. Antun Hangi, a teacher in the service of the Habsburg state, made another contribution to this growing body of imperial knowledge. His pioneering ethnographic study, titled *The Life and Customs of Muslims in Bosnia-Herzegovina* (1900), appeared in both Serbo-Croatian and German editions as an expert's guide to "Muhammedan sensibilities"; "being with them as a friend, going to their houses, I got to know them so well that I wanted to describe their life to their compatriots in Croatia," Hangi wrote.[83]

Governor Kállay's directives noted the originality of Hörmann's enterprise, but also stressed the historical elements of folklore as evidence of Muslims' "Bosnian ancestry" (*bosnischen Abstammung*) and "old Bosnian customs."[84] These references to "ancestry" clearly invoked the much-debated historical theories claiming the Bosnian Muslims were the direct descendants of the medieval heretical community known as the Bogumils. By asserting the Muslims' ancestral difference from Catholics and Orthodox before the conversion to Islam, the Bogumil (or Bogomil) theory was supposed to provide a sense of national continuity and imply defiance of pressures imposed by their neighbors. Though always contested and later widely discredited, the proliferating references to Bogumil Muslim ancestry, continuity, and past glories closely followed the templates of the already established patriotic histories of Czechs, Serbs, Hungarians, Croats, and other nationalities.[85] Safvet-beg Bašagić's history of Bosnia (1900), for example, rehearsed such tropes in an attempt to light "the old pride in the hearts of our young generation, urging it to seek after Eastern and Western education and to contribute something to the progress of our homeland."[86] History of the nationalist kind, in other words, would establish a sense of enduring Bosnian Muslim distinction, while ethnographic studies would demonstrate the continuing richness of their patriotic traditions.

Among other things, the Habsburg patriotic projects intensified the already existing lines of national difference drawn around Bosnian Muslims in the South Slavic national imaginaries. Historians like Robert Donia have written extensively on the tense and delicately balanced relationships between the Habsburg officials and different Bosnian Muslim actors, many of whom openly rejected Austro-Hungarian authority over Islamic religious and educational affairs while simultaneously remaining generally supportive of Habsburg economic programs and policies.[87] Moreover, some Bosnian Muslim intellectuals responded favorably to the overtures from Kállay's government; in particular, the works of Kapetanović, Hörmann, and Bašagić became increasingly popular as symbols of the distinct culture of Bosnian

Muslims.[88] In the long term, Kállay's sponsorship of folklore collections and journals like *Bošnjak* provided a critical boost for an emerging sense of Muslim national distinction and enabled the creation of a new repertoire of Muslim patriotism that would endure well into the twentieth century.[89]

The rise of intense interest in Muslim culture was part of a wider imperial-nationalist competition over Bosnian matters. Alongside Muslim-oriented projects, the Habsburg government promoted the Provincial Museum (*Landesmuseum*, established in 1884) as a central institution that would exhibit and apply the latest scientific advances in ethnology, archaeology, history, and natural sciences to pertinent subjects in Bosnia.[90] Archaeological excavations in particular offered prominent public displays even in countryside districts where scientists like Carl Patsch hoped they would "arouse local patriotism, thus inciting interest for the benefit of provincial history."[91] The museum's amply subsidized journal, quickly becoming one of the leading scientific publications in the Balkans, often issued statements that combined antiquarian interests with patriotic-sounding appeals to various Bosnian publics. As one article characteristically put it:

> Our homeland Herceg-Bosnia hides many antiquities. . . . But ruin has befallen our antiquities, in which we and our ancestors can recognize ourselves. . . . Thus let us get to work! We now have a treasury in which we can preserve . . . our native valuables and advance them into the infinite future, which is why we have our museum in Sarajevo, and our newspapers. . . . Let us write down from the grandfather, the grandmother, the father, the uncle, the mother, the aunt—that story: about the castle, the city, the church, the chapel, the mosque, the graveyards, the battlefields, etc. . . . Let us go and dig out those old stones. . . . Here is work for a worthy custodian of our dear proud Herceg-Bosnia![92]

In fact, like the appearance of first newspapers in Bosnia, the development of new museums and journals was seen as an already "nationalist" domain in which Austro-Hungarian officials had to compete with established Croatian and Serbian institutions. In regard to Bosnia's museum, Serbian and Croatian scholars acknowledged and often admired its high-quality scientific contributions. "In Bosnia and Herzegovina, the young science of anthropology is better developed than in Croatia," the Zagreb-based *Vienac* observed in 1900.[93] The fact that this land, long deprived of the kind of bourgeois associational life thriving in central Europe, "finally has its own national museum must cheer every scholar," noted the famed Croatian biologist Špiro Brusina in 1905; but it "truly hurts when one thinks that an older brother [Croatia] cannot compete with its younger kin [Bosnia]" in terms of funding and cutting-edge work appearing at the turn of the century.[94]

Whereas some South Slavic intellectuals welcomed the new Habsburg institutions, most Serbian and Croatian publicists rejected them as "foreign" interventions that did not adequately reflect Bosnia's true spirit of patriotism. Thus when a young literary critic reviewed the state of journalism in Bosnia for a Croatian nationalist publication in 1903, he deplored the lack of "good" newspapers and counseled that the province "needs first and foremost a nationally conscious and serious press, which would help [Bosnia] in its difficult political and economic troubles." Such nationalist writers particularly deplored the Habsburg government-sponsored journal *Nada*, which had become one of Kosta Hörmann's signature imperial projects (published 1895–1903). According to nationalist-minded critics, *Nada* was a bad influence, as it allegedly featured too few "genuinely" Bosnian writers (in fact, it did publish many of the leading local and regional figures in literature and the fine arts).[95]

Nada was indeed an unusual journal, established by the Austro-Hungarian administration as an elite cultural forum for Bosnia, but its pages were not filled with programmatic statements urging pride in any particular kind of homeland. Instead, its preferred form of discussion was literary debate about the merits of past and contemporary belles lettres. Patriotism was not shunned in these conversations, for it was embraced as a feeling alongside any number of sentiments—erotic desire, fear, envy, hope, and so on—that could inspire artistic expressions. "Lyrical poetry expresses feelings, and is patriotism not a feeling too?" asked one *Nada* contributor in 1903 and praised South Slavic works full of "true patriotic sentiments," not of meaningless "patriotic tirades."[96] Similar references to patriotic feelings proliferated in this Habsburg-sponsored journal at the turn of the century. Works of emerging writers were found to be brimming with "patriotism, erotica, pure lyricism, even reflections and satire."[97] Others still, like the poems of Safvet-beg Bašagić, were noted for their deft fusions of "flames of patriotic reflection" and expressions "overflowing with erotic effervescence."[98] Literature understood in this way could certainly be—and often was—accused of not being "nationalist" enough, yet it was also not without its own notions of fin de siècle patriotic sentiments.

In these ways, imperial-sponsored projects—such as Muslim folklore collections and new literary journals—became sites of intense debate over the meanings of patriotism that attracted political attention across the Habsburg Monarchy. Most South Slavic nationalists perceived the Habsburg embrace of patriotic idioms not only as usurpations of their "authentic" genres but also as sinister Habsburg machinations designed to "divide and rule" the South Slavs. When it came to Bosnia, "there is something that must terribly pain any patriotic Serb of any faith," Stevan Kaćanski wrote in 1888, "and that is the principle *divide et impera*."[99] Slovene and Croatian writers similarly wrote that the Habsburg policies in Bosnia pitted South Slavic groups against one another, enabling the Monarchy to disrupt Yugoslav unity in this crucial province.[100] Moreover, because Bosnia was a truly joint Austro-Hungarian territory, debates over imperial policy had not only provincial but also empire-wide ramifications. As Kállay himself stressed in

1897, his work as imperial minister "concerned not only Bosnia but other state affairs" as well that went beyond the partial interests of any single nationality; his administration in Bosnia followed "neither Czech, nor Polish, nor German, nor Hungarian politics," but only "the politics of the entire Monarchy."[101]

Using similar reasoning, Czech, Slovak, and other nationalist politicians eagerly cited Bosnia as the embodiment of what they saw as failed imperial management of national relations in the Monarchy as a whole.[102] The famed Czech politician Tomáš Masaryk (and later president of Czechoslovakia), for example, got deeply involved in debates over Habsburg Bosnia in the 1890s, reading about the issues, traveling to Sarajevo, and writing about the need to revise imperial policies in this crucial province. In several long and much-debated speeches before the Austro-Hungarian delegations in 1892 and 1893, Masaryk outlined a slew of charges against the empire's work in this province. A "police regime" ruled Bosnia, Masaryk stated; nationalist expressions were sharply curtailed while the Habsburg administration promoted "Bosnian" language, history, and folklore over Serbian and Croatian claims to the same matters. The plight of the peasants remained woefully neglected while Austro-Hungarian policies favored Bosnian Muslim nobility over Serbs and Croats. The fact that glowing government reports had whitewashed and downplayed the poverty and many problems of the province made the situation even worse. Drawn from his personal observations and from Czech and South Slavic journalistic reports, Masaryk's indictments covered a familiar mix of liberal and nationalist politics, demanding greater transparency and popular responsibility in governing Bosnia.[103]

At the very end of this speech, however, Masaryk felt compelled to add his own unusual commentary on "patriotism" and imperial policy. "To be honest, I did not expect to hear so much spoken about patriotism in this forum," he pointedly noted. Referring to the Habsburg embrace of "patriotic" sentiments in Bosnia, Masaryk said: "Generally, it makes me uncomfortable when educated men who feel true patriotism speak such a great deal about patriotism. I personally cannot bring myself to say '*I feel patriotic*.' I believe that those who are true patriots do not even need to say so."[104]

Keeping up his part in this debate over the authenticity and utility of patriotism, the Habsburg governor Kállay was ready to state his case. Delving into the details of the school regulations, economic investments, and agrarian policies, Kállay attempted to recognize and ultimately refute each of the major issues raised by his critics, particularly by Masaryk. When it came to the issue of "nationalities" in Bosnia, the governor acknowledged the patriotic inclinations of the populace in Bosnia—issuing stilted praise of Serbs, Muslims, and Croats while stating that he "had nothing to fear from them"—but also asserted his earlier arguments about Bosnian national distinction. After "spending much time studying ethnography" and history, Kállay claimed that the Habsburg government was merely following standard practices in "calling all inhabitants of Bosnia Bosnians." Those who wanted to declare themselves as Serbs and Croats could do so, but the Habsburg government vowed not take sides in any Serbian-Croatian arguments.[105] Having staked the Habsburg position as basically neutral, Kállay simultaneously "assigned the greatest weight to Muhammedan lords as the state-conscious element" in Bosnia. If *divide et impera* meant state management of divergent interests, Kállay said, then the Habsburg government practiced that principle, "something that every government would do, regardless of its political form, including a democratic one."[106] Alternating between "neutrality" and support for particular groups, Habsburg policies thus actively encouraged rather than suppressed the spread of patriotic causes, which increasingly involved emerging constituencies such as the Bosnian Muslims—and unsettled the already declared patriots, including observers like Tomáš Masaryk.[107]

Such widening debates raised "uncomfortable" questions about the political character of patriotism: Could imperial projects in Bosnia produce patriotic sentiments and institutions that could rival those of Croatian, Serbian, or Czech causes? If patriotism cannot be established by statements like "I feel patriotic," then what counts as an authentic expression of patriotism? What consequences could Habsburg sponsorship of Bosnian Muslim folklore, language, and history have for Muslims themselves and for other Habsburg debates over nationalism?

On the one hand, the imperial-national competition over Bosnia heightened the nationalist anxieties about the instability of their own political projects, which revolved around standardized and easily reproducible idioms of patriotic passion (slogans, grammars, textbooks, and so on). Serbian and Croatian reactions to Austro-Hungarian initiatives in Bosnia—which quickly generated idioms of "pride in the homeland" patterned on already available models—anxiously and constantly characterized them as "insufficiently" or "not genuinely" national. The Habsburg authorities' entry into the nationally contested terrain of Bosnia (announced by publications of Bosnian grammars, museumization of the Bosnian past, etc.) had the effect of exposing the generic qualities of nationalism as a set of pliable and widely usable political forms.

But on the other hand, the Habsburg authorities were themselves destabilized by their entry into the South Slavic national polemics over Bosnia. Having attempted to cultivate certain venues of patriotic activity, Austro-Hungarian officials like Kállay and Hörmann found themselves in domains—folklore, language, history, print media—already dominated (or at least claimed) by Serbian and Croatian national movements. In the first two decades of Habsburg rule, the committed imperial promotion of the Bosnian cause produced a number of new journals, books, and enduring institutions like the Provincial Museum. With Kállay's death in 1903, many of these particular projects came to an abrupt end. *Nada*, for example, ceased publication in the same year, having lost its primary backer. The new minister Istvan Burián soon officially moved away from sponsorship of "Bosnianness" altogether. In perhaps the most telling instance of imperial retreat from certain domains of patriotism, the Habsburg administration in 1907 adopted "Serbo-Croatian" instead of "Bosnian" as the new formal name of the vernacular language in the province.[108]

Some issues were clearly recognized as a lost cause. However, imperial competition with nationalist politics in Bosnia, even while conceding defeat in some areas, had eagerly taken up other political fields, thus keeping anxieties about the authenticity, utility, and cultivation of patriotism alive for many decades.

The Empire Writes Back: Bosnia as a Habsburg "Sleeping Beauty"

Just as eastern European nationalists were keen to speak to the wider world about their causes, stressing their suffering under imperial oppression and calling for political recognition from a variety of liberal audiences, Habsburg officials competed with such nationalist depictions, promoting their views of Bosnia before local as well as international audiences. The divergence between imperial and nationalist presentations of Bosnia was clear. One Serbian newspaper in 1889 complained that the Austro-Hungarian administration "tries very hard to project a most rosy picture onto a most sorry state of this miserable land, which was not this miserable even under the Turks!"[109] Beginning under Kállay's rule and continuing until the dissolution of the Monarchy, Austro-Hungarian authorities concentrated on two areas in the effort to present a favorable picture of Bosnia. In the first place, they strove to counter the discourses of national suffering that South Slavic activists developed since the early nineteenth century, a body of writing that they perceived as false and deliberately negative publicity about the province. At the same time, they increasingly focused on international promotion of a "sleeping beauty" view of Bosnia, presenting the province as a charming region far removed from political disturbances. Bosnian Muslims appeared especially prominently in this imperial imaginary as guarantors of Bosnia's exotic, fairytale character.

Monitoring, suppressing, and counteracting negative depictions of imperial projects in Bosnia ranked high on the list of Austro-Hungarian administrative priorities. The Monarchy's officials, attentive to the potential impact of nationalist print media, scrutinized regional newspapers (including those based in Serbia and Croatia) and tightly regulated journalistic codes in Bosnia.[110] Well into the first decade of the twentieth century, various clerks compiled disparate newspaper clippings into extensive reports on the state of journalism in Belgrade, Dubrovnik, Zagreb, Cetinje, Zadar, Novi Sad, and throughout Bosnia-Herzegovina.[111]

Going far beyond governmental monitoring of public opinion, a network of contracted informants, who for the most part did not know of one another, supplied imperial officials with secretly obtained sources of many kinds: snippets of coffeehouse conversations, telegram scraps from newspaper offices, rumors, intercepted letters, and so on. "I regularly check the paper wastebasket whenever I am in the office. So today I found in the basket this crumpled-up Greek letter that ended up there by mistake," a certain informant named "Jovo" reported in 1905. The letter, intended for Serbian politicians in Sarajevo and Budapest, was dutifully translated to German and filed away as information on "the Serbian opposition."[112] Similarly obtained documents were sometimes photographed, a copy sent to Vienna while the original was repackaged and placed back into circulation.[113] By 1907, even "notes on telephone conversations" about suspected "agitators" ended up in Habsburg archives shortly after the introduction of this mode of communication to the province.[114]

Habsburg surveillance of the nationalist opposition extended well beyond southeast Europe. Whenever prominent newspapers in Germany, Britain, or Russia published critical writings on Bosnia, Austro-Hungarian officials took note and filed reports about what they saw as inaccurate reports about the Monarchy's work in the Balkan province. Kállay's regime was particularly sensitive to these matters, but later officials in the service of ministers like Aehrenthal were similarly eager to intervene into European journalistic debates when necessary. In 1908 and 1909, for example, Austro-Hungarian officials keenly defended their work after facing much criticism during a major diplomatic crisis caused by their unilateral annexation of Bosnia. In the midst of diplomatic turmoil, articles in British newspapers like *The Daily Mail* made "the case for Austria," citing "progress of the two provinces" and far-reaching "benefits to commerce."[115] When more critical reports appeared in the same newspaper in 1909, the Habsburg ambassador to Britain filed memoranda complaining about the English journalists' presentation of the "depressing state" of Herzegovina coupled with their praise for the "splendid fighters" of Montenegro.[116] By 1910, the Habsburg officials had mounted another series of highly publicized events focusing on the emperor Franz Joseph's short and sole visit to Bosnia. Lavish ceremonies in Sarajevo, Mostar, and other towns prompted numerous headlines across Europe about "the wise emperor" and the "great welcome by his new subjects" in the Balkans.[117]

Even when activists left Bosnia, patterns of imperial-nationalist competition continued and extended into new contexts and audiences. Đorđe Čokorilo, a Bosnian Serb nationalist who authored many anti-Habsburg articles, was occasionally censored and jailed by Austro-Hungarian authorities for various infractions, ranging from failure to pay fines to arguments over "insulting" word choices.[118] After numerous run-ins with the Habsburg government, however, Čokorilo fell out of favor with the more moderate

Serbian politicians in 1905 and lost his once prominent place in Bosnian journalism.[119] After emigrating to the United States, Čokorilo then tried his luck again as a publicist among the South Slavic immigrants in Chicago. Even in this new context, however, familiar patterns of imperial-nationalist competition continued. In 1908, Čokorilo sent to the Habsburg government in Sarajevo several posters announcing "massive protests" in Chicago against the Habsburg annexation of Bosnia. At a time when no armed conflict had taken place in the province in almost three decades, Čokorilo told his American audience that "once again, explosions of deadly guns echo across the blood- and tear-soaked Bosnia-Herzegovina." While the "people of this downtrodden land are being thrown into chains," South Slavs had to show that they did not have "such a cold heart" as to ignore the pleas of their suffering Bosnian brothers, Čokorilo wrote.[120] Habsburg authorities investigated the Chicago reports, but their assessment found that Čokorilo, despite his attempt to "represent his actions as the actions of the South Slavs living in America," was largely operating alone (and rather unsuccessfully) in his intention "to stoke hatred against the dynasty, the monarchy, and especially against the Bosnian government."[121]

But while individuals like Čokorilo could be written off as vocal but relatively isolated troublemakers, the profusion of "sad Bosnia" discourses during the nineteenth century was a more worrisome development for Austro-Hungarian authorities. The writings of Stevan Kaćanski in the 1880s, for example, built on the well-established nationalist repertoire depicting Bosnia as "the saddest of all Slavic lands." This view, which originated under Ottoman rule, intensified throughout the Habsburg period. "How sad, indescribably sad, is the picture of Bosnia-Herzegovina today!" wrote Kaćanski in 1888.[122] Imperial officials were concerned over the impact of such nationalist broadsides against the Monarchy, which denounced every aspect of Habsburg rule in Bosnia, from insufficiently nationalist education to pervasive censorship to agrarian policies. "Derogatory depictions of our Monarchy," one Austro-Hungarian observer wrote, could instill "chauvinistic" and "destructive" sentiments among the Bosnian reading public.[123] Other officials had similar anxieties. When Emil Kasumović, an Austro-Hungarian consular official, came across a nationalist pamphlet comparing Habsburg conduct in Bosnia to British scorched-earth campaigns in the Boer War, he wrote a scathing report pointing out its false assertions and misleading claims of violated rights. Such invocations of national suffering in Bosnia, often depicting Habsburg tormentors assaulting and "colonizing" helpless Bosnian women, make "a mockery of human rights" discourses, Kasumović wrote in 1902.[124]

To combat the proliferating nationalist writings, Austro-Hungarian administration made sustained efforts to present a much more positive international image of Bosnia. At first, it was government officials like János Asbóth, Lajos Thallóczy, and Kosta Hörmann who directly worked with

Kállay to produce new works that staked out different arguments attesting to Austria-Hungary's many successes in governing and improving Bosnia. Asbóth's book was particularly important, as it appeared with government support in Hungarian, German, and English already by the 1890s.[125]

But to reach new international audiences, Habsburg officials soon turned to journalists and writers not directly associated with the government. The work that set the tone for many of these projects was Heinrich Renner's luxuriously produced travel account first published in 1896. Renner, a Berlin-based journalist who arrived to Bosnia in 1878 to report on Habsburg and Balkan affairs for German and American newspapers, became well acquainted with the province, traveling "through Bosnia-Herzegovina, up and down and all over" (*Durch Bosnien und die Herzegovina, Kreuz und Quer*, as the title put it). After writing up his impressions, Renner showed his manuscript to several acquaintances in the Habsburg provincial administration, who were impressed and intrigued by the work. Sensing potential to present a popular and decidedly positive picture of Bosnia, Austro-Hungarian officials not only aided Renner with further travel arrangements but also meticulously copyedited his prepared manuscript in 1895, furnishing the author with corrected historical dates, local statistics, and Serbo-Croatian, Turkish, and Arabic expressions that appeared throughout the detailed travelogue.[126] When the book appeared with a Berlin publisher a year later, it received very favorable reviews and quickly sold out, leading to a second revised edition in 1897 and a Serbo-Croatian translation in 1900.[127]

Habsburg sponsorship of the *Nada* journal and the Provincial Museum had already paved the way for projects like Heinrich Renner's travel guide. In the course of preparing his book, Renner consulted museum officials, stayed in government-built hotels, relied on Habsburg officials for translations, and used nearly three hundred illustrations—depicting Bosnian mountains, rivers, towns, costumes, buildings, and industries—provided by artists and photographers working for *Nada*. Between stirring descriptions of local landscapes, Renner sometimes wrote about Habsburg policies, occasionally even defending them from "the fiercest and most unfair attacks from the delegations of Young Czechs" (like Masaryk).[128] But most of the time, Renner steered away from political issues. His book was presented as deeply researched yet accessible to a broad audience thanks to its deliberately "casual, conversational style" that does "not presume special knowledge" of the region. Its conclusion neatly summed up its tone and message. "This much is certain: Bosnia and Herzegovina are not only rich in scenic and ethnographic matters, but are also the most interesting areas to visit in the European East thanks to their rapid cultural and economic development." A visit to this "romantic" and "charming" land—not the "sad Bosnia" of the past but a new, "happy Bosnia" under Habsburg management—was recommended not only to "tourists, economists, and scholars" but also to "numerous colonial policymakers in Europe" who would see how a judicious government policy could transform a wild "Oriental" area into "a worthy companion of its sister European countries."[129] In other words, Austria-Hungary's work in Bosnia was like an imperial fairy tale: "The Bosnian Sleeping Beauty (*das bosnische Dornröschen*) slept through centuries of enchanted sleep and it was not until her resurrection, when the imperial troops crossed the borders, that she entered into a new era. Then the overgrown thicket around Sleeping Beauty's castle was cleared, and after barely two decades of restless and hard work, Bosnia is becoming well known and respected before the world. What has been done in this country is almost unprecedented in the colonial history of all peoples and times."[130]

Encouraged by the success of Renner's travel guide, the Habsburg administration continued to explore similar publicity venues and found another suitable partner in the English travel writer Maude Holbach in the first decade of the twentieth century. Holbach had already made a name for herself as the author of a travel account of Dalmatia in 1908; after exploring neighboring Bosnia-Herzegovina, she looked to publish a similar work on these provinces a year later. Once again, Habsburg officials stepped in, offering their expert advice and local services to Holbach. Divergent priorities, however, soon caused a conflict of interests for the author. Holbach's London publisher (John Lane) wanted her to write more about contentious Bosnian politics in the wake of the 1908 annexation crisis, but her Habsburg advisers urged her to stay the course and produce a largely apolitical guide for tourist purposes. "Had it been more political," the London editors wrote, Holbach's book could have received better subsidies from the publisher, but in the end, the apparently better Habsburg support prevailed.[131] The work appeared in 1910 as a guide to "a primitive pastoral land where shepherds still play upon their flutes and shepherdesses wander with distaff in hand spinning as they watch their flocks; a land untouched by the fret and hurry of modern life, still wrapped in ancient peace." The introduction explicitly addressed certain negative associations with Bosnia: "all of Europe has heard of the persecution of Christians in Mohammedan land, [but] one-half of the population here remained Christian," causing Holbach to wonder "whether the Western world has not done the Turk an injustice and painted him blacker than he deserved." Aside from brief comments on how much "Austria has done for this country," her account mostly stayed away from political debates and focused on the "picturesque" aspects of Bosnia.[132] Though not as popular as Renner's travelogue, Holbach's book still participated in the same international project of promoting Bosnia as an enchanting Habsburg land, full of mysterious mountains, exotic costumes, and folk singers.[133]

The enterprising publisher and writer Milena Mrazović made major contributions to these efforts through a series of well-received books. Born in Croatia in a family of Habsburg officials, Mrazović moved to Bosnia as a child and lived in Sarajevo almost her entire adult life, from 1879 to 1919.

Her numerous stories and sketches attest to her enduring fascination with the province, especially with the familiar yet exotic presence of Bosnian Muslims. Originally written and published in German, many of her pieces were translated into English and Russian, reaching international audiences that relatively few Bosnian writers could claim at the turn of the century. Mrazović's breakthrough book, *Selam: Sketches and Tales of Bosnian Life* (1893), firmly declared her intention "to bring about a more practical knowledge of both the land and people" of Bosnia, focusing once again on Bosnian Muslims.[134] Summarizing her literary career in 1900, Mrazović wrote: "As the backdrop of my memories stands an Oriental Bosnia—a fairytale figure of an earlier time of my youth."[135] Indeed, while the first Bosnian Serb patriotic journal took the name "Fairy" (*Bosanska Vila*, founded 1885), it was the advocates of the Habsburg state who wholeheartedly embraced this fairy-tale iconography of patriotism and remade it for their own imperial purposes.[136]

Development of tourism was crucial to the Habsburg effort to counter the perception of Bosnia as a contested, dangerous, and possibly violent region. As one British Member of Parliament claimed in 1891, "everyone is aware that a great European war, originating in all probability in the Balkan Peninsula, is one of the few political certainties of our time; and how far the destinies of Bosnia and Herzegovina will be affected by it, it is impossible to say." Austro-Hungarian authorities sought to overturn such fears by several means, including through the establishment and international promotion of a network of tourist amenities that tamed the once-wild Balkan province. They would have been relieved to hear the same English politician conclude after a tour of the provinces that Habsburg political life "is a question which evidently need not agitate the prospective tourist. . . . I confidently recommend the attractions of a visit not only to Bosnia, but also to Herzegovina and Montenegro."[137] A travel writer reporting for a popular Berlin journal in 1885 was impressed by Bosnia's natural attractions; he suggested that this discovered territory should be rightly called "Franz Joseph's Land" since the Habsburg emperor had opened it up for the world to admire, even though he had not yet personally stepped foot in this province.[138]

The Austro-Hungarian investment into making Bosnia appealing to foreign tourists was inseparable from the government's broader economic and political projects. Newly constructed railway lines made previously remote areas much more accessible to potential visitors while hotels began to appear even in small towns like Kiseljak and Foča by the turn of the century. Julius Pojman, an enterprising government official in Sarajevo, established a "tourist club" in the Bosnian capital and published an illustrated guide to the province in 1903.[139] The journal *Nada*, having already helped establish Renner as an authority on Bosnia, proudly pointed to recent French and German travel guides as proof that "Bosnia and Herzegovina are tourist lands of the future."[140] At the same time, tourist guides for "Croatian youth and travelers" began to appear in Zagreb, often retracing Renner's routes and reprinting the same pictures provided by "Kosta Hörmann, . . . whose noble efforts for the improvement of our people are widely attested."[141] In 1902, the American journalist William Eleroy Curtis wrote that the Habsburgs "decided to make the country attractive to strangers and tourists, who would advertise it." Reflecting on his extensive visit to Bosnia, Curtis approvingly noted that newly introduced "amusements and pleasures of all kinds"—including "theaters, operas, parks, museums, gardens, cafes, military bands, parades, ceremonials," and so on—"proved remarkably important in diverting [locals'] minds from politics and opening to them a new world."[142] The Italian English writer Luigi Villari was more critical, pointing out that "the *Fremdenindustrie*, however, is not as yet very flourishing, for the country, in spite of its fine mountain scenery and its picturesque Oriental character, is too far out of the way of the ordinary tourist from Western Europe to compete with Switzerland, Tirol, or the German baths." Nonetheless, the government's efforts "to attract tourists to Bosnia-Herzegovina" were deemed successful enough for Vienna's "first colonial experiment."[143]

These efforts to generate positive tourist publicity about Bosnia continued up to the outbreak of the First World War. In 1913, the imperial government encouraged readers of the London-based *Globe Trotter* to visit Bosnia, providing a discount to its members and suggesting a number of local highlights. The *Globe Trotter*, in turn, praised the Austro-Hungarian government, featuring Sarajevo on its July cover and printing a guide to the country in French, German, and English. "The special charms and attractive features of Bosnia-Hercegovina, that picturesque southern extremity of the Austro-Hungarian Empire, lying at the very gate of Occident and Orient," were illustrated by numerous photographs "kindly loaned by the government." The accompanying text stressed Bosnia's physical proximity to—as well as cultural distance from—the comforts of Europe: "The life in market-places and bazars shows the same picture that henceforward will repeat itself through the whole of Asia, even to the confines of the Chinese frontier, so that the tourist visiting Bosnia-Herzegovina may really get a fair impression of genuine Oriental life" during a sojourn to these lands.[144] In other words, curious European travelers who wanted a taste of "the Orient" could skip longer, possibly dangerous trips to "the East" and go instead to a safe and nearby—but still exotic—corner of the Habsburg Monarchy.

In their effort to reach international publics and to impress audiences at home, the Habsburg government took the Bosnia show on the road, so to speak, by establishing opulent Bosnian exhibits at numerous fairs and world expositions. By the 1890s, imperial celebrations had already featured exhibits of Bosnian materials, but at the turn of the century these presentations began to assume major new dimensions. In 1896, for example, the Budapest Millennium Exposition featured an elaborate Bosnian pavilion organized by Kosta Hörmann and Henri Moser. It featured displays of "Oriental" Bosnian architecture in the "pseudo-Moorish style," designed by engineers from Vienna, Prague, and Budapest. "Living exhibits" of "Muhammedans" added a mysterious ambiance, "sitting cross-legged on the windowledge, smoking and sipping coffee, dreamily looking out to the horizon."[145] In 1898, a similarly ornate stage was constructed for Bosnia-Herzegovina during the Emperor's jubilee exhibition in Vienna, highlighting again the conspicuously Orientalized constructions housing Bosnian crafts, costumes, carpets, wares, and so on. Austro-Hungarian newspapers took special note of Franz Joseph's own visit to the Bosnian pavilion in Vienna, a highly publicized event that occurred twelve years before the emperor would actually travel to the province. Through such virtual tours, performed even by the emperor himself, Bosnia became an important part of the repertoire of imperial patriotism that was being staged and promoted in Vienna, Budapest, and Sarajevo.[146]

The 1900 Paris World Exposition marked the high point of Habsburg objectification of Bosnia. Strolling past the American exhibit, visitors to the Paris event encountered three pavilions belonging to the Habsburg Monarchy, one each for Austria, Hungary, and Bosnia — with Bosnia forming a kind of an imperial supplement, a third dimension of the Dual Monarchy. In terms of attendance and publicity, the 1900 Paris Exposition was by far the most successful such event, attracting almost 50 million visitors to a massive urban site housing the representations of twenty-two participant states. The Bosnian pavilion in particular impressed many visitors. On entering the bazaar-like structure, "one saw, on the ground floor, the panoramas of Serajevo [*sic*]" flanked by vistas of the Jajce waterfalls and the Buna springs near Mostar; "real water flowed, and a splendid rainbow appeared over the waterfall, an illusion produced by means of electric light." Actors dressed as Bosnian merchants offered their wares while a "Bosnian orchestra composed of twenty musicians, two being women in national costume," played on the second floor.[147]

Ringing the entire pavilion was Alphonse Mucha's masterpiece: a massive frieze depicting Bosnian landscapes, legends, and historical scenes (about 40 meters long and 3 meters high). Already in 1898, the Habsburg government began planning this project and offered the contract to Mucha, a world-famous art nouveau painter and declared Czech patriot with a penchant for Pan-Slavic themes.[148] Mucha's homage to Bosnia, based on his travels in the province and studies of local folklore, presented twelve panels depicting the progress of Bosnian history. Mucha was certainly familiar with the popular nineteenth-century images of "sad Bosnia"; according to the artist's son Jiří, Mucha "originally wanted to portray the suffering of this nation of people that had been constantly humiliated by foreign occupation," sketching "dark and dramatic compositions." Given different instructions from the Habsburg organizers, however, "Mucha was forced to change the compositions into scenes portraying different eras, starting with prehistoric times" and continuing to prosperous Habsburg rule. After all, the aim was to present the imperial provinces in the best possible light.[149] Beginning with three prehistoric ages, Mucha traced the region's past through Roman rule, the arrival of the Slavs, and the Ottoman period, culminating in the Austro-Hungarian present, which featured juxtaposed portraits of Bosnia's three major confessions: Catholics and Orthodox gathered around their respective priests while Muslim men stood before an architect holding a small-scale model of a mosque (in a departure from earlier Ottoman discourses, Jews were left out of this fin de siècle Habsburg picture of Bosnia). Interspersed throughout the frieze were blue-hued floral motifs and folktale figures. The towering final scene was "The Allegory of Bosnia-Herzegovina": a young, dark-haired, and lavishly costumed woman enthroned above the exhibit grounds, her head bowed down as if in modesty or submission, her arms extended in "offering her products to the World Exposition." Shepherds, workmen, and other young women and men stood by her side, staring back at the viewer and holding the bounty of the land: fruits, tobacco, timber, sheep, horses, grains, etc. (see figure 5.3.)

In effect, Mucha's centerpiece was a grand art nouveau rendering of the Habsburg imperial fairy tale, depicting a Bosnian Sleeping Beauty roused from centuries of sleep by wise imperial governance. The work, like the Bosnian pavilion itself, was very positively received. One French reviewer wrote that Mucha's paintings, particularly the centerpiece, beautifully complemented the spirit of "the young land" where "legends still

Figure 5.3 *The Allegory of Bosnia-Herzegovina*, by Alphonse Mucha, 1900. The Habsburg Monarchy set up three pavilions at the Paris World Exposition, one each for Austria, Hungary, and Bosnia. Mucha's frieze, about 40 meters long and 3 meters high, ringed the entire Bosnian pavilion.

live on in wild mountains, where modern life has not clipped the wings of popular imagination. To Bosnians, there are still mysterious forests, inhabited by fairies, who are virgins with ethereal bodies."[150] Viewed in longer nineteenth-century perspective, Mucha's portrait of Bosnia presented a counterresponse to the familiar nationalist depictions of "sad Bosnia." In the 1860s, the work of another Czech painter, Jaroslav Čermák, had provided an iconic image of Bosnian suffering in the form of a naked Christian woman being enslaved by dark-skinned Turkish thugs (a representation explored in chapter 2). The two images have clearly different valences—Čermák's depicting Turkish destruction, Mucha's highlighting Austrian flourishing—but their similarities are just as conspicuous. Like Čermák, Mucha represented Bosnia as a fertile young woman whose light complexion stands apart from some of the darker-colored "Turkish" figures in her midst. The two images display overlapping investments in notions of masculine protection and rule over this female figure, whose honor and recognition were at stake in both cases; whether raped by Turkish brutes or rescued by an Austrian king, Bosnia still remained a woman at the disposal of men in power.[151] In these senses, Čermák and Mucha were engaged in projects of marketing their respective visions of Bosnia to wider European audiences, which rewarded both artists with prestigious medals at exhibitions in Paris.

In reaching out to a variety of domestic and international audiences, the Bosnian pavilions became crucial arenas for the empire's attempt to re-present itself before its own subjects and officials. Recognition from abroad, of course, was very significant; in the eyes of Habsburg officials, exhibition medals and tourist reviews stood as proof that other Europeans admired Austria's work in Bosnia even when some local "malcontents" did not. The exhibitionary order that emerged during the nineteenth century, as Tim Mitchell and many other scholars have shown, revolved around public sites of representations (museums, world fair exhibits, etc.) designed to demonstrate European imperial superiority over the colonial subjects.[152] The history of the Habsburg project in Bosnia, however, highlights how such concerns entailed not only objectification of colonized subjects but also fundamental rethinking of imperial self-conception in light of new anxieties over the emerging national movements.

From its outset, the Habsburg project in Bosnia was a work of remaking the empire itself, a sustained attempt to refashion how the Austro-Hungarian state related to nationalist contestations, political pressures, and colonial aspirations of the late nineteenth century. Bosnia proved to be an exemplary terrain for working through these challenging issues. Resolving to make a "model province" (*Musterstaat*) out of the former Turkish borderland, the Habsburg administration tried to dispel the already present Serbian and Croatian nationalist movements and create—among imperial officials as well as provincial residents—a sense of patriotic discovery and pride in the newly acquired province.[153] Seen in this light, the fairy tale of Bosnia's awakening, developed and presented in tourist guides, fiction books, and exposition pavilions, was a template of what the Habsburg Empire could be—a model of a revitalized Austro-Hungarian state whose quiet power and charm captured the imaginations of its citizens and international audiences.

In doing so, the Habsburg administration went far beyond countering and suppressing the most challenging nationalist currents in Bosnia; it actively adopted nationalist forms and repurposed patriotic idioms for its endeavors. This entailed, among other things, the codification and glorification of parts of Bosnia's past, the development of new institutions and symbolic registers, and the organization of elaborate self-presentations before a variety of audiences. Habsburg projects in Bosnia integrated ethnographic and folkloric pursuits, the very hallmarks of nineteenth-century nationalist activity, and featured them very prominently in the establishment of new print media, cultural associations, and international exhibits. Even the very trope of "awakening" the Bosnian Sleeping Beauty was already provided by and associated with national revival projects. The folktale itself came from the romantic repertoire of the Grimm brothers and, as the political scientist Ron Suny noted, it remained a commonplace metaphor for "national awakening" ever since.[154] That the Habsburg imperial authorities eagerly took on the role of the patriotic awakener in Bosnia stands as a telling instance of the ubiquity and the appeal of nationalist political forms.

Rethinking Imperial Patriotism

It can be tempting to interpret Ottoman and Habsburg approaches to patriotism as "alternatives" to the more familiar kinds of nationalism. After all, certain aspects of Habsburg and Ottoman state reform clearly fostered "supranational," "regional," or "local" affiliations and loyalties that stood at odds with the established national movements.[155] Moreover, the fact that the Ottoman and Habsburg Empires collapsed during the First World War while nationalist forces triumphed often prompts somewhat nostalgic "what could have been" considerations that make imperial projects appear decidedly different from the nation-centered and violent histories that unfolded in the wake of 1914.

But while there were clear differences and declared antagonisms between imperial and national forces, we should not lose sight of the crucial role that empires have historically played in spreading nationalism and actively generating new national projects. To be clear, this is not a matter of the now-commonplace observation that imperial administrative practices have often unintentionally encouraged the creation of new patriotic attachments and rival political imaginings (by designating provincial units, for example, or by categorizing imperial populations in censuses and maps).[156] As the case of Bosnia shows, the rise of new patriotic projects in this province was not an inadvertent side effect of some unrelated administrative act—instead, it was the stated point of carefully cultivated Ottoman and Habsburg efforts and policies, especially those directed toward Bosnian Muslim constituencies. In the Habsburg context in particular, Bosnian Muslims came to play a double role in the development of imperial patriotism: they were identified as a potential "state-building element" in this province itself and were exoticized as an "Oriental" presence that guaranteed Bosnia's difference from other Habsburg provinces. Such imperial patriotic projects intensified the already existing lines of national difference drawn around Bosnian Muslims as (br)others in the South Slavic national imaginaries.[157]

Although a number of writers have already called attention to the intersections of imperial and national projects—"In theory, there is an abyss between nationalism and imperialism; in practice, it can and has been bridged," Hannah Arendt wrote in the 1950s—few historians have considered the ramifications of imperial histories for our understanding of nationalism. Focus on imperial patriotic activities allows us to challenge "the idea of a natural succession 'from empire to nation-state'" and to explore how empires and nations "often operate in similar ways," as Krishan Kumar recently urged scholars to do.[158] The emergence of print media in Bosnia presents one domain that illustrates the inseparability of imperial-national political practices. Although there were competing imperial and national publications by the end of the nineteenth century, these press media were born together, developing shared languages and initiatives. Even in areas where the Ottoman and Habsburg Empires had to catch up with South Slavic nationalists—as was the case with ethnography, for example—the imperial states quickly learned to appropriate such fields of activism for their programs. Although scholars have explored how twentieth-century Communist states have used ethnography for the political affirmation of particular nationalities, as was the case in the Soviet Union, the earlier nineteenth-century forays of Ottoman and Habsburg states into similarly patriotic arenas remain less well known.[159] Indeed, while Yugoslav "socialist patriotism" explicitly drew on Communist repertoires of internationalism and class struggle, many of its practices—which simultaneously monitored the nationalist opposition and affirmed the brotherhood and unity of different nationalities—also implicitly paid homage to the pioneering imperial initiatives of the nineteenth century.[160]

Ottoman and Habsburg endeavors in Bosnia frequently resignified the meanings of "patriotism," mobilizing them for different aims: advocating a break with "the old customs and superstitions," for example, or depicting imperial rule as a form of patriotic awakening, or soliciting international recognition for disparate political ventures. The proliferation of patriotic projects under Ottoman and Habsburg rule underscores what Theodora Dragostinova called the increasingly widespread fluency in "speaking national," that is, the capacity to invoke patriotic and nation-based rhetorics for a variety of purposes.[161] In this sense, Ottoman and Habsburg officials also learned to "speak national" fluently and passionately by the end of the nineteenth century. Their interventions, which actively generated new patriotic initiatives and repertoires in Bosnia, thus illuminate the underlying accessibility, translatability, and multiplicity of nation-forms across so many different political contexts.

Another Bosnia

Any history of nationalism in Bosnia must necessarily confront questions about how its findings illuminate current ethnic divisions and the legacies of the violence of the 1990s.[1] This expectation—that the country's past should explain its divisive present—not only structures academic grant formulas, which routinely require their applicants to state the "policy relevance" of humanistic or social scientific research, but also underpins broader understandings of this region. During and after the Bosnian War of 1992–1995, evening newscasts, parliamentary speeches, and newspaper editorials across Europe and the United States commonly invoked "ancient ethnic hatreds" as explanatory historical factors driving the violence. In the subsequent years, the name "Bosnia" itself has become a global synonym for "ethnic cleansing," enabling UN secretary generals and American presidents to speak of having the "determination to never again permit another Bosnia."[2] In wider scholarship as well, Bosnian and Yugoslav issues appear mostly as violent reminders of the contradictions of modernity. "The Serb-Croat wars," wrote the philosopher Charles Taylor, "disconcert us because they mix an unquestionably modern discourse—self-determination, rule by the people, et cetera—with other elements that seem to us alien to (what we understand as) modernity." For Taylor and many other writers, "the Bosnian savagery" is "quintessentially modern," a sign of our times, but it still partakes of a discrete kind of modernity that sets it apart from Western "liberal nationalism" and thus requires special explanation.[3]

This framing encourages a related expectation: that scholars should also suggest some "solutions" to the situation in contemporary Bosnia, usually by establishing a consensus on conflicting historical claims, presenting proposals for reconciling Serb-Croat-Muslim parties, or creating a more stable political framework for the country. Diplomats, political scientists, and various intellectuals continue to discuss ethnic quotas and possible border changes twenty years after the outbreak of the 1992–1995 war. Even the noted philosopher Slavoj Žižek—who in the 1990s described "('Muslim') Bosnia" as the shining legacy of Yugoslavia and its "multicultural tolerance"—proposed in a 2012 interview that it would be best to redraw some Balkan borders around Bosnia and Kosovo. "It's a horrible thought," Žižek conceded, "touching on very traumatic things," but there was no alternative except to let ethno-territorial consolidation run its course: "I would let Bosnia-Herzegovina disintegrate into two parts," he explained, which would "stabilize the situation because the current situation, where Bosnia-Herzegovina is kept under external pressure, seems so unproductive, and that is why tensions are renewed again and again." Perhaps major gains could be made by even "small changes" on the map.[4]

In such debates, one encounters again and again the temptation to "solve" national disputes, to bring the work of nationalism to some kind of satisfactory conclusion or productive end point. Over the course of the twentieth century, the primary means for implementing such solutions across the world has been the demarcation of ethno-territorial units, made nationally homogeneous through assimilation, migration, expulsion, murder, genocide, and related geopolitical strategies. The underlying assumption is that such changes "stabilize the situation" in the long term and provide a relatively satisfactory answer to seething tensions in a variety of contested multiethnic areas.

Nation-making understood in this sense appears like a giant jigsaw puzzle. This game is a commonplace metaphor for national disputes, one that has been often invoked since at least the nineteenth century. In this model, thousands of old and new pieces, interlocking shapes, and particular physical constraints limit possibilities for movement and change. Nonetheless, many believe that with enough creativity, attention, and time, the challenging puzzle pieces of nation-making can be made to fit together and produce a stable, perhaps even pleasing geopolitical picture in the end.[5]

Back to Grounded Theory

To study nationalism in Bosnia is thus to enter a field already framed by the assumption that the ultimate subject of any such inquiry will be, in one way or another, ethnic violence and ethno-territorial structures. My strategy in engaging this framework has been to displace or subvert its basic assumptions in order to present a different understanding of the histories of nationalism in Bosnia. In doing so, I have borrowed from and improvised on anthropological and literary methods that proceed not by rejecting prior terms or assumptions but by delving into their logics and extending them. As Marilyn Strathern has written, "displacement can only come from a previous position. It thus extends"—takes on and transforms—"that previous position rather than refutes it."[6] Consequently, my historical account does not dismiss the emphasis on violence in order to replace it with an emphasis on intercommunal peace, nor does it privilege the expectation that this study will ultimately explain wartime and postwar Bosnia. In either case, such moves risk locking our analyses into fixed positions revolving around binaries (violence-nonviolence, present-past) that reinforce each other and repose already established claims rather than produce new directions for research.[7]

Instead of continuing such cycles, my approach has aimed to identify and work within certain unavoidable registers of narrating and analyzing South Slavic national movements. The turn to the empirical, which Claudio Lomnitz has called "grounded theory," affords multiple advantages. It helps do justice to the richness of the diverse sources, archives, and materials that speak to the histories of nationalism in Bosnia. This strategy also has the benefit of opening up subjects that may initially seem parochial—such as the literatures on national suffering in Bosnia—by revealing how they constituted integral parts of related transnational developments across the Balkans and Western Europe, thus making these provincial findings speak to broader political concerns. Moreover, it allows us to challenge the more predictable readings of these histories and to outline an interpretation of nationalism as a dynamic and still proliferating political form.

I have made use of these grounded-theoretical strategies of displacement in several ways. In taking up the oft-posed prompt, "whose is Bosnia?" this book overtly engages with a central nationalist debate but seeks to displace the dramatic narratives that usually follow this question and lead to already established political positions. Instead of providing explanations of different possible answers ("Bosnia is Serbian," "Bosnia is Muslim," "Bosnia is no man's land," and so on), this study revisits the historical materials and narrative strategies that such answers rely on. I have taken up central subjects in South Slavic national histories, such as the work of Vuk Karadžić or the 1914 Sarajevo assassination, and have delved into them, bringing out the genealogies, tensions, and debates that animated them. To be clear, this approach does not aim to move beyond "the classics" of national histories so as to replace them with some other (perhaps more politically appealing) figures and explanations; rather, it strives to provide new insight into these inescapable national sites.

Crucially, this approach has led me to conceptualize nationalism differently from most scholarly accounts, understanding it not as a finite movement that ends in some momentous achievement (the establishment of a state, the partition of territories and populations, etc.), but as a political project that is fundamentally open-ended and impossible to complete. I did not originally set out to write about these ideas, but as I researched and wrote about South Slavic national politics I increasingly realized I had to confront and explicate these peculiar workings of nation-making. My strategy in analyzing these phenomena has been generally twofold. On the one hand, I focused on the proliferation of national forms across diverse political contexts in and around Bosnia, showing how particular nationalist genres, practices, and idioms—such as folkloric ethnography—enabled the generation of ever-more patriotic projects in the South Slavic political space, including Serbian-Croatian ventures as well as Ottoman and Habsburg imperial initiatives. On the other hand, I explored the compulsion that certain subjects—like suffering or youth—have exercised on these national movements, compelling activists to continually reengage with their demands and implications for nation-making. Analysis of these proliferating and compelling national forms not only helps explain how nationalist politics historically came to saturate areas like Bosnia but also provides insight into nationalism as a dynamic and open-ended project.

National narratives relating to Bosnian Muslims form a major theme of this book, appearing not as a separate chapter but as a distinct thread that reveals certain aspects of South Slavic and Ottoman-Habsburg politics. In particular, I have focused on struggles over the national belonging of Bosnian Muslims as a way of exploring the figure of the (br)other. Since "(br)other" is not an independent term defining a substance but an interpretive device for analyzing claims of sameness and otherness, it needs to be read primarily in its historical contexts, which the preceding pages have explored at length. Here I limit myself to a few remarks that clarify the (br)other figure and point out how it works to further the goals of this book.

To show the complexity of meanings of "brotherhood" in South Slavic national politics, one need not resort to a mythical referent, such as the biblical story of Cain and Abel, which already anticipates a focus on fratricide. A different, and in many ways more direct, path to understanding the (br)other as co-national can be found within the nationalist productions analyzed in this study, such as Vuk Karadžić's *The Serbian Dictionary*, the first national publication of its kind (1818, revised 1852). As usual, Vuk provided corresponding German and Latin terms for his definitions and then offered illustrations drawn from South Slavic proverbs, folk poetry, and other ethnographic material. Here, for instance, is Vuk's entry for the word "brother" (*brat*):

Brother: m., *der Bruder*; *frater*;

[1]   He who helps me is a *brother* to me.

[2]   A: Who gouged out your eye?
       B: My *brother*.
       A: That is why it's so deep.

[3]   There is no summer until St. George's day
       Nor a *brother* until his mother births him
       At home I have nine dear *brothers*.[8]

To see this entry as evidence of either harmonious fraternity or terrifying fratricide is to miss the range and movement that it displays. Instead of trying to determine whether this text speaks more to brotherly solidarity or conflict, it is more productive to consider the simultaneity of different senses and relations among them. The entry outlines, on the one hand, the extended and transferrable meaning of brother as a nonfamilial affinity (appearing proverbially as "He who helps me is a brother to me" in the first example) while, on the other hand, it also asserts bonds of directly shared familial ancestry and ancestral space (multiple brothers birthed by the same mother and inhabiting the same home, as in the third example cited from folk poetry). The middle passage is drawn from Vuk's collection of proverbs; presented in a question-and-answer form and alluding to a nineteenth-century Slavic folk tale, it brings into focus fraternal violence and its intensity, emphasizing a wound—not death—dealt by one's brother.[9] This difference is significant not to make eye-gouging appear less bad than murder, but to simply note that the focus is not on fratricide but on ongoing and ambivalent fraternal relations. Even when raising the possibility of murder, most brother-related discussions in the nineteenth-century South Slavic national canon dwell on the living antagonisms and intimacies between brothers; to cite another widely known proverb from Vuk's collection, "Brother leads a brother over a pit, but does not push him into it."[10] As one Croatian scholar wrote in 1889, "the proverbs that show the unethical mutual relations of brothers are far more numerous" than ones concerned with the normative "ethical bond" of "brotherly love."[11] In both "ethical" and "unethical" cases, the intensity of brotherly relations is often highlighted—"That's why it's so deep"—and left unresolved.

Within the proliferating nineteenth-century debates over the meanings of South Slavic brotherhood, "the Turks" occupied particularly conspicuous roles. Some Serbian and Croatian national activists tried to distinguish between "the Turks" (meaning non-Slavic Ottoman rulers) and "our Turks" (meaning Bosnian Muslims). In heralding a new patriotic age that would unite South Slavic brothers across religious and regional boundaries, national activists were fond of citing the well-known saying: "Cherish your brother, his faith be yours or other (when he acts and behaves like a brother)."[12] The proverb, appearing in Vuk's and many other folkloric collections, thus encapsulated the patriotic imperative as one of cross-confessional solidarity, though with a condition that stipulated amiable "brotherly" relations.

At the same time, as many examples in this book have shown, openly anti-Turkish writings became exceptionally popular at this time, ranging from folk poetry depicting battles between Turkish villains and South Slav heroes to nineteenth-century classics like *The Death of Smail-aga* (1846) or *The Mountain Wreath* (1847). Widely popular references to Turks—like the saying, "There is no greater butcher [or blood-antagonist, *krvnik*] than a turned-Turk"—sometimes directly specified Slavic converts to Islam as the greatest threat to the national being and appeared alongside calls for cross-confessional brotherly unity.[13]

Yet even in the more extreme cases of the dehumanization of the Turks in the South Slavic national imaginary, implications of shared bonds continued to reappear. An 1887 collection of Serbian folklore from Croatia told the following tale about "the Turks": "There are Turks with tails, with a tail like a dog. They come into our lands too; they cannot sit down, but must curl their tails, cross their legs, and thus squat. They can smell a baptized Christian soul; our blood tastes sweet to them. — (Yes, our turned-Turks are not like that.)[14]

In cases like this, there is no need to find an explicit mention of the term "brother" in order to observe this figure at work. The story's concluding remark conveys some of the ways in which the figure of the (br)other reappears across processes that scholars often describe as Othering, assimilation, dehumanization, and inclusion: it appears as a parenthetical clarification, an almost casual and affirmative remark: yes, of course, those belonging to "our" own people are not like dogs, "they" do not have a taste for "our" blood because a part of "them" is "us." After the parenthesis is closed and the inconclusive clarification has been made, the passages from "ours" to "theirs," from "brother" to "Other," remain implicitly open. To capture these sliding meanings and reversible processes of national identification, my approach has been to double-write the term "(br)other" strategically, inscribing it not always, but at selective points, in order to foster different expectations and sensitivities in interpreting various discussions of national community and identity.

This approach helps us clarify one reason, among several, why this history matters. In exploring nineteenth-century South Slavic movements, this book has addressed issues of difference, assimilation, and violence in specific contexts — in discussions of national suffering or in youth heroism, for example — but it has done so without claiming that these histories "add up" to account for the violence of the 1990s or the contemporary situation in the country. Of course, historical inquiries can help us reconsider such subjects, but only if they move beyond unhelpful notions of "history repeating itself" and engage more creatively with different senses of historical legacy and with particular contexts of violence, which require extensive and careful local analysis.[15] In light of these general points, I consider one brief example of how the history of nineteenth-century political imaginaries can be useful in interpreting some moments of the nationalist present in Bosnia.

In 2005, the road sign for the ethnically cleansed village of Urkovići near Srebrenica was defaced shortly after some Muslim refugees returned to claim their former homes in what is now the Serbian entity. Someone had added a "T," so the defaced sign read [T]Urkovići. As Carl Dahlman and Gerard Toal, who highlight this case in their study of refugee return in postwar Bosnia, wrote: "This change was an intimidating reminder to villagers that some saw them not as returning neighbors but 'Turks.' A recovering place was publicly marked as enemy space. Disclosed in this seemingly minor local gesture is the foundational act of geopolitics upon which ethnic cleansing rests globally: the re-mapping of fellow neighbors as foreign enemies."[16]

While I agree with Dahlman's and Toal's interpretation, which stresses that "Bosnia's struggles are indeed within a long European historical tradition,"

I also want to point out how certain nationalist engagements with history, such as the [T]Urkovići sign, work: not by simple repetition but by active improvisation, defacing, and double-writing within particular repertoires and contexts. This study has, in part, aimed to identify such national repertoires in Bosnia and to explore the ambiguities and possibilities inhering within them, especially as they concern "Turks" and "brothers." As this book has shown, processes of nationalization targeting Bosnian Muslims have not been unidirectional or marked by more or less steady Othering, but have been rather reversible, alternating and slipping between claims of belonging and enmity, underlying sameness and extreme difference. In light of these dynamics, it is worth emphasizing that nation-making does not culminate in "the re-mapping of fellow neighbors as foreign enemies" and thus end with the destruction of the Other, but instead repeatedly exposes the inescapable and undecidable figure of the (br)other within the national community.

The point is not in some "continuity" of the (br)other—a figure too shifting and changeable to be continuous—but rather in his irrepressibility. It would be easy to dismiss this kind of (br)otherhood as an exceptional Balkan ailment, a complication localized to one corner of the world, but such claims would run against the historical record and structural workings of modern nationalism at large. As Zygmunt Bauman has written, "no attempt to assimilate, transform, acculturate or absorb the ethnic, religious, linguistic, cultural and other heterogeneity and dissolve it in the homogeneous body of the nation was, or indeed could be, unconditionally successful." Violence, however devastating, is ultimately incapable of erasing the (br)others within; "their numbers and nuisance power seem to grow with the intensity" of strategies aimed to eliminate them. Bauman's perspective helps us see (br)otherhood not as an aspect of timeless human "nature" but as a historical-structural condition of modern national societies whose classification schemes are inevitably disturbed by "strangers," those who come to stand "for the treacherousness of friends, for the cunning disguise of the enemies, for fallibility of order, vulnerability of the inside."[17]

The political upheavals and the massive violence of the twentieth century have profoundly altered the relations between different communities in Bosnia, tearing neighbors, friends, and families apart in the name of ethnic difference and territorial partition. But throughout these changes, elusive bonds of (br)otherhood remain central to the work of nationalism, defying claims of resolution and exposing the inherent incompleteability of nation-making projects.

Game Over

In summing up these histories, perhaps it is useful to reconsider the jigsaw puzzle as a foundational metaphor for nationalism and propose another comparison drawn also from the repertoire of common games. As this book understands it, the key analog of nationalism is not the familiar jigsaw puzzle, which presumably has a correct solution of some sort, but Tetris, one of the icons of twentieth-century puzzle video games. In Tetris, there is no "solution," no prescribed "end," no stages that the action goes through on its way to a triumphant conclusion. All one does is struggle to align the unceasing stream of falling, differently shaped blocks into continuous rows. The player is rewarded for every properly unified row, but the satisfaction is brief because each line, as soon as it is completed, disappears; more blocks continue to fall. This peculiar setup—emphasizing the conspicuously incomplete lines and sinister breaks in continuity rather than the consolidated achievements—has been cited as a major factor in explaining why such a seemingly simple game has become so popular and addictive.[18] In addition to resembling the ambitions and anxieties of nation-builders to continually realign and reorder their volatile domains, Tetris can illuminate nationalism because it is premised on what game analysts call a "no-victory condition," a structural design that makes the game impossible to complete. No matter how adept a player is at unifying rows, the game eventually and always ends the same way: the mounting obstacles overwhelm and topple the entire construction, until one starts over again.

Notes

ABiH   Arhiv Bosne i Hercegovine (State Archive of Bosnia and Herzegovina)

AFM   Archive of the Franciscan Monastery, followed by town name: Fojnica (FO), Kreševo (KR), Kraljeva Sutjeska (KS), Sarajevo (SA), Tolisa (TO)

AH   Arhiv Hercegovine u Mostaru (Archive of the Herzegovina Canton in Mostar)

AHAZU   Arhiv hrvatske akademije znanosti i umjetnosti (Archive of the Croatian Academy of Arts and Sciences)

AS   Arhiv Srbije (State Archive of Serbia)

ASANU   Arhiv srpske akademije nauka i umetnosti (Archive of the Serbian Academy of Arts and Sciences)

ATK   Arhiv Tuzlanskog kantona (Archive of the Tuzla Canton)

BIFZ   *Bosna u tajnim političkim izvještajima Frantiśeka Zacha iz Beograda*, ed. Václav Záček (Sarajevo: ANUBiH, 1976) (Bosnia in the secret reports of František Zach)

GPKH-PLG   *Građa za povijest književnosti hrvatske*, vol. 26, *Pisma Ljudevitu Gaju*, ed. Josip Horvat and Jakša Ravlić (Zagreb: JAZU, 1956) (Letters to Ljudevit Gaj)

HAS   Historijski arhiv Sarajevo (Historical Archive of the City of Sarajevo)

HHStA   Haus-, Hof- und Staatsarchiv (Austrian State Archives, Vienna)

IFJ-SD   *Ivan Franjo Jukić: Sabrana djela*, 3 vols., ed. Boris Ćosić (Sarajevo: Svjetlost, 1973) (Collected works of Ivan Franjo Jukić)

MB-PP   *Mlada Bosna: Pisma i prilozi*, ed. Vojislav Bogićević (Sarajevo: Svjetlost, 1954) (Young Bosnia letters)

NSK   Nacionalna i sveučilišna knjižnica u Zagrebu (National and University Library in Zagreb)

OiP   Vladimir Gaćinović, *Ogledi i pisma*, ed. Todor Vujasinović (Sarajevo: Svjetlost, 1956) (Writings and letters of Vladimir Gaćinović)

SDVK   *Sabrana djela Vuka Karadžića*, 36 vols., ed. Golub Dobrašinović et al. (Belgrade: Prosveta, 1965) (Collected works of Vuk Karadžić)

Introduction

1. Milutin Garašanin (1843–1898) was the son of the famed Serbian
prime minister Ilija Garašanin (1812–1874), known as the architect of Serbia's
nineteenth-century expansion; on his life and sources, see Anon., "Milutin
Garašanin," *Bosanska vila* 13, no. 5 (1898): 5; J. M. Žujović, "Milutin Garašanin,"
Godišnjak Srpske kraljevske akademije 12 (1899): 213–220; and Momčilo Žeravčić,
ed., *Milutin Garašanin: Lični fond* (Belgrade: Arhiv Srbije, 1977). Quotations from
M. Garašanin, *Dokolice* (Belgrade: Horovic, 1892), 88–89. All translations are
mine unless otherwise indicated.

2. Garašanin, *Dokolice*, 88–89.

3. On Milutin Garašanin's activities regarding Bosnia, see Milorad Ekmečić,
Bosanski ustanak, 1875–1878, 3rd ed. (Belgrade: SANU, 1996), 146; and Predlog
za organizaciju i prepremu ustanka u Bosni, 26 January 1865, FMG no. 6, AS.

4. Garašanin, *Dokolice*, on "phraseology," 1; on patriotism, 90–91.

5. Benedict Anderson, *Imagined Communities: Reflections on the Origins and
Spread of Nationalism*, 3rd ed. (London: Verso, 2006), 4, 41, 81.

6. Homi K. Bhabha, ed., *Nation and Narration* (London: Routledge, 1990), 1.

7. Balibar suggested "excess of nationalism" and "supplement of nationalism"
as terms to describe "an internal contradiction" that, in his view, consists of the
tensions between proclaimed national equality and continuing class antagonisms;
this understanding retraces Anderson's notion of "an imagined community"
without considering alternate interpretations of this tension. See Étienne Balibar,
Masses, Classes, Ideas: Studies on Politics and Philosophy before and after Marx
(London: Routledge, 1994), 202–204.

8. Miroslav Hroch, *Social Preconditions of National Revival in Europe:
A Comparative Analysis of the Social Composition of Patriotic Groups among
the Smaller European Nations*, trans. Ben Fowkes, 2nd ed. (New York:
Columbia University Press, 2000); and Hroch, "From National Movement to the
Fully-Formed Nation: The Nation-Building Process in Europe," in *Mapping the
Nation*, ed. Gopal Balakrishnan (London: Verso, 1996), 78–97.

9. For example, Eugen Weber, *Peasants Into Frenchmen: The Modernization
of Rural France, 1870–1914* (Stanford, CA: Stanford University Press, 1976); Peter
Sahlins, *Boundaries: The Making of France and Spain in the Pyrenees* (Berkeley:
University of California Press, 1989); Celia Applegate, *A Nation of Provincials: The
German Idea of Heimat* (Berkeley: University of California Press, 1990); Jeremy
King, *Budweisers into Czechs and Germans: A Local History of Bohemian Politics,
1848–1948* (Princeton, NJ: Princeton University Press, 2002); and Marnix Beyen
and Maarten Van Ginderachter, eds., *Nationhood from Below: Europe in the Long
Nineteenth Century* (New York: Palgrave Macmillan, 2012).

10. Pero Slijepčević (Slepčević), *Privatna inicijativa u nacionalnom radu* (Geneva:
Kurir, 1918), 19–20.

11. Claudio Lomnitz, *Deep Mexico, Silent Mexico: An Anthropology of
Nationalism* (Minneapolis: University of Minnesota Press, 2001), xv–xix and 127.

12. For example, Sanjay Seth, "Rewriting Histories of Nationalism: The Politics
of Modern Nationalism in India, 1870–1905," *American Historical Review*
104, no. 1 (1999): 95–116; and Pheng Cheah, *Spectral Nationality: Passages of
Freedom from Kant to Postcolonial Literatures of Liberation* (New York: Columbia
University Press, 2003).

13. Maria Todorova, "The Trap of Backwardness: Modernity, Temporality, and the Study of Eastern European Nationalism," *Slavic Review* 64, no. 1 (2005): 140–164; and Todorova, *Imagining the Balkans*, 2nd ed. (Oxford: Oxford University Press, 2009).

14. Lomnitz, *Deep Mexico*, xv–xix and 127.

15. Scholarship on intellectuals and nationalism is enormous; for an introduction, see Ronald Grigor Suny and Michael D. Kennedy, eds., *Intellectuals and the Articulation of the Nation* (Ann Arbor: University of Michigan Press, 1999); Dominic Boyer and Claudio Lomnitz, "Intellectuals and Nationalism: Anthropological Engagements," *Annual Review of Anthropology* 34 (2005): 105–120; and Zygmunt Bauman, "Intellectuals in East-Central Europe: Continuity and Change," *East European Politics and Societies* 1, no. 2 (1987): 162–186. On activists as key protagonists of national movements, see esp. Pieter Judson, *The Guardians of the Nation: Activists on the Language Frontiers of Imperial Austria* (Cambridge, MA: Harvard University Press, 2006); and Tara Zahra, *Kidnapped Souls: National Indifference and the Battle for Children in the Bohemian Lands, 1900–1948* (Ithaca, NY: Cornell University Press, 2008).

16. Pursuit of these questions still remains focused on cultural and intellectual production, but it helps move us away from rigid conceptions of "elites," "ordinary people," and "agency"; the last term in particular has often become a byword for resistance to authority rather than a category for analyzing wider relations of power. For a trenchant critique of such understandings of agency, see Saba Mahmood, *Politics of Piety: Islamic Revival and the Feminist Subject* (Princeton, NJ: Princeton University Press, 2005), 1–39, 153–188.

17. On the nation as an abstraction, see Anderson, *Imagined Communities*, 6–7; and Lomnitz, *Deep Mexico*, xv, 6–7.

18. The questions that I pose here are not meant to present a totalizing theory of nationalism; I am well aware of the problematic character of the universalizing and Eurocentric impulses of modern social sciences, including the discipline of history. In fact, it is precisely because nationalist assumptions encourage totalizing perspectives—fostering a worldview in which "every nation" both takes a standardized, universally recognizable form and possesses a supposedly unique national content—that nationalism requires extensive grounded-theoretical scrutiny. On a formative nationalist vision of "a world of nations," see Giuseppe Mazzini, Stefano Recchia, and Nadia Urbinati, eds., *A Cosmopolitanism of Nations: Giuseppe Mazzini's Writings on Democracy, Nation Building, and International Relations* (Princeton, NJ: Princeton University Press, 2009).

19. Hazim Šabanović, *Bosanski pašaluk: Postanak i upravna podjela* (Sarajevo: ANUBiH, 1982), 35–58, 115–174; and Ahmed Aličić, *Uređenje bosanskog ejaleta od 1789 do 1878 godine* (Sarajevo: Orijentalni institut, 1983), 17–44, 120–132. In this study I use the word "Bosnia" as shorthand for the entire province of Bosnia-Herzegovina; I use "Herzegovina" when referring to this region located southeast of central Bosnia.

20. Ratimir Gašparović, *Bosna i Hercegovina na geografskim kartama od prvih početaka do kraja XIX vijeka* (Sarajevo: ANUBiH, 1970); and Anita Burdett, ed., *The Historical Boundaries between Bosnia, Croatia, Serbia: Documents and Maps, 1815–1945* (Cambridge, UK: Archive Editions, 1995).

21. On Ottoman categories, see Ömer Barkan, "Tarihi Demografi Araştırmaları ve Osmanı Tarihi," *Türkiyat Mecmuası* 10 (1951): 1–27. On Bosnia, see Đorđe

Pejanović, *Stanovništvo Bosne i Hercegovine* (Belgrade: SANU, 1955), 12–28; and Jusuf Mulić, "Prilog istraživanju mogućnosti procjenjivanja broja stanovnika u Bosni i Hercegovini u vrijeme osmanske vlasti," *Hercegovina* 13 (2001): 35–68.

22. Pejanović, *Stanovništvo Bosne i Hercegovine*, 23–46; and Vojislav Bogićević, *Pismenost u Bosni i Hercegovini: Od pojave slovenske pismenosti u IX vijeku do kraja austrougarske vladavine u Bosni i Hercegovini 1918 godine* (Sarajevo: Veselin Masleša, 1975). Most of the population in Bosnia spoke some variant of Serbo-Croatian, but it should be stressed that Albanian, Ladino, Italian, Turkish, Hungarian, Arabic, Greek, Czech, and other languages were also present. For archival examples of various languages in use in nineteenth-century Bosnia, see Zbirka pisama, ZOP No. 979, ABiH.

23. A typical nationalist map of the Balkans, in this case Greek, explained: "There are five colors on the map, one each for Romanians, Serbs, Bulgarians, and Albanians. For Greeks there are two colors, one for Greeks inside the kingdom of Greece, one for Greeks in Turkey. There is no color for Muslims and Turks" (or for any "others"). Stojan Novaković (Šar-Planinac), "Grčke misli o etnografiji balkanskog poluostrva," *Otadžbina* 25 (1890): 234–235.

24. On these issues, see Pieter Judson, "Frontiers, Islands, Forests, Stones: Mapping the Geography of a German Identity in the Habsburg Monarchy, 1848–1900," in *The Geography of Identity*, ed. Patricia Yaeger (Ann Arbor: University of Michigan Press, 1996), 382–406; and Gerard Toal and Carl T. Dahlman, "A Distinctive Geopolitical Space," *Bosnia Remade: Ethnic Cleansing and Its Reversal* (Oxford: Oxford University Press, 2011), 46–82.

25. For example, Leopold von Ranke, *The History of Servia and the Servian Revolution, with a Sketch of the Insurrection in Bosnia*, trans. Louisa Kerr, 3rd ed. (London: H. G. Bohn, 1853); Karl Marx, *The Eastern Question: A Reprint of Letters Written, 1853–1856*, ed. Eleanor Marx Aveling (London: Sonnenschein, 1897); and generally see David Roessel, *In Byron's Shadow: Modern Greece in the English and American Imagination* (Oxford: Oxford University Press, 2002).

26. On such notions of "Europe," see Holly Case, *Between States: The Transylvanian Question and the European Idea during World War II* (Stanford, CA: Stanford University Press, 2009); and Case, "Being European: East and West," in *European Identity*, ed. Jeffrey T. Checkel and Peter J. Katzenstein (Cambridge: Cambridge University Press, 2009), 111–131.

27. Robert Lee Wolff, *The Balkans: Many Peoples, Many Problems* (Madison, WI: USAFI, 1944).

28. Cf. Mihovil Pavlinović, *Hrvatski razgovori* (Zadar: Narodni list, 1877); and Apollon Maikov, *Bosna je srpska: Ili odgovor na "Razgovore" Don-Mih. Pavlinovića*, 2nd ed. (Novi Sad: Srpska narodna štamparija, 1878).

29. For example, Ćiro Truhelka, *Hrvatska Bosna, mi i oni tamo* (n.p., 1907) and R. M., *Hrvatska Bosna: Mi i "tamo oni"* (Mostar: Narod, 1908).

30. For example, Emerich Bogović, *Zur bosnischen Frage* (Zagreb: Hartman, 1880); Lazo M. Kostić, *Čija je Bosna?: Mišljenja stranih naučnika i političara o etničkoj pripadnosti Bosne i Hercegovine* (Toronto: Bratstvo, 1955); Enver Redžić, "Komunistička partija Jugoslavije i pitanje Bosne i Hercegovine," *Prilozi* 5 (1969): 10–26; and Đoko Slijepčević, *Pitanje Bosne i Hercegovine u XIX veku* (Cologne: n.p., 1981).

31. Ivo Banac, "Separating History from Myth: An Interview," in *Why Bosnia?: Writings on the Balkan War*, ed. Rabia Ali and Lawrence Lifshultz (Stony Creek, CT: Pamphleteer's Press, 1993), 138–139. Also Banac, *The National Question in Yugoslavia: Origins, History, Politics* (Ithaca, NY: Cornell University Press, 1984).

32. *No Man's Land* was the title of the Oscar-winning 2001 film by Danis Tanović.

33. Slavoj Žižek, *Did Somebody Say Totalitarianism?: Five Interventions in the (Mis)use of a Notion* (London: Verso, 2001), 232; and Žižek, "Caught in Another's Dream in Bosnia," in Ali and Lifshultz, *Why Bosnia?*, 233–240.

34. On the tensions of "speaking for" subaltern subjects, see the discussion in Rosalind Morris, ed., *Can the Subaltern Speak?: Reflections on the History of an Idea* (New York: Columbia University Press, 2010).

35. "Whose is . . . ?" is a favorite format of nationalist questions about "ambiguous" or "controversial" places, persons, or cultural artifacts. "Whenever I teach," wrote Aleksandar Hemon, "I encounter the question that, in this or that way, many students have posed: Whose is the writer Danilo Kiš? To what culture does he belong? . . . The question presents a problem for me because I am not able to answer it without getting tripped into protofascist sentences in which terms like 'mixed marriage' figure prominently." Aleksandar Hemon, "Čiji je pisac Danilo Kiš?" *Sarajevske sveske* 8 (2005): 9–11. On similar tropes elsewhere, see Sumantra Bose, *Contested Lands: Israel-Palestine, Kashmir, Bosnia, Cyprus, and Sri Lanka* (Cambridge, MA: Harvard University Press, 2010).

36. This reading draws heavily on Roland Barthes, *S/Z*, trans. Richard Miller (New York: Hill & Wang, 1974).

37. Timothy Garton Ash, "The Last Revolution," *New York Review of Books*, 16 November 2000, 11, emphasis mine.

38. Gale Stokes, "Solving the Wars of Yugoslav Succession," in *Yugoslavia and Its Historians: Understanding the Balkan Wars of the 1990s*, ed. Norman M. Naimark and Holly Case (Stanford, CA: Stanford University Press, 2003), 193–207, emphasis mine. Mihailo Crnobrnja's survey openly states its genre in its title: *The Yugoslav Drama*, 2nd ed. (Montreal: McGill-Queen's University Press, 1996).

39. On the dramatic and the epic, see Bertolt Brecht, *Brecht on Theater: The Development of an Aesthetic*, ed. John Willett (New York: Hill and Wang, 1964).

40. Nikola Trišić-Triša testimony, 11 December 1952, in *Sarajevski atentat: 28. VI 1914: Pisma i saopštenja*, ed. Vojislav Bogičević (Sarajevo: Svjetlost, 1965), 94.

41. Ivan Franjo Jukić, *Zemljopis i poviestnica Bosne* (Zagreb: Gaj, 1851), 17–18.

42. For example, Anderson discussed "fratricide" and "unbrotherly" relations mainly as an issue of "memory and forgetting," that is, how later national mythologies reframe past conflicts and divisions to project images of national unity onto historical accounts. This analysis, although insightful in some aspects, does not adequately consider the basic relations that sustain the living ambivalent bonds of brotherhood. Anderson, *Imagined Communities*, 6–7, 199–203.

43. Jacques Derrida, *The Politics of Friendship*, trans. George Collins (London: Verso, 1997), esp. viii–ix, 33–34, 88–89, 96–97, 236–240. As Derrida stated in an interview, in this book he "tried to analyze what happened to Greek thought with the advent of Christianity, especially with the concept of brotherhood. The way the Christian concept of brother transformed the Greek concept of brotherhood was

at the same time something new, an inauguration, a mutation, a break, but this break, at the same time, was developing something which was potentially inscribed in the Greek tradition." See John Caputo, ed., *Deconstruction in a Nutshell: A Conversation with Jacques Derrida* (New York: Fordham University Press, 1997), 10. On Christian underpinnings of the secular democratic category of "fraternity," see Mona Ozouf, "Fraternity," in *A Critical Dictionary of the French Revolution*, trans. Arthur Goldhammer (Cambridge, MA: Harvard University Press, 1989), 694–703.

44. Zygmunt Bauman's notion of "the stranger" is important here; see his *Modernity and Ambivalence* (Cambridge, MA: Polity, 1991), esp. 61–62. On broader considerations (which also inspired Bauman's work on "the stranger"), see Jacques Derrida, *Dissemination*, trans. Barbara Johnson (London: Athlone, 1981), esp. 95–100, 219–222; and Derrida, *Positions*, trans. Alan Bass (Chicago: University of Chicago Press, 1981), 42–43.

45. As Carole Pateman has written, fraternal politics are not a reinscription of a nuclear family model onto society: "Modern civil society is not structured by kinship and the power of fathers; in the modern world, women are subordinated to men as *men*, or to men as a fraternity." "Fraternity" itself is a "term that is usually missing in discussions of the social contract and civil society, [and] must be restored to its rightful place" in analyses of modern political concepts, especially of nationalist ideologies. Pateman, *The Sexual Contract* (Stanford, CA: Stanford University Press, 1988), 3, 77–115.

46. I thank the anonymous "reviewer one" for these insightful interpretations of the (br)other dynamics.

1. The Land of the People

1. Ivan Lorković, "Veliko djelo," *Novo doba* 1 (1898): 104.

2. Stojan Novaković, "Jedan razgovor iz najstarije srpske istorije," in *Srpska čitanka za niže gimnazije i realke* (Belgrade: Državna štamparija, 1870), 9–17; cf. Miroslav Kraljević, *Požeški djak, ili: Ljubimo milu svoju narodnost i grlimo sladki svoj narodni jezik* (Požega: Kraljević, 1863).

3. Anon., "Domovina, ili Država i narod," serialized in *Danica Ilirska* 6 (1840); Karol Libelt, "Ljubav otadžbine," serialized in *Kolo* 7 (1850): esp. 31–46; Ivan Lorković, "Rački," in *Narodna misao* (Zagreb: Dionička tiskara, 1897), 78–218; Stjepan Deželić, *Hrvatska narodnost, iliti duša hrvatskoga naroda: Poviestno-filozofička razprava* (Zagreb: Hartman, 1879); cf. Milovan Milovanović, "Načelo narodnosti u međunarodnom pravu i međunarodnoj politici," *Otadžbina* 22 (1889): 321–345.

4. One example among countless such nineteenth-century collections: "Everything that the people has made by itself, without foreign influence, possesses its own particular and pure character. This characteristic particularity, this immeasurable treasure, it bequeaths to its successors . . . in shapes that can hold the most of this treasure, as created by the people's spirit, the people's genius, its entire wisdom and knowledge." Miloš Milojević, *Pesme i običai ukupnog naroda srpskog*, 3 vols. (Belgrade: Državna štamparija, 1870).

5. Ernest Renan's 1882 essay originally titled "Qu'est-ce qu'une nation?" appeared in Serbian a year later as *Šta je narod?* (Belgrade: Sv. Sava, 1883).

6. Gliša Geršić, "Nacionalno načelo u devetnajestom veku, a posebice njegov odnošaj prema pravu narodnog samoopredeljenja (plebiscitu)," *Glasnik Srpskog učenog društva* 47 (1879): 78–176, quotations from 113–117.

7. Ibid., 118.

8. See Étienne Balibar, "Demos-Ethnos-Laos," Zulfia Karimova and Andriy Vasylchenko, "Narod," and Marc Crépon, Barbara Cassin, and Claudia Moatti, "People-Race-Nation," in *Dictionary of Untranslatables: A Philosophical Lexicon*, ed. Barbara Cassin, trans. Steven Rendall et al. (Princeton, NJ: Princeton University Press, 2014), 201–203, 701–703, 751–764.

9. Definitions of the terms *ethnos* and *demos* have often been mapped onto related dichotomies, such as Eastern-Western and ethnic-civic nationalism; see Bernard Yack, "The Myth of the Civic Nation," in *Theorizing Nationalism*, ed. Ronald Beiner (Albany: State University of New York Press, 1999), 103–118.

10. James Clifford, "On Ethnographic Self-Fashioning: Conrad and Malinowski," in *The Predicament of Culture: Twentieth-Century Ethnography, Literature, and Art* (Cambridge, MA: Harvard University Press, 1988), 92–113; and esp. Ian Hacking, "Making Up People," in *Historical Ontology* (Cambridge, MA: Harvard University Press, 2002), 99–114.

11. For example, Peter Burke, *Popular Culture in Early Modern Europe* (New York: Harper & Row, 1978); Timothy Baycroft and David Hopkin, eds., *Folklore and Nationalism in Europe during the Long Nineteenth Century* (Leiden: Brill, 2012); and Serhiy Bilenky, *Romantic Nationalism in Eastern Europe: Russian, Polish, and Ukrainian Political Imaginations* (Stanford, CA: Stanford University Press, 2012). On the centrality of folklore studies to Balkan nation-formations, see Joel M. Halpern and E. A. Hammel, "Observations on the Intellectual History of Ethnology and Other Social Sciences in Yugoslavia," *Comparative Studies in Society and History* 11, no. 1 (1969): 17–26; Carol Silverman, "The Politics of Folklore in Bulgaria," *Anthropological Quarterly* 56, no. 2 (1983): 55–61; Slobodan Naumović, "Identity Creator in Identity Crisis: Reflections on the Politics of Serbian Ethnology," *Anthropological Journal on European Cultures* 8, no. 2 (1996): 39–128; Klaus Roth, "Folklore and Nationalism: The German Example and Its Implications for the Balkans," *Ethnologia Balkanica* 2 (1998): 69–79; and Ivo Žanić, *Flag on the Mountain: A Political Anthropology of War in Croatia and Bosnia-Herzegovina, 1990–1995* (London: Saqi, 2007).

12. Terence Ranger and Eric Hobsbawm, eds., *The Invention of Tradition* (Cambridge: Cambridge University Press, 1992); and an important critique by Charles Briggs, "The Politics of Discursive Authority in Research on the 'Invention of Tradition,'" *Cultural Anthropology* 11, no. 4 (1996): 435–469.

13. This approach also draws on and contributes to debates over populism, in particular its relation to nationalism. For example, see Ernesto Laclau, *On Populist Reason* (London: Verso, 2005); Jacques Rancière, *Short Voyages to the Land of the People* (Stanford, CA: Stanford University Press, 2003); and Francisco Panizza, *Populism and the Mirror of Democracy* (London: Verso, 2005).

14. Ratimir Gašparović, *Bosna i Hercegovina na geografskim kartama od prvih početaka do kraja XIX vijeka* (Sarajevo: ANUBiH, 1970).

15. Dositej Obradović, "Ljubezni Haralampije [1783]," in *Život i priključenija Dimitrija Obradovića* (Belgrade: Knjažesko-Srbska knjigopečatniia, 1833), xvii–xviii.

16. Obradović, "Vostani Serbije [1804]," in *Život i priključenija Dimitrija Obradovića*, 137–138; and Obradović, *Pěsna o izbavlěniju Serbie* (Vienna: Kurzbeck, 1789).

17. Ljudevit Gaj, "Oglasz za *Novine horvatzke* i *Daniczu*," *Danica ilirska* 1 (1835), n.p. (announcement issued 20 November 1834).

18. Phillip E. Moseley published Russian archival documents in "A Pan-Slavist Memorandum of Liudevit Gaj in 1838," *American Historical Review* 40, no. 4 (1935): 704–716, quotation from report dated 1 November 1838.

19. Ferdo Šišić, *Hrvatska povijest*, vol. 3 (Zagreb: Dionička tiskara, 1913), 270.

20. Dunja Rihtman Auguštin, "Vuk Karadžić: Past and Present," in *Ethnology, Myth, and Politics: Anthropologizing Croatian Ethnology* (Aldershot, UK: Ashgate, 2004), 13–21.

21. Ingrid Merchiers, *Cultural Nationalism in the South Slav Habsburg Lands in the Early Nineteenth Century: The Scholarly Network of Jernej Kopitar, 1780–1844* (Munich: Sagner, 2007).

22. Wilfried Potthoff, ed., *Vuk Karadžić im europäischen Kontext: Beiträge des internationalen wissenschaftlichen Symposiums der Vuk Karadžić—Jacob Grimm-Gesellschaft* (Heidelberg: Winter, 1987).

23. For example, Bogoslav Šulek, "Srbi i Hrvati," *Neven* 8 (1856): 1–12; cf. Ante Starčević, *Ime Serb* (Zagreb: K. Albrecht, 1868); and Starčević, *Pasmina Slavoserbska po Hervatskoj* (Zagreb: Lav. Hartmán, 1876).

24. The literature on Karadžić is substantial in English, German, and Russian, and is vast in Serbo-Croatian; this list highlights only a few works. For example, Vuk Karadžić, *Songs of the Serbian People*, ed. and trans. Milne Holton and Vasa Mihailovich (Pittsburgh, PA: University of Pittsburgh Press, 1997); Duncan Wilson, *The Life and Times of Vuk Stefanović Karadžić, 1787–1864: Literacy, Literature, and National Independence in Serbia* (Ann Arbor: Michigan Slavic Publications, 1986); Ljubomir Stojanović, *Život i rad Vuka Stefanovića Karadžića* (Belgrade: Makarije, 1924); Miodrag Popović, *Vuk Stef. Karadžić* (Belgrade: Nolit, 1964); and Meša Selimović, *Za i protiv Vuka* (Sarajevo: Svjetlost, 1967). On recent reinterpretations, see Marko Živković, *Serbian Dreambook: National Imaginary in the Time of Milošević* (Bloomington: Indiana University Press, 2011), 91–93, 161–167, and 186–187. The collected writings of Vuk Karadžić were published in thirty-six volumes as *Sabrana dela Vuka Karadžića* (hereafter *SDVK*-subset and volume number), ed. Golub Dobrašinović et al. (Belgrade: Prosveta, 1965).

25. Despite nationalist disagreements, the consensus is this: "Today, Vuk's language is the basis of modern BCS [Bosnian-Croatian-Serbian]." Ronelle Alexander, *Bosnian, Croatian, Serbian: A Grammar with Sociolinguistic Commentary* (Madison: University of Wisconsin Press, 2006), 383. On the history of the question, whose is Vuk's language?, see Vojislav Nikčević, "Čiji je takozvani Vukov jezik?," *Kritika* 12 (1970): 370–385; and Robert Greenberg, *Language and Identity in the Balkans: Serbo-Croatian and Its Disintegration* (Oxford: Oxford University Press, 2004).

26. Vuk Stefanović Karadžić, "Predslovie," in *Mala prostonarodnja slaveno-serbska pjesnarica* (Vienna: J. Schierer, 1814), 15–16.

27. Vuk Karadžić, "Predgovor," in *Srpski rječnik, istolkovan njemačkim i latinskim riječma* (Vienna: P. P. Armeniern, 1818), xvi–xx.

28. Vuk Karadžić and Sava Tekelija, *Pisma visokopreosveštenome gospodinu Platonu Atanackoviću, pravoslavnome vladici budimskome o srpskome pravopisu,*

sa osobitijem dodacima o srpskom jeziku (Vienna: P. P. Armeniern, 1845), 85–86.
On his case for Herzegovinian, see Karadžić, trans., *Novi Zavjet Gospoda našega*
Isusa Hrista (Vienna: P. P. Armeniern, 1847); also Karadžić, *Srpski rječnik*, 2nd ed.
(Vienna: Armeniern, 1852).

29. Karadžić, *Kovčežić za istoriju, jezik i običaje Srba sva tri zakona* (Vienna:
Armeniern, 1849), 12–16.

30. Karadžić, "Predslovie," 14.

31. Emphasis in original; Karadžić, "Predgovor," *Srpski rječnik* (1818), xvii.

32. Ibid., ix; and Karadžić, *Kovčežić*, 13–16.

33. For example, see the collection of vehemently anti-Vuk—but rarely
antipeasant—arguments by contemporary Serbian intellectuals in Miroslav Jovanović
and Tatjana Subotin-Golubović, eds., *Protiv Vuka: Srpska građanska inteligencija 18.*
i 19. veka o jeziku i njegovoj reformi (Belgrade: Stubovi kulture, 2004).

34. Obradović, "Ljubezni Haralampije [1783]," xv.

35. Emphasis in original; Karadžić, *Kovčežić*, 11.

36. Vladimír Macura, "The Center," in *Mystifications of a Nation: The "Potato*
Bug" and Other Essays on Czech Culture, trans. Hana Píchová and Craig Cravens
(Madison: University of Wisconsin Press, 2010), 27–35.

37. Josef Dobrovský 1816 letter quoted in Vidaković, "Predislovie," in *Skupljeni*
gramatički i polemički spisi Vuka Stef. Karadžića, vol. 1 (Belgrade: Štamparija
Kraljevine Srbije, 1894), 115. Jacob Grimm defended Vuk against Dobrovský's
charges; see Grimm's 1825 letter in "Aus Jacob Grimms Briefwechsel mit slavischen
gelehrten," in *Untersuchungen und Quellen zur germanischen und romanischen*
Philologie, ed. August Sauer (Prague: Bellmann, 1908), 615–620.

38. See Vuk, "Druga recenzija [1817]," in *Skupljeni gramatički spisi Vuka*,
163–166. Almost thirty years later, the same charges were raised by Jovan Steić,
"Jezikoslovne primědbe na predgovor g. Vuka Stef. Karadžića k prevodu Novog
Zavěta," *Glasnik Družtva srpske slovenosti* 2 (1849): 1–42.

39. Karadžić, "Pravi uzrok i početak skupljanja našijeh narodnijeh pjesama,"
in *Skupljeni gramatički i polemički spisi Vuka Stef. Karadžića*, vol. 3 (Belgrade:
Štamparija Kraljevine Srbije, 1896), 66.

40. Karadžić, "Predslovie," 19.

41. Karadžić, "Predgovor," *Srpski rječnik* (1818), xvii.

42. "I was born and raised in a house where my grandfather and uncle,
like many other Herzegovinians who wintered [there] nearly every year, sang
and told songs all winter long." Karadžić, "Predgovor," *Narodne srpske pjesme*
[junačke], vol. 4 (Vienna: P. P. Armeniern, 1833), xl; Karadžić, "Predgovor,"
Srpski rječnik (1818), xiii; also see Vuk's references to his family's specifically
Herzegovinian background in *Život i običaji naroda srpskoga* (Vienna: L. Sommer,
1867), 72.

43. Jovan Subotić, "Někē čerte iz pověstnice Serbskog knjižestva," *Serbskii*
Lětopis 4 (1846): 121.

44. Karadžić, *Kovčežić*, 15.

45. Kopitar, cited in *Bartholomäus Kopitars Briefwechsel mit Jakob Grimm*, ed.
Max Vasmer (Berlin: Akademie der Wissenschaften, 1938), 57.

46. Šafarik letter, 11 October 1830, in *Korespondence Pavla Josefa Šafaříka*
s Františkem Palackým, ed. Věnceslava Bechyňová and Zoe Hauptová (Prague:
Československá akademie věd, 1961), 93.

47. Peter Burke, "The Discovery of the People," in Burke, *Popular Culture*, 3–22.

48. Karadžić, "Predgovor," *Narodne srpske pjesme [junačke]* (1834), 4: vii–xvii. On Filip Višnjić, see Nikola Krstić, "Beleške pokojnog vladike Mušickog o Filipu Višnjiću," *Glasnik srbskog učenog društva* 20 (1866): 236–243.

49. Karadžić, *Narodne srpske pjesme [ženske]*, vol. 1 (Leipzig: Breitkopf, 1824), xvii–xix.

50. As Svetlana Slapšak noted, "The gender-genre division of Vuk Karadžić [was] never closely examined by South Slavic scholars"; see "Women's Memory and an Alternative Kosovo Myth," in *History of the Literary Cultures of East-Central Europe: Junctures and Disjunctures in the 19th and 20th Centuries*, vol. 4, ed. Marcel Cornis-Pope and John Neubauer (Amsterdam: John Benjamins, 2010), 265–266. Also see Janko Jurković, "O ženskih karakterih u naših narodnih pjesmah," *Rad JAZU* 30 (1875): 1–19.

51. Karadžić, *Narodne srpske pjesme [ženske]* (1824), 1: xx–xxxi.

52. V. Vrčević, "O ovoj knjizi," in *Srpske narodne pripovijetke, ponajviše kratke i šaljive* (Belgrade: Državna štamparija, 1868), iv–v. Even Vrčević himself admitted: "I left out many of the humorous tales that I heard since printing press length and decency will not permit it." For another approach to folklore and humor, see the work of Friedrich Salomo Krauss, e.g., *Slavische Volkforschungen* (Leipzig: Wilhelm Heims, 1908).

53. Karadžić, *Narodne srpske pjesme [junačke]* (1833), 4: x.

54. On "The Herzegovinian," see Vuk–Kopitar correspondence, 5 July, 9 July, 17 July, 27 August, 6 September, 20 September, 1 October; Vuk–Grimm, 6 November; and Vuk–Goethe, 8 November; all dated 1823; 224–225, 228, 231, 246–247, 253, 264–266, 273–274, 308–309, 311–312, *SDVK-P* 21. Vuk retained several prints of this image; Vuk MS. 8552/212 (1823), ASANU. This image was certainly inspired by the *guslar* Filip Višnjić, but according to the art historian Vojislav Jovanović, "the model was very likely Vuk himself," resulting in a "very Herzegovinian look." Vojislav M. Jovanović, "O liku Filipa Višnjića i drugih guslara Vukova vremena," *Zbornik Matice srpske za književnost i jezik* 2 (1954): 67–96.

55. Johann Gottfried von Herder, *Ideen zur Geschichte der Menschheit*, vol. 3 (Stuttgart: Cottäschen, 1827 [1787]), 43–45; also Burke, *Popular Culture*, 8.

56. Cf. title pages to Vuk Stefanović (note the infrequent use of the Karadžić surname in the early editions), *Pismenica serbskoga iezika po govoru prostoga naroda* (Vienna: Schierer, 1814) with the later title pages of Vuk Stef. Karadžić, *Narodne srpske pjesme [ženske]*, 1 (1824); and *Narodne srpske pjesme [junačke]*, vol. 4 (1833). On Vuk's efforts to attain the titles of "Doctor," "Professor," and "Academic," which were honorarily granted by numerous institutions, see: Vuk–Kopitar, 6 September, 23 October, 19 November, 5 December 1823; Vuk–Grimm, 31 December 1824; Vasilijević–Vuk, 20 January 1825; Vuk–Grimm, 3 February 1825; 253–254, 287–290, 318–319, 331–333, 531–532, 541, 558–559, *SDVK-P* 21; and Kopitar–Vuk, 25 January 1831, 367–368, *SDVK-P* 23.

57. Vuk Karadžić, *Servian Popular Poetry*, trans. John Bowring (London: Davison, 1827), xxx–xxxiii; and John Bowring, "Popular Poetry of the Servians," *Westminster Review* 6 (1826): 23–39, esp. 28. Also see Bowring–Vuk, 15 February 1829; Vuk–Kopitar, 30 January 1832; Vuk–Bowring, 28 April 1832, 48, 597–598, 658, *SDVK-P* 23.

58. Karadžić, "Glas narodoljubca, 1819," 35, *SDVK-OJ* 13.

59. Karadžić, *Kovčežić*, 13–14.

60. That is, "pravi *self-made-man,* onakav kakav je bio i Vuk." Todor Stefanović Vilovski, "Srpska zora i njeni saradnici," *Brankovo kolo za zabavu, pouku i književnost* 14 (1908): 307.

61. Karadžić, "Ero," *Srpski rječnik* (1818), 163; "Hero," *Srpski rječnik* (1852), 804; and esp. *Srpske narodne pripovjetke* (Vienna: Sommer, 1870), 301–305; and *Narodne srpske poslovice* (Cetinje: Narodna štamparija, 1836), 119, 135, 262–263, 272.

62. Karadžić, *Narodne srpske pjesme [ženske]* (1824), 1: xx.

63. Todorova, *Imagining the Balkans,* 162–164.

64. After Serbia gained formal autonomy in 1833, Jovan Stejić wrote to Vuk: "Christianhood (*Rišćanluk*) is happy, it got a lot of what it wanted: a small tribute of 50,000 ducats, several districts, and those villages on the other side of the Drina in Bosnia. In Belgrade town the present Turks remain, but they now belong entirely to Serbians' rule and jurisdiction: their mother will be sorry (*jadna im majka*)." Letter dated 3 October 1833, 234, *SDVK-P* 24. Stejić was deeply disappointed when he learned that Belgrade would still nominally remain under Turkish jurisdiction; 10 October 1833, 237–238, *SDVK-P* 24.

65. Attributed to Karadžić, "O stanju Srba u Hercegovini pod Ali-pašom Stočevićem" (ed. Radovan Samardžić), 470–476, *SDVK-IS* 15; and Karadžić, *Život i običaji naroda srpskoga,* 258–261.

66. For example, Karadžić, *Narodne srpske pjesme,* vols. 2, 3 (Vienna: P. P. Armeniern, 1823); vol. 4 (1833); and *Srpske narodne pjesme [junačke],* vol. 4 (Vienna: P. P. Armeniern, 1862), esp. 130–164.

67. Karadžić, *Narodne srpske poslovice,* 9, 25, 39, 75, 158, 162, 332–333.

68. Karadžić–Danilo I Njegoš, 21 April 1854, 540, *SDVK-P* 29.

69. Karadžić and Sava Tekelija, *Pisma Atanackoviću* (Vienna: P. P. Armeniern, 1845), 85–95.

70. Karadžić, *Kovčežić,* 8.

71. Karadžić–Kopitar, 25 October 1830, 324–325, *SDVK-P* 23; Karadžić–Kopitar, 519–520, *SDVK-P* 23; Vuk even hoped for help from British or German biblical societies, but no such aid came at the time.

72. Karadžić, *Kovčežić,* 2–3.

73. Karadžić and Tekelija, *Pisma Atanackoviću,* 20.

74. Leopold von Ranke, *Die serbische Revolution: Aus serbischen Papieren und Mittheilungen* (Hamburg: Friedrich Pertes, 1829), 6, 36; and Leopold von Ranke, *Serbien und die Türkei im neuzehnten Jahrhundert* (Leipzig: Duncker & Humblot, 1879), 24–25.

75. Karadžić, "Predgovor," *Srpski rječnik* (1818), xx. It is noteworthy that many other Serbo-Croatian words derived from Turkish were *not* marked as such in Vuk's dictionary, perhaps because Vuk was not even aware of their Turkish derivation; e.g., *bubreg* or kidney; *dugme* or button; *biser* or pearl.

76. Karadžić, *Srpski rječnik* (1852), entry *kara,* 264.

77. Lukijan Mušicki–Karadžić, 1817, in *Vukova Prepiska,* vol. 2 (Belgrade: Državna štamparija, 1908), 192.

78. Subotić, "Něke čerte," 122–123.

79. Steić, "Jezikoslovne primědbe," 6–8.

80. To the contrary, a number of authors in English-language scholarship (Andrew Wachtel, Ronelle Alexander, Robert Greenberg, and *The Encyclopedia*

Britannica among others) erroneously assume that he extensively traveled throughout Bosnia and Herzegovina. Only a handful of Yugoslav writers have addressed his absence from Bosnia and Herzegovina, usually in an apologetic way. See Golub Dobrašinović, "Vukovo interesovanje za Bosnu," *Prilozi za književnost, istoriju, jezik i folklor* 26 (1960): 86–89; Vladimir Stojančević, "Jedna velika neispunjena želja Vukova," *Kovčežić: Prilozi i građa o Dositeju i Vuku* 12 (1974): 74–77; Muhsin Rizvić, *Između Vuka i Gaja* (Sarajevo: Oslobođenje, 1989).

81. Karadžić, "Predgovor," *Srpski rječnik* (1852), 1.

82. Karadžić, *Kovčežić*, 2–3.

83. Pavle Karanović–Karadžić, 5 October 1835, 558–559, *SDVK-P* 24. On a similar attempt of a writer from Herzegovina to reach out to Vuk, see Jovan Popović Mostarski–Vuk, 26 January, 31 January, 24 February 1822, 46–47, 52–55, 70–71, *SDVK-P* 21.

84. Pavle Karanović–Ljudevit Gaj, 17 May 1837, R-4702/b, NSK.

85. Pavle Karano-Tvrković, "Kratko zemljopisanije o Bosni," *Srbskii spomenici* (Belgrade: Tipografija knjažestva Srbije, 1840), iii–xxii.

86. Dimitrije Tirol, "Njekoliko rječi o Srbkim Spomenicima i njiovom Pseudo-Sabiratelju Pavlu Karano-Tvrkoviću," *Serbskii narodnii list* 6, no. 23 (1841): 180–182; Vuk Karadžić, "G. pop Pavle Karano-Tvrtković i Srbskii Spomenici," *Peštansko-budimski skoroteča*, nos. 24–25 (1842): 146–148, 153–155; Karadžić, "Opet g. pop Pavle Karano-Tvrtković," *Peštansko-budimski skoroteča*, nos. 27–28 (1843): 211.

87. Karadžić, "G. pop Pavle Karano-Tvrtković i Srbskii Spomenici," 153–155.

88. Leopold von Ranke–Vuk Karadžić, 31 January 1833, 50–51, *SDVK-P* 24; Karadžić–Ranke, 16 November 1833, 256–257, *SDVK-P* 24.

89. Leopold von Ranke, "Die letzten Unruhen in Bosnien," *Historisch-politische Zeitschrift* 2 (1834): 233–304. An English translation followed soon; see Ranke, *The History of Servia and the Servian Revolution, with a Sketch of the Insurrection in Bosnia*, trans. Louisa Kerr, 3rd ed. (London: H. G. Bohn, 1853).

90. Vuk Karadžić, *Srpske narodne pjesme iz Hercegovine (ženske)* (Vienna: Sommer, 1866); see introduction by Vrčević, iii–vi.

91. Vrčević, "Kratka biografija," n.d., MS no. 7380/7, ASANU; Vrčević, "Posveta i predgovor za *Hercegovačke pjesme*," 1864, MS no. 9154, ASANU. On Vrčević's long-standing interest in Bosnia and Herzegovina, see Vrčević–Miklošić, March–May 1857, in *Arhivska građa o Vuku Karadžiću*, ed. Golub Dobrašinović (Belgrade: Arhiv Srbije, 1970), 486–488.

92. Vrčević, *Srpske pjesme iz Hercegovine*, iv.

93. Vrčević, "Posveta besmrtnom duhu, ocu srbske narodnosti, Vuku Karadžiću," 1864, MS no. 9154, ASANU: "O Vuk! You are now in the kingdom of ghosts . . . while your name echoes across the earth." Working as a Habsburg consular official in Trebinje in the 1860s, Vrčević published articles on many subjects: Herzegovinian trials of werewolves; descriptions of nineteenth-century battles; histories of medieval monasteries; Bosnian Muslim epic poetry; customary law procedures on marriage, murder, and property; popular jokes; documents for Montenegrin political history, and so on. Vrčević's contributions were widely noted, but his legacy pales in comparison with his namesake Karadžić. For example, see: Vrčević, "Seoska osuda na smrt novoga vukodlaka," *Pravo* 11, no. 23 (1875): 335–340; *Narodne satirično-zanimljive podrugačice skupio ih po Boki Kotorskoj,*

Crnoj-gori, Dalmaciji, a najviše po Hercegovini, 2nd ed. (Dubrovnik: Pretner, 1888); *Hercegovačke narodne pjesme, koje samo Srbi Muhamedove vjere pjevaju* (Dubrovnik: Pretner, 1890); *Razni članci Vuka Vrčevića* (Dubrovnik: Pretner, 1891).

94. Ognjeslav Utješenović-Ostrožinski, *Misli o važnosti, pravcu i sredstvima unapređivanja književnosti srbsko-hrvatske* (Belgrade: Valožić, 1869), 16.

95. Editorial board, *Zora: Književni rad Srpskog đačkog društva u Beču* (Vienna: Kovač, 1875), 9, 27–28.

96. Golub Dobrašinović, *Vukovi prenumeranti: Pretplatnici i dobrotvori Vukovih dela, 1814–1862* (Belgrade: Beogradsko čitalište, 2001).

97. Blaž Josić–Ljudevit Gaj, 11 December 1839, R-4702/b, NSK.

98. Vatroslav Jagić, "Srpske narodne pjesme iz Bosne i Hercegovine," *Rad JAZU* 2 (1868): 205–206.

99. Bono Perišić–Ljudevit Gaj, 12 June 1849, ZP XIX no. 312, AFM-FO; also see Ivan Franjo Jukić–L. Gaj, 1838 and 22 June 1839, R-4702/b, NSK; and Martin Nedić, 12 May 1839, 4 October 1839, 14 June 1849, R-4702/b, NSK.

100. Samuilo Ilić–Karadžić, 7 August 1827, 506–508, *SDVK-P* 22; Dimitrije Vladislavljević, 15 November 1827, 599–601, *SDVK-P* 22.

101. Ivan Franjo Jukić, "Samo za sada," *Danica ilirska* 8, no. 36 (1842): 142.

102. Ivan Franjo Jukić, *Bosanski prijatelj*, vol. 1 (Zagreb: Tiskarnica Lj. Gaj, 1850), 33.

103. Jukić [posthumously published], "Putovanje iz Sarajeva u Carigrad godine 1852," *Bosanski prijatelj* 3 (1861): 71–91.

104. Karačić letter, 24 June 1848, Pisma box 2, folio 4, AFM-KS; and "Protocollum provinciae Bosnae Argentinae," Circular, 8 May 1849, 1835–1870 volume, folio 112–113, AFM-SA.

105. Blaž Josić–Grga Martić, 13 August 1867, folio 4, OGM 165, AFM-KR.

106. Lozić, "Starine Livna okružja," 1864, Rijetkosti 142/3, folio 10, AFM-KR; and "Sasatavak narodnog rječnika," n.d. (ca. 1860s), folio 12.

107. Stefan Herkalović–Ljudevit Gaj, 30 November 1837, 200–205, *GPKH-PLG*.

108. Herkalović–L. Gaj, 10 February [1839], 209–210, *GPKH-PLG*. Vjekoslav Babukić made a related historical claim about the language of the medieval Bosnian kings: "Anyone can see that this is pure Illyrian (*čist ilirski*), only mixed here and there with Church Slavonic formulations"; "Starine ilirske," *Danica ilirska* 6, no. 30 (1840): 118–119.

109. Antun Vakanović–L. Gaj, 26 March 1839, 476–477, *GPKH-PLG*; František Zach, report dated 27 January 1844, 61–62, *BIFZ*.

110. For example, Herkalović–L. Gaj, 3 June 1845, 218–219, *GPKH-PLG*.

111. Jukić–Herkalović, 28 September 1843, 162–164, *IFJ-SD* 3.

112. Jukić–Bono Perišić, 27 April 1841, 118, *IFJ-SD* 3.

113. Jukić–Perišić, 2 July 1841, 118–119, *IFJ-SD* 3.

114. Ibid.

115. Ivan Franjo Jukić, "Predgovor," *Zemljopis i poviestnica Bosne* (Zagreb: Tiskarnica Ljudevita Gaja, 1851), vii–x.

116. Jukić, "Molba I," at the end of *Bosanski Prijatelj* 1 (Zagreb, 1850). On a related attempt to establish a Bosnian museum, see Perišić, "Dissertatio de Nummis et de Museis: Koja je korist od Museah," 1867, Rijetkosti 142/3, folio 11, AFM-KR.

117. Jukić–Blaž Josić, 23 December 1840, 116, *IFJ-SD* 3.

118. For example, see Jukić, *Zemljopis*; and Jukić, *Bosanski prijatelj* 1 and *Bosanski prijatelj* 2 (Zagreb, 1851).

119. Jukić, *Zemljopis*, vii.

120. Grga Martić, Ivan Franjo Jukić, and O. Filip Kunić, *Narodne piesme bosanske i hercegovačke* (Osijek: Lehmann, 1858), viii–ix.

121. For example, see Jukić, *Bosanski prijatelj* 3 (Zagreb, 1861) and *Bosanski prijatelj* 4 (Sisak, 1870).

122. Jukić, *Zemljopis*, 17–18, 20–21.

123. As a committed Franciscan friar, Jukić was not fond of folk "customs," which he viewed as "superstitions" (*praznovierje*) that harmed true religious piety; folk poetry, however, was an exception and was prized as the primary marker of national spirit. See *Zemljopis*, 18–20; and his collections of folklore in the *Bosanski prijatelj* volumes.

124. Martić, Jukić, and Kunić, *Narodne piesme bosanske i hercegovačke*, xii.

125. For example, see Jukić's "Zemljopisno-povjesno opisanje Bosne," *Srbsko-dalmatinski magazin* 6 (1841): 17–43, and "Zemljopisno-pověstno opisanje Bosne," *Danica Ilirska* 7, nos. 28–32 (1841); similar pattern of dual Cyrillic- and Roman-script publication applied for most of the 1840s.

126. Anon., "Izvestija," *Glasnik družtva srpske slovesnosti* 3 (1851): 298.

127. Anon., "Iz književnosti," *Narodne Novine*, no. 238 (16 October 1851).

128. Kovačević, "Ustav politične propagande imajuće se voditi u zemljama slaveno-turskim," ca. 1850, FIG no. 647, AS; and Kovačević, "Topografsko statično opisanje," ca. 1851, FIG no. 651, AS. Stojan Novaković confirms the use of Kovačević's work in the Serbian state cabinet; see his *Balkanska pitanja i manje istorijsko-političke beleške o Balkanskom poluostrvu, 1886–1905* (Belgrade: Kraljevina Srbija, 1906), 497.

129. Toma Kovačević and his editor Ilija Rakić claimed that this was an original work, based on notes that Kovačević had given Jukić when they were both Bosnian Franciscan students; Kovačević, *Opis Bosne i Hercegovine* (Belgrade: N. Stefanović, 1865; 2nd ed. 1879), iii–xi. Already in 1866, Franjo Rački attacked Kovačević for plagiarizing Jukić: "Kritike," *Književnik: časopis za jezik i poviest hrvatsku i srbsku* 3 (1866): 156–157.

130. A German report based on Jukić–Kovačević works also appeared as "Statistische Angaben Kowatschewitj's Beschreibung von Bosnien (verfasst von Jukitj 1834 [*sic*], gedruckt in Belgrad 1851 [*sic*])," in Otto Blau, *Reisen in Bosnien und der Hertzegowina* (Berlin: Reimer, 1877), 224–228.

131. For this reading, I draw on Jacques Derrida, "The Law of Genre," in *Acts of Literature*, ed. Derek Attridge (New York: Routledge, 1992), 221–252.

132. On these long-term developments, see Naumović, "Identity Creator in Identity Crisis," 39–128.

133. Stefan Verković, *Veda slovena: Bŭlgarski narodni pesni ot predistorichno i predkhristiiansko doba* (Belgrade, 1878; and Sofia, 1881); and Verković, *Narodne pesme makedonskih Bugara: Ženske pesme* (Belgrade: Pravitelstvena knjigopečatnja, 1860).

134. For example, Matthias Murko, *Deutsche Einflüsse auf die Anfänge der slavischen Romantik*, 2 vols. (Graz: Styria, 1897); Jovan Skerlić, *Istorija nove srpske književnosti*, 2nd ed. (Belgrade: Cvijanović, 1914); and Radivoj Simonović, *Pogreške naših filologa* (Sremski Karlovci: Manastirska štamparija, 1907).

135. Nikola Andrić, "Otkud Vuku 'Zidanje Skadra'?" *Glas Matice hrvatske*, nos. 12, 14–18 (1908); and a defense by Jovan Tomić, "Evo, otkud Vuku," *Srpski književni glasnik*, nos. 3–6 (1908).

136. Jovan Cvijić, *Pregled geografske literature o balkanskom poluostrvu za 1894 godinu* (Belgrade: Radikalna štamparija, 1894), 19. Jovan Cvijić (1865–1927), like almost all Serbian intellectuals, paid homage to Vuk as "the founder of the Serbian literary language and of modern Serbian literature" and a figure indelibly associated with "Herzegovina and Bosnia." See Cvijić, *Aneksija Bosne i Hercegovine i srpski problem* (Belgrade: Državna štamparija, 1908), 20–21.

137. For example, Jovan Erdeljanović, "Milićević kao ispitivač narodnog života," *Delo* 49 (1908): 321; and Pavle Popović, *Iz književnosti* (Belgrade: Gece Kon, 1906), 130–132.

138. On Cvijić's career and work, see Milorad Vasović et al., eds., *Sabrana dela Jovana Cvijića*, 13 vols. (Belgrade: SANU, 1987), esp. vol. 1.

139. N.T.K., "Vukova slava," *Bosanska vila* 12 (1897): 316, 334, 369; and Andra Gavrilović, ed., *Spomenica o prenosu praha Vuka Stef. Karadžića iz Beča u Beograd 1897* (Belgrade: Državna štamparija, 1898), 31–51, 90–91, 250.

140. Gavrilović, *Spomenica o prenosu praha Vuka*, 270–274, 318, 327, 370.

141. Ibid., 329.

142. Tihomir Đorđević, ed., *Karadžić: List za srpski narodni život, običaje i predanje*, 4 vols. (Belgrade, 1899–1903).

143. Sima Tomić, "Vukov rad na etnografiji," *Delo: List za nauku, književnost i društveni život* 15 (1897): 470–485; and Vuk Karadžić, *Skupljeni istorijski i etnografski spisi Vuka Stef. Karadžića* (Belgrade: Kraljevina Srbija, 1898). As Momčilo Ivančić wrote, "Vuk is not just the first Serbian philologist and grammatician but also the first ethnographer"; "Život i književni rad Vuka Stefanovića Karadžića," *Otadžbina* 7, no. 20 (1888): 323.

144. "Proslava Vukova rođenja Sarajevo," 1937, PKD-108, folio 138, ABiH. However, by the interwar period, the Croatian ultranationalist rejection of Vuk effectively transformed him from a generally leading South Slavic figure (recognized as such by many Slovene, Croatian, Montenegrin, and Bosnian intellectuals) into a decidedly Serbian icon. Also see Miodrag Popović, "Vuk među Ilirima," *Kovčežić: Prilozi i građa o Dositeju i Vuku* 6 (1964): 5–18; and Viktor Novak, *Vuk i Hrvati* (Belgrade: Naučno delo, 1967).

145. Antun Radić, "Književne novosti," *Zbornik za narodni život i običaje južnih slavena* 3 (1898): 309.

146. Antun Radić, "Proučavanje građe," in *Osnova za sabiranje i proučavanje građe o narodnom životu* (Zagreb: Dionička tiskara, 1897), 86.

147. Antun Radić, "Način sabiranja," *Osnova* (1897): 73.

148. A few examples from the ethnographic guide: "(46) Some sounds, by which animals are attracted, chased off, or nudged, will be easily written down . . . and others will be more difficult to write down. . . . But everyone should try to write them down as best as one can. (47) Classification of certain material should be done by that division of illnesses and medicines for the insane (in section II, chap. 2, B., and IV. 9, pp. 18 and 25). . . . (110) Conversations and jokes are only mentioned here, as conversations belong to XII, and jokes to section X." Radić, "Način sabiranja," 75–85.

149. Ibid., 73–75.

150. Antun Radić, "Izvješće o putovanju njegovu po Bosni i Hercegovini," *Zbornik za narodni život i običaje južnih Slavena* 4 (1899): 292–324, quotation from 293.

151. In this way, the nationalist notion of *narod* resembles the workings of myth; alibi "is, as one realizes, a spatial term." Roland Barthes, *Mythologies*, trans. Jonathan Cape (New York: Noonday, 1972), 122.

152. Jules Michelet, *Le peuple* (Paris: Hachette, 1846), appearing in English translation by G.H. Smith as *The People* (New York: Appleton, 1846); Roland Barthes, *Michelet* (Berkeley: University of California Press, 1992), 184–188; also see Barthes, "Michelet Today," in *The Rustle of Language*, trans. Richard Howard (New York: Hill & Wang, 1986), esp. 206–207.

2. The Land of Suffering

1. Velimir Gaj, "Viesti o Bosni i Hercegovini," *Književna zabava hrvatskosrbska* 3 (1868): 150–153. Also see Gaj, *Balkan-Divan* (Zagreb: Gaj, 1878).

2. Ernest Renan, "What Is a Nation?" (1882), in *Nation and Narration*, ed. Homi K. Bhabha, trans. M. Thom (London: Routledge, 1990), 19.

3. Benedict Anderson, *Imagined Communities: Reflections on the Origins and Spread of Nationalism*, 3rd ed. (London: Verso, 2006), 7.

4. For surveys of this literature, which overwhelmingly focuses on medical and religious aspects of suffering, see Iain Wilkinson, *Suffering: A Sociological Introduction* (London: Polity, 2004); and Jeff Malpas and Norelle Lickiss, eds., *Perspectives on Human Suffering* (New York: Springer, 2012).

5. Dipesh Chakrabarty, *Provincializing Europe: Postcolonial Thought and Historical Difference*, 2nd ed. (Princeton, NJ: Princeton University Press, 2007), 117–148; and Chakrabarty, *Habitations of Modernity: Essays in the Wake of Subaltern Studies* (Chicago: University of Chicago Press, 2002), 101–114.

6. Oscar Wilde, *The Essays of Oscar Wilde* (New York: Cosmopolitan, 1916), 6. The young Wilde, like Byron, Tennyson, and Gladstone before him, also wrote about national suffering in the Balkans; e.g., "On the Massacre of the Christians in Bulgaria [1877]," in *Poems* (Boston: Roberts, 1882), 13.

7. The stress on empathy is now commonly accepted as grounds for the historical emergence of the modern subject endowed with altruistic sensibilities and human rights; see Lynn Hunt, *Inventing Human Rights: A History* (New York: Norton, 2007); and Steven Pinker, *The Better Angels of Our Nature: Why Violence Has Declined* (New York: Penguin, 2011). Others have criticized such universalizing (and usually feel-good) narratives of empathy on a number of grounds; e.g., see Bertolt Brecht, *Brecht on Theatre: The Development of an Aesthetic*, trans. John Willett (New York: Hill and Wang, 1964); Veena Das, A. Kleinman, and M. Lock, eds., *Social Suffering* (Berkeley: University of California Press, 1997); and Karen Halttunen, "Humanitarianism and the Pornography of Pain in Anglo-American Culture," *American Historical Review* 100, no. 2 (1995): 303–334.

8. Wendy Brown, *States of Injury: Power and Freedom in Late Modernity* (Princeton, NJ: Princeton University Press, 1995), 73–74.

9. Asma Abbas, *Liberalism and Human Suffering: Materialist Reflections on Politics, Ethics, and Aesthetics* (New York: Palgrave MacMillan, 2010), 1–17, 73–94.

10. The histories of Bulgaria, Macedonia, and Kosovo offer many examples in this regard; e.g., Ivan Vazov, *Pod igoto* (Sofia, 1888), or *Under the Yoke*, trans. M. Alexieva and T. Atanassova (New York: Twayne, 1976); also Gregorij Kapčev,

Macedonija ili glas roba, 2nd ed. (Zagreb: Scholz, 1898); and Hadži Serafim Ristić, *Plač stare Srbije* (Zemun: Sopron, 1864).

11. For example, Charles and Barbara Jelavich, *The Establishment of Balkan National States, 1804–1920* (Seattle: University of Washington Press, 1977). On Bosnia's "balance sheet," see Robin Okey, *Taming Balkan Nationalism: The Habsburg "Civilizing Mission" in Bosnia, 1878–1914* (Oxford: Oxford University Press, 2007), 217–250.

12. New histories of emotion and affect have shown how historians can analyze what Barbara Rosenwein has called "emotional communities." For a discussion of these issues, see Jan Plamper, ed., "The History of Emotions: An Interview with William Reddy, Barbara Rosenwein, and Peter Stearns," *History and Theory* 49, no. 2 (2010): 237–265.

13. On the making of European humanitarianism in relation to the Ottoman realms, see Davide Rodogno, *Against Massacre: Humanitarian Interventions in the Ottoman Empire, 1815–1914* (Princeton, NJ: Princeton University Press, 2012); Nina Athanassoglou-Kallmyer, *French Images from the Greek War of Independence, 1821–1830* (New Haven, CT: Yale University Press, 1989); and Saba Mahmood, "Religious Freedom, the Minority Question, and Geopolitics in the Middle East," *Comparative Studies in Society and History* 54, no. 2 (2012): 418–446.

14. Emmeline Pankhurst, "Why We Are Militant (1913)," in *Suffrage and the Pankhursts*, vol. 8, ed. Jane Marcus (London: Routledge, 1987), 153–162.

15. Mato Topalović, "Tužna Bosna," *Danica Horvatzka, Slavonzka y Dalmatinzka* no. 14 (1835): 53.

16. Pjesmotvorni spisi, Razgovor Vilah Ilirkinjah, 1835, FMN, AFM-TO; Razgovor koga vile ilirkinje imadoše u pramalitje, 1835, R-3111, NSK; and Veselje vilah ilirskih, a tugovanje vile Bosanske, 1838, R-3817, NSK; published as Anon. [Nedić], *Razgovor koga Vile Ilirkinje imadoše u Pramalitje* (Karlovac: I. Pretner, 1835).

17. Anon. [Nedić], *Razgovor koga Vile Ilirkinje imadoše u Pramalitje*.

18. Jukić, Tužna Bosna neće da više tuguje, 1838, R-4702/b, NSK.

19. Topalović, "Tužna Bosna," in *Pjesmarica ili sbirka rado pjevanih pjesamah*, ed. Gjuro Deželić (Zagreb: Albrecht, 1872), 136–139; and Vjekoslav Klaić, *Hrvatska pjesmarica: Sbirka popjevaka za skupno pjevanje* (Zagreb: Matica hrvatska, 1893), 6–7, 195. On Karas, see Lebensbild, Karas, ca. 1850s, R-7306, NSK.

20. Mirko Bogović, *Stĕpan, poslĕdnji kralj bosanski: Drama u pet činah* (Zagreb: Narodna tiskarnica, 1857).

21. Stevan Vladislav Kaćanski, "Jadna Bosna," *Velika Srbija* no. 1, 14 January 1888.

22. *Bosna: Glasnik potlačenog srpstva*, ed. Kosta Jezdimirović, Šabac, 1889–1892.

23. "Aoj, Bosno, sirotice kleta" was recorded by the Serbian King's Guard Orchestra for the Gramophone Company, CHARM-Kelly Catalogue no. 13658 (1909). The song was a hit; when a group of gymnasia students from Serbia first glimpsed the Bosnian border in 1909, "they gazed with sadness and yearning across the Drina River and unconsciously began to sing" this tune. It was also a favorite of the Young Bosnia revolutionary organization before 1914. See Anon., *Spomenica Muške gimnazije u Kragujevcu, 1833–1933* (Kragujevac: Šumadija, 1934),

199–200; and "Saveznik-Četnik" (1912), in *Bosanski omladinci i sarajevski atentat*, ed. Božo Čerović (Sarajevo: Trgovačka štamparija, 1930), 169–170.

24. Ljudevit Pivko, *Proti Avstriji, 1914–1918* (Ljubljana: Obzorja, 1991), 439.

25. See *Stenografske beleške Narodne skupštine Kraljevine Jugoslavije*, Plenary 23 (1932), 43 and 49; Plenary 6 (1936), 257; Plenary 15 (1938), 442; Plenary 27 (1938), 513.

26. Pavao Ritter Vitezović, *Bossna captiva, sive regnum et interitus Stephani ultimi Bosniae regis* (Trnava: n.p., 1712); and Vitezović, *Croatia rediviva: Regnante Leopoldo magno caesare deducta* (Zagreb, 1700), as cited by Ivan Kukuljević Sakcinski, *Jugoslavenska knjižnica* (Zagreb: Albrecht, 1867), 10, 30.

27. Robert Davis, *Christian Slaves, Muslim Masters: White Slavery in the Mediterranean, the Barbary Coast, and Italy, 1500–1800* (New York: Palgrave Macmillan, 2003); Davor Dukić, *Sultanova djeca: Predodžbe Turaka u hrvatskoj književnosti ranog novovjekovlja* (Zadar: Thema, 2004).

28. Kenneth Setton, *Western Hostility to Islam and Prophecies of Turkish Doom* (Philadelphia: American Philosophical Society, 1992); Gillian Weiss, *Captives and Corsairs: France and Slavery in the Early Modern Mediterranean* (Stanford, CA: Stanford University Press, 2011), 2, 170–172.

29. Muhamedlia, Teološka rasprava o Kuranu, 1840, R-3891, NSK.

30. Recent examples include Tijana Krstić, *Contested Conversions to Islam: Narratives of Religious Change in the Early Modern Ottoman Empire* (Stanford, CA: Stanford University Press, 2011); E. Natalie Rothman, *Brokering Empire: Trans-Imperial Subjects between Venice and Istanbul* (Ithaca, NY: Cornell University Press, 2011); Molly Greene, *Catholic Pirates and Greek Merchants* (Princeton, NJ: Princeton University Press, 2010); Daniel Jütte, "Interfaith Encounters between Jews and Christians in the Early Modern Period and Beyond: Toward a Framework," *American Historical Review* 118, no. 2 (2013): 378–400.

31. Stories of Christians enslaving and then emancipating their Muslim captives in a gesture of enlightenment were known to nineteenth-century South Slavic patriots; see Anon., "Dobročinstvo i zahvalnost," trans. Anka Obrenović, *Danica ilirska* 2, no. 20 (1836): 77–80. Also see Osman Ağa Timişvari, *Die Autobiographie des Dolmetschers Osman Aga aus Temeschwar* (London: Gibb Memorial Trust, 1980).

32. Gjuro Palmotić, *Suxanjstvo srechno*, ca. 1680s, R-3969, NSK. On these tropes, see Joe Snader, *Caught between Worlds: British Captivity Narratives in Fact and Fiction* (Lexington: University of Kentucky Press, 2000); and Daniel Vitkus, ed., *Piracy, Slavery, and Redemption: Barbary Captivity Narratives from Early Modern England* (New York: Columbia University Press, 2001).

33. Miodrag Popović, *Vidovdan i časni krst: Ogled iz književne arheologije* (Belgrade: Slovo ljubve, 1976).

34. For example, V. M. G. Medaković, *Hristjani na balkanskom poluostrvu i njihova sudbina* (Belgrade: Napredna stranka, 1885), 1–2.

35. On these changes, compare *Historica memoria quomodo Turcae Bosniae regnum ceperunt* (n.d., ca. sixteenth century), R-3254, NSK, and *Nobilium regni Bosnae familiae* (n.d., ca. seventeenth century), R-4026, NSK, with the following: Petar Luković Bunić, *Muhamed Drugi u Bosni: Tragedija* (1849), R-3715, NSK; Ljudevit Vukotinović, "Mato Gerebić," "Ivan Vojković," and "Sužan Ličanin," *Danica Ilirska* 1, nos. 12–18 (1835); Ivan Švear, *Ogledalo Iliriuma* (Zagreb:

Suppan, 1839); Antun Knežević, *Krvava knjiga, ili spomenik na 405 godina poslije propasti slavnoga kraljevstva bosanskoga* (Zagreb: Albrecht, 1869); Vjekoslav Klaić, *Poviest Bosne do propasti kraljevstva* (Zagreb: Dionička tiskara, 1882); and two parallel Croatian-Serbian plays, Mirko Bogović, *Stĕpan, poslĕdnji kralj bosanski: Drama u pet činah* (Zagreb: Narodna tiskarnica, 1857) and Mita Popović, *Stevan, poslednji kralj bosanski: Tragedija u pet radnja, Javor*, nos. 18–22 (1884).

36. Jukić, "Opisanje Bosne," *Danica ilirska* 7, no. 30 (1841): 122.

37. Petar Protić, "Bosanka," in *Neven-sloge* (Belgrade: Družina mladeži srbske, 1849), 86.

38. Ognjeslav Utješenović, "Jeka od Balkana," "Echo vom Balkan," *Augsburger Allgemeine Zeitung*, 18 February 1842; "Jeka od Balkana," *Danica Ilirska* 9, no. 10 (1842): 37–38; "L'écho du Balkan, ou larmes des Chrétiens de la Bulgarie, de la Herzogovinie et de la Bosnie," *Le Correspondant* 4 (1843): 66–69; and an additional German translation by Johann Friedrich Heinrich Schlosser, ed., *Wanderfrüchte: Sammlung auserlesener Poesien aller Zeiten in Uebertragungen* (Mainz: Kirchheim, 1856), 309–314. Also see Ivan Kukuljević Sakcinski, ed., *Bibliografija jugoslovenska*, vol. 1 (Zagreb: Albrecht, 1860), 166. Quotation from Utješenović, *Vila Ostrožinska: Sitne pjesme i osnova estetike*, 2nd ed. (Vienna: L. Sommer, 1871), 16.

39. Utješenović, "Jeka od Balkana."

40. Anon., "Les Chrétiens en Bulgarie et en Bosnie," *Le Correspondant* 4 (1843): 62–66.

41. Anon., editorial on "Echo vom Balkan," *Augsburger Allgemeine Zeitung*, 18 February 1842.

42. Ognjeslav Aranicki, *Ognjeslav Utješenović-Ostrožinski* (Zagreb: Tipografija, 1933), 19.

43. Mato Topalović, *Odzivi rodoljubnog serca, Bosanskim gorama* (1847), R-3807, NSK.

44. Jukić, *Zemljopis i poviestnica Bosne* (1851), 10.

45. Ibid., 154.

46. Karadžić–Talvi, 13 May 1853, 156–157, *SDVK-P* 10. The African Institute in Paris, a prominent society dedicated to the "abolition of slavery and the civilization of Africa," admitted Vuk as an honorary member in 1847; see Miodrag Ibrovac, "Vuk i Francuzi," in *Vukov zbornik*, ed. Viktor Novak (Belgrade: Naučno delo, 1966), 439–440.

47. Ban, *Na čemu smo sa istočnim pitanjem*, n.d. (ca. 1860s), FIG no. 1507, AS.

48. Jukić, *Zemljopis i poviestnica Bosne* (1851), 154.

49. Michel-Rolph Trouillot, *Silencing the Past: Power and the Production of History* (Boston: Beacon Press, 1995), 85–86. Susan Buck-Morss, *Hegel, Haiti, and Universal History* (Pittsburgh, PA: University of Pittsburgh Press, 2009), 21–22.

50. Despite writing in 1871, Nićifor Dučić did not once mention the American Civil War; he specifically invoked the American Revolution as the exemplary overthrow of "slavery." See his "Iskrena riječ Srpkinjama," *Mlada Srbadija* 2, no. 10 (1871): 147. To be clear, slavery was in fact thriving in the nineteenth-century Ottoman Empire, but few South Slavic nationalists expressed interest in the kind of slave trade taking place in the Mediterranean, favoring instead comparisons with the Atlantic. Meanwhile, slavers across the Ottoman Empire enslaved and traded millions of people, especially women from the

Caucasus and from northern and sub-Saharan Africa. Emerging nineteenth-century South Slavic patriots, however, almost never mentioned this ongoing Mediterranean slave trade in their invocations of the national slavery of the Balkan *raya*. Even Vuk Karadžić's entry on "slave" (*rob*), minimal in 1818 but expanded in the 1852 edition, describes ransom slavery and the enslavement of women as practices of past Turkish wars, not the ongoing reality for millions of Caucasian and African women and men in the Ottoman Empire; see *Srpski rječnik* (1852), 651. Many scholars have documented the vast scope and brutality of this system; e.g., see Ehud R. Toledano, *Slavery and Abolition in the Ottoman Middle East* (Seattle: University of Washington Press, 1998); Madeline Zilfi, *Women and Slavery in the Late Ottoman Empire: The Design of Difference* (Cambridge: Cambridge University Press, 2010); and Alison Frank, "The Children of the Desert and the Laws of the Sea: Austria, Great Britain, the Ottoman Empire, and the Mediterranean Slave Trade in the Nineteenth Century," *American Historical Review* 117, no. 2 (2012): 410–444.

51. John Stuart Mill, *Utilitarianism Explained and Exemplified in Moral and Political Government* (London: Longman, 1864), 328–331.

52. Ivan Kukuljević Sakcinski, "Die Nationalität in Kroatien und Slavonien," *Luna: Agramer Zeitung*, 24 September 1842.

53. Ivan Kukuljević Sakcinski, "Bratja: Narodna novella," *Različita děla*, vol. 2 (Zagreb: Gaj, 1843), esp. 23–24, 29–30. This kind of imagery is conspicuously absent from his later account of his first trip to Bosnia; see Kukuljević Sakcinski, *Putovanje po Bosni* (Zagreb: Župan, 1858).

54. See Ján Kollár, *Slávy dcera: Lyricko-epická baseň pěti zpěvích* (Prague: Kober, 1862), 232; and Utješenović, *Vila Ostrožinska*, 16–17.

55. Ognjeslav Utješenović, 3 January 1844, R-3981-B, NSK.

56. Jukić, "Kokošija vojska, ili Patnja čovieka sa ženom," *Bosanski prijatelj* 1 (1850): 111–114.

57. Anon., "Les Chrétiens en Bulgarie et en Bosnie," 66.

58. Tadija Smičiklas, *Dvijestogodišnjica oslobodjenja Slavonije*, vol. 1 (Zagreb: JAZU, 1891), 65.

59. Leopold von Ranke, *A History of Servia and the Servian Revolution*, trans. Louisa Kerr (London: J. Murray, 1847), 459–462.

60. Leopold von Ranke, *The History of Servia and the Servian Revolution, with a Sketch of the Insurrection in Bosnia*, trans. Louisa Kerr, 3rd ed. (London: H. G. Bohn, 1853), 365.

61. Ranke, *History of Servia* (1847), 459–462. A complete translation in Serbian appeared as Ranke, *Srbija i Turska u devetnaestom veku*, trans. Stojan Novaković (Belgrade: Dimitrijević, 1892). For a similar argument, see Anon., *Das serbische Volk und seiner Bedeutung für die orientalische Frage und für die europäische Civilisation* (Leipzig: Gustav Mayer, 1853).

62. Jukić, "Opisanje Bosne," 122. On similar concerns, see Milovan Janović, "Pismo uredniku," *Matica: List za književnost i zabavu* 1 (1866): 135.

63. Annette Wieviorka, *The Era of the Witness*, trans. Jared Stark (Ithaca, NY: Cornell University Press, 2006); and Bain Attwood, "In the Age of Testimony: The Stolen Generations Narrative, 'Distance,' and Public History," *Public Culture* 20, no. 1 (2008): 75–95.

64. Stefan Herkalović–Ljudevit Gaj, 10 February 1839, 209–210, GPKH-PLG.

65. Anon. (P.), "S bosanske granice," *Srbija: Političko-ekonomni list*, 26 August 1868. Months later, another article began similarly: "Whenever you receive

news from [Ottoman Bosnia], do not hope for anything good. There is nothing else to describe but misery, suffering, and grief." "Bosna," *Srbija: Političko-ekonomni list*, 4 November 1868.

66. František Zach, 14 June 1844, 112–114, *BIFZ.*

67. Kovačević, 8 October 1848, FIG no. 269, AS.

68. Brođanin, 20 December 1849, ZOP no. 804, ABiH.

69. Brođanin, 4 September [n.d., ca. 1848] and 23 November 1849, ZOP no. 804, ABiH; for Serbian press reports on Ottoman Bosnia, see *Srbske novine*, October–December 1850 and March–May 1851.

70. Anon., *Die Christen in Bosnien: Ein Betrag zur näheren Kenntniss der Verhältnisse der bosnischen Raaja zu den Türken* (Vienna: Carl Gerold, 1853); and Anon., ["Iz Allg. Ztg. od ednog Srbina"], "Hristjani u Bosni: Prilog za bolě poznavaně otnošenija bosanske raje i Turaka," *Sedmica*, nos. 26, 27, 29, and 31 (1853).

71. Anon., *Christen in Bosnien*, 15, 17–20, 28–29.

72. Anon., [Matija Mažuranić], *Pogled u Bosnu: ili kratak put u onu krajinu učinjen 1839–40 po jednom domordcu* (Zagreb: Tisak Lj. Gaj, 1842), quotations from 18–19, 27, 51–52, 59, 67–69.

73. Mažuranić, *Pogled u Bosnu*, ii. An unpublished draft, apparently postdated "1843–1844," opened with a similar sentiment: "My desire to get to know the people and its customs inspired me so much that I dared to leave the civilized world and undertake a journey to Turkey, to see and witness for myself the widely known and infamous cruelty of wild Muhammedans against the Christians." See Mažuranić, *Put jednog inostranca po turskoj Carevini*, 1843, R-5530, no. 1, NSK.

74. Mažuranić, *Pogled u Bosnu*, 25, 41.

75. Regarding his two-year residence in Ottoman Bosnia, Matija Mažuranić wrote in 1848: "I don't know when I will return home, because, I fear, I am born only for this land. The Turks love me very much for my great wisdom, as they say, and the *raya* more and more put their faith in me, so from here on out there can be no other way, either a crown on the head, or a stake in the ass." He traveled for most of the 1840s and returned to Croatia in the 1850s. Matija–Antun Mažuranić, 25 August 1848, 26 November 1848, 30 September 1849, and 13 January 1859, R-5838-B, NSK.

76. Matija Mažuranić, *A Glance into Ottoman Bosnia*, trans. Branka Magaš (London: Saqi Books, 2007), 133. Also see critical commentary by Ekrem Čaušević and Tatjana Paić-Vukić, "Pogled u Bosnu Matije Mažuranicća kao povijesni izvor," *Prilozi za orijentalnu filologiju* 56 (2006): 177–191.

77. Emphasis mine. The story then reverts to the "I" voice of the French officer, often alluding to but rarely assuming the "we" voice of the *raya* in the subsequent narrative. Anon. ("Iz zapisnika jednog francuskog oficira"), "Ajduk Janko," serialized in *Matica: List za književnost i zabavu* 3 (1868): 548; italics mine.

78. For example, Miroslav Hurban, "Narodni i književni život Slovakah," *Kolo* 1 (1842): 99–108; Dragutin, "Svět pismeni i nepismeni," *Danica ilirska* 13, no. 44 (1847): 175; and Ivan Macun, *Cvetje slovenskiga pesničtva* (Trieste: Lloyd, 1850), 2–4, 147–149, 222–226.

79. Anon., "O načinu kojim se narodnost i kod obladanih narodah sačuvati može," *Danica ilirska* 5, no. 43 (1839): 171.

80. Jakov Ignjatović, "Srbin i njegova poezija," *Danica: List za zabavu i književnost* 1 (1860): 118–120. This important treatise was serialized in *Slavisches*

Centralblatt and separately published in German as *Der Serbe und seine Poesie* (Bautzen: Schmaler, 1866).

81. Partha Chatterjee, *The Nation and Its Fragments: Colonial and Postcolonial Histories* (Princeton, NJ: Princeton University Press, 1993).

82. Franjo Rački, "Besjeda predsjednikova," *Rad JAZU* 1 (1867): 44–46.

83. Ignjatović, "Srbin i njegova poezija," 340.

84. The modern term *fantazija* made its way into South Slavic languages from the German *Phantasie*, especially in the sense of perceptive imagination necessary for any kind of knowledge; that was the lesson taught in Slovene, Croatian, and Serbian textbooks since the mid-nineteenth century. See Janko Pajk, "O vaji fantazije [1866]," in *Izbrani spisi* (Maribor: Skaza, 1872), 150–151; Andrija Matić, "Znanje i obrazovanje," *Javor* 15 (1887): 429–430; Pavle Padejski, "Važnost zemljopisne nastave i ocena raznih metoda," *Otadžbina* 26 (1890): 501–507; and Božo Knežević, *Principi istorije*, vol. 1 (Belgrade: Državna štamparija, 1898), 212. For other senses of *fantazija*, see Henry Buckle, "Kći pustinje," *Vienac* 4 (1872): 398–400; Anon., "Marko Kraljević: Istorijska slika," in *Srbadija Almanah* (Novi Sad: Pajević, 1884), 124–127; and Henrik Dernburg, "Fantazija u pravu," *Mjesečnik pravničkog družtva u Zagrebu* 20 (1894): 492–502, 533–540.

85. August Šenoa, "O poetici," in his *Antologija pjesničtva hrvatskoga i srbskoga, narodnoga i umjetnoga* (Zagreb: Matica hrvatska, 1876), ii–xlviii, here ii–vi. Though Šenoa mostly discusses South Slavic sources, his synthesis of fantasy and history clearly invokes nineteenth-century historicist thought, particularly as developed by Wilhelm von Humboldt and Theodor Mommsen; see, e.g., Frederick Beiser, *The German Historicist Tradition* (Oxford: Oxford University Press, 2012), 208.

86. Šenoa, "O poetici," xxxv.

87. Originally Ivan Mažuranić, "Smèrt Čengić-age," in *Iskra: zabavni sastavci*, ed. Ivan Havliček (Zagreb: Gaj, 1846), 181–228. There are three English-language translations, the most recent being *Smail-aga Čengić's Death*, trans. Charles A. Ward (Zagreb: Association of Croat Writers, 1969). For an annotated edition, see Mažuranić, *Smrt Smail-age Čengića*, ed. Davor Kapetanić (Zagreb: JAZU, 1968).

88. On the 1840 event, see Jevto Milović, "Arhivska dokumenta o pogibiji Smail-age Čengića," *Zbornik istorije književnosti* 4 (1964): 209–259; on the Čengićes, see Hamdija Kreševljaković, *Čengići: Prilog proučavanju feudalizma u Bosni i Hercegovini* (Sarajevo: Grafički zavod, 1959).

89. Mažuranić, *Put jednog inostranca po Turskoj carevini*; and *Reise Beschreibung eines Europaers*, 1843–1844, R-5530, no. 3, NSK.

90. Mažuranić, *Put jednog inostranca po Turskoj carevini*. These drafts included *krstoseri* ("Christ-shits"), but such expressions were softened to *krsti* and *pseta* ("Christlings, dogs") in the final published work.

91. For example, Andrew Wachtel, *Making a Nation, Breaking a Nation: Literature and Cultural Politics in Yugoslavia* (Stanford, CA: Stanford University Press, 1998), 28, 42–45; and Aleksa Djilas, *The Contested Country: Yugoslav Unity and Communist Revolution, 1919–1953* (Cambridge, MA: Harvard University Press, 1996), 24. On the centrality of Njegoš in Yugoslav politics, see Milovan Đilas, *Njegoš: Pjesnik, vladar, vladika* (Belgrade: Zodne, 1988); and Ivo Žanić, *Flag on the Mountain: A Political Anthropology of War in Croatia and Bosnia* (London: Saqi, 2007), 364–388.

92. Šenoa, "O poetici," xviii.

93. Ivan Mažuranić, *Smrt Smail-age Čengijića* (Zagreb: Župan, 1876), 2–3.

94. "Curses like a Vlach on a stake (*psuje kao Vlah s koca*); because a man who is impaled on a stake, not fearing any greater evil, then curses to the Turks anything that comes into his mouth, hoping they will finish him off"; *Srpske narodne poslovice*, ed. Vuk Karadžić (Vienna: Armeniern, 1849), 266. Also see the entry on *kolac* ("stake") in *Rječnik hrvatskoga ili srpskoga jezika*, vol. 5, ed. Đura Daničić (Zagreb, 1906), 177–178; and Tihomir Đorđević, "Nabijanje na kolac," *Policija* 6–7 (1920): 420–428.

95. Here Jacques Rancière's notions of "mute speech" in literature are helpful; see his *Mute Speech: Literature, Critical Theory, and Politics* (New York: Columbia University Press, 2011).

96. Mažuranić, *Smrt Smail-age* (1876), 33–35, 54.

97. Franjo Marković, "Predgovor," in *Smrt Smail-age* (1876), xl. Indeed, in Mažuranić's depiction of the Herzegovinian countryside, no "peasants" or synonymous terms (*seljak, kmet*, etc.) appear aside from the nameless and collective *raya*.

98. Mažuranić, *Smrt Smail-age* (1876), 33–35, 54.

99. Ibid., 21, 39.

100. By 1968, some 150 editions of *The Death of Smail-aga* were printed in over thirty languages, including German, French, Russian, Italian, and English; the poem had become a part of high school curricula by the 1860s. See Davor Kapetanić, "Bibliografija izdanja," in Mažuranić, *Smrt Smail-age Čengića* (Zagreb: Jugoslavenska akademija znanosti i umjetnosti, 1968), 151–183.

101. For example, Vjekoslav Klaić, "Nešto o tehnici Čengić-age," *Hrvatska lipa* 1 (1875): 246–248, 262–263, 273–274, 281.

102. Ivan Mažuranić and Matija Mažuranić, *An die Monarchen Europas*, 1843–1844, R-5530, no. 3, NSK.

103. August Šenoa, "Na Balkanu," "Lanac," "Munja Od Gabele," in *Izabrane pjesme* (Zagreb: Hartman, 1908); Đorđe Jakšić, "Jevropi," "Prve žrtve," and "Jevropski mir," in *Pesme Đure Jakšića* (Belgrade: Državna štamparija, 1873); and Stevan Kaćanski, "Srbi i Turci," *Srbska narodnost*, no. 3 (1862).

104. On related dynamics and senses of the term "Europe," see Holly Case's extraordinary study, *Between States: The Transylvanian Question and the European Idea during World War II* (Stanford, CA: Stanford University Press, 2009).

105. For example, Nikola Šimić and Milutin Tomić, "Smrt Smail-age Čengića," *Iskra*, nos. 8–16 (1885); Marko Dragović, "Čiji je spjev Smrt Smail-age Čengića," *Obzor* 29 (1888); and Vladimir Mažuranić, "Poziv na predbrojbu pjesama Ivana Mažuranića," *Svjetlo*, no. 42 (1894).

106. Grga Martić, 16 April 1893, R-5530, no. 2, NSK; Martić added that a number of other issues "hinder the reliability" of the account and speculated that the author was not Ivan but Matija Mažuranić.

107. For telling commentary on how Grga Martić's poetry "never measured up to master Mažuranić," see Gjuro Šurmin, "U pomen fra Grga Martića," *Savremenik: Ljetopis društva hrvatskih književnika* 1 (1906): 13–14.

108. Milorad Živančević, *Ivan Mažuranić* (Zagreb: Globus, 1988), 32.

109. Marković, "Predgovor," vii. Šenoa was even more blunt, stating that "there cannot be a more artificial poem than Čengić-aga, but there cannot be one that is closer to the folk either" ("O poetici," xxxvi).

110. Šenoa, "Nova jeka od Balkana," *Pozor* 9, no. 225 (1861): 142; Utješenović, trans., "Jék od Balkana," *Jezičnik* 19 (1881): 4–6.

111. For example, Jakšić, "Raja," "Padajte braćo," "Što nisam," "Ljubav," "Katkad," "Osman-aga," "Bura na moru," "Dve zastave," and especially "Prve žrtve" and "Bratoubica," in *Pesme*.

112. Đorđe Jakšić, "Mučenica," *Danica: List za zabavu i književnost* 3 (1862): 173–177.

113. "Jakšić is a master artist in the psychological sketching of the inner life of the human soul," commented Stevan Popović in "Naša novija lirika," *Letopis Matice srpske* 121 (1880): 101; also see a favorable Russian review of Jakšić, including *The Martryress*, by Dmitriĭ Nikolskiĭ, "Ocherki serbskoĭ literatury," *Izviestiia S. Peterburgskago slavianskago blagotvoritel'nago obshchestva* 3 (1886): 117–121.

114. E. Thamner and W. Sphor, "Le salon d'Anvers," *La Belgique Contemporaine* 2 (1861): 181.

115. Théophile Gautier, *Abécédaire du salon de 1861* (Paris: Dentu, 1861), 99–100; also see Anon., "Belgium," *The Spectator*, no. 1730, 24 August 1861, 907; and Édouard Gerney, "Salon de 1861," *Le Moniteur de la Mode* 3 (1861): 433.

116. Jaroslav Čermák, *Razzia de bachi-bouzoucks dans un village chrétien de l'Herzégovine*, Čermák acquisition file 1861, Dahesh Museum of Art, New York (consulted in 2011).

117. Ognjeslav Utješenović, "Jedna slika od Jaroslava Čermaka," *Matica: List za književnost i zabavu* 5 (1870): 61–65; and Utješenović, "Roblje," *Vienac* 9 (1870): 129–130 and 138–140. Interest in Čermák reprints—at least four hundred were sent from Paris to Zagreb alone—spiked with the Herzegovinian Uprising of 1875; see *Vienac* 7 (1875): 472, 537, 559, 570, 804. On Uroš Predić's praise for Čermák, see "Biografija," *Godišnjak SKA* 28 (1919): 298.

118. William Gladstone, *Bulgarian Horrors and the Question of the East* (London: Murray, 1876) and *Lessons in Massacre* (London: Murray, 1877). Also see Peter Loewenberg, "Gladstone, Sin, and the Bulgarian Question," in his *Fantasy and Reality in History* (Oxford: Oxford University Press, 1995), 93–107; Irvin Cemil Schick, "Christian Maidens, Turkish Ravishers: The Sexualization of National Conflict in the Late Ottoman Period," in *Women in the Ottoman Balkans: Gender, Culture, and History*, ed. Amila Baturović and Irvin Cemil Schick (New York: I. B. Tauris, 2007), 273–304; and Martina Baleva, *Bulgarien im Bild: Die Erfindung von Nationen auf dem Balkan in der Kunst des 19. Jahrhunderts* (Cologne: Böhlau, 2012).

119. For example, Jovan Jovanović Zmaj, "Turčinu na novu godinu 1878," in *Pevanija Zmaj-Jovana Jovanovića*, vol. 3 (Novi Sad: M. Popović, 1882), 1177–1179.

120. U spomen zauzeća Sarajeva, Zagreb, 1878, NKHZ 13, VII-218, ABiH; and "Sarajevo je naše," *Slovenski gospodar* (Maribor), 29 August 1878.

121. Mita Živković, "Sarajevo: Prilog poznavanju srpskih krajeva i prilika," *Brastvo* 4 (1890): 144–195.

122. Mita Živković, "Pravda u Bosni," in *Bosančice: Kratke priče iz Bosne* (Belgrade: Srpska književna zadruga, 1897), 66–67.

123. *The Encyclopedia Britannica* (1899), "Servia," 21: 691.

124. Marković, "Predgovor," xii, xxxiv; italics mine.

125. F. Cherubin Šegvić, "O epu," in *Smrt Smail-age Čengijića* (Zagreb: Albrecht, 1894), 6.

126. Vladimir Lunaček, "Za Ivana Mažuranića," *Obzor*, no. 58 (1914): 1–2; and Lunaček, "O Mažuranićevom Čengić-agi," *Kritika* 3, no. 10 (1922): 453–468.

127. Mučenica od Đ. Jakšića sa produženjem L. Kostića, ca. 1880s, R-10.960, Arhiv Matice Srpske.

128. Vladimir Borota, "Dva naraštaja," *Vienac*, nos. 29–32 (1892).

129. Vaso Pelagić, "Austrija kao civilizator u Bosni i Hercegovini," *Straža* 1 (December 1878): 526–530.

130. Sloboda (Niš), *Iz Bosne*, 10 February 1889, ZMF Präs BH 158/1889, ABiH; and ZMF Präs BH 1178/1904, ABiH.

131. Already in 1878, the Croatian representative Klaić complained that Austro-Hungarian rule could bring about "denationalization" (*Entnationalisierung*) of the inhabitants of Bosnia-Herzegovina; see *Stenographische Sitzungs-Protokolle der Delegation des Reichsrates*, Session 1 (1878), 198–199; also see ZMF Präs BH 811/1901, and 112/1905, 593/1905, 1314/1908, and 1196/1910, ABiH.

132. J. Miodragović, "Govor prilikom proslave Sv. Save," *Brastvo* 6 (1894): 319–329.

133. See Okey, *Taming Balkan Nationalism*, 217–250.

134. This idea resonates with the notion of "injury play" by Abbas, *Liberalism and Human Suffering*, 53–56, 75–81.

135. On Kočić's activities, see ZMF Präs BH 1263/1910, 1264/1910, 1359/1910, 1372/1910, and 345/1911, ABiH.

136. Petar Kočić, "Jazavac pred sudom," in *S planine i ispod planine* (Belgrade: Davidović, 1907), 83–110, here 91–93.

137. Ilija Ivačković, "Nove zbirke srpskih pripovedaka," *Nova iskra* 6 (1904): 343–346.

138. Branko Čubrilović, *Petar Kočić i njegovo doba* (Zagreb: Tipografija, 1934), 26.

139. Kočić, "Jazavac pred sudom," 98, 110.

140. Similar tropes abound in nationalist writings. Aleksa Šantić's now-famous poem "My Homeland" (1908) sums up patriotic sensibility thus: "I bear the pain of all the wounds of my people / My soul suffers and cries with it. . . . Within me moan the souls of millions / My every sigh, my every tear / Wails and calls out with their pain." Aleksa Šantić, "Moja otadžbina," in *Pjesme* (Belgrade: Srpska književna zadruga, 1911).

141. Jovan Skerlić, "Mlada srpska poezija i pripovetka," *Hrvatsko kolo* 1 (1905): 441; and D.M., "Naš književni život," *Bosanska vila* 9 (1907): 138.

142. Radovan Perović-Tunguz (Nevesinjski), "Iz zemlje plača," *Delo* 40 (1906): 314–315. On Perović's "fantasy," see D.M., "Naš književni život," 138. Also see Polimac, "Na ćupriji mutne Drine," *Brastvo*, nos. 12–13 (1908): 356–357.

143. Kočić, "Naša riječ," *Otadžbina*, no. 1, 15 June 1907.

144. Kočić, "Težak," *Otadžbina*, no. 1, 15 June 1907.

145. Ibid; also see Kočić (or often Anon.), "Molitva," no. 3; "Mi vas preziremo," no. 16; "Osuđeni narod," no. 18; "Šarlatani," no. 19; "Iridenti (neoslobođeni)," no. 20, all in *Otadžbina*, no. 1, 15 June 1907; and "Porezi pod Turcima," nos. 6–7; "Orijentalizam našeg pravosuđa," no. 8; "Za srpski jezik," no. 37; "Pljačkanje kmetova," no. 50; "Jesmo kolonija," no. 64; "Za srpski jezik i ćirilicu," no. 79; "Iz naroda," no. 83; "Austriaco-Hungarica," no. 122, all in *Otadžbina*, nos. 1–2 (1911–1912).

146. Serbische Organisation, 12 December 1907, ZMF Präs BH: 1363/1907, ABiH.

147. Benko, Delo, 18 June 1911, ZMF Präs BH 264/1911, ABiH.

148. Emil Reich, "The Crisis in the Near East: The Austro-Hungarian Case," *The Nineteenth Century and After* 64, no. 8 (1908): 713.

149. Lj. Dvorniković, "Književnost," *Nada*, no. 14 (1903): 194–195 (review of Tugomir Alaupović, *Probrane pjesme*, Zagreb, 1902). Also see Alaupović, *Naše rane* (1898), which one critic praised thus: "At times the ambiance is truly magical. The plague is described beautifully, while the scene by the destroyed tower of Omar and the description of hunger remind one of the powerful style of Mažuranić in the most beautiful pages of *Smail-aga*. Does one need greater praise?" *Novi Viek* 3 (1898): 123–124.

150. Želimir Juričić, *The Man and the Artist: Essays on Ivo Andrić* (Lanham, MD: University Press of America, 1986), 115; and Roger Petersen, *Western Intervention in the Balkans: The Strategic Use of Emotion* (Cambridge: Cambridge University Press, 2011), 134.

151. Petar Džadžić, "Književno delo, istorija, stvarnost," in *Književnost, istorija, savremenost*, ed. Branislav Milošević (Belgrade: Rad, 1979), 48.

152. Ivo Andrić, *The Bridge on the Drina*, trans. L. Edwards (Chicago: University of Chicago Press, 1977), 40–59.

153. Lynda E. Boose, "Crossing the River Drina: Bosnian Rape Camps, Turkish Impalement, and Serb Cultural Memory," *Signs* 28, no. 1 (2002): 71–96; and Toma Longinović, *Vampire Nation: Violence as Cultural Imaginary* (Durham, NC: Duke University Press, 2011), 131–132.

154. See Andrić's comments in Ljubo Jandrić, *Sa Ivom Andrićem* (Belgrade: Srpska književna zadruga, 1977), 121.

155. Gyatri Spivak, "Echo," in *The Spivak Reader*, ed. Donna Landry and Gerald McLean (London: Routledge, 1996), 175–202; John Hollander, *The Figure of Echo: A Mode of Allusion in Milton and After* (Berkeley: University of California Press, 1981); and Joan W. Scott, "Fantasy Echo: History and the Construction of Identity," *Critical Inquiry* 27 (2001): 284–304.

3. Nationalization and Its Discontents

1. Martin Nedić, Zapamćenja, n.d. (ca. 1860s), FMN, AFM-TO.

2. František Zach, 23 March 1844, 77–79, *BIFZ*.

3. Blasius Josić, "Carmen" (1852, 1853), "Festis" (1855), Pisma II, folio 4, ZP, AFM-KS; Josić continued to write, though he kept a low patriotic profile, composing poetry in Latin at a time when his companions embraced "the pure speech of the peasant."

4. František Zach, 24 November 1843, 35–38, *BIFZ*.

5. František Zach, 23 March 1844 and 27 April 1844, 77–79 and 101–102, *BIFZ*.

6. Kovačević, 15 May 1848, FIG no. 263, AS; also see Kovačević, 8 October 1848, FIG no. 269, AS.

7. Kovačević, 28 December 1847, FIG no. 234, AS.

8. Kovačević, 8 October 1848, FIG no. 269, AS.

9. Kovačević, "Projekt za podizanje bune," 20 February 1862, in *Politička akcija Srbije u južnoslovenskim pokrajinama Habsburške Monarhije, 1859–1874*, ed. Vojislav Vučković (Belgrade: Naučno delo, 1965), 69–81.

10. Eric Hobsbawm, *Bandits*, 2nd ed. (London: Weidenfeld, 2000 [1969]); esp. chap. 6 (Haiduks) specifically regarding the Balkans. Also see Dimitrije Djordjević

and Stephen Fischer-Galaţi, *The Balkan Revolutionary Tradition* (New York: Columbia University Press, 1981); Dimitrije Djordjević, "Balkan Revolutionary Organizations in the 1860s and the Peasantry," in *The Crucial Decade: East Central European Society and National Defense, 1859–1870,* ed. Bela K. Kiraly (Boulder, CO: East European Monographs, 1984), 270–283; and Frederick Anscombe, "The Balkan Revolutionary Age," *Journal of Modern History* 84, no. 3 (2012): 572–606.

11. Anon., "O načinu kojim se narodnost i kod obladanih narodah sačuvati može," *Danica ilirska* 5, nos. 40–43 (1839): 157–159, 162–164, 166–168, 170–171.

12. Miroslav Hurban, "Narodni i književni život Slovakah," *Kolo* 1 (1842): 99–108.

13. This has been the recent consensus: "Most national movements in East Central Europe during the nineteenth century sought autonomy within, not secession from, multinational empires." Taking this as the presumed historical norm, "nationalist movements in the Ottoman state were an exception." See Rogers Brubaker, Margit Feischmidt, Jon Fox, and Liana Grancea, *Nationalist Politics and Everyday Ethnicity in a Transylvanian Town* (Princeton, NJ: Princeton University Press, 2006), 32–35.

14. Medo Pucić, "Bosanske davorije [1841]" and "Karađurđevka [1847]," in *Pjesme Meda Pucića Dubrovčanina* (Pančevo: Jovanović, 1879), 203–280 and 304–313.

15. Fran Kurelac, *Fluminensia, ili koječega na Rěci* (Zagreb: Antun Jakić, 1862), 133.

16. Anon., "O načinu kojim se narodnost," *Danica ilirska* 5, no. 40 (1839): 157.

17. Linas Eriksonas and Leos Müller, eds., *Statehood before and beyond Ethnicity: Minor States in Northern and Eastern Europe, 1600–2000* (Brussels: Peter Lang, 2005).

18. Giuseppe Mazzini, *La questione d'Orient,* 2nd ed. (Rome: G. Mazzini, 1877); and Karl Marx, *The Eastern Question: A Reprint of Letters Written 1853–1856 Dealing with the Events of the Crimean War,* ed. Eleanor Marx Aveling (London: Sonnenschein, 1897).

19. Anon., "The Future of Turkey," *The New York Daily Times,* 9 May 1854. Serbian newspapers made similar observations, asserting in 1866 that when it came to the Balkans, regional states could not afford to be left out of "decisive changes in the European map." *Srbske novine,* no. 79 (9 July 1866).

20. On the intertwined histories that helped constitute both "regional" questions and larger dynamics of state-making (and the very notion of Europe), see Holly Case, *Between States: The Transylvanian Question and the European Idea during World War II* (Stanford, CA: Stanford University Press, 2009).

21. Keith Brown emphasized these aspects of revolutionary organizations in his book on turn-of-the-century Macedonia; see *Loyal unto Death: Trust and Terror in Revolutionary Macedonia* (Bloomington: Indiana University Press, 2013).

22. Michel Foucault, *Security, Territory, Population: Lectures at the Collège de France, 1977–1978,* trans. Graham Burchell (New York: Picador, 2007), 275, 288.

23. Platon Kulakovskiĭ, *Illirizm: Izsliedovanie po istorii khorvatskoĭ literatury perioda vozrozhdenia* (Warsaw: Tipografija varshavskago uchevnogo okruga, 1894), 293–295, 083–086; Philip E. Moseley, "A Pan-Slavist Memorandum of Liudevit Gaj in 1838," *American Historical Review* 40, no. 4 (1935): 704–716; Jaroslav Šidak, "'Tajna politika' Lj. Gaja i postanak njegovih 'memoranduma' knezu Metternichu 1846–47," *Arhivski vjesnik* 13 (1970): 397–434; and Ljubiša

Doklestić, "O pokušaju ustanka u Bosni 1840 i o tajnoj politici Gajeva kruga prema Bosni 1843–44," *Historijski zbornik* 35 (1982): 15–41.

24. For related commentary on secrets and national politics, see Eugen Kvarternik, *Politička razmatranja*, vol. 1 (Zagreb: Gaj, 1861), 15–16, 46–47.

25. For example, Dušan Berić, " 'Proekt' Ljubomira Ivanovića iz 1866 godine o ustanku hrišćana u evropskoj Turskoj," *Zbornik za istoriju Matice srpske* 27 (1983): 151–172.

26. Kovačević, 24 November 1850, FIG no. 654, AS.

27. Anon., O konstituciji i revoluciji u društvu, 1862, FIG no. 163, AS.

28. Cf. Section 11, § 110, "Ustav Knjažestva Serbije (1835)," and Section 2, § 23, "Ustav za Knjažestvo Srbiju (1869)," in *Ustavi Kneževine i Kraljevine Srbije, 1835–1903* (Belgrade: SANU, 1988), 56 and 95.

29. Vasa Čubrilović, ed., *Oslobođenje gradova u Srbiji od Turaka 1862–1867 godine* (Belgrade: SANU, 1970); Ženi Lebl, *Do "Konačnog rešenja": Jevreji u Beogradu, 1521–1942* (Belgrade: Čigoja, 2001), 82–11; and Dietmar Müller, *Staatsbürger auf Widerruf: Juden und Muslime als Alteritätspartner im rumänischen und serbischen Nationscode Ethnonationale Staatsbürgerschaftskonzepte, 1878–1941* (Berlin: Harrasowitz, 2005).

30. See esp. Ivo Banac, "The Confessional 'Rule' and the Dubrovnik Exception: The Origins of the 'Serb-Catholic' Circle in Nineteenth-Century Dalmatia," *Slavic Review* 42, no. 3 (1983): 448–474.

31. Dragoslav Stranjaković, "Kako je postalo Garašaninovo *Načertanije*," *Spomenik Srpske kraljevske akademije* 91 (1939): 63–115. On Garašanin and the *Načertanije*, see Nikša Stančić, "Problem Načertanija Ilije Garašanina u našoj historiografiji," *Historijski zbornik* 22 (1969): 179–196; and David MacKenzie, *Ilija Garašanin: Balkan Bismarck* (Boulder, CO: East European Monographs, 1985).

32. For example, Vaclav Začek, ed., *Epistolarni dnevnik Františeka Zaha, 1860–1878* (Novi Sad: Matica srpska, 1987).

33. Nationalists themselves drew these connections, comparing Serbian and Polish claims to independence in light of the Eastern Question; e.g., Ban, "Na čemu smo sa istočnim pitanjem," n.d. (ca. 1860s), FIG no. 1507, AS.

34. On abiding Polish interest in Ottoman Balkan affairs, see Jerzi Skowronek, *Polityka bałkańska Hotelu Lambert, 1833–1856* (Warsaw: Uniwersytet Warszawski, 1976); and Antoni Cetnarowicz, *Tajna dyplomacja Adama Jerzego Czartoryskiego na Bałkanach* (Cracow: Uniwersytet Jagielloński, 1993). Many leading Serbian-Croatian writers embedded their national questions within the Eastern Question; e.g., see Mihailo Polit-Desančić, *Die orientalische Frage and ihre organische Lösung* (Vienna: Franz Leo, 1862); Vladimir Jovanović, *The Serbian Nation and the Eastern Question* (London: Bell and Daldy, 1863); Vladimir Jovanović, *The Emancipation and Unity of the Serbian Nation, or, The Regeneration of Eastern Europe by the Reconstitution of the Nationalities* (Geneva: Trübner, 1871); and Eugen Kvaternik, *Istočno pitanje i Hrvati: Historično-pràvna razprava* (Zagreb: Albrecht, 1868).

35. Stranjaković, "Kako je postalo *Načertanije*," 77–79.

36. Ibid., 87–89.

37. Ibid., 80–81.

38. Mackenzie, *Ilija Garašanin*, 62–75; Damir Agičić, *Tajna politika Srbije u XIX stoljeću* (Zagreb: AGM, 1994), 11–40.

39. Stranjaković, "Kako je postalo *Načertanije*," 80–81.

40. Ban, "Nacrt ustava za vođenje političke propagande u zemljama sloveno-turskim," 16 May 1850, FIG no. 647, AS.

41. Spisak bosanski fratara, 1843, FIG no. 83, AS; S. Car, 17 July 1843, FIG no. 95, AS.

42. Mato Mikić, *Arkiva*, vol. 3 (entry for 1854), Manuscript collection, folio 204, AFM-KS; Mikić states that Kovačević (a "former Franciscan") "came from Serbia and gave two gold watches" to the monastery custos in Sutjeska.

43. Garašanin letters, January–March 1862, esp. 14 February 1862, FIG no. 1274, AS; and Garašanin, Austriska politika u Bosni, May 1869, II OJR sig. 17/1, no. 2, ASANU.

44. StAbt Bosnien, box 2 (1830–1837), box 3 (1840–1844), box 4 (1846–1910), and especially StAbt Türkei III (Grenzverhältnisse), box 18, HHStA.

45. Army General Staff, *Die Occupation Bosniens und der Hercegovina durch k.k. Truppen im Jahre 1878* (Vienna: K.K. Generalstab, 1879), 126, 892–893.

46. "The Austro-Serbian Alliance of 1881," in *The Secret Treaties of Austria-Hungary, 1879–1914*, ed. Alfred F. Pribram (Cambridge, MA: Harvard University Press, 1920), 51.

47. Kutschera Confidentenbericht, 20 January 1903, ZMF Präs BH 166/1903, ABiH.

48. Bezirksämter Mostar, Nevesinje, Gacko, Trebinje, Foča, Bileća, January 1903, ZMF Präs BH 224/1903, ABiH. Also see ZMF Präs BH 1178/1904 and 253/1906, ABiH.

49. Matija Mrazović, "Plan o pripremanju akcije u Bosni," April 1867, FMM, AHAZU; as this copy shows, the Serbian officers Orešković and Garašanin crossed out several proposed sections and rewrote the joint Serbian-Croatian proposal. This text is almost identical to Antonije Orešković and Ilija Garašanin, "Program jugoslovenske politike preložen od strane Garašanina Štrosmajeru," March 1867, in Vučković, *Politička akcija*, 273–281; also see 259–260, 290–291, 332–337, and 339–342.

50. Orešković and Garašanin, "Program jugoslovenske politike."

51. Brođanin, 4 October 1849, and 23 November 1849, ZOP no. 804, ABiH.

52. Brođanin, 4 September [ca. 1848], and 21 September 1850, ZOP no. 804, ABiH.

53. Brođanin, 1 March 1850, ZOP no. 804, ABiH.

54. Brođanin, 4 October 1849, ZOP no. 804, ABiH.

55. Orešković, "Predlog ratnog plana Srbije," 25 January 1863, in Vučković, *Politička akcija*, 96–101, quotation on 97.

56. Ibid., 98.

57. Okan–Ristić, Oslobođeně Bosne moguće ě samo pomoću strane koě države, 4 January 1869, II OJR sig. 12/3, no. 28, ASANU.

58. Gdi se koi nalazi od onih ljudi koi su za upotrebu u radnji isključivo bosanskoj, 5 August 1870, II OJR sig. 27/10, no. 368, ASANU.

59. Garašanin, n.d. (1866), FIG no. 1567, AS.

60. For example, see reports of Ristić, Garašanin, and Blaznavac for years 1865–1868 in Vučković, *Politička akcija*, 201–314.

61. Dučić, Izvještaj, 1 March 1874, II OJR sig. 17/1, no. 20, ASANU; and numerous requests for state support in organizing *čete*: Okan, Projekt, 17

September 1868, II OJR sig. 27–10, no. 366, ASANU; Garašanin, Izvještaj, 22 December 1868, sig. 3/14, no. 1395; Okan, 9 December 1868, sig. 12/5, no. 583; Orešković, Plan o turskom ratu, October 1870, sig. 26/4, no. 403; Ljubibratić, Promemorija (ca. 1875), sig. 17/1, no. 303, ASANU.

62. Garašanin, n.d. (1866), FIG no. 1567, AS.

63. Garašanin, Plan, 1858, FIG no. 1072, AS.

64. On first Serbian attempts to aid schools in Bosnia, see Vaso Vojvodić, "Rad Srbije na pomaganju prosvete u Bosni i Hercegovini," in *Iz knjizževne istorije i prosvete* (Novi Sad: Slavija, 1989), 87–166.

65. The case of the Hadžiristić family is indicative of the dilemmas of Bosnian Christian elites during the late Ottoman period. As an established merchant family in Sarajevo, the Hadžiristićes appear to have enjoyed a good working relationship with Ottoman authorities, Russian and Austrian consuls, and Serbian Orthodox clergy. By the 1860s, however, some of the young educated men like Kosta Hadžiristić developed new ties with Belgrade literary and patriotic societies that advocated Serbian nationalism and overthrow of Ottoman rule. Nonetheless, rather than side with the new national forces, many of the members of the Hadžiristić family remained suspicious of plans for Serbian nationalist uprisings in Bosnia. On these dynamics, see: esp. folio 1 (Kosta Hadžiristić letters), folio 3 (letters to the Russian consul), folio 4 (Đorđe Lazarević and Vaso Hadži Ristić letters), and folio 6 (various letters), 1850s–1860s, O-HR-220, HAS; Kosta Hadži-Ristić Dogadajnik, IZ, no. 9275, folio 69, ASANU; and Todorović–Hadži Ristić, Defteri, n.d., TK IX-1-20, ABiH. Also see O-T-387 (1860–1874) and O-R-230 (1830–1874), HAS.

66. Petranović, Đe sam bio i šta sam radio, 10 December 1869, II OJR sig. 17/1, no. 6, ASANU.

67. B. Petranović to Stevo Petranović, 10 April 1869, II OJR sig. 12/3, no. 37, ASANU; Dimitrije Mita Klicin, *Spomenica Steve Petranovića nacionalnog borca, 1835–1913* (Novi Sad: Dunavska štamparija, 1937).

68. Risto Šušljić, Građa za istoriju srpskih škola u Bosni i Hercegovini do okupacije, SZ no. 35, sect. 3, Arhiv Nacionalne i univerzitetske biblioteke Bosne i Hercegovine.

69. Petranović, Đe sam bio i šta sam radio.

70. Ibid.

71. See B. Petranović, *Srpske narodne pjesme iz Bosne (ženske)* (Sarajevo: Bosansko-vilajetska štamparija, 1867); also Petranović, *Svečanost pri dočeku preosveštenog mitropolita bosanskog gospodina Dionisije* (Sarajevo: Bosansko-vilajetska štamparija, 1868). On favorable Ottoman reports about Petranović's school, see "Vilajetske vjesti," *Bosna*, no. 17 (5 September 1866); and "Izvješća," *Sarajevski cvjetnik*, no. 3 (16 January 1869).

72. Stojan Novaković, foreword to B. Petranović, *Srpske narodne pjesme iz Bosne i Hercegovine: Epske pjesme starijeg vremena* (Belgrade: Državna štamparija, 1867); also Novaković, "Običaji srpskog naroda u Bosni," *Glasnik srpskog učenog društva* 28 (1869), 29 (1870), and 30 (1871): 176–227, 237–255, and 313–361. Also see "Protokoli sednica," *Glasnik Srpskoga učenog društva* 3 (1866): 429; F. Mauerer, "Jedan bosanski učitelj i spisatelj," *Danica: List za zabavu i književnost* 10 (1869): 89–92; and anon., "Beleške," *Matica: List za književnost i zabavu* 5 (1870): 188.

73. Matić, 28 May 1866, Akta SUD no. 40/1866, ASANU.

74. Vladislav Skarić, *Sarajevo i njegova okolina od najstarijih vremena do austro-ugarske okupacije* (Sarajevo: Bosanska pošta, 1937), 223–224; also see Thomas Herkalović, *Vorgeschichte der Occupation Bosniens und der Hercegovina* (Zagreb: Hartman, 1906), 15–16.

75. Petranović, Đe sam bio i šta sam radio, 10 December 1869, II OJR sig. 17/1, no. 6; and Petranović, 12 August 1875, sig. 17/1, no. 228, ASANU. In his correspondence, Petranović blamed the Serbian merchants of Sarajevo for being inadequately patriotic and openly hostile to his activist work; it did not help that the increasingly wary Ottoman authorities then seized on the merchants' complaints and hastened his departure.

76. Okan, 11 December 1869, II OJR sig. 26/7, no. 484, ASANU.

77. Dučić, 15 December 1869, II OJR sig. 26/7, no. 426, ASANU. On Nićifor Dučić's literary and historical works, see his *Književni radovi*, 6 vols. (Belgrade, 1899).

78. Novak Kilibarda, the literary critic and Montenegrin politician, later compiled and exposed the many inventions and forgeries that Petranović's work was based on; see Kilibarda, ed., *Srpske narodne pjesme iz Bosne i Hercegovine: Sakupio Bogoljub Petranović*, 3 vols. (Sarajevo: Svjetlost, 1989).

79. Petranović, Đe sam bio i šta sam radio, II OJR sig. 17/1, no. 6, ASANU; Okan, 21 April 1873, sig. 12/3, no. 104, ASANU.

80. As quoted in S. Ljubibratić and Kruševac, "Prilozi za proučavanje hercegovačkih ustanaka, 1857–1878 godina," *Godišnjak istoriskog društva Bosne i Hercegovine* 7 (1955): 198–199.

81. As quoted from an August 1875 report in Milorad Ekmečić, *Ustanak u Bosni, 1875–1878*, 3rd ed. (Belgrade: SANU, 1996 [1960]), 104.

82. For example, Vidojević, 20 August 1875, II OJR sig. 12/5, no. 321, ASANU; and Dučić–Ristić, 21 August 1875, sig. 26/12, no. 622, ASANU. Contemporary reports, like Arthur Evans's 1876 account, made the point clearly: "That the insurrection was brought about by foreign agitators is strongly disproved by the fact that the outbreak took the Serbian Revolutionary Society—the Omladina itself—by surprise." Arthur Evans, *Through Bosnia and the Herzegovina on Foot during the Insurrection, August and September 1875*, 2nd ed. (London: Longmans, 1877), 332.

83. Ljubibratić, January 1875, FMLj, no. 142; no. 143, 16 February 1875; no. 144-a, 25 February 1875; no. 145, 5 March 1875, AH.

84. "Herzegovina," *New York Herald*, 6 November 1875, 4. On the outbreak of the uprising, see Hannes Grandits, "Violent Social Disintegration: A Nation-Building Strategy in Late-Ottoman Herzegovina," in *Conflicting Loyalties in the Balkans: The Great Powers, the Ottoman Empire, and Nation-Building*, ed. Nathalie Clayer et al. (New York: I. B. Tauris, 2011), 110–134.

85. "Herzegovina," 4; David Harris, *A Diplomatic History of the Balkan Crisis of 1875–1878* (Stanford, CA: Stanford University Press, 1936); and Mihailo D. Stojanović, *The Great Powers and the Balkans, 1875–1878* (Cambridge, UK: The University Press, 1968).

86. The entire crisis is recounted and analyzed in great detail by various authors in *Međunarodni naučni skup povodom 100-godišnjice ustanaka u Bosni i Hercegovini, drugim balkanskim zemljama i istočnoj krizi 1875–1878 godine*, ed. Rade Petrović, 3 vols. (Sarajevo: ANUBiH, 1977).

87. For example, Jovan Ristić, *Jedno namestništvo, 1868–1872* (Belgrade: Štamparija Kraljevine Srbije, 1894); Ristić, *Knez Mihailo i zajednička radnja balkanskih naroda* (Belgrade: Štamparija Kraljevine Srbije, 1894); Antonije Orešković, *Malo više svetlosti* (Belgrade: S. Nikolić, 1895); and Orešković, *Da smo jednom načisto* (Belgrade: S. Nikolić, 1898).

88. For example, Vaso Čubrilović, *Bosanski ustanak, 1875–1878* (Belgrade: Srpska kraljevska akademija, 1930); and Milorad Ekmečić, *Ustanak u Bosni, 1875–1878*, 3rd ed. (Belgrade: SANU, 1996 [1960]), esp. 87–89, 394–397. Here quoted: Vojislav Vučković, "Neuspela politička akcija Matije Bana, 1860–1861," *Istoriski časopis* 9–10 (1959): 381–409; and Milorad Ekmečić, "Nacionalna politika Srbije prema Bosni i Hercegovini i agrarno pitanje (1844–1875)," *Društvo istoričara Bosne i Hercegovine* 10 (1959): 197–219.

89. Dejan Djokić, ed., *Yugoslavism: Histories of a Failed Idea, 1918–1992* (Madison: University of Wisconsin Press, 2003); and John Lampe, "The Failure of the Yugoslav National Idea," *Studies in East European Thought* 46, no. 1 (1994): 69–89.

90. Stranjaković, "Kako je postalo *Načertanije*," 89–90.

91. Dučić, Izvještaj o školama [1868–1874], 1 March 1874, II OJR sig. 17/1, no. 20, ASANU.

92. Okan–Ristić, Oslobođenĕ Bosne.

93. Okan, Projekt. On Ristić's career, see Vladimir Stojančević, ed., *Život i rad Jovana Ristića: Povodom 150-godišnjice rođenja* (Belgrade: SANU, 1985).

94. Okan–Ristić, Oslobođenĕ Bosne.

95. Rade Petrović, "Ideja o prodaji Bosne i Hercegovine šezdesetih godina XIX stoljeća," *Balcanica* 8 (1977): 279–299.

96. Garašanin letters, 14 February 1862; and Anon., Organizovana propaganda izvan Srbije, 1862, FIG no. 1265, AS. On agents' wages, which ranged from 25 ducats (Bogoljub Petranović) to 8 ducats for three operatives (Jovan Gluščević and his brothers), see Dučić, March 1868, II OJR sig. 9/6, no. 463, ASANU. On Gluščević's monetary requests, see Kaljević–Ljubibratić, 15 August 1868, FMLj no. 19, AH.

97. Stevo Petković [to the Serbian government], 12 March 1872, II OJR sig. 12/3, no. 70, ASANU.

98. Ibid.

99. See S. Petković, 25 March 1872, II OJR sig. 12/3, n.d., no. 71; Petković, 24 March 1872, no. 72; n.d., no. 73; and Petković, n.d., no. 124, ASANU.

100. Fasilis–Antić, 31 July 1872, II OJR sig. 17/5, no. 178, ASANU; letters from Perovićes and Radulović, 20 May 1871, II OJR sig. 17/5, no. 176; 17 December 1871, II OJR sig. 17/5, no. 177; 4 March 1873, II OJR sig. 17/5, no. 181, ASANU. As these documents show, the Ottoman authorities arrested Leontije Radulović and Serafim and Jovan Perović in Herzegovina in 1870 and exiled them to Fezzan (Libya), which "the Turkish government uses just as the Russian government uses Siberia" (quotation from Fasilis, above).

101. Pelagić, "Prethodno dve-tri rieči," in *Rukovođa za serbsko-bosanske, ercegovačke, starosrbijanske i makedonske učitelje, škole i obštine* (Belgade: Državna štamparija, 1867), 4–5.

102. Pelagić, § 36, in *Rukovođa*, 45.

103. Dučić, 15 December 1869.

104. Dučić, 23 September 1872, II OJR sig. 26/7, no. 463, ASANU.

105. Mehmed Alagić, "Povijest jedne porodice: Memoari Mehmedi-Faika Alagića iz Konjica" [1894], ed. Vojislav Bogičević, in *Spomenik SANU* 110 (1961): 56.

106. Škarić–Ristić–Dučić, 1869–1870, II OJR sig. 17/1, nos. 214, 216, 219, 224, ASANU; and A. Andrić, Stanje u Bosni, 1862, FIG no. 1390, AS. On continuing Serbian interest in Bosnian Franciscans, also see N. O.–Garašanin, 18 February 1867, FIG no. 1665, AS.

107. Mujić et al.–Ristić, 30 May 1870, II OJR sig. 17/3, no. 167, ASANU; and Grigorović, Nekoliko slova na javno pismo, 10 April 1872, sig 12/3, no. 312, ASANU.

108. Zastava, 1873, Fototeka no. 368/III, ATK.

109. Živko Crnogorčević, *Memoari Živka Crnogorčevića* (Sarajevo: ANUBiH, 1966), 19; and Anon. (Dobri Bošnjanin), "Jedna fotografija iz 1873," *Narod*, no. 85 (9 December 1921).

110. Anon. (Dobri Bošnjanin), "Jedna fotografija iz 1873."

111. Here my analysis concerns only this formulaic dimension of patriotic expression and not the other aspects that the photograph presents (from the framing and composition of the patriotic society to the men staring back at the viewer). On "metapictures," see W. J. T. Mitchell, *Picture Theory: Essays on Verbal and Visual Representation* (Chicago: University of Chicago Press, 1994), 35–82.

112. Đorđe Popović, "Srpski grb i srpska zastava," *Srbadija: Časopis za zabavu i pouku* 1 (1881): 424–426.

113. Jovan Dragašević, "Jeka od gusala," in *Pesme* (Belgrade: Državna pečatnica, 1869), 41–42; also see Dragašević, *Istinske priče: Avtobiografija u odlomcima* (Belgrade: Kimpanović, 1888).

114. Dragašević–Bošković, 6 October 1891, PO 57–469, AS.

115. For "chronic ethnic confusion among Bosnian Muslims," see Sabrina P. Ramet, "Primordial Ethnicity or Modern Nationalism: The Case of Yugoslavia's Muslims Reconsidered," in *Muslim Communities Reemerge: Historical Perspectives on Nationality, Politics, and Opposition in the Former Soviet Union and Yugoslavia*, ed. Edward Allworth (Durham, NC: Duke University Press, 1994), 125. Other scholars have estimated that "most Bosnian Muslims avoided taking sides between the two Christian communities, feeling that the demands for their 'nationalization' undermined Muslim unity." Ivo Banac, "Bosnian Muslims: From Religious Community to Socialist Nationhood and Post-Communist Statehood, 1918–1992," in *The Muslims of Bosnia-Herzegovina: Their Historic Development from the Middle Ages to the Dissolution of Yugoslavia*, ed. Mark Pinson and Roy P. Mottahedeh (Cambridge, MA: Harvard University Press, 1994), 134.

116. Robert Donia, *Sarajevo: A Biography* (Ann Arbor: University of Michigan Press, 2006), 94; also see his excellent study *Islam under the Double Eagle: The Muslims of Bosnia and Hercegovina, 1878–1914* (Boulder, CO: East European Monographs, 1981).

117. For example, Muhamed Hadžijahić, *Od tradicije do identiteta: Geneza nacionalnog pitanja bosanskih Muslimana* (Sarajevo: Svjetlost, 1974); and Šaćir Filandra, *Bošnjaci i moderna: Humanistička misao Bošnjaka od polovine XIX do polovine XX stoljeća* (Sarajevo: BKC, 1996).

118. "Čemu se imamo nadati," *Bošnjak*, no. 28, 4 July 1900.

119. In reviewing the career of one "Serbian Muhammedan" (Avdo Hasanbegov Karabegović), a Belgrade literary critic wrote in 1902 that "many hated him

precisely because he called himself a Serb and because he, against all their advice, did not want to reject that name. He hated them for the same reasons." Svetozar Ćorović, *Pjesme Avda Hasanbegova Karabegovića* (Belgrade: Ćućić, 1902), v.

120. Ban, Na čemu smo sa istočnim pitanjem.

121. Dučić, Iz Bosne, n.d. (ca. 1860s), II OJR sig. 26/7, no. 500, ASANU.

122. Ibid. On Belgrade mosques, see Ljubomir Nikić, "Džamije u Beogradu," *Godišnjak grada Beograda* 5 (1958): 151–206.

123. Sima Lazić, *Srbi u davnini* (Zagreb: Albrecht, 1894), 35. The proverb was noted in ethnographic collections in the early nineteenth century and much used as a slogan for interconfessional unity, particularly in reaching out to Muslims; e.g., see R.K., "Braći muhamedove vjere (Kardaš'in sev hangi dindar olsun)," *Brastvo: Društvo svetog Save* 8 (1899): 149–150.

124. Njegoš's epic poetry, however, attached clear conditions of "brotherly" acceptance in addressing conversions to Islam: "Cherish your brother, his faith be yours or other / But only when he should act like a brother; / For with us, they do not want to be brotherly / But in their Turkish way they are murderly." Petar II Petrović Njegoš, ed., "Sinovi Ivanbegovi," in *Srbsko ogledalo* (Belgrade: Srbska knjigopečatnja, 1846), 5.

125. František Zach, 14 June 1844, 112–114, *BIFZ*.

126. Kovačević, 15 May 1848, FIG no. 263, AS.

127. Cf. A. Andrić, Stanje u Bosni, 1862, FIG no. 1390, AS; with Okan–Ristić, 18 March 1869, II OJR sig. 12/3, no. 31; and Okan, 14 April 1869, II OJR sig. 12/3, no. 36, ASANU.

128. Uzelac, 12 July 1871, II OJR sig. 26/12, no. 650; and Uzelac, 20 August 1871, II OJR sig. 26/12, no. 662, ASANU.

129. Matija Ban, *Meїrima ili Bošnjaci: Pozorištno dělo u pet razděla* (Novi Sad: Medaković, 1851). The play was performed and reprinted in South Slavic, Czech, and Russian languages; e.g., see *Mejrima ili Bošnjaki: Drama v pjati dejstvijah,* trans. P. A. K. (Moscow: Katkov, 1876).

130. Ban, Razgovori o Turcima i Hrišćanima, 1866, FIG no. 1570, AS.

131. Vlašić, Razgovor sa Pomakom iz sela Dospala u obziru narodnosti, 9 June 1869, II OJR sig. 17/1, no. 4, ASANU.

132. Anon., Patriočeske misli i predlozi, 1863, FIG no. 1405, AS.

133. Okan–Ristić, 1 October 1868, II OJR sig. 12/3, no. 23, ASANU. According to Vasić, the two *bey*s were "Adži-beg Tuzla-pašić" and "Ibrahim-beg Osman-begović"; see Gruber–Orešković, 23 August and 8 September 1867, in Vučković, *Politička akcija*, 308–309, 311–312; also see Izvěstije, 1 March 1869, sig. 12/3, no. 30, ASANU.

134. General-Consulat in Odessa, 3 October 1895, ZMF Präs BH 1270/1895, ABiH; and Über die bosnischen Emigranten in Russland, 17 October 1895, ZMF Präs BH 1293/1895; also see ZMF Präs BH 1249/1895, 1252/1895, 1270/1895, 361/1896, and 835/1896, ABiH.

135. CM Dragiša, 31 May 1901, ZMF Präs BH 790/1901, ABiH; also Memoranda, 1901, ZMF Präs BH 825/1901, 1093/1901, 1147/1901, 244/1902, and 1283/1902, ABiH.

136. CM Pobrić, 19 February 1905, ZMF Präs BH 261/1905, ABiH.

137. CM Filan, 2 February 1903, ZMF Präs BH 278/1903, ABiH.

138. Äusserung über serb. moslimische Coalition, 4 February 1909, ZMF Präs BH 354/1909, ABiH. Fadilpašić reportedly stated that "as soon as Muslims get their

religious educational autonomy they will step out of the [Serb-Muslim] executive committee because they don't want to work with the Serbs." Also see ZMF Präs BH 510/1909, ABiH.

139. J. Dragašević, 18 February 1873, PO 56–465, AS; Ljubibratić, n.d., FMLj no. 1302, AH; and Ljubibratić, n.d. (probably 1880s), no. 1318, AH.

140. Proglas braći Srbima muhamedanskog zakona (1875), FMLj no. 155a; Draga braćo Muhamedanci i Hrišćani (1878), no. 1540; also Ljubibratić, 5 September 1875, no. 189; Ljubibratić, 10 September 1877, no. 561; and especially Ljubibratić, O muslimanima, 1883, nos. 1523 and 1524, AH.

141. Okan–Ristić, 3 October 1873, II OJR sig. 12/3, no. 116, ASANU. Also see Petković, "U srbskom prevodu Koran," *Vienac* 36 (1872): 580. Finally, see the Serbian translation based largely on the French source by Albert Kazimirski de Biberstein: *Koran*, trans. Mićo Ljubibratić (Belgrade: Državna štamparija, 1895).

142. CM Filan, 26 June 1901, ZMF Präs BH 1063/1901, ABiH. In addition to the Qur'an, a number of Serbian publications were devoted to "Serbian Muhammedans": e.g., Milenko Vukićević, *Znameniti Srbi Muslomani* (Belgrade: Srpska književna zadruga, 1906) or the Belgrade journal *Bosansko-hercegovački glasnik* (1896–1898 and 1905–1909); on such publications in Bosnia, see ZMF Präs BH 207/1898, 1279/1906, 1302/1906, and 52/1907, ABiH.

143. CM Filan, 21 May 1905, ZMF Präs BH 679/1905, ABiH.

144. CM Pobrić, 18 February 1905, ZMF Präs BH 255/1905; and CM Filan, 8 June 1905, ZMF Präs BH 751/1905, ABiH. The Bosnian Muslim writer S. Avdo Karabegović was employed by the Serbian state as a teacher for Muslim children in Mali Zvornik from 1905 until his death in 1908; Dušan Šijački, ed., *Avdina spomenica* (Belgrade: Savić, 1909), 38–39.

145. Anon., "Kronika," *Zora* 4 (1899): 36.

146. Đikić, 19 October 1900, Ministarstvo narodne privrede, F XII, no. 43, AS.

147. Jusuf Pečenković, 17 January 1938, in *Sarajevski atentat: Pisma i saopštenja*, 42–43.

148. For example, Sulejman Pašić-Skopljak, Osman Đikić, and S. A. Karabegović, *Pobratimstvo* (Belgrade: Dimitrijević, 1900). The collection was favorably received in Belgrade; e.g., M. S., "Pobratimstvo," *Letopis Matice srpske* 205 (1900): 97–98.

149. Musa Ćazim Ćatić, "Moji doživljaji u Carigradu," *Bošnjak*, no. 28 (1903): 3.

150. Betreffend Mehmed Spahić, 15 January 1900, ZMF Präs BH 76/1900, ABiH; and Mehmed Spahić, "Historija moga srbovanja," serialized in *Osvit*, nos. 20–25 (1899). Also see ZMF Präs BH 1443/1898, 457/1900, and 52/1907, ABiH.

151. Zapisnik šerijatske sudačke škole, 12 February 1902, ZVS 56–542, 1902, ABiH; and Sposobnik pitomaca, 30 July 1902, ZVS 56–546, 1902, ABiH.

152. V. Šola–Spužević, 2 December 1903, NKHZ 14, VII-242, ABiH.

153. 1899, NKHZ 15, IX-2/16; 1902, NKHZ 14, VII-240; 1902, NKHZ 15, IX-2/33; and 1902, NKHZ 8, VI-9, ABiH announces the publication of Mehmed-Dželaluddin Kurt, *Hrvatske narodne ženske pjesme (muslimanske)* (Mostar: Hrvatska tiskara, 1902).

154. CM Novak and CM Filan, 20 January 1905, ZMF Präs BH 104/1905; also see ZMF Präs BH 1453/1903, 157/1905, 254/1905, ABiH.

155. My point is not to refute or valorize these qualities as somehow "resistant" to nationalism—it is simply to note them as integral parts of the

dynamics of nationalization. For an example of this widespread discourse of "nationalization," see the work of the Serbian-Muslim nationalist Šukrija Kurtović, *O nacionalizovanju Muslimana* (Sarajevo: Narod, 1914); and an endorsement by the renowned scholar Jovan Skerlić, "O nacionalizovanju Muslimana," *Srpski književni glasnik* 32 (1914): 307–310.

156. Đorđe Pejanović, "Osman Đikić, njegova sredina i prilike," *Srpska omladina* 3–4 (1912): 61–65.

157. Vojo Vasiljević, 23 August 1913, 98, *MB-PP*.

158. Risto Radulović, "Politička zrelost," *Narod*, no. 42 (22 September 1907); also see "Naši muslimani," *Narod*, no. 142 (9 November 1911).

159. Todor Ilić, n.d. (1913), 104–105, *MB-PP*.

160. Jacques Rancière, *The Ignorant Schoolmaster: Five Lessons in Intellectual Emancipation* (Stanford, CA: Stanford University Press, 1991), 6.

161. Eugen Weber, *Peasants into Frenchmen: The Modernization of Rural France, 1870–1914* (Stanford, CA: Stanford University Press, 1976), 114. As Tara Zahra has shown, this basic principle underpinned proliferating nationalist contestations over children and youth; see Zahra, *Kidnapped Souls: National Indifference and the Battle for Children in the Bohemian Lands, 1900–1948* (Ithaca, NY: Cornell University Press, 2008).

4. Year X, or 1914?

1. Miloš Pjanić, August 1913, 149–151, *MB-PP*.

2. Pjanić was sentenced in connection with the 1912 attempt on the Habsburg governor of Croatia; see "Politički veleizdajnički procesi, 1914–1915," 467–468, *MB-PP*.

3. Leo Pfeffer, *Istraga u sarajevskom atentatu* (Zagreb: Nova Evropa, 1938), 132. On Pfeffer's notes on the Princip trial, see Pfeffer 1914–1915, ZOP, no. 855, ABiH. For a similar account of radicalization, see Milo Borić, "Od 'napredne' do 'nacionalističke' omladine," *Književni sever* 5 (1929): 309–314.

4. Vladimir Dedijer, *The Road to Sarajevo* (New York: Simon & Schuster, 1966); David McKenzie, *Apis, the Congenial Conspirator: The Life of Colonel Dragutin T. Dimitrijević* (Boulder, CO: East European Monographs, 1989); and McKenzie, *The "Black Hand" on Trial: Salonika 1917* (Boulder, CO: East European Monographs, 1995).

5. Eric Hobsbawm, *The Age of Empire, 1875–1914* (New York: Vintage, 1989), 145, 169, 227–228.

6. Although historians have generally stressed the modern construction of "youth" as a social category, the relationship between nationalism and the rise of youth as a political subject has been much cited yet little explained. For example, see John R. Gillis, *Youth and History: Tradition and Change in European Age Relations, 1770–Present* (New York: Academic Press, 1974); and Sergio Luzzatto, "Young Rebels and Revolutionaries, 1789–1917," in *A History of Young People in the West*, vol. 2, ed. Giovanni Levi and Jean-Claude Schmitt (Cambridge, MA: Belknap Press, 1997), 174–231. For a critical reconsideration of these issues, see James D. Straker, *Youth, Nationalism, and the Guinean Revolution* (Bloomington: Indiana University Press, 2009).

7. Benedict Anderson, *Imagined Communities: Reflections on the Origins and Spread of Nationalism* (London: Verso, 1983), 119.

8. Claudia Verhoeven, *The Odd Man Karakozov: Imperial Russia, Modernity, and the Birth of Terrorism* (Ithaca, NY: Cornell University Press, 2009), 7.

9. It is worth remembering that "all those qualities which today we look upon as enviable possessions—freshness, self-assertion, daring, curiosity, youth's lust for life—were regarded as suspect" throughout the nineteenth century, Stefan Zweig wrote in his legendary memoir. In 1880s Vienna, "Youth was a hindrance in all careers, and age alone was an advantage," leading many male university graduates to sport "mighty beards and gold spectacles" in order to look more "experienced" and "respectable." Stefan Zweig, *The World of Yesterday*, trans. Helmut Ripperger (New York: Viking, 1964), 33–34. Also see Kristina Popova, "Jugend und Alter," in *Historische Anthropologie im südöstlichen Europa: Eine Einführung*, ed. Karl Kaser et al. (Vienna: Böhlau, 2003), 199–215.

10. Picasso's words—"It takes a very long time to become young"—fittingly capture the protracted search for youth as a modern political subject. Cited in Jean Cocteau, *The Hand of a Stranger* (New York: Libraries Press, 1969), 20.

11. Vuk Karadžić, *Srpski rječnik, istolkovan njemačkim i latinskim riječma* (Vienna: P. P. Armeniern, 1818), 405, 508.

12. Teodor Mandić, "Uspomene iz našeg crkveno-narodnog života," *Letopis Matice srpske* 204 (1900): 7. Also compare Janko Drašković, *Mladeži ilirskoj* (Zagreb: Suppan, 1836) with Drašković, *Hrvatska omladina* (Zagreb: Milaković, 1885).

13. For example, *Preodnica: Srpska omladina u Pešti* (Budapest, 1863). Also see Jovan Skerlić, *Omladina i njena književnost (1848–1871): Izučavanja o nacionalnom i književnom romantizmu kod Srba* (Belgrade: Srpska kraljevska akademija, 1906); and Gale Stokes, *Legitimacy through Liberalism: Vladimir Jovanović and the Transformation of Serbian Politics* (Seattle: University of Washington Press, 1975).

14. The corrective concluded, "So gentlemen reformers, it is *mladež* that should mean *juventus* or *die Jugend*." Jevstatije Mihajlović, *Obrana jezika srbskog od izopačivanja i prostačenja něgovog i kirilice od Vukovice* (Zrenjanin: Pleiz, 1863), 118. Confusion over the term was apparent in universities; when the Serbian painter Uroš Predić enrolled in a Viennese academy in the 1870s, a professor asked him if he was an *omladinac*. "When I said that I was, he looked at me with suspicion, but calmed down when I explained that *omladina* merely means *die Jugend*, so that every young Serb is an *omladinac*." Uroš Predić, "Biografija," *Godišnjak Srpske kraljevske akademije* 28 (1921): 288–289.

15. Stanoje Bošković, "Jedno pismo o 'srpskoj omladini,'" *Javor* 1 (1862): 189–191.

16. Vladimir Jovanović, *Za narod i slobodu* (Novi Sad: Platonova štamparija, 1868), 200–204.

17. Ibid., 183–184, 197.

18. Ibid., 215–216.

19. Anon., "Nekoliko vojničkih pitanja, namjenjeno oslobođenju celog Srpstva," *Mlada Srbadija* 2, no. 13 (1871): 193–194.

20. Ničifor Dučić, "Iskrena riječ Srpkinjama," *Mlada Srbadija* 2, nos. 10–12 (1871): 145–150, 161–164, 183–186.

21. For example, Anon., "Crnogorac ili stradanja Hrišćana u Turskoj od H. Levičnika," *Matica: List za književnost i zabavu* 1 (1866): 742; and Jovan Jovanović Zmaj, "Sentomaš" [1855], *Srbski Letopis* 100 (1859): 78–83; Zmaj, "Pesma starog srpskog mača," "Gvožđe," "Srbinu," "Omladina," "Krv i suze," in

Pevanija Zmaj-Jovana Jovanovića (Novi Sad: Popović, 1882), 189–190, 199–202, 222–231, 235–246; and Laza Kostić, "Puška," "Omladini," "Žrtva šejtanu," "Harem," "Razgovor sa uvučenom srpskom zastavom," "Suzni," "Iz Abdulaha," in *Pesme Laze Kostića*, 2 vols. (Novi Sad: Zadružna štamparija, 1873), 35, 58–68, 144–163, 203–204.

22. Sima Popović, "1867: Posvećeno Đačkoj legiji," *Vila: List za zabavu, književnost i nauku* 3 (1867): 54–55.

23. Laza Kostić, "Rajo, tužna rajo," *Srbski Letopis* 101 (1860): 60.

24. Đura Jakšić, "Padajte braćo (1862)," in *Pesme* (Belgrade: Državna štamparija, 1873), 69–70.

25. V. Jovanović, *Za slobodu i narod* (1868), 221–225, 271–275.

26. Though hundreds of Serbian, Croatian, Slovene, Russian, and Italian volunteers were initially reported in Bosnia-Herzegovina, by 1877 most had returned home or moved to other fronts; see articles in Rade Petrović, ed., *Međunarodni naučni skup povodom 100-godišnjice ustanaka u Bosni i Hercegovini, drugim balkanskim zemljama i istočnoj krizi 1875–1878 godine*, 3 vols. (Sarajevo: ANUBiH, 1977); and Giuseppe Barbanti-Brodano, *Garibaldinci na Drini, 1876* (Belgrade: Kultura, 1958).

27. For example, Anon. (Ernst Eckstein, ed.), "Serbien von 1858 bis 1875," *Unsere Zeit: Deutsche Revue Der Gegenwart* 9 (1875): 594–595.

28. A telegram from Sarajevo to the Belgrade journal *Jedinstvo* stated: "We Bosnian Serbs . . . with the exception of a few followers in Banja Luka publicly declare our mistrust in Pelagić, whatever he writes in our name publicly or secretly is lying." Ninkovics, 19 June 1872, OJR, sig. 12/3, no. 75, ASANU. Also see Kosta Hadži–Ristić Događajnik, entries for 1866 and 1867, IZ, no. 9275, folio 69, ASANU.

29. For example, Jovanović-Zmaj, "Srbinu" [1875], "Vidov-dan," "Bojna pesma" [1876], "Nova godina" [1877], "Brankova zelja," "K naslovnoj slici Ilustrovane kronike" [1878], "Jadna majka," in *Pevanija Zmaj-Jovana Jovanovića* (Novi Sad: Popović, 1882), 200–202, 222–225, 244–250, 250–253, 257–260, 306–308.

30. Editorial, "Srpska omladina u Austro-Ugarskoj," *Pobratimstvo* 1, no. 8 (1881): 529–531.

31. For example, Redovnička omladina bosanska u Đakovu, *Bosanske narodne pripovjedke* (Sisak: Vončina, 1870).

32. Kosta Hadži–Ristić Događajnik, 1868–1869, IZ, no. 9275, f. 59, ASANU.

33. Von Haymerle-Andrássy, 2 March 1878, *Actenstücke aus den correspondenzen des ministeriums über orientalische angelegenheiten* (Vienna: K. K. Staatsdruckerei, 1878), 72.

34. On this background, see Robin Okey, *Taming Balkan Nationalism: The Habsburg "Civilizing Mission" in Bosnia, 1878–1914* (Oxford: Oxford University Press, 2007), 65–73, 221–223; and Mitar Papić, *Školstvo u Bosni i Hercegovini za vrijeme austro-ugarske okupacije, 1878–1918* (Sarajevo: Veselin Masleša, 1972). On government sponsorship of Bosnian university students in Vienna, see Institut für bosnisch-hercegovinische Hochschüler, May–June 1905, ZVS 116–30 and 116–32, ABiH.

35. Bericht des Dr. von Thallóczy über seine Inspizierungsreise in Bosnien-Hercegovina, 1904, ZMF Präs BH 1282/1904, ABiH.

36. Papić, *Školstvo u Bosni*, 84–89.

37. For example, Prvijenac, tajni đački list u Tuzli, 1904, ZOP no. 671, ABiH; Srpska svijest, tajni đački list u Sarajevu, 1895, ZOP no. 672; and Appel, 31 May 1901, ZMF Präs BH 1302/1901, ABiH. Also see Milan Janković, *"Sloboda" i "Jugoslavija"* (Belgrade: Gregorić, 1939).

38. Bericht des Dr. von Thallóczy über seine Inspizierungsreise, 1904; on Bosnian Serb student associations in Prague, see Sloboda, klub Srba akademičara iz BH, 3 March 1906, ZVS 19-467-9/1906, ABiH.

39. Bericht des Dr. von Thallóczy über seine Inspizierungsreise, 1904.

40. Otvoreno pismo—Offener Brief an die hohen österreichisch-ungarischen Delegationen, 30 May 1901, ZMF, Präs BH 857/1901, ABiH.

41. CM Sriemac, 16 August 1901 (one of the signatories, Aleksandar Babić, was "afraid to come home since he signed the memorandum and his dad is mad at him for that"), ZMF Präs BH 1170/1901, ABiH.

42. "Jadno," *Naš život*, June 1906, ZMF Präs BH 841/1906, ABiH.

43. Jugoslovenski klub protocol, 11 February 1908, ZMF Präs BH 348/1908, ABiH.

44. K., "Dopis," *Novo Doba: List sjedinjene hrvatske, srpske i slovenačke omladine* 1 (1898): 370–376. Similar debates continued; see Aiglon, "Srpski i hrvatski đak u Beču," *Zora: Glasnik srpske napredne omladine* 1, no. 8 (1910): 360–362.

45. Jovan Erdeljanović, "Nemci na slovenskom jugu," *Delo* 35 (1905): 83.

46. CM Sriemac, 1 June 1901, ZMF Präs BH 811/1901, ABiH.

47. Appel, 14 June 1901, ZMF Präs BH 858/1901, ABiH. The governor-lieutenant Johann Appel advised that the administration "refrain from using in the future any of the twenty [Memorandum] signatories" in its services. The Serbian merchant leaders then tried to support the Bosnian students in Vienna with stipends, though their efforts withered. Also see ZMF Präs BH 184/1902, 300/1902, 302/1902, and 27/1903, ABiH.

48. CM Pokret omladine, 1 March 1902, ZMF Präs BH 270/1902, ABiH.

49. Rad omladine (Brkić), October 1902, ZMF Präs BH 1349/1902, ABiH.

50. CM Pokret omladine, 1 March 1902.

51. Rad omladine (Brkić), October 1902. Also see CM Pobrić, 13 June 1905, ZMF Präs BH 777/1905, ABiH.

52. Anon., "Moralna snaga," *Novo doba: List sjedinjene hrvatske, srpske i slovenačke omladine* 1 (1898): 49–52.

53. CM Mirko, 23 September 1903, ZMF Präs 1246/1903, ABiH.

54. For example, *Kalendar "Prosvjeta" za prestupnu godinu 1912* (Sarajevo: Srpska dionička štampa, 1911), frontispiece motto.

55. Vladimir Andrić and Kosta Majkić, "T. G. Masarik," *Pregled* 1, no. 3 (1910): 140–153.

56. Mohamedanischer Schulverein, October 1885, ZVS 39-20, 1885, ABiH; and Hajrudin Ćurić, *Muslimansko školstvo u Bosni i Hercegovini do 1918. godine* (Sarajevo: Veselin Masleša, 1983).

57. Rad omladine (Brkić), October 1902.

58. Klub muslimanske omladine, 9 April 1914, ZVS 18-311/1914, ABiH. Among the more nationalist Muslim youth, Muhamed Mehmedbašić, Mustafa Golubić, Đulaga Bukovac, and Ibrahim Fazlinović were involved in Serbian-Croatian secret societies, including the plan for the 1914 assassination.

59. On literacy and other figures, see Vojislav Bogićević., *Pismenost u Bosni i Hercegovini: Od pojave slovenske pismenosti u IX v. do kraja austrougarske vladrine u Bosni i Hercegovini* (Sarajevo: Masleša, 1975), 284–287.

60. "Could this small number of our graduated sons, even if they were united, ever say, 'We're the people,' or 'We're the voice of the people'? . . . Various attempts of different groups of our educated youth have not shown any distinct readiness, any strength of direction," stated one editorial; see "Naša omladina," *Srpska riječ*, no. 168 (17 December 1905).

61. For example, Dahlen, 28 December 1879, ZVS 3015, 1879; and ZMF Präs BH 157/1905 and 1330/1906, ABiH.

62. For example, CM, 4 April 1897, ZMF Präs BH 406/1897; and especially CM Blažo, 13 May 1897, ZMF Präs BH 680/1897, ABiH.

63. Slavy, 1 February 1881, ZMF Präs BH 473/1881; and ZMF Präs BH 244/1902, 378/1902, and 1496/1903, ABiH.

64. Bericht des Dr. von Thallóczy über seine Inspizierungsreise, 1904.

65. Srpski Soko Brčko, Banjaluka; and Hrvatski Sokol Sarajevo, Travnik, 1906, ZVS 19-262/1906 and ZVS 19-270/1906, ABiH; Pravila društava Srpski Soko Mostar, Ključ, Kalinovik, Vranjak, Trebinje; Hrvatski Sokol Konjic, Čapljina; Muslimanski Soko Mostar, Ljubinje, Čapljina, Tuzla, Sarajevo, 1911–1912, ZVS 18-286/1912, ABiH. On the first Sokols in Bohemia, see Claire Nolte, *The Sokol in the Czech Lands to 1914: Training for the Nation* (New York: Palgrave, 2002).

66. Klub srpsko-hrvatske nacionalističke omladine, 22 January 1914, ZVS 18-300/1914, ABiH.

67. CM Klein, Report A, n.d., and Bosansko-hercegovački komitet, Report B, n.d. (1905), ZMF Präs BH 1535/1905, ABiH.

68. CM, Report C, 8 December 1905, ZMF Präs BH 1535/1905, ABiH. On Kočić's difficulties in mobilizing the peasants, see ZMF Präs BH 1263/1910, 1264/1910, 1359/1910, 1372/1910, and 345/1911, ABiH.

69. Černy, 12 December 1905, ZMF Präs BH 1535/1905, ABiH.

70. Kutschera and Benko, 20 December 1905, ZMF Präs BH 1535/1905, ABiH.

71. On this and other related Kočić cases, see ZMF Präs BH 1161/1907, 1170/1907, 1181/1907, 1188/1907, 1198/1907, 1205/1907, 1222/1907, 1226/1907, 1234/1907, 1252/1907, 1308/1907, ABiH; and esp. Serbische nationale Organisation, 27 October 1907, ZMF Präs BH 1336/1907; Bericht Otadžbina, 4 April 1908, ZMF Präs BH 515/1908; and Disziplinarsache, 9 September 1908, ZMF Präs BH 1446/1908, ABiH.

72. Albori, 3 December 1906, ZMF Präs BH 1330/1906, ABiH.

73. Benko, 3 November 1907, ZMF Präs BH 1248/1907, ABiH.

74. Quotations from Albori, 10 April 1905, ZMF Präs BH 500/1905, ABiH; and Albori, 18 April 1905, ZMF Präs BH 540/1905; also see ZMF Präs BH 458/1905, 576/1905, 630/1905, ABiH.

75. "Censur 'Atentat na obraz srpskog naroda,'" 29 April 1905, ZMF Präs BH 596/1905, ABiH; and Albori, 15 August 1904, 1057/1905; also see "Slobodna štampa-cenzura," *Srpska riječ* no. 74 (24 May 1905).

76. Albori, 6 February 1906, ZMF Präs BH 133/1906; and CM Trifić, 7 March 1906, ZMF Präs BH 272/1906, ABiH.

77. The military court found Grđić "guilty" on many charges, but the death penalty was dropped. See Stephan Sarkotić, ed. and trans., *Der Banjaluka-Prozess*,

vol. 2 (Berlin: Arbeitsausschuss Deutscher Verbände, 1933), 551–579. Wartime Habsburg prosecution specifically targeted Bosnian high school and university students; see Popis đaka srednjih škola protiv kojih su vođeni postupci, 1914–1918, ZOP no. 88, ABiH.

78. Albori, 2 February 1905, ZMF Präs BH 164/1905; also see Opća učiteljska skupština, July 1906, ZMF Präs BH 1201/1906, ABiH.

79. CM Tintor, 7 September 1908, ZMF Präs BH 1498/1908, ABiH.

80. Attentat auf den Landeschef, 5 August 1910, ZMF Präs BH 1229/1910; also see ZMF Präs BH 926/1910 and 1375/1910; and ZMF Gen 6541/1910, ABiH.

81. Polizeidirektion Graz, 28 September 1910, ZMF Präs BH 1466/1910, ABiH; also see ZMF Präs BH 1636/1910. The anarchist insignia in question, depicting a man with long black hair against a red background, derived from the book cover of Peter Kropotkin, *Die Französische Revolution* (Leipzig: Theodor Thomas, 1909). Very similar sketches appeared on other Young Bosnia correspondences; see Mlada Bosna IV-4-5, 2 April 1914, ZOP no. 911, ABiH.

82. In particular see "Über das Attentat auf Landeschef," 18 August 1910, ZMF Präs BH 1229/1910, ABiH.

83. Vladimir Dedijer, *The Road to Sarajevo* (New York: Simon & Schuster, 1966), 243–249.

84. Nevesinje, 3 October 1909, IB no. 4657, ABiH.

85. Nikola Dakić, "Izvještaj," 21 June 1912, 314–318, *MB-PP*.

86. Wendy Bracewell, "'The Proud Name of Hajduks': Bandits as Ambiguous Heroes in Balkan Politics and Culture," in *Yugoslavia and Its Historians: Understanding the Balkan Wars of the 1990s*, ed. Norman Naimark and Holly Case (Stanford, CA: Stanford University Press, 2003), 22–36; and Ivo Žanić, *Flag on the Mountain: A Political Anthropology of War in Croatia and Bosnia* (London: Saqi, 2007).

87. The most influential interpretation in this vein comes from Vladimir Dedijer, who argued that the Sarajevo assassins were inspired by a folk tradition of "Kosovo tyrannicide"; see Dedijer, *Road to Sarajevo*, 237–259. For a trenchant critique of Dedijer, see Ivan Čolović, "Sarajevski atentat i kosovski mit," *Peščanik*, http://pescanik.net/2014/06/sarajevski-atentat-i-kosovski-mit/ (accessed 12 July 2014).

88. Friedrich Salomo Krauss and Tihomir Đorđević, "Erotische und skatologische Sprichwörter und Redensarten der Serben, gesammelt von Vuk Stefanović Karadžić," *Anthropophyteia* 4 (1907): 300–301. On the relationship between "women's" (*ženske*) and "heroic" (*junačke*) folk poems, also see Ivan Radetić, "Prilozi k tumačenju naših narodnih pjesama: Poštenje junačko," *Književnik* 3 (1866): 251–256.

89. Friedrich Krauss also documented a range of ironic references to "heroes" in South Slavic folklore; some peasant stories involved groups of men praising their penises as heroes (*u zdravlje naši kuraca, naši junaka!*) while women responded with praise for their vaginas for having ultimately triumphed over heroes turned cowards (*Vaši su kurci kukavci. Istom kad poleti na naše pice, jeste li ga vidile, kako se junači? . . . Živile naše pice radosnice!*). Krauss, "Südslavische Volksüberlieferungen," *Anthropophyteia* 1 (1904): 132.

90. On such modernist writings and legacies, see Dimitrije Mitrinović and Henry Christian Rutherford, eds., *Certainly, Future: Selected Writings* (Boulder, CO: East European Monographs, 1987).

91. "Suvi zulumi" (Šošljaga-Kočić), 1908, ZOP no. 787, ABiH; on Kočić's influence, see Ljubomir Dučić, 22 December 1936, in V. Bogičević, ed., *Sarajevski atentat: 28. VI 1914. Pisma i saopštenja* (Sarajevo: Svjetlost, 1965), 32.

92. Gaćinović, "Mlada Bosna," 1910, 70–72, *OiP*.

93. On the popularity of Gaćinović's essay (published in Belgrade in 1912 and "circulating from hand to hand and often copied"), see 1914 trial notes in V. Bogičević, ed., *Sarajevski atentat: Stenogram glavne rasprave protiv Gavrila Principa i drugova* (Sarajevo: Arhiv NRBiH, 1954), 314, 434; and later recollections by Aca Blagojević, 3 July 1929, V. Vasiljević, 19 December 1950, and Kosta Gnjatić, 4 April 1962, in Bogičević, ed., *Sarajevski atentat: Pisma i saopštenja*, 27, 75, 100.

94. Gaćinović, "Smrt jednog heroja," 1912, 280–283, 285, 287, *MB-PP*.

95. Ibid., 283, 286.

96. Historiography has focused overwhelmingly on the influences of Russian anarchist thought while neglecting other forces that shaped the Young Bosnian movement. Part of this Russo-centric assessment comes from Gaćinović's later writings themselves. A year after the outbreak of the First World War, Gaćinović wrote in a fawning text to Leon Trotsky that it was the Young Bosnians' imitation of "Russian ideals" — "We were your, if you will, colony of ideas" — that brought about the 1914 assassination. Young Bosnian writings themselves, however, show a much greater range of influences. See Gaćinović–Trotsky, "Sarajevski atentat: Gde je početak," 1915, 80–96, *OiP*; cf. Trotsky's deeply critical views of Balkan nationalist politics in *The Balkan Wars, 1912–13: The War Correspondence of Leon Trotsky*, ed. George Weissman and Duncan Williams, trans. Brian Pearce (New York: Monad, 1980).

97. In her survey of *omladina* movements before 1914, Mirjana Gross concluded that Yugoslav conceptions of youth "most often bore the attribute '*future*,'" but her note on this temporal register has been little explored; Gross, "Nacionalne ideje studentske omladine u Hrvatskoj uoči I svjetskog rata," *Historijski zbornik* 21 (1968): 140. On explicitly futurist and surrealist writings in Bosnia, see *Šiš-Miš, Glasilo bihaćkih futurista: Vanstranački futurističko-kubistički Nolimetangere-Nebarkaj list*, 24 February 1914, ZOP, no. 903, ABiH.

98. Gaćinović, "Smrt jednog heroja," 288, 291.

99. Gaćinović, "Onima koji dolaze," 1910, 69–70, *OiP*.

100. Gaćinović, "Smrt jednog heroja," 288.

101. On this background to Young Bosnia, see the essays in the special issue of *Pregled* 64, nos. 7–8 (1974).

102. Srpska svijest, tajni đački list u Sarajevu, 1895.

103. Thomas Carlyle, *On Heroes, Hero-Worship, and the Heroic in History* (London: James Fraser, 1841); Thomas Carlyle, *O herojima, heroizmu i obožavanju heroja u istoriji*, trans. B Knežević (Belgrade: Državna štamparija, 1903). Also see Branislav Petronijević, "O herojima," *Delo* 31 (1904): 76–83, 234–246; Cherubin Šegvić, "Geneza najnovijih pojava u hrvatskoj književnosti," *Hrvatsko kolo* 1 (1905): 444–462; and Nikolaj Velimirović, "Tvorci istorije: Karlajlova i Tolstojeva teorija," *Delo* 71 (1914): 55–69.

104. Marko Car, "O herojima i obožavanju heroja," *Bosanska vila* 19, no. 19 (1904): 356–357; also see Car, "Ljubomir Nedić," *Letopis matice srpske* 222 (1903): 11.

105. Risto Radulović, "Seljak i politika," *Pregled* 3, no. 2 (1912): 65–69; also Radulović, "Pojave pravog nacionalizma," *Narod*, no. 276 (2 March 1912).

106. Gaćinović, "Krik očajnika," 1912, 73–77, *OiP.*

107. Slobodan Jovanović, "Toma Karlajl," *Srpski književni glasnik* 11 (1904): 908, 914.

108. Die antiungarischen Demonstrationen in BH, March–April 1912, ZOP no. 925, ABiH; and Ungarfeindliche Demonstrationen, 4 March 1912, ZMF Präs BH 423/1912, ABiH.

109. Šahinagić fotografija, 1912, ZOP no. 876, ABiH; also Klofač, 7 March 1912, 125, *MB-PP.*

110. Janković, *"Sloboda" i "Jugoslavija,"* 21.

111. Antun Cuvaj, *Građa za povijest školstva kraljevina Hrvatske i Slavonije,* vol. 10 (Zagreb: Zemaljska tiskara, 1913), 285–286.

112. Andrić, quoted in *Bosanski omladinci i sarajevski atentat,* ed. Božo Čerović (Sarajevo: Trgovačka štamparija, 1930), 255. Luka Jukić was given the death penalty, but his sentence was commuted to life imprisonment.

113. Luka Jukić–Drljević, 20 April 1912, 128–129, *MB-PP.*

114. Borivoje Jevtić, "Nove generacije," *Srpska omladina* 1, no. 5 (1913): 89–91.

115. On such atrocities, see the Carnegie Endowment for International Peace, *Report of the International Commission to Inquire into the Causes and Conduct of the Balkan Wars* (Washington, DC: Carnegie Endowment, 1914); on general background, see Richard C. Hall, *The Balkan Wars, 1912–1913* (London: Routledge, 2000).

116. For example, see the (mostly unsigned) contributions of the Sarajevan journal *Srpska riječ,* 1913: "Pred Skadrom," no. 13; "Je li Sarajevo u Arnautluku," no. 20; "Najnovije iz Srbije," no. 27; "Iz omladinskih krugova," no. 34; "Ispod Skadra," no. 43; "Neznanim junacima," no. 53; "Pred kraj rata" and "Srpske haubice," no. 75; "Pad Skadra," "Tebe Boga hvalimo" and "Prva žrtva kosovske ideje," no. 82; "Iz doline plača," no. 83; "Vidov-dan," no. 127; and "Zločin ili bezumlje," no. 128.

117. Božo Madžar, "Balkanski ratovi i iznimne mjere u Bosni i Hercegovini," *Godišnjak društva historičara Bosne i Hercegovine* 35 (1984): 63–73.

118. Napredak (BG)–Pjanić, 24 October 1912, 139–141, *MB-PP.*

119. Ivan Meštrović's much-celebrated production before 1914 "closely followed his motto: 'We must create a cult of heroes!'" See Duško Kečkemet, *Umjetnost Ivana Meštrovića* (Split: Slobodna Dalmacija, 1962), 12.

120. Dimitrije Mitrinović, "Liga za umetničku kulturu jugoslovenstva i Balkana," *Delo* 68 (1913): 396. On racial theories of struggle in the South Slavic context, see Dr. E. Miler, "Predrasuda o rasama" and "Woltmann," *Savremenik* 2 (1907): 46–48, 366–367. For general background, see Marius Turda and Paul J. Weindling, eds., *"Blood and Homeland": Eugenics and Racial Nationalism in Central and Southeast Europe, 1900–1940* (Budapest: Central European University Press, 2007).

121. Balkanski rat fotografija, 1912–1913, ZOP no. 852, ABiH; also see Gaćinović izvještaj, 22 May 1912, ZOP no. 900, ABiH

122. Oton Župančič, "Dan svih živih," *Srpska omladina* 1, no. 10 (1913): 180.

123. Anon., "Slike iz Balkanskog rata," *Srpska omladina* 1, no. 9 (1913): 171–172. Also see Milan Pribićević, *Naš najveći junak* (Rijeka: Trbojević, 1913).

124. Anon., "Prestanak jednog pokoljenja," *Srpska omladina* 1, no. 9 (1913): 166–167.

125. Augustin Ujević, "Borba nacionalističke omladine," *Naprednjak* 2, no. 50 (1912): 1–2; and Ujević, "Za novu omladinu," *Bosanska vila* 28, no. 17 (1913):

246–248. Also see Cvjetko Ćorović, Nešto o ženama i njihovoj budućnosti, 1914, ZOP no. 871, ABiH.

126. Vladimir Čerina, "Prije i poslije Kosova," *Vihor: List za nacijonalističku kulturu* 1, no. 2 (1914): 21–25. Also see Čerina, "Pjesnik nas sutrašnjih," *Savremenik* 9 (1914): 323–370, which opens with the epigraph: "A genius is a hero: a superman."

127. Borivoje Jevtić, "Ideje i dela," *Srpska omladina* 1, nos. 6–7 (1913): 125–127. Also see Tin Ujević, "Ispunjeni zavjet," *Bosanska vila* 28, no. 1 (1913): 1–3.

128. Borivoje Jevtić, "Nepobeđeni," *Srpska omladina* 1, no. 5 (1913): 98–99.

129. Čabrinović, another assassin, reportedly exclaimed immediately after the assassination, "I am a Serbian hero." Dedijer, *Road to Sarajevo*, 319. When asked, "Did you find in the writings of the broader Sarajevo youth circles anything that was of decisive importance for your intention?," Gavrilo Princip said, "Yes, I did, I found *The Death of a Hero*, namely, Žerajić and a few other writings that I can't recall now." See Bogičević, ed., *Sarajevski atentat: Stenogram*, 55, 314.

130. Gaćinović died in Switzerland in 1917. In his letters, he referred to the assassination as the act of a Young Bosnian collectivity— "how much sacrifice, poetry, light, and enthusiasm is there in these young groups"—and very rarely mentioned Princip as the assassin. "But the political moment deceived them, and instead of a glorious inauguration, this enormous event became a day of national crucifixion and martyrdom," Gaćinović wrote in late 1914, referring to Austria's brutal wartime persecutions in Bosnia and Serbia. Gaćinović–Merđep, 20 October 1914, 210–213, *OiP*.

131. For example, Mihajlo Milanović, *Narodni junak Gavrilo Princip ili ubistvo Ferdinanda i Sofije* (Sarajevo, 1919); Stevan Žakula, *Od Terezina do Sarajeva: Uspomene povodom desetogodišnjice prenosa kostiju vidovdanskih heroja* (Belgrade: Jugoštampa, 1930); and Anon., ed., *Današnjica i Mlada Bosna: Uloga i značaj Vladimira Gaćinovića* (Sarajevo: Petar Živković, 1937). Also see Stjepko Ilijić, "Toma Carlyle i kult heroja," *Savremenik* 15 (1920): 121–123.

132. Vladimir Nazor, *Kristali i sjemenke* (Zagreb: Nakladni zavod Hrvatske, 1949), 303; and Josip Barković, *Omladina Jugoslavije u NOB* (Zagreb: Epoha, 1967). On later twentieth-century hero appropriations, see Vera Katz, "Ideološka upotreba otkrivanja spomen-ploče Gavrilu Principu u odgoju i obrazovanju generacija u Bosni i Hercegovini," *Prilozi* 37 (2008): 113–126; and Ivan Čolović, "A Criminal-National Hero? But Who Else?," in *Balkan Identities*, ed. Maria Todorova (New York: New York University Press, 2004), 253–268.

133. As Dominick LaCapra has written, similar visions of violence, such as those of Georges Sorel (*Reflections on Violence*, 1908), were "symptomatic of broader currents in the early twentieth century, and modernity more generally—currents exacerbated but not caused by World War I and the Great Depression." See LaCapra's important essay "Toward a Critique of Violence," in *History and Its Limits: Human, Animal, Violence* (Ithaca, NY: Cornell University Press, 2009), 90–122.

134. For example, Reinhart Koselleck, *Futures Past: On the Semantics of Historical Time*, trans. Keith Tribe (New York: Columbia University Press, 2004), esp. 255–276; Kathleen Davis, *Periodization and Sovereignty: How Ideas of Feudalism and Secularization Govern the Politics of Time* (Philadelphia: University of Pennsylvania Press, 2008); Daniel Rosenberg and Susan Harding, eds., *Histories*

of the Future (Durham, NC: Duke University Press, 2005); David Lloyd, *Irish Times: Temporalities of Modernity* (Dublin: Field Day, 2008); and Roxanne Panchasi, *Future Tense: The Culture of Anticipation in France between the Wars* (Ithaca, NY: Cornell University Press, 2009).

135. Giorgio Manganelli, *Centuria*, trans. Henry Martin (New York: McPherson, 2005), 72.

5. Another Problem

1. Editorial board, "Našim čitaocima," *Nada*, no. 1 (1895): n.p.

2. Oscar Jászi, *The Dissolution of the Habsburg Monarchy* (Chicago: University of Chicago Press, 1961 [1929]), e.g., 144; István Deák, *Beyond Nationalism: A Social and Political History of the Habsburg Officer Corps, 1848–1918* (Oxford: Oxford University Press, 1990). However, recent scholarship has greatly changed this picture by showing the growth of intertwined liberal and nationalist forces; esp. see Pieter Judson, *Exclusive Revolutionaries: Liberal Politics, Social Experience, and National Identity in the Austrian Empire, 1848–1914* (Ann Arbor: University of Michigan Press, 1997); and Judson, *Guardians of the Nation: Activists on the Language Frontiers of Imperial Austria* (Cambridge, MA: Harvard University Press, 2006).

3. George Polya, *Mathematical Discovery: On Understanding, Learning, and Teaching Problem Solving* (New York: John Wiley, 1981), 271.

4. Daniel L. Unowsky, *The Pomp and Politics of Patriotism: Imperial Celebrations in Habsburg Austria, 1848–1916* (West Lafayette, IN: Purdue University Press, 2005); and Laurence Cole and Daniel L. Unowsky, eds., *The Limits of Loyalty: Imperial Symbolism, Popular Allegiances, and State Patriotism in the Late Habsburg Monarchy* (New York: Berghahn, 2009). On early modern debates, see Balázs Trencsényi and Márton Zászkaliczky, eds., *Whose Love of Which Country?: Composite States, National Histories, and Patriotic Discourses in Early Modern East Central Europe* (Leiden: Brill, 2010); and Robert von Friedeburg, ed., *"Patria" und "Patrioten" vor dem Patriotismus: Pflichten, Rechte, Glauben und Rekonfigurierung europäischer Gemeinwesen im 17. Jahrhundert* (Wiesbaden: Harrasowitz, 2005), particularly the essay by Reinhart Koselleck.

5. Julia Phillips Cohen, *Becoming Ottomans: Sephardi Jews and Imperial Citizenship in the Modern Era* (Oxford: Oxford University Press, 2014); Michelle Campos, *Ottoman Brothers: Muslims, Christians, and Jews in Early Twentieth-Century Palestine* (Stanford, CA: Stanford University Press, 2010); Darin Stephanov, "Minorities, Majorities, and the Monarch: Nationalizing Effects of the Late Ottoman Royal Public Ceremonies, 1808–1908" (PhD thesis, University of Memphis, 2012); Alexander Vezenkov, "Reconciliation of the Spirits and Fusion of the Interests: 'Ottomanism' as an Identity Politics," in *We, the People: Politics of National Peculiarity in Southeastern Europe*, ed. Diana Mishkova (Budapest: Central European University Press, 2009), 47–78; Rashid Khalidi, "Ottomanism and Arabism in Syria before 1914: A Reassessment," in *The Origins of Arab Nationalism*, ed. Rashid Khalidi and Reeva S. Simon (New York: Columbia University Press, 1993), 50–69. Quotation from the title of W. W. Haddad and W. Ochsenwald, eds., *Nationalism in a Non-National State: Dissolution of the Ottoman Empire* (Columbus: The Ohio State University Press, 1977).

6. Of course, there were many differences between the Ottoman and the Habsburg states in their respective conceptions of imperial rule (e.g., after the 1867 Compromise, Franz Joseph held different titles as the emperor-king in Austria and Hungary, respectively). But both the Habsburg and Ottoman states were inheritors of older dynastic polities that continued to act as (and refer to themselves as) "empires." On comparative imperial histories, see e.g., Karen Barkey and Mark von Hagen, *After Empire: Multiethnic Societies and Nation-Building in the Soviet Union and the Russian, Ottoman, and Habsburg Empires* (Boulder, CO: Westview, 1997).

7. Benedict Anderson, *Imagined Communities: Reflections on the Origins and Spread of Nationalism*, 3rd ed. (London: Verso, 2006).

8. Jürgen Habermas, *The Structural Transformation of the Public Sphere: An Inquiry into a Category of Bourgeois Society* (Boston: MIT Press, 1991 [1962]); quotation from Geoff Eley, "Nations, Publics, and Political Culture: Placing Habermas in the Nineteenth Century," in *Habermas and the Public Sphere*, ed. Craig Calhoun (Boston: MIT Press, 1992), 289–339.

9. CM Jovo, 6 April 1905, ZMF Präs BH 475/1905, ABiH.

10. For example, Andrea Orzoff, *Battle for the Castle: The Myth of Czechoslovakia in Europe, 1914–1948* (Oxford: Oxford University Press, 2009); and Cathleen M. Giustino, "Rodin in Prague: Modern Art, Cultural Diplomacy, and National Display," *Slavic Review* 69, no. 3 (2010): 591–619.

11. On related Habsburg projects elsewhere in the Monarchy, see esp. Larry Wolff, *The Idea of Galicia: History and Fantasy in Habsburg Political Culture* (Stanford, CA: Stanford University Press, 2010); and Timothy Snyder, *The Red Prince: The Secret Lives of a Habsburg Archduke* (New York: Basic Books, 2008).

12. On similar dynamics around imperial and (trans)national publics, see the excellent study by Sarah Abrevaya Stein, *Making Jews Modern: The Yiddish and Ladino Press in the Russian and Ottoman Empires* (Bloomington: Indiana University Press, 2004).

13. Anon., "Vilajetske vjesti," *Bosna*, no. 1 (16 May 1866): 1. Here I cite the content in Serbo-Croatian using the Julian calendar rather than the Hegira calendar; the same newspaper issues carried roughly the same text in Ottoman Turkish.

14. Stojan Novaković, "Književne prilike," *Mlada Srbadija* 1 (1870): 91–93.

15. Ljudevit Gaj, "Proglas," *Danica Ilirska* 5, no. 47 (1839): 185.

16. Anon., "Dopis," *Zastava*, no. 24 (1866); also no. 126 (1870).

17. Muhamed Hadžijahić, "Pokušaj osnivanja štamparije i novina u Sarajevu 1853. godine," *Bibliotekarstvo* 10 (1964): 27–40; Todor Kruševac, *Bosansko-hercegovački listovi u XIX veku* (Sarajevo: Veselin Masleša, 1978); and Jozo Džambo, *Buchwesen in Bosnien und der Herzegowina (1800–1878): Zur Problem der Lesersoziologie* (Frankfurt: Peter Lang, 1985).

18. Determining authorship in these Ottoman newspapers is difficult, as few pieces were individually signed. Moreover, archival documentation related to the Ottoman press was destroyed in the bombardment of the Oriental Institute in Sarajevo in 1992.

19. Stojan Novaković, "Književnost," *Vila*, no. 19 (5 July 1868): 456.

20. The first bilingual (Ottoman-Bosnian) publications, like the agrarian Sefer Law of 1859, used a pre-reform Serbian dialect. For example, see Kanunname—Uredba (1859), ZOP no. 613, ABiH. For Ottoman laws printed in Serbo-Croatian, see manuscripts C-8772 or R-7665, National Museum of

Bosnia-Herzegovina Library. The 1866 Ottoman *Bosna* adopted Vuk's standard
two years before the Belgrade Serbian Learned Society (*Srbsko učeno društvo*) did,
which held on to its own and ultimately unsuccessful linguistic dialect until 1869.

21. "Vilajetske vjesti," *Bosna*, no. 1 (16 May 1866); "Znanje i obrazovanost,"
Sarajevski cvjetnik, no. 12 (10 June 1872).

22. "Priposlato," *Sarajevski cvjetnik*, no. 46 (13 November 1869).

23. Mehmed Hulusi, "Vilajetske vjesti," *Neretva*, no. 1 (19 February 1876).

24. "Poučne zabave," *Bosanski vjestnik*, no. 22 (3 September 1866); Editorial,
Bosanski vjestnik, no. 23 (10 September 1866); "Poučno,"*Bosna*, nos. 13–15
(April–May 1870).

25. Mehmed Šaćir Kurtćehajić, "Preporuke," *Sarajevski cvjetnik*, no. 25 (20 June 1870).

26. Hulusi, "Vilajetske vjesti," *Neretva*, no. 1 (19 February 1876).

27. See from *Sarajevski cvjetnik*: "Vilajetske vjesti," no. 17 (24 April 1869);
"Novinarstvo kod nas," no. 23 (5 June 1869); "Unutrašnje vjesti," no. 25
(20 June 1870); "O vilajetske novine!" no. 40 (3 October 1870); "Javna
korešpondencija," no. 4 (23 January 1871).

28. See Kurtćehajić letter in Safvet Bašagić, *Bošnjaci i Hercegovci u islamskoj
književnosti* (Sarajevo: Svjetlost, 1986 [1912]), 204.

29. "Vilajetske vjesti," *Sarajevski cvjetnik*, no. 45 (8 January 1872); "Unutrašnje
vjesti," *Bosna*, no. 12 (19 April 1870).

30. For example, see "Različitosti" and "Inostrane vjesti" in *Sarajevski
cvjetnik*: no. 27 (4 July 1870), no. 16 (24 April 1871), no. 33 (16 October 1871),
no. 36 (6 November 1871), no. 4 (25 March 1872); "Vilajetske vjesti," no. 36
(6 November 1871); and "Našu staru želju opet izjavljujemo," no. 39 (27
November 1871).

31. A typical exhortation read: "Our advancement in a material sense . . .
depends also on the advancement of field agricultural economy." See "Materijalni
napredak," *Sarajevski cvjetnik*, no. 14 (3 April 1869); in the same periodical,
see "Zemljodjelstvo," no. 9 (27 February 1869); "Narodna privreda," no. 13
(27 March 1869); "Što se ne posije neće roditi," no. 20 (24 April 1869);
"Unutrašnje vjesti," no. 22 (29 May 1869); "Uloga javne radionice," no. 37 (11
September 1869); nos. 1, 18, 31 (January, May, August 1870); and nos. 19, 31
(May, October 1871). See also "Vjesti," *Bosna*, no. 130 (1868).

32. "Sujevjerje," *Sarajevski cvjetnik*, no. 38 (18 September 1869).

33. Kurtćehajić, "Sujevjerje," *Sarajevski cvjetnik*, nos. 28, 38, 39, 40, 41,
42 (July–October 1869). Also "O obrazovanju," *Sarajevski cvjetnik*, no. 10 (6
March 1869).

34. Kurtćehajić, "Patriotizam," *Sarajevski cvjetnik*, no. 30 (25 July 1870).

35. "U Sarajevu," *Bosanski vjestnik*, no. 1 (7 April 1866); also "Podlistak,"
Sarajevski cvjetnik, nos. 6–8 (January–February 1869).

36. Basiret, "Primjedba," *Sarajevski cvjetnik*, no. 7 (13 February 1871); also
"Domaće vjesti," *Bosanski vjestnik*, no. 10 (11 June 1866).

37. Kurtćehajić, "Patriotizam."

38. See *Sarajevski cvjetnik*, no. 14 (4 April 1870), no. 15 (11 April 1870), no. 17
(25 April 1870), no. 9 (29 April 1872), no. 14 (1 July 1872).

39. "Spisak," *Bosna*, no. 222 (20 August 1870).

40. Despite featuring some of the first primers using the new Serbo-Croatian
standard, the Ottoman Bosnian textbooks were left out of Charles Jelavich's survey

of South Slavic educational policies; Jelavich, *South Slav Nationalisms: Textbooks and Yugoslav Union before 1914* (Columbus: The Ohio State University Press, 1990).

41. See *Naravoučenije o čoveku i njegovim dužnostima*, trans. Georgije Jovanović (1866); *Bukvar za osnovne škole u vilajetu bosanskom* (1867); [Miloš Mandić], *Kratka sveštena istorija za osnovne škole u vilajetu bosanskom* (1868) and *Prva čitanka za osnovne škole u vilajetu bosanskom* (1868); Jovan Džinić, *Prvi bosansko-srpski kalendar za prostu godinu 1869* (1868); also *Početni zemljopis za katoličke učione u Bosni* (1871); all published by *Vilajetska štamparija* in Sarajevo.

42. Anon., *Početni zemljopis za katoličke učione u Bosni* (Sarajevo: Vilajetska štamparija, 1871), 16–17.

43. For example, "Vilajetske vjesti," *Sarajevski Cvjetnik*: no. 3 (16 January 1869), no. 7 (13 February 1869), no. 21 (22 May 1869), no. 42 (16 October 1869), no. 2 (17 January 1870), no. 10 (7 March 1870), no. 28 (11 July 1870), no. 45 (7 November 1870), no. 8 (27 February 1871), no. 35 (30 October 1871), no. 47 (22 January 1872).

44. Bogoljub Petranović, *Srpske narodne pjesme iz Bosne (ženske)* (Sarajevo, 1867); in *Bosanski vjestnik*, see "Marko Kraljević i sv. nedelja," no. 7 (21 May 1866); "Narodne pjesne: O krsnom imenu," no. 8 (28 May 1866); "Svatovske," nos. 9–17 (June–July 1866); "Narodne pjesne bosanskijeh Muslomana," nos. 20–22 (August 1866).

45. Jovan Džinić, *Prvi bosansko-srpski kalendar za prostu godinu 1869* (Sarajevo, 1868).

46. For example, *Srbija: Političko ekonomni list* for the year 1868: "S bosanske granice," 3 June; "U Sarajevu," 23 June; "U Bosni," 13 August; "S bosanske granice," 12 September; "S bosanske granice," 15 September; "Iz Hercegovine," 6 October; "S bosanske granice," 17 October; "Iz Bosne," 24 November; "Iz Sarajeva," 8 December; "Iz Sarajeva," 15 December; "Sarajevske škole," 26 December.

47. Kurtćehajić, "Vilajetske vjesti," *Sarajevski cvjetnik*, no. 13 (3 April 1871).

48. Kurtćehajić, "Vilajetske vjesti," *Sarajevski cvjetnik*, no. 21 (23 May 1870).

49. "Iz Krupe," *Sarajevski cvjetnik*, no. 51 (18 December 1869).

50. "Iz Biograda" and "Vilajetske vjesti," *Sarajevski cvjetnik*, nos. 2, 13 (January, April 1871). Also see Ženi Lebl, *Jevreji u Beogradu, 1521–1942* (Belgrade: Čigoja, 2001), 82–142; and Čubrilović, ed., *Oslobođenje gradova u Srbiji od Turaka* (Belgrade: SANU, 1970).

51. For example, Nikola Jovanović, *O jevrejskom pitanju u Srbiji* (Belgrade: Stefanović, 1879); and Vaso Pelagić, *Vjerozakonsko učenje Talmuda ili ogledalo čivutskog poštenja* (Novi Sad: A. Pajević, 1872). On Serbia's repressive laws and abuses of Jews in the 1860s and 1870s, see the British diplomatic reports in B. Destani, ed., *Ethnic Minorities in the Balkan States*, vol. 1 (Cambridge, UK: Archive Editions, 2003), 88–127.

52. "Izrailitska alijancija," *Sarajevski cvjetnik*, no. 35 (29 August 1870).

53. For example, see *Sarajevski cvjetnik* for: "Jevreji u Srbiji," no. 42 (16 October 1869); "Prava Jevreja u Rusiji," no. 2 (24 January 1870); "Jevreji u Poljskoj," no. 13 (3 April 1871); "Rusija," no. 15 (17 April 1871); "Srbija traži Mali Zvornik," no. 4 (25 March 1872); "Vilajetske vjesti," no. 47 (22 January 1872).

54. "Iz Biograda (dopis)," *Sarajevski cvjetnik*, no. 2 (9 January 1871). As Julia Cohen shows, this particular image of Jews as a model Ottoman community has a long and troubled history linked to various attempts to depict "the Ottomans as a foil to the persecutory regimes of Europe"; see *Becoming Ottomans*, 2, 132–142. Interestingly, Mehmed-beg Kapetanović continued Kurtćehajić's earlier line of arguments in the Habsburg period (1878–1914), often alluding to similar positions of Muslim and Jewish subjects in Ottoman, Habsburg, and Russian states. Not unlike some Ottoman Jewish responses discussed in Cohen's book, Kapetanović vehemently denounced the pogroms against Jews in Russia and eastern Europe while simultaneously downplaying the significance of the Armenian massacres in the Ottoman Empire; c.f. Anon., "Armensko pitanje," *Bošnjak*, no. 16 (1895); and "Kad će već prestati to proganjanje bijednih Jevreja," *Bošnjak*, no. 44 (1899): 2.

55. For example, "Srbija," *Sarajevski cvjetnik*, no. 42 (16 October 1869).

56. Quotation from "Inostrane vjesti," *Sarajevski cvjetnik*, no. 26 (26 June 1869), 4. Also see in *Sarajevski cvjetnik*: no. 20 (15 May 1869) and no. 12 (27 March 1871); also "Dopis od jednog Poljaka," no. 3 (18 March 1872) and no. 13 (17 June 1872).

57. "Iz Biograda (dopis)," 1.

58. The death of Kurtćehajić from tuberculosis in 1872 contributed to the slump in editorial quality in the last years of the Ottoman Bosnian press.

59. Martina Baleva, "The Empire Strikes Back: Image Battles and Image Frontlines during the RussoTurkish War of 1877–1878," *Ethnologia Balkanica* 16 (2012): 273294.

60. Under the reign of Abdülhamid II, the Ottoman government continued to develop new patriotic initiatives; see Campos, *Ottoman Brothers*; Stephanov, "Minorities, Majorities, and the Monarch"; and Wendy Shaw, *Possessors and Possessed: Museums, Archaeology, and the Visualization of History in the Late Ottoman Empire* (Berkeley: University of California Press, 2003).

61. Tomislav Kraljačić, *Kalajev režim u Bosni i Hercegovini, 1882–1903* (Sarajevo: Veselin Masleša, 1987), 74; Robin Okey, *Taming Balkan Nationalism: The Habsburg "Civilizing Mission" in Bosnia, 1878–1914* (Oxford: Oxford University Press, 2007); Robert Donia, *Islam under the Double Eagle: The Muslims of Bosnia and Hercegovina, 1878–1914* (Boulder, CO: East European Monographs, 1981); and Clemens Ruthner, "Habsburg's Little Orient: A Post/Colonial Reading of Austrian and German Cultural Narratives on Bosnia-Herzegovina, 1878–1918," in *Wechsel-Wirkungen: The Political, Social, and Cultural Impact of the Austro-Hungarian Occupation of Bosnia-Hercegovina, 1878–1918*, ed. Ursula Reber et al. (New York: Peter Lang, 2008). Russian, French, and British conquests raise similar questions about the ways in which European empires managed Islam; e.g., see Michael Khodarkovsky, *Russia's Steppe Frontier: The Making of a Colonial Empire, 1500–1800* (Bloomington: Indiana University Press, 2002); Adeeb Khalid, *The Politics of Muslim Cultural Reform: Jadidism in Central Asia* (Berkeley: University of California Press, 1998); and David Motadel, ed., *Islam and the European Empires* (Oxford: Oxford University Press, 2014).

62. On the evolution of Kállay's policies, see Mustafa Imamović, *Pravni položaj i unutrašni politički razvitak Bosne i Hercegovine, 1878–1914* (Sarajevo: Svjetlost, 1976), 69–127.

63. Kraljačić summed up the consensus thus: "The attempt to solve the national question in Bosnia-Herzegovina by introducing the Bosnian nation was from its outset sentenced to a historical failure. There were no political and other conditions necessary for its success" (*Kalajev režim u Bosni*, 272). But the failure to fully realize some planned goals should not blind us to the longer-term significance and broader consequences of these developments.

64. Although differing on points of emphasis, studies by Donia, *Islam under the Double Eagle*; Tomislav Kraljačić, *Kalajev režim u Bosni i Hercegovini, 1882–1903*; and Okey, *Taming Balkan Nationalism* have documented in detail the Habsburg attempts to incorporate Bosnian Muslims into the Monarchy. Also see Fikret Adanir, "The Formation of a 'Muslim' Nation in Bosnia-Hercegovina," in *The Ottomans and the Balkans: A Discussion of Historiography*, ed. Fikret Adanir and Suraiya Faroqhi (Leiden: Brill, 2002), 267–304.

65. Adolf Strausz, *Bosnien, Land und Leute: Historisch-ethnographisch-geographische Schilderung*, vol. 2 (Vienna: Gerold, 1884), v–vi and 145–148. On more economic arguments, see Josef Neupauer, *Wie könnte die europäische Cultur nach Bosnien verpflanzt werden?* (Vienna: Feitzinger, 1884).

66. Ljuboje Dlustuš, "Školske prilike u Bosni i Hercegovini od okupacije do danas," *Školski vjesnik* 1 (1894): 3–4.

67. Bericht k.u.k. diplo. Agenten in Cairo an den Minister des Aeussern Goluchowski, 10 January 1901, ZMF Präs BH 109/1901; also see ZMF Präs BH 295/1901 and 799/1901, ABiH.

68. Bericht des k.u.k. Botschaft für die vereinigten Staaten von Amerika, 29 November 1903, ZMF Präs BH 1489/1903, ABiH.

69. Memorandum des kaiserlich-russischen Justiz-Ministeriums ueber den Wirkungskreis des mohammedanischen Rechtes in Russland, 16 December 1904, ZMF Präs BH 1270/1904, ABiH.

70. Anon., *Die Lage der Mohammedaner in Bosnien, von einem Ungarn* (Vienna: Holzhausen, 1900), 125–126. Although many scholars have assumed that Kállay was the author of this work, the evidence instead points to Lajos Thallóczy. See Robin Okey, "A Trio of Hungarian Balkanists: Béni Kállay, István Burián, and Lajos Thallóczy in the Age of High Nationalism," *Slavonic and East European Review* 80, no. 2 (2002): 246.

71. Ernennung des Vakuf-Inspektors Hulusi, 19 October 1904, ZMF Präs BH 884/1884 and ZMF Präs BH 1093/1904, ABiH.

72. *Sarajevski list*, no. 83 (27 June 1884).

73. Among others, *Behar* intermittently used Ottoman Turkish, whereas *Muallim* actively advocated and used Arabic script to write Serbo-Croatian in the 1910s; see "Za arapsko pismo," no. 3, and "O arapskom pismu kod nas," *Muallim* no. 10 (1911): 33–37, 163–169.

74. See *Vatan*: Sejfulah, "Vatanımız bulunan Bosna ve Hersek," no. 1 (1884); "Bosna'da asar-i atika taharriyati," no. 11 (1884); "Şehrimizdeki müzehane," no. 157 (1887); "Müzehanenin resmi kuşadı," no. 177 (1887); Hulusi, "Elsine-i şarkiye kongresi," no. 267 (1889); "Bosna'da asar-i atika hafriyatı," no. 290 (1890); "Saray'da arkeoloji ve antropoloji konferansı," no. 513 (1894).

75. "Şu bu," *Vatan*, serialized in nos. 289–302 (1890); cf. "Cumle-i Müntehabe-i," *Vatan*, no. 361 (1891).

76. A. G., "Dragi gospodine," *Bošnjak* 1, no. 3 (16 July 1891).

77. Bošnjak, 11 June 1891, stated that "we chose the Roman script for our journal because most Muhammedans read and write in Roman letters now"; as cited in NKHZ 14, VII-236, ABiH.

78. Anon., "Svačije poštujemo, a svojim se dičimo," *Bošnjak* 1, no. 4 (23 July 1891).

79. Mehmed-beg Kapetanović-Ljubušak, *Narodno blago* (Sarajevo: Zemaljska štamparija, 1887); and Kapetanović-Ljubušak, *Istočno blago*, 2 vols. (Sarajevo: Spindler & Löschner, 1896). For a salient example of Kapetanović-Ljubušak's reworking of Vuk's terrain, see his discussion of proverbs concerning "brothers" and "brotherhood" in *Istočno blago*, vol. 1 (1896), 13–14, 61, 85, 128, 200–201, 323–324.

80. Kosta Hörmann, *Narodne pjesme Muhamedovaca u Bosni i Hercegovini*, vol. 1 (Sarajevo: Zemaljska štamparija, 1888), iii–xiii. Also see Đenana Buturović, *Studija o Hörmannovoj zbirci muslimanskih narodnih pjesama* (Sarajevo: Svjetlost, 1976).

81. "Vuk Stefanović Karadžić," Čitanka za zemaljske škole (1906), ZVS 2-47/1906, ABiH.

82. Luka Marjanović, "Književna pisma," *Vienac* 20 (1888): 478–479. Marjanović published his Bosnian Muslim folklore collection ten years later; see Luka Marjanović, ed., *Hrvatske narodne pjesme: Junačke pjesme (muhamedovske)*, vols. 3–4 (Zagreb: Matica hrvatska, 1898–1899).

83. Antun Hangi, "Predgovor prvom izdanju," *Život i običaji muslimana u Bosni i Hercegovini*, 2nd ed. (Sarajevo: Daniel Kajon, 1906), n.p.

84. Kállay, 2 January 1888, ZMF Präs BH 17/1888, ABiH.

85. For example, Johann von Asbóth, *Bosnien und die Herzegowina: Reisebilder und Studien* (Vienna: Hölder, 1888), 23–94.

86. Safvet-beg Bašagić Redžepašić [Mirza Safvet], *Kratka uputa u prošlost Bosne i Hercegovine, 1463–1850* (Sarajevo: Vlastita naklada, 1900), 199 and 208. For a comprehensive assessment of the Bogomil theories in light of later historical research, see John V. A. Fine, *The Bosnian Church: Its Place in State and Society from the Thirteenth to the Fifteenth Century* (London: Saqi, 2007 [1975]).

87. My focus here is on the politics of imperial patriotism, not the Bosnian Muslim autonomy movements and parties that emerged by 1906; on these issues, see Donia, *Islam under the Double Eagle*.

88. Hajdar Fazlagić, "Kako bi nam narod zavolio knjigu," *Školski vjesnik* 1 (1894): 750–753.

89. When Bosnia emerged as an independent state in the 1990s, for instance, its proponents resurrected many symbols produced by the Habsburg patriotic projects: the Bogomil historical theories, the medieval gravestones images promoted by Austro-Hungarian archaeologists, etc. For example, see Pål Kolstø, "Državni simboli u novim državama: Znakovi jedinstva i podjele," *Prilozi* 33 (2004): 185–208.

90. Verzeichnis, Paris, 1900, ZVS 40-149-45/1900, ABiH; the Habsburg government was keen to show off the range of new scientific activities based in Bosnia (anthropology, archaeology, ethnography, dermatology, metallurgy, ornithology, meteorology, viticulture, etc.) at the world exposition in Paris in 1900.

91. Karlo Pač, "Rimska nalazišta u kotaru novljanskom," *Glasnik Zemaljskog muzeja*, no. 1 (1898): 493–502.

92. Petar Mirković, "Manastir Panagjur," *Glasnik Zemaljskog muzeja*, no. 1 (1889): 12–15.

93. O. N., "Kakvi je naraštaj u Bosni i Hercegovini," *Vienac* no. 23 (1900): 499–500.

94. Spiridon Brusina, "Naravoslovne crtice sa sjevero-istočne obale Jadranskog mora," *Rad JAZU* 163 (1905): 38–40.

95. Henrik Glück, "O književnosti i o novinstvu u Bosni-Hercegovini," *Hrvatska misao*, no. 1 (1903): 281–291. On *Nada*, which featured leading South Slavic writers like Silvije S. Kranjčević and Antun G. Matoš, see Boris Ćorić, *Nada: Književnohistorijska monografija, 1895–1903* (Sarajevo: Svjetlost, 1978).

96. Vinko Kisić, "Književnost," *Nada*, no. 20 (1903): 318–319.

97. Anon., [Review of Vuko Pećanac, *Carmina selecta*], *Nada*, no. 24 (1903): 333.

98. Anon., [Review of Mirza Safvet, *Trofanda*], *Nada*, no. 18 (1896): 359.

99. "Velika Srbija: Red je na Bosnu" (1888), 19–20, ZMF Präs BH 654/1888, ABiH.

100. For example, Anon., "Hrvatstvo i Srbstvo u Bosni i Hercegovini," *Slovanski svet* 9 (1894): 299–300; and "Hrvati pa Srbi," *Slovanski svet* 12 (1899): 113–114.

101. Kállay, *Stenographische Sitzungs-Protokolle der Delegation des Reichsrates*, Session 33, 1897, 198 (all *Protokolle* volumes published in Vienna by Hof- und Staatsdruckerei).

102. For example, Masaryk and Herold, *Stenographische Sitzungs-Protokolle der Delegation des Reichsrates*, Session 29, 1893, 186, 195; Kállay response, 199; Slama, *Stenographische Sitzungs-Protokolle*, Session 32, 1896, 150; and Wolf, *Stenographische Sitzungs-Protokolle*, Session 37, 1901, 238.

103. Masaryk, *Stenographische Sitzungs-Protokolle*, Session 28, 1892, 151–159, 166–167, 241–243.

104. Ibid., 159.

105. Kállay, *Stenographische Sitzungs-Protokolle*, Session 31, 1895, 292. On Kállay's work as a historian of Serbia and Bosnia, see Beni Kállay, *Istorija srpskog naroda*, trans. Gavrilo Vitković, 2 vols. (Belgrade: Ćurčić, 1882).

106. Kállay, *Stenographische Sitzungs-Protokolle*, Session 28, 1892, 169–170. The democratic practice of *divide et impera* was also noted by James Madison: "*Divide et impera*, the reprobated axiom of tyranny, is under certain qualifications, the only policy, by which a republic can be administered on just principles"; *James Madison: The Theory and Practice of Republican Government*, ed. Samuel Kernell (Stanford, CA: Stanford University Press, 2003), 349.

107. On Masaryk's long-term interest in Bosnia, see Ladislav Hladký, "T. G. Masaryk i Bosna i Hercegovina," *Prilozi* 30 (2001): 117–141.

108. Landessprache, offizielle Bezeichnung derselben "srpsko-hrvatski jezik," 14 October 1907, IB no. 168539, ABiH; also see Burián, *Stenographische Sitzungs-Protokolle der Delegation des Reichsrates*, Session 40, 1904, 365–366.

109. *Sloboda* (Niš), 10 February 1889, ZMF Präs BH 158/1889, ABiH. "For us Bosnia is the land of tears and wailing," wrote a Serbian nationalist journalist, "but for the [Habsburg] state officials, it is a real El Dorado." "Mi i oni," *Otadžbina*, no. 21 (1907), 1.

110. Naredba glede umnožavanja literarnih i umjetničkih proizvodina, 30 October 1881, ZVS 27-48/3, 1881, ABiH. Press regulations were significantly relaxed later: e.g., Pressgesetz, 21 January 1907, ZMF Präs BH 53/1907; and Pressgesetz, 18 March 1907, ZMF Präs BH 320/1907, ABiH.

111. ZMF Präs BH, ABiH contains numerous and extensive such reports titled *Revue Journalstimmen*: e.g., 241/1899, 440/1905, 762/1905, 1254/1906, 1265/1907, and 1495/1910.

112. CM Jovo, 30 March 1905, ZMF Präs BH 444/1905. On Habsburg assessments of informants, see ZMF Präs BH 1348/1909, 354/1909, and 1100/1907, ABiH.

113. Bericht der k.u.k. Gesandtschaft in Belgrad, 20 August 1908, ZMF Präs BH 1376/1908; Serbische Propaganda und Bandenorganisierung, 4 January 1909, ZMF Präs BH 330/1909; Amtsmeldung, Konfident B, 1 May 1909, ZMF Präs BH 1177/1909, ABiH.

114. Telephon-Meldung, 9:20h, 10 November 1907, ZMF Präs BH: 1327/1907, ABiH.

115. For example, compare: Anon., "Austria's Defence" and "The Case for Austria: Why Bosnia and Herzegovina Were Annexed," *The Daily Mail*, no. 3972 (2 January 1909); Anon., "Making Trouble," *The Daily Mail*, no. 4014 (20 February 1909); and Anon., "Austrian Explanations," *The Daily Mail*, no. 4170 (21 August 1909).

116. Mensdorff Memorandum, 5 February 1909, ZMF Präs BH 413/1909, ABiH.

117. Anon., "Emperor Francis Joseph," *The Daily Mail*, no. 3954 (12 December 1908); "The Emperor's Jubilee," *The Daily Mail*, no. 3945 (2 December 1908); and esp. "The Wise Emperor," *The Daily Mail*, no. 4411 (30 May 1910).

118. Wortverstümmelung in Srpska riječ, 10 April 1905, ZMF Präs BH 500/1905, ABiH.

119. CM Trifić, 12 August 1905, ZMF Präs BH 1051/1905; and Benko, 3 March 1906, ZMF Präs BH 237/1906, ABiH.

120. Zbor balkanskih Slovena, Chicago, 4 July 1906, ZMF Präs BH 846/1906; and Ujedinjeno srpstvo Chicago, 30 June 1906, ZMF Präs BH 753/1906, ABiH. Also see Đorđe Čokorilo, "Sa puta po Americi," *Narod*, no. 67, 1908.

121. The claims about the street demonstration come from Čokorilo's account. Based on research in the Chicago History Museum Archives, most city newspapers did not report the event. Nonetheless, Habsburg authorities continued to monitor nationalist writings from the United States. See Kalendar Ujedinjeno Srpstvo Chicago, 8 February 1909, ZMF Präs BH 368/1909; and Narodna odbrana, 26 December 1913, ZMF Präs BH 133/1914, ABiH.

122. "Velika Srbija: Red je na Bosnu" (1888), 45, ZMF Präs BH 654/1888, ABiH.

123. Appel, 21 February 1902, ZMF Präs BH 227/1902, ABiH.

124. E. Kasumović, 30 January 1902, ZMF Präs BH 172/1902; also see ZMF Präs BH 80/1902, 106/1902, and 408/1902, ABiH.

125. For example, János Asbóth, *Bosznia és a Herczegovina: Uti rajzok és tanulmányok* (Budapest: Pallas, 1887); Asbóth, *Bosnien und die Herzegowina*; and Asbóth, *An Official Tour through Bosnia and Herzegovina, with an Account of the History, Antiquities, Agrarian Conditions, Religion, Ethnology, Folk lore, and Social Life of the People* (London: Sonnenschein, 1890).

126. Redakteur Renner, 8 November 1895, ZMF Präs BH 1383/1895; e.g., see corrections of Arabic words (*Chalifa, Zikr,* the call to prayer, etc.). Also see ZMF Präs BH 521/1895, ABiH.

127. Heinrich Renner, *Durch Bosnien und die Hercegovina, kreuz und quer: Wanderungen*, 2nd ed. (Berlin: D. Reimer, 1897); and Renner, *Herceg-Bosnom uzduž i poprijeko* (Zagreb: Hrvatska dionička tiskara, 1900). The first edition of five thousand copies sold out within a year, leading to a second edition with sixty more images; see D. Franić, "Književna obznana," *Nastavni vjesnik* 6 (1897): 206–208.

128. Renner, *Durch Bosnien*, 54.

129. Ibid., vi and 566–567.

130. Ibid., vi–vii.

131. Privatschreiben Dr. Küh an M. Holbach, 28 May 1909, ZMF Präs BH 1341/1909, ABiH; and Korrespondenz, 8 June 1909, ZMF Präs BH 1390/1909. For her part, Maude Holbach underlined that "I do not wish Mr. Lane [the London publisher] to know that the book is being subsidized in Austria," while Lane publishers wanted more on Bosnian politics. Also see ZMF Präs BH 843/1908, 279/1909, and 2034/1909. Meanwhile, John Lane Company's advertisements tried to frame Holbach's book as a commentary on the 1908 annexation crisis: "The political troubles which occurred not long ago in the Balkans should make this book especially popular;" see "Bosnia," *The International Studio* 39 (1909), 11.

132. Maude Holbach, *Bosnia and Herzegovina: Some Wayside Wanderings* (London: John Lane, 1910), 15–22.

133. On the widely positive reception of Holbach's work, which usually described it as a "tourist guide" to Bosnia's "interesting and unspoiled peoples and the unhackneyed beauty and quaintness of this remote part of Europe," see Anon., "Book Reviews," *Photo-Era Magazine* 24 (1910), 240; Anon., "Notes," *The Nation* 90 (1910), 215; and Anon., "Book Reviews," *Bulletin of the American Geographical Society* 42 (1910), 624–625.

134. Milena Mrazović, *Selam: Sketches and Tales of Bosnian Life*, trans. Mrs. Waugh (London: Jarrold, 1899), 5–6; originally *Selam: Skizzen und Novellen aus dem bosnischen Volksleben* (Berlin: Deutsche Schriftsteller-Genossenschaft, 1893).

135. Milena Preindlsberger-Mrazović, *Bosnisches Skizzenbuch: Landschafts- und Kultur-Bilder aus Bosnien und der Hercegovina* (Dresden: Pierson, 1900), vi; also see Preindlsberger-Mrazović, *Bosnische Volksmärchen, mit Illustrationen von Ewald Arndt* (Innsbruck: Edlinger, 1905).

136. *Bosanska Vila*, a biweekly Bosnian Serb journal based in Sarajevo, was published from 1885 to 1914.

137. T. W. Legh, M.P., "A Ramble in Bosnia and Herzegovina," *The New Review* 5 (1891): 470–480.

138. Karl Braun-Wiesbaden, "Reise-Eindrücke aus Bosnien und der Herzegowina," *Nord und Süd* 34 (1885): 349–364, here 350.

139. Julius Pojman and Carl Neufeld, *Illustrierter Führer durch Bosnien und die Herzegowina*, 4th ed. (Vienna: Hartleben, 1913 [1907]).

140. K.N., "Književnost," *Nada*, no. 18 (1902): 251.

141. Julije Kempf, *Od Save do Adrije: Bosnom i Hercegovinom* (Zagreb: Pedagoško-književni zbor, 1898), i.

142. William Eleroy Curtis, *The Turk and His Lost Provinces: Greece, Bulgaria, Servia, Bosnia* (Chicago: F.H. Revell, 1903), 296–297.

143. Luigi Villari, "Austria-Hungary's Colonial Experiment," *The Monthly Review* 8 (1902): 72–87, here 85, 87.

144. Editorial board, "Bosnia and Hercegovina," *The Globe Trotter* 43 (1913), cover image and 66–73.

145. Editorial board, *Bosna i Hercegovina na milenijskoj izložbi u Budimpešti godine 1896* (Budapest: Pesti könyynyomda-részvény-társaság, 1896), 110–111.

146. Das Buch vom Kaiser, 1898, ZOP, ABiH; "Jubilarna izložba," "Franjo Josip," *Nada*, nos. 11, 16, and 24 (1898); and Unowsky, *Pomp and Politics of Patriotism*, 170–171.

147. Henri Moser organized the logistics, arranging everything from electricity to toilets for the Bosnian Pavilion; see Moser, 28 December 1899, ZVS 40-149-4/ 1900, ABiH. For a report, see James Penny Boyd, *The Paris Exposition of 1900: A Vivid Descriptive View and Elaborate Scenic Presentation of the Site, Plan, and Exhibits* (Chicago: Dominion, 1900), 491–492.

148. Weltausstellung Paris (1899–1900), ZVS 40-149/1900, ABiH.

149. Alfred Weidinger, "Alphonse Mucha and the Pavilion for the Ottoman Provinces of Bosnia-Herzegovina at the Exposition Universelle in Paris in 1900," in *Alphonse Mucha*, ed. Agnes Husslein-Arco et al. (New York: Prestel, 2009), 49–55, here citing Jiří Mucha, 52.

150. Abel Fulcran César Fabre, "Mucha—Un maitre décorateur: Après une visite au Pavillon de Bosnie," *Le Mois Littéraire et Pittoresque* 17 (1900): 579–598; also Charles Lavine, "Au Pavillon de la Bosnie: Les fresques de Mucha," *Le livre d'or de l'exposition de 1900* (Paris: Cornély, 1900), 123–124; and M. Léra, "En Bosnie-Hérzegovine," *Le Monde Moderne* 14 (1901): 734–746.

151. The sexual dimension of Habsburg representations of Bosnia-Herzegovina was brought out in a 1909 French-language caricature; it depicted Emperor Franz Joseph as a hoary eighty year old holding two young women perched on his lap, the caption reading: "Conquests once again at my age: Bosnia and Herzegovina." Postcard in author's private collection. Similarly themed cartoons appeared in the Ottoman press; see *Kalem: Mizâh gazetesi/Journal humoristique*, no. 8 (1908): 7; and no. 22 (1909): 7–8, 10.

152. Edward Said, *Orientalism* (New York: Vintage, 1978); Timothy Mitchell, *Colonising Egypt* (Berkeley: University of California Press, 1991); and Vanessa R. Schwartz and Jeannene M. Przyblyski, eds., *The Nineteenth-Century Visual Culture Reader* (London: Routledge, 2004).

153. On Bosnia as a *Musterstaat*, see Gustav Steinbach, "Eine Kolonie Österreich-Ungarns," *Die Nation* 13 (1896): 482–485.

154. Ronald Grigor Suny, *The Revenge of the Past: Nationalism, Revolution, and the Collapse of the Soviet Union* (Stanford, CA: Stanford University Press, 1993), 3.

155. For example, Hannes Grandits, *Herrschaft und Loyalität in der spätosmanischen Gesellschaft: Das Beispiel der multikonfessionellen Herzegowina* (Vienna: Böhlau, 2008).

156. For example, Anderson, *Imagined Communities*; and Frederick Cooper and Jane Burbank, *Empires in World History: Power and the Politics of Difference* (Princeton, NJ: Princeton University Press, 2010), 213, 363–365.

157. On the twentieth-century legacies, see Adanir, "Formation of a 'Muslim' Nation."

158. Krishan Kumar, "Nation-States as Empires, Empires as Nation-States: Two Principles, One Practice?," *Theory and Society* 39, no. 2 (2010): 119–143; Kumar, "Nation and Empire: English and British National Identity in Comparative

Perspective," *Theory and Society* 29, no. 5 (2000): 575–608; and Hannah Arendt, *The Origins of Totalitarianism* (New York: Meridian, 1958), 153.

159. Francine Hirsch, *Empire of Nations: Ethnographic Knowledge and the Making of the Soviet Union* (Ithaca, NY: Cornell University Press, 2005); and Yuri Slezkine, "The USSR as a Communal Apartment, or How a Socialist State Promoted Ethnic Particularism," *Slavic Review* 53, no. 2 (1994): 414–452.

160. Tito himself wrote: "As to whether or not we are nationalist, I can say the following: we are just so much nationalist as it is necessary to foster healthy socialist patriotism in our country, and socialist patriotism is substantially what internationalism is." Josip Broz Tito, *Yugoslav Communists and the International Workers' Movement* (Belgrade: Socialist Thought, 1983), 186. Also see Franjo Tolić, ed., *Savez komunista Bosne i Hercegovine u borbi za bratstvo, jedinstvo i ravnopravnost* (Sarajevo: SKBiH, 1977).

161. Theodora Dragostinova, "Speaking National: Nationalizing the Greeks of Bulgaria, 1900–1939," *Slavic Review* 67, no. 1 (2008): 154–181.

Epilogue

1. My approach in this conclusion directly draws on strategies of "displacement" proposed by Saba Mahmood, *Politics of Piety: Islamic Revival and the Feminist Subject* (Princeton, NJ: Princeton University Press, 2005); Marilyn Strathern, *The Gender of the Gift: Problems with Women and Problems with Society in Melanesia* (Berkeley: University of California Press, 1988); and Roland Barthes, *The Pleasure of the Text*, trans. Richard Miller (New York: Hill and Wang, 1975); see esp. Mahmood, *Politics of Piety*, 189–192.

2. For example, Federal Register, ed., *William J. Clinton: Public Papers of the Presidents of the United States*, vol. 1 (Washington, DC: National Archives, 1999), 705; and Kofi Annan (with Nader Mousavizadeh), *Interventions: A Life in War and Peace* (New York: Penguin, 2012), 91.

3. Charles Taylor, "Nationalism and Modernity," in *The Morality of Nationalism*, ed. Robert McKim and Jeff McMahan (Oxford: Oxford University Press, 1997), 31–32, 42–52; for Taylor's commentary on "a 'fair' resolution for Bosnia," see *A Secular Age* (Cambridge, MA: Harvard University Press, 2007), 659–660, 706.

4. Slavoj Žižek, "Intervju sa Al Jazeera Balkans, 2012," http://www.youtube.com/watch?v=cDaE8LkO6AU (accessed 12 May 2014).

5. The first European jigsaw puzzle games were precisely maps ("dissected maps") made by the London cartographer John Spilsbury in the 1760s. Geographic puzzle games have remained popular since the eighteenth century. In recollections of his childhood in 1910s Manchester, for example, Elias Canetti wrote about assembling a jigsaw puzzle map of Europe blindfolded, feeling each country by its shape. See Jill Shefrin, *Neatly Dissected for the Instruction of Young Ladies and Gentlemen in the Knowledge of Geography: John Spilsbury and Early Dissected Puzzles* (Los Angeles: Cotsen, 1999); Elias Canetti, *Tongue Set Free*, trans. Joachim Neugroschel (New York: Seabury, 1979), 47; and Samuel van Valkenburg, *European Jigsaw: An Atlas of Boundary Problems* (New York: Foreign Policy Association, 1945).

6. Strathern, *Gender of the Gift*, 11–21. In a different context but a related interpretive vein, Roland Barthes wrote: "By subtle subversion I mean, on the

contrary, what is not directly concerned with destruction, [but something that] evades the paradigm, and seeks . . . [not] a synthesizing term, but an eccentric, extraordinary term" (*Pleasure of the Text*, 54–55).

7. The circular quality of some arguments around "tolerance" retrace familiar dichotomies; for example, see Robert Hayden, "Antagonistic Tolerance: Competitive Sharing of Religious Sites in South Asia and the Balkans," *Current Anthropology* 43 (2002), 205–231; and Glenn Bowman, "Orthodox-Muslim Interactions at 'Mixed Shrines' in Macedonia," in *Eastern Christians in Anthropological Perspective*, ed. Chris Hann and Hermann Goltz (Berkeley: University of California Press, 2010), 195–219.

8. Vuk Karadžić, "Brat," *Srpski rječnik* (1852), 40; to make the three examples distinct, I have marked them in Arabic numerals. Characteristically, Vuk's entry for "sister" (*sestra*) provides only the bare bones of the German and Latin terms.

9. Also phrased as "Brothers gouge out eyes the deepest"; Vuk Karadžić, ed., *Srpske narodne poslovice*, 2nd ed. (Vienna: Armeniern, 1849), 28, 157; and Vicko Skarpa, ed., *Hrvatske narodne poslovice* (Šibenik: Hrvatska tiskara, 1909), 243–245. On a related folk tale, see "Pravda i krivda," in *Srpske narodne pripovijetke*, ed. Vuk Karadžić (Vienna: Armeniern, 1853), 106–109; and P. A. Rovinskii, "Chernogoriia v eia proshlom i nastoiashtem," *Sbornik otdieleniia russkago iazika i slovesnosti Imperatorskoi akademii nauk* 69 (1901): 596–598. For references to this proverb in political debates, see Stipan Ivichevich, "Vlašichi su skladna bratja mila: Bratja što su," *Zora dalmatinska*, no. 9 (1847): 65–68; Stojan Novaković, *Balkanska pitanja* (1906), 480–481; and Antun Radić, "Braća," *Dom*, no. 13 (1901): 217–200.

10. Karadžić, *Srpske narodne poslovice*, 28. Also see Milo Jovović, "Brat je mio, koje vjere bio," *Bosanska vila* 9, no. 3 (1894): 34; other examples are discussed in chapter 3.

11. Franjo Marković, "Etički sadržaj naših narodnih poslovica," *Rad JAZU* 96 (1889): 177–178.

12. Karadžić, *Srpske narodne poslovice*, 29.

13. A related proverb stated: "There is no butcher without one's own brother"; Karadžić, *Srpske narodne poslovice*, 203 and 215. On *krvnik* as blood antagonist, see Đura Daničić, ed., *Rječnik hrvatskoga ili srpskoga jezika*, vol. 5 (Zagreb: JAZU, 1898), 706–707.

14. Nikola Begović, *Život i običaji Srba-graničara* (Zagreb: Narodne novine, 1887), 202.

15. For examples of such research in Bosnia, see Max Bergholz, "Sudden Nationhood: The Microdynamics of Intercommunal Relations in Bosnia-Herzegovina after World War II," *American Historical Review* 118, no. 3 (2013): 679–707; and "The Strange Silence: Explaining the Absence of Monuments for Muslim Civilians Killed in Bosnia during the Second World War," *East European Politics and Societies* 24, no. 3 (2010): 408–434. On such issues more broadly, see Veena Das, *Life and Words: Violence and the Descent into the Ordinary* (Berkeley: University of California Press, 2007).

16. Gerard Toal and Carl T. Dahlman, *Bosnia Remade: Ethnic Cleansing and Its Reversal* (Oxford: Oxford University Press, 2011), 320.

17. Zygmunt Bauman, *Modernity and Ambivalence* (Cambridge: Polity, 1991), 53–74.

18. Mikhail Kulagin, a Soviet computer engineer and coworker of the game's creator, Alexey Pajintov, described *Tetris* (1984) as "a game with a very strong negative motivation. You never see what you have done well, and only your mistakes are seen on the screen and you always want to correct them." Quoted from *Tetris: From Russia with Love*, BBC 4 Documentary, dir. Magnus Temple, Ricochet Digital Production, February 9, 2004.

Index

Locators followed by f and m indicate figures and maps.